Ex Libris

Hugh & Georgie O'Shaughnessy

THE
ECONOMIC DEVELOPMENT
OF GUYANA
1953-1964

THE ECONOMIC DEVELOPMENT OF GUYANA
1953–1964

BY

WILFRED L. DAVID

Lecturer in Economics
University of Guyana
and
Economic Adviser
Ministry of Economic Development
Guyana

CLARENDON PRESS · OXFORD

1969

Oxford University Press, Ely House, London W.1

GLASGOW NEW YORK TORONTO MELBOURNE WELLINGTON
CAPE TOWN SALISBURY IBADAN NAIROBI LUSAKA ADDIS ABABA
BOMBAY CALCUTTA MADRAS KARACHI LAHORE DACCA
KUALA LUMPUR SINGAPORE HONG KONG TOKYO

MADE AND PRINTED IN GREAT BRITAIN BY
WILLIAM CLOWES AND SONS, LIMITED
LONDON AND BECCLES

PREFACE

THIS study is a revised version of a thesis accepted for the degree of Doctor of Philosophy at Oxford University. It is a comprehensive analysis of some of the more important development problems facing a small, open and dependent economy. Although the main emphasis is on a relatively short period of twelve years, the conclusions and policy recommendations apply in varying degrees to most economies at a similar stage of economic development, especially those in the Caribbean.

I cannot pretend to list all the sources of help received, but several persons and institutions merit special mention. I am particularly grateful to my supervisor and teacher, Lady Hicks, for her encouragement and sympathetic guidance and her criticisms which have helped considerably in moulding all sections of the present work; also to Sir John Hicks for invaluable help.

I should also like to thank the Principal and Fellows of Linacre College, Oxford, for the kind consideration given to my efforts during my graduate years at Oxford, and the Board of Management of the George Webb Endowment Fund of Oxford University for substantial financial assistance.

Professor Charles Kennedy, of the University of Kent, and Mr. A. D. Hazlewood, of the Oxford University Institute of Economics and Statistics, made useful suggestions for the expansion of certain themes, for which I am grateful.

Numerous Government Departments, Organizations, and other persons in Guyana and overseas were also helpful in the preparation of this study. My particular thanks go to Mrs. Esme Gordon of the Ministry of Economic Development, who undertook the laborious task of typing the manuscript and checking the proofs, to Messrs. S. L. Carmichael, A. D. Augustin, W. Bascom for reading revised drafts, and to my colleagues at the Universities of Guyana and the West Indies for helpful comments.

Finally, I should like to express my gratitude to Mr. Victor O'Connell of Linacre College, Oxford, who so kindly undertook the revision of the final manuscript, competently and with exacting care; also to my wife who has worked as typist and has borne the burden of having this study intrude our home for more than three years.

W. L. D.

Georgetown
March 1969

CONTENTS

LIST OF TABLES

LIST OF FIGURES

CURRENCY CONVERSION RATIOS

Pre-1967 Devaluation	*Post-1967 Devaluation*
£1 Sterling = $4·80 Guyana	£1 Sterling = $4·80 Guyana
£1 Sterling = $4·80 W. Indian	£1 Sterling = $4·80 W. Indian
US$1·00 = $1·71 Guyana	US$1·00 = $2·00 Guyana
£1 Sterling = US$2·80	£1 Sterling = US$2·40

The ratios used in this book are those that applied before the 1967 devaluation.

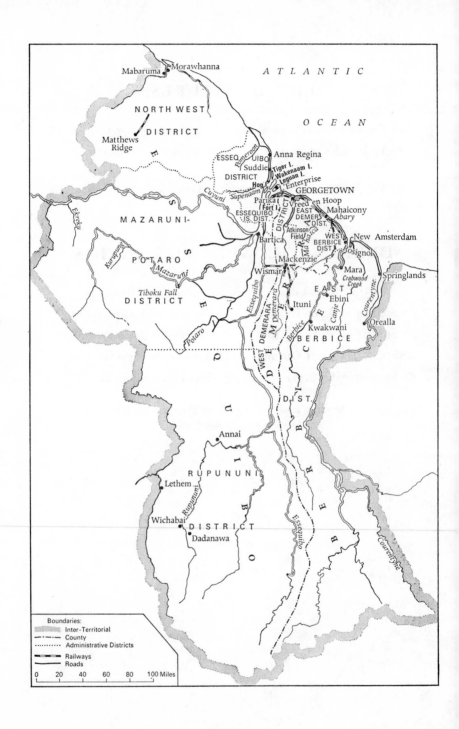

ATLANTIC

OCEAN

Mabaruma • • Morawhanna

NORTH WEST

DISTRICT

Matthews
Ridge

E

S

S

E

MAZARUNI-

POTARO

Tiboku Fall
DISTRICT

Ekreku

Kurupung

Mazaruni

Potaro

Q

U

I

B

O

ESSEQ
DISTRICT
Suddie

Pomeroon

UIBO

Anna Regina

Cuyuni

Supenaam

Hog I.

Tiger I.
Wakenaam I.
Leguan I.

Enterprise

Parika

Fort I.

ESSEQUIBO
IS. DIST.

GEORGETOWN

Vreed en Hoop

EAST
DEMER
A DIST.

Mahaicony

Abary

WEST
DEMER
A DISTRICT

Atkinson
Field

Mahaica

WEST
BERBICE
DIST.

New Amsterdam

Bartica

Essequibo

Mackenzie

Wismar

WEST
DEMERARA

Demerara

EAST
DEMER
A DIST.

Rosignol

Mara
Crabwood Creek

Courentyne

Springlands

EAST

Ebini

Ituni

Canje

Berbice

Kwakwani

BERBICE

DIST.

Orealla

B

E

R

B

I

C

E

Annai

RUPUNUNI

Lethem

Rupununi

Wichabai
Dadanawa

DISTRICT

Essequibo

Courentyne

Boundaries:
Inter-Territorial
County
Administrative Districts
Railways
Roads

0   20   40   60   80   100 Miles

INTRODUCTION

GUYANA lies on the northern coast of South America between Venezuela on the west and Surinam on the east. It is the most southerly point of the group of countries which comprise the Commonwealth Caribbean. By the standards of the West Indies Guyana is a large country and even when measured on a world scale it is not small. It covers an area of 83,000 square miles and has a population of about 750,000. But only the coastal strip and the bauxite town of MacKenzie have been of any major social and economic importance, for the bulk of the population lives in these areas. If it is considered that about 90 per cent of the population inhabit just under 2 per cent of the total land area then a clearer picture emerges of a population density comparable with those of most of the other countries in the Commonwealth Caribbean.

This study is focused on the performance of the Guyanese economy during the post-war period—with special reference to the years 1953–64. 1953 was a year of major political significance. In April 1953 elections were held under a new constitution which granted a substantial measure of self-government. 1964, likewise, witnessed an important political event. In 1964, elections were held under the system of proportional representation, prior to the attainment of fully independent status under the name of GUYANA in May 1966. Thus the period reviewed in this study could be regarded as a transitional phase in the country's political, social, and economic development, and can be described as a period when the Guyanese economy was at the crossroads.

By criteria that are commonly used to measure economic advance, the country's performance was poor. G.D.P. grew by about 6 per cent and G.N.P. by about 5·6 per cent between 1953 and 1961, but it was not possible to maintain this pace in the years after 1961, for these were years marred by a high degree of political and social unrest. Thus we may divide the period into eight years of very slow growth of income per head followed by three years of sharp decline. The slow growth of income per head was directly related to the rapid growth of population. The average annual increase of population between 1953 and 1961 was about 3 per cent, so that the increase in output per head was just over 1 per cent per annum. This rapid growth of population is one of the country's major economic problems. In this study we are concerned with an examination of the nature of the development that Guyana experienced during the period under review and the structural changes connected with economic progress.

It is useful at the outset to define explicitly what we mean by 'economic development' and the ways it is connected with investment. A variety of criteria for measuring economic development have been suggested in the literature. For some commentators development is best measured by the growth of aggregate output. Others suggest the growth of real income *per capita* and the rate of growth of industrial production; but the concept of capital formation has traditionally held a high place among the variables stressed.

Investment is a many-sided actor on the economic scene. It is the *primum mobile* with a simultaneous performance as income generator, capacity creator, employment stimulator, and as such has been a unique force in development economies. The traditional model of developing countries presents the problem of investment as a scarcity of total output and income. Given the low level of *per capita* real incomes characterizing these countries, the model assumes that average and marginal consumption propensities are high, that savings are low, and that formation of new productive investment is therefore limited. The low level of investment in turn sharply restricts the rate of growth of real output, and allowing for population growth, a tendency towards static equilibrium results with no growth in real *per capita* output and no tendency towards such growth. Thus the notion that capital accumulation is the crux of the development problem is firmly embedded in the early post-war literature on the problem of economic development, and was the foundation of early efforts at development planning. Practical experience of the difficulties involved in the establishing of a self-sustaining growth process is causing the gradual rejection of this theory.

Experience with development problems and development

planning has amply demonstrated that economic development is not a simple matter of generating enough capital investment, though capital is a necessary catalyst. It is a far more complex problem of generating the human skills and knowledge required for working with, and managing, the capital, and this in turn requires a transformation of the economic, social, legal, and cultural environment. Appreciation of this problem has been reflected in the creation of facilities for pre-investment surveys through the United Nations Special Fund, the evolution of techniques of manpower planning to complement investment planning, and a growing emphasis on education and technical assistance in the developing countries.

Thus in our analysis economic development is interpreted widely. On the general level development is regarded as having taken place if the real income *per capita* increases over time. Like any other single criterion this definition has its limitations. The averaging of aggregate real income over the total population neglects the manner in which income is distributed throughout the economy. This consideration assumes a special relevance in the Guyanese context. Apart from the problem of low average income *per capita*, the country has been plagued since the 1930s by the problem of chronic unemployment of a relatively large proportion of the labour force. We have therefore investigated the extent to which economic development, measured by the growth of real income *per capita*, is accompanied by the absorption into productive employment of the unemployed and of new recruits to the labour force.

This twin problem of income and employment is examined within the framework of both resource allocation and resource expansion. In this sense development inculcates the freezing of a complex of resources of various compositions into definite uses for a certain period of time. This requires decisions as to types and forms with respect to uses, that is, decisions on the nature of the complex resources to be employed in these uses, and the choice of time periods during which these resources are to be frozen into given uses.

This broad approach allows us scope for analysis and enables us to discuss the limits within which the Guyanese economy has to operate, i.e. the limits determined by those natural resources that are available and exploitable, and the limits determined by the manpower of a growing population. This means that the evolution of the economy may be analysed in terms of a broad conceptual scheme which takes into account the production functions that have to be altered so as to raise productivity; the economic resources that are available at various 'prices' for re-allocation both directly in the new production functions, and indirectly in the secondary effects of innovation and general development; and thirdly, the socio-cultural structure, which conditions the desire, direction, and feasibility of economic change, including the socio-economic propensities that express the habits and values of the society. It is in this sense that we consider important the skills of the inhabitants, their further development through education and training, and, in general, the people's 'Will to Economize'.

In Guyana, as in most developing countries, statistics covering many important topics are neglected. The author has supplemented considerably the sources mentioned by means of direct requests for additional data to the various institutions and government departments. Despite this the available data still often lacks refinement. Throughout this study attention is drawn to the reservations with which the available evidence ought to be interpreted. But the available statistical data, though often crude, does enable us to obtain an approximation adequate for an appreciation of the general features of Guyana economy.

The economy of Guyana can be sub-divided into the following sectors:

A. *The Public Sector* (Government)
B. *The Propulsive Private Sector*
   1. Households
   2. The foreign-owned Export Sector (Sugar and Bauxite)
C. *The Dependent Private Sector*
   I. Rice and Forestry
   II. Other Agriculture (including Stock-raising)
   III. Light Manufacturing Industry
   IV. Service Sectors (Distribution, Transport, etc.)

This rough division presents a scheme which underlies our analysis of the economy.

We begin our analysis by an examination of the growth of production and income, first in aggregate terms and then in relation to some of the key sectors of the economy. Chapter I therefore presents a picture of the behaviour of national income, expenditure, and investment. The next chapter deals with the growth of population, labour force, and employment. These magnitudes assume tremendous importance in Guyanese conditions where the pressure of population on the limited resources so far exploited and made available on the coastal strip is one of the key factors determining the pace of economic advance and where unemployment in both the rural and urban areas is a major problem facing those charged with planning economic growth.

Chapter III deals with agriculture, traditionally the most important sector in the Guyanese economy. In this chapter the behaviour of the main variables in the propulsive sugar sector, and the dependent rice, stock-raising, and forestry sectors is examined. The generation of income from secondary sources is illustrated by reference to developments in the mining sector. The manufacturing sector has not been given separate treatment because it has mainly taken the form of processing of primary products such as sugar and rice, and its contribution to the growth of income has been insignificant.

The study proceeds with an analysis of the role of external trade and payments, for the external sector has been the largest propulsive sector in the development of the economy. Chapter VI deals mainly with the monetary and fiscal aspects of development including the sources of funds for financing economic development, as well as the disaggregation of investment into its various components. Chapter VII is concerned with the extent to which the growth of public expenditure contributed to the development process by facilitating the adaptation of social and economic infrastructure.

Finally we trace the salient features of the evolution of economic planning, and, in the light of our findings in respect of the structural weaknesses of the economy, outline the possible paths for future economic development.

I

THE GROWTH OF NATIONAL INCOME, EXPENDITURE, AND INVESTMENT

1. *The Growth of Income and Output*

The present chapter traces the growth of national income, expenditure, and investment during the period 1953 to 1964 and brings into focus the trend displayed by certain key variables closely connected with these aggregates. Subsequent chapters will analyse investment behaviour and development within the more important sectors of the economy.

A distinctive feature of the modern economic growth of nations is a sustained and substantial rise in national income and product *per capita*. The emphasis on a sustained and substantial rise in these two basic economic indicators is particularly important because of its implications for the structure and conditions of modern economic growth and investment, and because of their requirements in the way of the society's adaptability to change. The difficulties of measuring economic growth lie precisely in this point that it may call for major structural changes and correspondingly large modifications in the social and institutional conditions under which greatly increased product *per capita* will be attained. Yet for purposes of measurement the changing components of the structure must be reduced to a common denominator—income.

A nation's total income like the individual's total income is a reflection of the total value of its economic activity. It is the aggregate expressed in money terms of all the needed goods and services produced by the mass of individuals and institutions which constitute the nation. But although this magnitude should provide a useful index of the total national economic activity considered in relation to its own past and potential future, and to the total activity of other nations, unfortunately in its crude form international income is far from being an accurate reflection of the value of economic activity, since the concept gives rise to theoretical and practical difficulties [1] not the least of which is the application of the sophisticated techniques developed in advanced countries to the problems of the development countries. [2]

In the advanced countries techniques of national income accounting have been brought to a high level of refinement and the national accounts usually provide a sound basis for economic analysis and investment policy, but whether these techniques can usefully be applied to a development country like Guyana is questionable. National Income Series for the economy of Guyana go back for nearly twenty years, and are based on simplified versions of the accounts recommended by the United Nations. [3] The strict adherence to the United Nations System has enabled the calculators to bypass many serious difficulties and distorting factors, so that the national income estimates do provide a useful first approximation to a kind of economic thermometer.

The truth of this judgement rests on the fact that there is no important section of the Guyanese population that is outside the money system, and even where production for home use is important, it never completely supplants production for sale. For although the economy is basically agricultural, only about 4·7 per cent of household consumption is non-cash. [4] If the monetization of the economy is a necessary concomitant of some measure of economic development, [5] then, at least in this

[1] The conceptual and practical difficulties surrounding the calculation and measurement of national income have been extensively discussed in the literature, but very incisive argumentation can be found in P. T. Bauer and B. S. Yamey, *The Economics of Underdeveloped Countries* (Cambridge, 1959), pp. 16–24; Phyllis Deane, *The Measurement of Colonial National Incomes* (Cambridge, 1948); *Colonial Social Accounting* (Cambridge, 1953); Milton Gilbert (ed.), *Income and Wealth*, Series III (Cambridge, 1953), especially papers by S. H. Frankel, F. Benham, and V. Rao.

[2] See Dudley Seers, 'The Role of National Income Estimates in the Statistical Policy of an underdeveloped area', *Review of Economic Studies*, Vol. XXI (1952–3), pp. 159–68.

[3] *A system of National Accounts & Supporting Tables, Studies in Methods No. 2,* United Nations (New York, 1953).

[4] A. Kundu, 'The Economy of British Guiana 1960–75', *Social and Economic Studies*, Vol. 12, No. 3 (Sept. 1963), p. 314.

[5] In tropical Africa, for instance, it has been estimated that approximately 70 per cent of the cultivated land and 60 per cent of the labour force of the indigenous agricultural economies is engaged in subsistence production. See *Enlargement of the Exchange Economy in Tropical Africa*, U.N. Dept. of Economic Affairs

respect, Guyana has been developing well. It follows that in an assessment of development in the economy over the 1953–64 period, the growth of national income can be regarded as a fairly reliable indicator and apparent increases are not merely manifestations of the increasing use of money as a medium of exchange.

Guyana, with an average annual household income for the post-war period of about £80, is a 'development country'[1] at a quasi-intermediate stage of economic development. This compares favourably with the level of *per capita* incomes achieved in most other development countries. Although this may be taken to mean that the people of Guyana are probably better off than some of their counterparts in other countries, their quest for higher living standards is no less intense than it is elsewhere. The situation is a classic demonstration of the race between development and discontent. The economic development of this country can be viewed therefore in the context of rapidly rising expectations, which have been moulded by an increasing nationalism[2] and centuries of contact with countries in Europe and North America. The fact that its average per capita income is higher than in other peripheral regions[3] gives Guyana an advantage in the advance towards the eradication of poverty

(New York, 1954), p. 3. For a discussion of some of the problems raised by subsistence activity see A. R. Prest, *The Investigation of National Income in British Tropical Dependencies* (London, 1957), p. 19.

[1] See U. K. Hicks, *Development Finance, Planning and Control* (Oxford, 1965), Ch. 1, for the introduction of this new terminology.

[2] The rise of nationalism in the developing regions in recent years has led these countries to desire a great acceleration in the transmission of the growth process. Nationalism as a motivation for the acceleration of economic growth is, however, a two-edged weapon. On the one hand, it may be indispensable in motivating old societies in new states to bear the economic costs and absorb the social changes involved in modernization. On the other hand, in a variety of ways nationalist motivations operate to make the inauguration of economic growth extremely inefficient, possibly to the point of ineffectiveness. For a fuller discussion of nationalism in relation to economic development see Harry G. Johnson, 'A Theoretical Model of Economic Nationalism in New States', *Political Science Quarterly*, Vol. LXXX, No. 2 (June 1965), pp. 169–85.

[3] See P. Rosenstan-Rodan, 'Economic Aid to Underdeveloped Countries', *Review of Economics and Statistics*, Vol. XLIII, No. 2 (May 1961), Table 1b. In this and several United Nations Sources which give League Tables of development countries, it is evident that Guyana is near the top of the League of countries which together comprise two-thirds of the world's population, but obtain only about one-seventh of the world's revenue. The top of the income bracket is taken as US$300 G.N.P. *per capita*.

and its inherent evils. Indeed, Guyana is better prepared to receive and assimilate the power of contemporary technology than were the more advanced countries at the time of their capitalistic evolution.

Table 1, which presents the National Income Series, is intended to give an indication in broad terms of the behaviour of some of the main economic aggregates. On the surface it seems that the economy has been growing rapidly in almost every

TABLE

NATIONAL INCOME SERIES

AT CURRENT

			(*Million*
	1953	1954	1955
1. Personal consumption expenditure	136·1	143·7	146·2
2. Government consumption expenditure	21·8	22·2	26·0
3. Gross capital formation, public and private	24·5	38·4	46·0
4. Exports of goods and services	85·5	87·9	93·1
5. Imports of goods and services	72·8	80·9	95·4
6. Net indirect taxes	19·2	19·7	27·5
7. Gross domestic product at factor cost	175·8	191·7	191·5
8. Net income payments to the rest of the world	10·3	9·9	9·4
9. Capital consumption allowances	7·6	7·8	8·9
10. National income	157·9	174·0	173·2
11. Household *per capita* net incomes (1959 constant prices)	359	374	341
12. Terms of trade 1956 = 100	102	102	98
13. Terms of trade 1961 = 100	—	—	—

Sources:
(a) C. O'Loughlin "The Economy of British Guiana 1952–56", *Social and Economic Studies*, Vol. 8, No. 1 (1959).
(b) A. Kindu "Inter-Industry Table for the Economy of British Guiana 1959, and National Accounts 1957–60", *Social and Economic Studies*, Vol. 12, No. 1 (1962).

Note:
Background to National Incomes Estimates. The Central Statistical Bureau began making estimates around 1958. At that time the available data was extremely limited. The Income Tax Records, which were open to O'Loughlin and later to Kundu, were not available to the Bureau. In the circumstances, only estimates of G.D.P. by industrial origin were made and certain measures, such as depreciation and household savings, were practically impossible to measure. However, income tax data later became available to the Bureau, and one of the officers of the Bureau spent several months collecting information. For these and other reasons, there may be

field. Between 1953 and 1964 the rate of growth of gross domestic product averaged about 6 per cent per annum. But this must be qualified [1] when account is taken of the fluctuating nature of the economy—very high *per capita* incomes being recorded in 1954 and 1961—the recession in 1958 and the slow recovery in 1959, as reflected in the low *per capita* income for that year. When full account is taken of these factors, the real

[1] See note to Table 1 below.

I

FOR GUYANA 1953-64

PRICES

Guyana dollars)								
1956	1957	1958	1959	1960	1961	1962	1963	1964
158·5	167·4	171·2	178·2	202·0	209·5	202·1	161·9	223·8
28·4	32·2	32·8	33·5	35·8	33·4	38·0	36·6	46·6
48·0	62·6	68·5	56·9	82·4	76·4	55·6	50·9	53·6
98·2	114·6	104·0	110·8	143·4	166·4	190·4	194·0	192·1
110·9	120·9	119·2	113·7	168·3	169·8	150·6	139·6	179·6
26·5	26·7	28·4	30·6	32·2	34·5	32·0	31·1	36·7
207·0	231·6	234·1	239·4	263·5	289·8	307·2	275·5	302·9
11·1	14·6	11·2	11·4	23·6	23·2	37·0	28·5	29·8
8·4	9·7	8·5	8·8	12·2	17·9	19·5	16·2	17·2
187·4	201·5	207·5	212·4	227·6	248·6	250·7	230·8	255·9
356	352	347	338	361	384	362	312	N.A.
100	112	106	111	108	112	115	N.A.	N.A.
74·5	87·7	82·6	82·3	91·0	100·0	98·7	113·0	114·9

(c) A. Kundu "The Economy of British Guiana 1960–75", *Social and Economic Studies*, Vol. 12, No. 3 (1963).

(d) *Quarterly Statistical Digest*, December 1964 (Statistical Bureau, Georgetown, Guyana) and Central Statistical Office, *Analysis of Domestic Product (1960–4)*.

N.A. = Not available.

differences in both method and accuracy in the data for the periods 1953–6, 1957–9, and 1960–4, which came from different sources. It was rather difficult, therefore, to derive continuous series for the 1953–64 period which would be consistent between the periods 1953 to 1956, 1957 to 1959, and 1960 to 1964. However, all the figures are merely the best data available; and now that the Statistical Bureau is functioning on a sound basis, with a good filing system which permits reference to the derivation of figures for previous years, it should be expected that there will be an improvement in the reliability of the statistical material available.

growth rate for the period is unlikely to be more than a mere 3 per cent per annum.[1]

Despite the fact that the period 1961–4 was one of severe political unrest with a consequent loss of confidence, gross domestic product continued to increase until 1962, but although the fall registered in 1963 was not tremendous, the fall in household *per capita* incomes to its lowest level for the period 1953–64 is very significant. The atmosphere of general stagnation which prevailed over the years 1961–4 would probably have led to an outright decline in gross domestic product had it not been for the very unexpected rises in sugar prices.

It may be noticed that the national income series given in Table 1 are in current prices and therefore do not reveal the behaviour of real output. Most statistics indicate that the growth rate of output between 1953 and 1961 was around 3 per cent per annum, with services, especially government services growing faster than commodity output. *Per capita* real output reached its maximum point in 1961, and thereafter declined because of strikes and political uncertainty. The figures since 1960 are shown in Table 2. From these it can be gleaned that G.D.P. at constant 1960 prices continued to increase up to 1962, dropped to its lowest in 1963, and failed to recover its 1961 or 1962 position in 1964.

Income per head increased rather slowly, owing to the fact that population was increasing at an accelerated pace. With an average increase in population of about 3 per cent the *per capita* increase in output was only about 1 per cent per annum.

Two other important factors must be taken into account in the evaluation of Guyana's G.D.P. growth. First the terms of trade effect must be considered (shown in Row 12 of Table 1).[2] Contrary to the experience of most development countries

---

[1] The Central Statistical Bureau have estimated that the annual growth rate of Gross Domestic Product was 3·4 per cent between 1952 and 1960 at constant 1957 prices.

[2] The validity of the hypothesis concerning the long-term deterioration of the terms of trade between primary products and manufactured goods is not our immediate concern. Our interest in this section arises from the fact that the main reasons explaining the favourable trend tend to make us sceptical of a substantial and sustained real growth rate. It is also significant in that exports are the governing dynamic of the economy—the ratio of exports to total G.D.P. being around 50 per cent. This aspect of development is treated more fully in Chapter V on foreign trade and payments.

TABLE 2

ESTIMATES OF REAL OUTPUT AT 1960 CONSTANT PRICES[a]

(Million Guyana dollars)	1960	1961	1962	1963	1964
Agriculture					
Sugar cane	35·2	34·8	34·9	34·0	32·7
Padi	11·7	13·1	13·1	10·0	14·5
Other crops	8·8	10·3	10·1	6·7	7·8
Livestock	3·4	7·0	9·1	6·9	8·3
Fishing	4·2	5·4	5·8	4·0	5·7
Forestry	6·6	6·9	6·1	5·0	6·2
Mining	29·1	36·5	46·0	38·3	47·6
Processing					
Sugar	11·1	10·8	10·8	10·5	9·1
Rice	2·2	2·4	2·6	1·9	2·7
Food and Tobacco	5·7	5·9	6·2	5·5	6·2
Other manufacturing	8·2	8·7	8·7	8·0	9·2
Distribution	37·2	39·8	37·3	28·7	38·4
Transport and communication	19·8	20·7	21·0	16·7	18·1
Engineering and construction	25·0	20·0	16·7	12·1	13·4
Rent of dwellings	8·2	8·4	8·5	8·7	8·3
Financial services	8·5	9·1	8·3	8·4	9·1
Other services	13·1	13·2	13·4	12·3	13·9
Government	25·6	27·7	27·7	25·4	28·2
Total (average)	264·0	281·0	288·0	243·0	279·0

Source: Central Statistical Bureau, *Analysis of Domestic Product 1960–4.*

[a] The estimates of Real Product are based on 1960 prices. The method adopted consists of totalling the value—added of each industry in the base year, weighted, in each year, by an index representing the volume of production in each industry based on 1960 levels of production. In a few cases, e.g. in Mining, the product in the current year was revalued at 1960 prices, and the 1960 value—added co-efficient applied to the gross value, to derive the current year value—added. There is no official index of production but it was possible to secure production statistics in Sugar, Rice, some other agricultural crops, Timber, Bauxite and Alumina, Manganese, Gold and Diamond, and some products in manufacturing. These together account for just less than 50 per cent of the G.D.P. in the base year. Therefore the deflated values in Sugar, Rice, Mining, Forestry, and most Manufacturing (including Processing) rest on fairly reliable bases.

The available information on the other sectors—Distribution, Transportation, Engineering and Construction, Services, etc. was scantier and the deflated values may not be very reliable. A rough index of government wages and salaries was used to deflate government. As in all estimates of real product made in the manner described, it is not only *price* changes that are eliminated, but any improvements in efficiency or technique leading to a reduction in the coefficient of secondary inputs, would not show up in the estimates.

during this period, the country's favourable terms of trade were mainly due to the fact that the prices she received for her exports increased considerably more than those she had to pay for imports. To understand the causes of this situation we should have to consider the Commonwealth Sugar Agreement which boosted the export price of sugar, the decline in the import prices of manufactured goods, and the prices negotiated for the country's bauxite exports. These prices usually reflect inter-company transfers and are to a large extent governed by other considerations than those determining open market prices. But this does not mean that there was anything illusory about the increase in real incomes brought about by this favourable movement in the terms of trade. The world demand for Guyana's exports became more urgent relative to the country's demand for world goods. The important fact, however, is that such a favourable trend may not continue. There are cogent reasons to expect the terms of trade to reverse direction. For unless it is certain that a country's products are due for a secular rise in price relative to import prices, prudence demands that investment planning should take account of increases in incomes due to increases in productivity alone.

Secondly, Row 8 of Table 1 (Net Factor Payments to the Rest of the World) highlights a further point of scepticism with regard to high estimates of G.D.P. and the country's real growth rate. For the estimates of G.D.P. in Guyana include factor incomes in the form of profits, interest, and dividends, which are paid abroad directly, and so do not get back into the domestic income stream. For a considerable part of Guyana's G.D.P. accrues as profits to non-resident owners of sugar and bauxite firms, and thus should not be counted as part of the true national income. Thus G.N.P., the income of Guyanese, did not grow as fast as G.D.P., the output of Guyana.[1] Since most of the

---

[1] The following estimates of the growth of G.N.P. between 1954 and 1963 have been given by the Central Statistical Bureau, Georgetown.

(*Thousand B.W.I. dollars*)

1954	1955	1956	1957	1958	1959	1960	1961	1962	1963
181·8	182·2	195·8	216·9	222·9	228	239·9	266·5	269·5	242·7

The dangers that surround the use of G.D.P. Estimates have been well analysed in A. P. Thorne, 'Size, Structure and Growth of the Economy of Jamaica', *Social and Economic Studies* (Supplement), Vol. 4, No. 4 (1955).

growth of output was due to the heavy importation of capital from abroad, both by private persons and the government, the share of overseas profits and of debt charges in output increased significantly.

On the other hand Guyana's residents did not receive any correspondingly large inflow of incomes from overseas, since their investments abroad are relatively small. Owing to favourable price movements already mentioned, the profits of sugar and bauxite enterprises increased substantially and more rapidly than did wage increases. This could be another reason why national income increases were less than G.D.P. increases. But it does not seem that the prices of bauxite, sugar, and other major exports are due for secular increases. Thus a fall in profits may go hand in hand with rises in wages due to trade union pressure. Attention therefore has to be focused on the need for increasing productivity and of the possible transfer of labour from low-yielding to high-yielding industries. But a certain *obiter dictum* must be added regarding the expatriation of factor incomes. The profits accruing to the sugar and bauxite interests yield the greater part of income tax revenue in the country. The taxation of profits yields around 35 per cent of the current revenues.

We have so far considered some of the main factors which must be borne in mind when estimating the performance of the national economy over the period under review. Too optimistic estimates of such a performance have failed to take account of the terms of trade effect, the fluctuating nature of the economy, and the export of profits and dividends due to the heavy importation of capital.[1] All these variables have to be taken into account in the determination of real economic development within the country. And when we add to these the falling value of money over the period, and the fact that popu-

[1] See K. Berrill, *Report on the British Guiana Development Programme 1960–64*, Sessional Paper No. 2 (1960), p. 7. On the basis of a recognition that the growth of output averaged 6 per cent per annum between 1952 and 1957, the author assumed that over the next five years (1960–4) the economy would have expanded at the rate of 6 per cent per annum. One cannot blame Berrill for failing to predict the series of pathological situations which characterized the economy after 1960, but it must be emphasized that he failed to consider national income estimates instead of G.D.P. estimates because he overlooked the terms of trade effect, the large inflow of investment capital, and consequently the large outflow of factor incomes.

lation growth was over 3 per cent, it would appear that expansion at the adjusted growth rate barely kept pace with the national increase. The growth experienced between 1953 and 1960 was just sufficient to maintain real incomes intact. This occurred because the period of vigorous growth between 1952 and 1957 was followed by one of slower growth between 1957 and 1960 which might have meant an actual decline in available *per capita* incomes. The political upheavals and consequent loss of confidence which characterized economic affairs after 1960 did not help to reverse this trend.

Guyana's performance over this period does not compare favourably with her Commonwealth Caribbean partners. Over the decade 1953–62 substantial economic progress was achieved by nearly all the major territories in the Commonwealth Caribbean. In Jamaica and Trinidad and Tobago, which were the fastest growing territories in the area, the G.D.P. at constant 1960 prices expanded between 1953 and 1961 at average annual rates of 7·8 per cent and 9·6 per cent respectively. On a *per capita* basis, real product in both countries grew at rates of over 6 per cent per annum. But in all the territories after 1957 there was a pronounced tendency for the domestic product to grow more slowly. On the basis of current prices, the average annual rate of growth in Jamaica between 1958 and 1962 was just over one-third of the figure achieved between 1954 and 1957, while in Trinidad and Tobago, the average rate of growth had slipped by some 5 percentage points. This trend was substantiated by the movements in real product, where the average rate of growth in Jamaica fell from 11·5 per cent in 1954–7 to 4·1 per cent in 1958–61, and in Trinidad and Tobago, from 11·1 per cent to 8·1 per cent.[1] Preliminary data suggest that real growth rate in both countries declined further in 1962 and 1963, mainly because of the effects of hurricanes, and post-independence depression.[2] If political stability is a necessary precursor of real

[1] *Trinidad and Tobago: Annual Abstracts of Statistics (Sundry years)*, Central Statistical Office, Port-of-Spain, Trinidad; *Jamaica: National Income and Expenditure*, Dept. of Statistics, Jamaica.

[2] However, the fluctuating nature of the economy and low level of *per capita* growth was also characteristic of Latin America during this period. During the second half of the fifties, real *per capita* income in the region as a whole rose by 1·4 per cent yearly, which was appreciably less than in the first half of the decade (1·9 per cent). The decline became more pronounced around 1957–9, with the

growth *per capita*, then perhaps unique political factors operated in Guyana. The suspension of the British Guiana Constitution in 1953 and the long period of unrest which ensued was one of them and the period of low confidence after 1960 was another. These distorting factors were, in the main, absent from the Trinidadian and Jamaican economic scene.

But if it is true that a certain minimum *per capita* income, i.e. level and rate of growth of income, has to be achieved in order that the economy may sustain a certain minimal level and rate of investment, then even this minimal point has not been reached in the country. The concept of a minimum rate of investment measures the rate needed to prevent *per capita* income from falling in the face of population growth.[1] A rate of investment somewhat above this minimum is the lowest target at which any deliberate attempt at investment planning should aim even though this may involve a heavy effort when population is growing rapidly. Although the 1953–64 period was characterized by heavy importation of capital, the argument is that because of low domestic real growth *per capita*, the quantum of investment generated locally may have been too low. This argument rests on the assumption that both the level and rate of growth of investment are functions of the level and rate of growth of income; and since the foreign component of investment is mainly determined by extraneous factors, a low level and rate of growth of domestic incomes must be the cause of some concern because of the implications for the rate of domestic investment.

An argument closely connected with the above is the following. Every *per capita* income-raising force brings into play global income-depressing forces. But at low *per capita* income levels, the income-depressing forces are more prominent than the income-

result that *per capita* income tended to remain stationary or to fall in the majority of Latin American countries. Brazil was an exception to the rule, since it continued to develop at a relatively rapid pace. From 1959 onwards, these trends were substantially modified, the rate of economic growth accelerated, and *per capita* income rose by 2·9 per cent in 1960 and 2·6 per cent in 1961, acquiring an impetus greater than that of the early fifties. This recovery was short-lived, however, for in 1962 *per capita* income again came to a standstill, and in 1963 tended to fall. United Nations, *Economic Survey of Latin America, 1963* (New York, 1965), Ch. I.

[1] United Nations: E.C.A.F.E., *Programming Techniques for Economic Development, Report of the First Group of Experts of Programming Techniques* (Bangkok, 1960), pp. 8–13.

raising ones, whereas the reverse is usually true at high *per capita* income levels.[1] What this suggests is that as long as the level and rate of growth of national income *per capita* remain at low levels, the greater are the possibilities of stagnation, and the more formidable becomes the task of attaining and sustaining a level and rate of investment somewhat above the minimum.[2]

We have not lost sight of the fact that the recent rate of growth in some of the very advanced countries has been very low [3] and that their present level of development is the result of a lengthy historical process. Countries, which recently embarked on their developmental process, cannot be expected to reach the level of the advanced countries in the space of a few decades. Reasons for the disparity between the advanced and developing countries abound though there is no prescriptive right or general law stating that all communities must develop simultaneously and equally. Linked with this attitude of mind is the emotional reaction to the 'growth' concept,[4] and the feeling that it is something of a disgrace to find one's country caught in the vicious circle of stagnation and poverty, even if the state of 'affluence' already achieved is well in advance of that attained by other peripheral regions. But if due regard is given to the simple historical perspectives of the problem and progress is related to time a clearer understanding is possible.

The evidence of secularly sustained growth in the nineteenth and twentieth centuries is confined to countries that have already achieved a certain measure of industrialization, or are peopled by communities that have had an industrial revolution

[1] This is just a variation of the popular Myrdal thesis that there exists a constellation of forces that interact in a circular and cumulative causal chain, giving rise to a vicious circle of poverty and stagnation, and underlining the fact that a development country like Guyana is 'poor because it is poor', where poverty is measured in terms of the level and growth of national income *per capita* and related aggregates. See G. Myrdal, *Economic Theory and Underdeveloped Regions* (London, 1957). It does not follow that one need accent all the conclusions and inferences that Myrdal seems to draw from this hypothesis. For a balanced and useful critique see P. T. Bauer, 'International Economic Development', *Economic Journal*, Vol. 69, No. 273 (March 1959), pp. 105–23.

[2] The validity of this argument may rest on a somewhat impressionistic premiss, as it may be difficult to verify it statistically.

[3] See United Nations: World Economic Surveys; Yearbooks of National Account Statistics; Statistical Yearbooks.

[4] T. Wilson, 'The Price of Growth', *Economic Journal*, Vol. LXXIII, No. 292 (December 1963), p. 605.

passed on to them as a heritage from their European ancestors. Elsewhere in today's 'pre-industrial societies' like Guyana, wherever dynamism has been experienced it has been as a result of the country's establishing profitable trading relationships with the industrially expanding areas. The governing dynamic has not come from within, there has not been established any worthwhile historical tradition, and because of this, the problem of economic development demands a careful historical and psychological explanation.

Insight into the nature of this problem has been provided by Professor Boulding. He states that

The greatest problem of colonial societies is that of the impact of the *import* of organisation on domestic organisation. The import of organisation is the prime characteristic of a colonial society. It imports political organisation from the mother country; it frequently imports religious organisation and education organisation through various sources, and it imports economic organisation from foreign corporations. Up to a point, this may be quite desirable, especially in the early stages of development. The danger, however, is that the import of organisation frustrates the development of domestic organisation. Dependency becomes a habit of mind. . . . Even though political independence may therefore be a will-of-the-wisp in the twentieth century, psychological independence is not. Domestic organisation may be an infant industry which needs to be protected against fierce competition of imports.[1]

2. *G.D.P. by Industrial Origin and Sources of Growth*

The composition of G.D.P. by industrial origin, as given in Table 3, shows the relative importance of the various sectors of the economy. The analysis of this composition as well as the contribution of the main sectors of the growth of domestic product over time ought to afford us some useful insights regarding the future direction of investment potentials within the country.

It is clear that the economy is mainly agricultural in the sense that over 25 per cent of G.D.P. originates in that sector,

---

[1] K. E. Boulding, 'Social Dynamics in West Indian Society', *Social and Economic Studies*, Vol. 10, No. 1 (March 1961), p. 31.

with another 9 per cent attributable to the processing of agricultural products such as the milling of rice and the semi-refining of sugar. According to the 1960 Population Census, 37 per cent of the working population or 59,790 persons were employed in agriculture. Although the percentage of labour force employed is somewhat higher than the percentage contribution to G.D.P., agriculture still remains the dominant activity.

A striking feature of the economy as revealed by the G.D.P. estimates by sectors is the relative stability in the ratios of the various sectors of the economy during the last twelve or thirteen years. When rapid development occurs within an economy there is generally a transformation of the relative importance of the agricultural and manufacturing sectors including processing activities, with the latter growing more rapidly. Occasionally, rapid development may take place even though major groups maintain a constant balance through alteration in the internal composition of a given sector. For example, new sub-sectors which possess greater man-hour productivity may develop in agriculture—such as livestock production and dairying. While the statistics on income generated within the economy are somewhat sketchy, there is little evidence of such a development within agriculture.

The major components in the producing sectors of the economy are sugar production and manufacturing, rice-padi cultivation and milling, and forestry. It is clear that the contribution of these four main activities seems to have been growing almost in equal proportion to G.D.P., while other industries are still in a comparatively early stage of development to have their impact felt on the economy.

Between 1953 and 1964 the average annual rate of growth in money terms of manufacturing industries other than processing of food and tobacco and the refining of mineral production was around 5 per cent.[1] The growth rate in money terms of the processing of food and tobacco products was 4 per cent. Data on production in real terms (1960 constant prices) are only available for the last five years. During this period the annual rate of growth of the manufacturing industry was only 3 per cent in

[1] See *Guyana Development Programme 1966–72*, Government Printery (Georgetown, 1966), Ch. XV.

TABLE 3

INDUSTRIAL ORIGIN OF G.D.P. AT FACTOR COST: PERCENTAGE DISTRIBUTION

	1954	1955	1956	1957	1958	1959	1960	1961	1962	1963	1964
Agriculture											
Sugar	10·5	9·6	10·3	12·3	12·9	12·5	13·4	12·5	11·5	15·7	11·5
Rice	10·8	8·9	7·9	2·5	3·7	3·9	4·5	4·5	4·3	3·7	5·0
Other				4·0	4·1	3·9	3·3	3·2	3·2	2·9	2·9
Total Agriculture	21·3	18·5	18·2	18·8	20·7	20·3	21·2	20·2	19·0	22·3	19·4
Forestry	2·3	2·1	2·6	4·0	4·2	3·5	2·5	2·4	2·1	2·1	2·4
Fishing	2·2	2·9	2·5	5·4	5·4	5·4	1·6	2·0	2·0	1·6	1·9
Livestock	2·4	3·1	2·1				1·3	2·4	3·2	2·8	2·6
Mining and Quarrying	12·7	9·9	11·3	8·6	6·3	7·1	11·0	12·9	16·3	13·0	17·1
Food Processing											
Sugar				5·6	5·3	4·8	4·2	4·8	5·5	8·7	5·5
Rice				0·7	0·9	0·7	0·8	0·9	0·7	0·6	0·7
Other[a]				2·1	1·9	1·8	2·1	2·3	2·3	2·3	2·3
Total Processing	9·3	10·3	8·0	8·4	8·1	7·3	7·1	8·0	8·5	11·6	8·5
Other manufacturing	3·2	3·3	3·2	3·4	3·4	3·6	3·1	2·9	3·1	3·2	3·3
Distribution	14·6	15·0	14·6	13·7	13·4	13·7	14·1	13·5	11·9	10·4	12·8
Transportation and communications	5·4	6·2	6·6	7·4	7·7	7·5	7·5	7·5	7·2	6·5	6·4
Engineering and Construction	8·4	9·6	10·3	10·8	10·8	10·5	9·5	7·2	6·8	5·3	5·1
Rent of dwellings	2·7	2·8	2·6	1·2	1·3	1·4	3·1	2·9	2·8	3·2	2·7
Financial services	2·6	2·6	1·9	2·7	3·1	3·3	3·2	3·1	2·9	3·2	3·0
Other services	2·6	2·9	2·8	5·9	5·8	5·9	5·0	4·6	4·5	4·6	4·5
Government	10·3	10·8	13·3	9·7	9·8	10·5	9·7	10·5	9·9	10·3	10·3
	100·0	100·0	100·0	100·0	100·0	100·0	100·0	100·0	100·0	100·0	100·0

Source: 1954–9, Kundu, 'The Economy of British Guiana 1960–75', loc. cit., p. 311 (except that headings on Forestry, and Fishing are reversed); O'Loughlin, 'The Economy of British Guiana 1952–56', loc. cit., p. 26; Kundu, 'Inter-Industry Table', p. 31). 1960–4, Central Statistical Office, *Analysis of Domestic Product*.

a Includes tobacco processing.

terms of constant prices, while the real output of the processing industry decreased slightly.[1]

Among the services and other related sectors contributing to G.D.P., Distribution, Building and Construction, Transport and Communications, and Government are by far the largest ones. Distribution is by far the most important service because of its handling of very large amounts of exports and imports; it should also be noted that most of the distributive services are provided by the three main activities—sugar, mining, and rice.

One may wonder why the distribution of goods and services (wholesale and retail) should absorb such a large share of the domestic product. One possible contributory factor may be the tendency for redundant labour to gravitate towards the retail sector of the distributive trades with low capital intensity and relatively easy entry.[2] The existence of a large number of retailers each handling a relatively small turnover tends to breed inefficiency and drive up the cost of distribution.[3] Another

---

[1] The slow growth of manufacturing industry is explained by the fact that the majority of new large and small establishments created since 1953 have been concentrated in the entertainment and service sectors rather than in productive sectors; and where there sprang up manufacturing establishments, several factors tended to limit their growth and viability. These included: insufficient markets for products and services; lack of market facilities; lack of finance; shortage of raw materials; lack of skilled labour; shortage of plant and equipment; laws or regulations affecting business; etc. It was found that the 'lack of finance' and 'insufficient markets' for the items being produced in some cases were the main difficulties being experienced. Shortage of investment capital seems to have been very severe in the case of establishments employing less than 15 persons, and special attention may have to be paid to the financing problems of establishments in this range. The reorganization of existing sources of capital for investment should be considered by the authorities so that special attention can be paid to the problems of smaller establishments and at the same time a wider distribution secured.

The difficulties in respect of insufficient markets arose because of competition from similar imported items, the price of locally produced goods, an oversupply in some cases, or insufficient promotion. See *Survey of Manpower Requirements and the Labour Force, British Guiana 1965*, Preliminary Report (Ministry of Labour and Social Security, Georgetown, 1965), especially Chs. 2 and 3. These findings were broadly confirmed on the basis of questions put to a cross-section of manufacturing businessmen in Guyana.

[2] For an interesting discussion of this point see R. H. Holton, 'Marketing Structure and Economic Development', *Quarterly Journal of Economics*, Vol. 67, No. 3 (August 1953), p. 345.

[3] There are at present over 240 large wholesale and retail establishments employing more than 6,000 persons (total). Since 1953 the majority of new establishments were either in some form of wholesale or retail trade, hotels, betting shops, or other entertainment centres. Indeed, a detailed examination showed few

factor has to do with the monopolistic nature of wholesale trade.

The chief dynamic factor in the growth of the economy over the period was the growth of exports, and it is significant that the exports of the four main products were the most important. Of the $98 million increase in G.D.P. during the seven years 1954 and 1961 the increase in exports accounted for $62 million. After 1961 the trend seems to have continued in the face of political and economic uncertainty. Production for the home market lagged, and the ratio of exports to G.D.P. rose from 44 per cent to over 50 per cent. Bauxite, sugar, and rice contributed almost equally to the increase of exports. Although in our later sectoral analysis of the economy, the behaviour of investments in rice, sugar, and mining will be fully analysed, we may at this stage outline the main factors that enabled these main export activities to sustain their contribution to the growth of domestic product.

Developments in the bauxite industry included both increases in output, the pioneering of a new trade in calcined bauxite, and the building of an alumina plant. The sugar industry benefited from increases in price under the Commonwealth Sugar Agreement, and from the chance of capturing a part of the United States market, following the reallocation of the Cuban quota after 1960. Heavy investment also occurred in this industry, partly in response to a rapid increase in wages, which increased by over 80 per cent in the course of 10 years. While output increased by one-third, the labour force was reduced by one-third;[1] but man-hours did not fall so much as the labour force, since the proportion of regular workers increased, while the number of casual workers declined sharply. This ten-

establishments in manufacturing. To take a particular example, of the 27 establishments formed in Lacytown during 1962–4, 10 could be described as hotels, betting shops, or other places of entertainment, another 10 in wholesale or retail trade, and only 3 in some form of manufacturing. When this pattern of the nature of new establishments is viewed against the need to limit imports and encourage local production, the results could be very disturbing, as the figures show that the major portion of the 'new effort' was being used in the provision of entertainment and services rather than the creation of goods. See *Survey of Manpower Requirements*, Ch. 2.

[1] E. P. Reubens and B. G. Reubens, *Labour Displacement in a Labour Surplus Economy: The Sugar Industry of British Guiana* (University of the West Indies, 1963), *passim*.

dency for strong trade union pressure to push up wage costs and consequently total unit costs, with the ultimate reduction in the competitive position of Guyanese sugar *vis-à-vis* Queensland sugar, has led to labour displacement within the industry with the introduction of more capital-intensive techniques; this has tremendous implications not only for the future of investment policy within the industry, but also for investing for employment in the country as a whole. The increase in rice production resulted from a large expansion of acreage, and rice continued to be sold to the B.W.I. islands at a fixed price, about 25 per cent above the world price.

The above analysis of G.D.P. by industrial origin and the main sources of economic growth puts the nature of investment and development planning in a clear light. The limited number of sectors responsible for the generation of national product tends to give weight to the claim that there is greater need for diversification of output for the economy as a whole, as well as within individual sectors. A primary aim of policy should be to encourage investments and create the necessary investment climate, so that productivity would be increased in existing industries, and the expansion of high-yielding industries with the requisite labour transfers from other low-yielding industries should be effected. This transfer of labour from low-yielding to high-yielding industries and our concern over increasing the level of productivity arises mainly in the light of our earlier finding that there was no substantial increase in output per head, even before the political disturbances of the early sixties. Output per head may be increased in either of the two ways mentioned above, i.e. by the transfer of labour from low-yielding to high-yielding industries, or by an increase in productivity, and by limiting population growth.

In the period under consideration the only high-yielding commodity industry whose labour force was expanding was the bauxite industry, which employs only 4 per cent of the total population. Productivity was more or less constant in cost sectors, and enough alternative employment opportunities were not offered so that labour could be transferred from low to high-yielding sectors. Thus attention has to be directed to the increase in efficiency, and the establishment of more high-yielding occupations.

3. *Consumption, Savings, and Investment*

Personal consumption expenditure can be regarded as giving an indication of changes in the general standard of living. The figures for personal consumption expenditure, household *per capita* incomes, and household net income all show a steady upward trend over the period. In the Guyana economy, with its very high dependence on external trade, private consumption expenditure must be assigned a dependent role, rather than an autonomous one, in the determination of economic change. It may therefore be valid to postulate that changes in income are one of the main determinants of private consumption expenditure; this postulate is of course different from those applied in the highly developed self-contained economies where the level of private consumption expenditure is an important determinant of the level of domestic production and hence of incomes. There are of course other relevant factors bringing about changes in the composition of private consumption expenditure. Among the most important are the demonstration effect, both domestic and international, and price changes which bring about a substitution of one good for another, or of services for goods. However, changes in disposable personal incomes must be a predominant factor.

In the case of the Guyanese economy the growth of household purchasing power was slower than the growth of output per head in spite of the fact that the purchasing power of exports over imports increased over the period. Workers in sugar, bauxite, and government service increased their real earnings by more than two-thirds, as can be seen from Table 4. Average real incomes were constant in spite of this, mainly because of a sharp increase in unemployment, but partly also because the real earnings of some other groups, such as clerks, declined.

A period of rapid growth involving relatively large injections of capital tends to be accompanied by some degree of inflation. This is attributable to the nature of the process which results in consumers' incomes increasing at a faster rate than the supply of consumer goods. An approximation to the degree of inflation is usually given by the Cost of Living Index. In the experience of Guyana there has been some increase in the cost of living, but it was just high enough to maintain real *per capita* incomes

TABLE 4

INDEX OF INCREASE IN REAL WAGES

	SUGAR			BAUXITE		CONSTRUCTION		GOVERNMENT PUBLIC WORKS		BUS DRIVER	COMMERCIAL	BAKERY	
Year	Male field workers	Skilled factory workers	Unskilled male adult factory workers	Class I electrician	Unskilled labour	Grade A carpenter	Unskilled labour	Male skilled Class I (urban)	Unskilled labour (urban)	Grade B	Adult sales clerk (urban)	Oven men	Delivery boys
1954	1·00	1·00	1·00	1·00	1·00	1·00	1·00	1·00	1·00	1·00	—	1·00	1·00
1955	0·93	1·03	1·03	—	—	—	—	—	—	—	—	0·97	0·97
1956	0·95	1·07	1·06	—	—	—	—	—	—	—	—	1·04	1·43
1957	1·11	1·20	1·17	1·35	1·24	1·08	1·16	1·44	1·56	1·09	1·00	1·03	1·41
1958	1·39	1·37	1·32	1·47	1·34	1·09	1·16	1·44	1·56	1·27	1·00	1·03	1·41
1959	1·28	1·30	1·32	1·58	1·41	1·07	1·14	1·48	1·68	1·46	0·98	0·95	1·39
1960	1·41	1·39	1·42	1·76	1·57	1·06	1·14	1·59	1·85	1·46	0·98	—	—
1961	1·72	1·58	1·56	1·74	1·56	1·05	1·12	1·57	1·83	1·32	0·97	—	—
1962	1·68	1·46	1·39	1·93	1·74	1·26	1·49	1·51	1·76	1·39	0·93	—	—
1963	1·99	1·62	1·61	1·90	1·72	1·24	1·47	1·49	1·73	1·37	0·92	—	—

Source: Annual Reports, Department of Labour, Georgetown, Guyana.

intact. But the increase in the cost of living would undoubtedly have been greater if a great deal of the purchasing power had not been diverted abroad through expenditure on imports which on average accounted for more than 45 per cent of G.D.P., and to food imports in particular which accounted for over 20 per cent of total imports.[1]

We have been arguing that the economy experienced only a moderate increase in prices over the period and in only a few years did the level of retail prices rise by more than 2 per cent to 3 per cent per annum. We have also mentioned the upward drift in real wages and wage costs in some of the more important sectors; but because of the openness of the economy, the upward drift of wage costs might not have had any appreciable effects on the domestic price level, and there may be some theoretical justification for this.

In small, open economies, such as Guyana, with automatic monetary mechanisms, increases in wage costs tend to have a greater effect on employment than on the level of internal prices. Because of their heavy dependence on foreign trade, international prices exercise a more predominant influence on domestic prices than the movements in local money costs. In a sense local price-levels are exogenously determined. Since these economies are unimportant buyers and sellers of internationally traded goods, they are price-takers in the international market,

---

[1] *Annual Accounts relating to External Trade*, Dept. of Customs and Excise, Georgetown, Guyana. A poor country tends to spend a higher proportion of its total expenditure on food, and it would appear that Engels' Law failed to have very much application in the country over this period. This must be considered in the light of the fact that food prices in Guyana tend to be lower than those obtained in other countries in the Commonwealth Caribbean and the greater tendency for rice, which is relatively cheap in Guyana to provide the basis for diet. Nevertheless, the pattern of expenditure indicates that there was little change in the food pattern during the period, any increases in income being spent mainly on transport, clothing, and household goods. The trade statistics show that the import content of consumer goods has been rising over the period, but there is much indication that the marginal propensity to import is directly related to the inelasticity of supply of local goods, as for instance, the substitution of tinned meat for fresh meat, powdered milk for fresh milk, etc. This is an indication of the lack of diversity of the economy which appears not to be supplying the local market to the extent that demand conditions make possible. Some of these findings have been given adequate support in a recent cross-sectional study of the elasticity of consumption expenditure in Guyana and Barbados.

See G. E. Gumper, 'West Indian Household Budgets', *Social and Economic Studies*, Vol. 9, No. 3 (1960), pp. 355–65.

and exert little, if any, influence on their export and import prices.

Given these features of domestic price formation, there are, in principle, at least three ways in which increases in wage costs may have adverse effects on employment. First, there is the *redistribution effect*. Since increases in money wages tend to be translated into increases in real wages, they may lead to a redistribution of real incomes away from entrepreneurs or from fixed incomes to wage-earners. In so far as this reduces savings and the profitability of investment, capital formation will be checked and so also will the expansion of employment.

Secondly, there is the *substitution effect*. A rise in wage costs may encourage entrepreneurs to substitute machines for labour. Thirdly, there is the *balance of payments effect*. This arises partly from the substitution effect, because machines are usually imported. But there may also be pressure on the balance of payments because of the redistribution effect, if the marginal import content of expenditure by households is higher than that of entrepreneurs. In any event, in so far as an increase in import expenditures involves (because of automatic operation of the monetary system) a reduction in the internal money supply, this will also tend to check domestic expenditure and employment.

Any analysis of income-consumption-investment relationships must take into account the distribution of income. Since the rate of economic development of a country depends strongly on its rate of capital formation, and hence also on its rate of savings, income distribution may be expected to play an important part in determining the pace of development through its influence on savings. In addition a similar causal link may be expected to operate through the effect of income distribution on the composition of demand. A second kind of mechanism, namely, the influence of economic development on the size of incomes, will arise from changes in the country's economic structure that take place during a growth process. The decreasing share of primary production in national product, the increasing importance of entrepreneurial incomes under circumstances of rapid technological change, and the replacement of independent workers by factory employees as the scale of production increases, are among the factors that may be expected to play a part in changing the size-distribution of incomes during the course of economic advancement.

There are no reliable statistics on income distribution in Guyana, but the following table calculated from Income Tax Returns should throw light on the problem. It is obvious from this that there does not exist the poor distribution of income

TABLE 5

DISTRIBUTION OF INCOME AMONG DIFFERENT INCOME GROUPS BASED UPON INCOME TAX RETURNS 1953–60 CHARGEABLE INCOMES FOR THE YEARS 1953–9

(1) *Percentages (No. of assesses)*

Income group	1953	1954	1955	1956	1957	1958	1959
Under 1,200	44·4	43·8	42·9	42·4	42·1	42·1	41·4
1,201–3,600	31·1	31·4	31·1	32·0	31·2	30·1	29·6
3,601–6,000	12·0	12·3	12·4	12·9	12·8	12·8	12·6
6,001–8,400	5·2	5·4	5·8	5·9	5·8	5·9	6·1
8,401–10,800	3·1	2·7	2·9	2·7	2·8	3·0	3·2
Exceeding 10,800	4·3	4·4	4·9	4·1	5·3	6·2	7·1

(2) *Percentages (percentages of total chargeable income) according to income groups*

Income group	1953	1954	1955	1956	1957	1958	1959
Under 1,200	17·2	16·6	16·1	16·3	15·6	15·0	14·3
1,201–3,600	24·2	24·2	23·3	24·6	23·1	21·5	20·4
3,601–6,000	19·0	19·1	18·5	19·8	19·0	18·2	17·3
6,001–8,400	14·2	14·1	14·6	15·2	14·4	14·2	14·0
8,401–10,800	8·4	8·9	9·0	8·3	8·6	9·3	9·3
Exceeding 10,800	17·0	17·1	18·5	15·8	19·4	22·0	24·7

Source: Dept. of Inland Revenue, Annual Reports. Files of the Dept. of Inland Revenue, Georgetown.

characterizing many development countries—especially in Latin America.[1] The constancy of distribution over time is also evident. But this is no reason for complacency. In the more advanced countries with egalitarian distributions of income, wide variations exist, but monetary and fiscal measures are effective in reducing inequalities and at the same time siphon-

[1] E.C.L.A., *Towards a Dynamic Policy for Latin America*, U.N. Economic and Social Council (April 1963), pp. 5–10.

ing off potential surpluses for public investment or providing the requisite incentives for investment in the private sector. The relatively equal distribution of income in Guyana helps to explain why actual and potential savings may be low and why a new class of profit-making entrepreneurs has failed to emerge within the country. Professor Arthur Lewis has agreed that

this new class is more thrifty than all the other classes (the landlords, the wage-earners, the peasants, the salaried middle classes), and their share of the national income increases relatively to that of all others. In private capitalism these entrepreneurs have made private profits, and have reinvested on private account; whereas in the U.S.S.R. the great increase in profits has been concealed as a 'turnover' tax which the planners have reinvested on public account. But in either case, the essential feature of the conversion from 5 to 12 per cent saving is an enormous increase of profits in the national income.[1]

Table 6 represents details about the flow of investments and savings. An important point which emerges is that total savings has been running at an average of 12 per cent of G.D.P. In this context we must consider the relevance of the judgement that the central problem in the theory of economic growth is to understand the process by which a community is converted from being a 5 per cent to a 12 per cent saver—with all the changes in attitudes, in institutions and in techniques which accompany this conversion.[2] In the case of Guyana there are certain factors which qualify this statement.

Given the large geographical size of the country and its small economic size, investment for development has been lumpy because of the large infrastructural requirements. Investment to curb unemployment might have also eaten deeply into savings. There have also been relatively few changes in the attitudes and

---

[1] W. A. Lewis, *The Theory of Economic Growth* (London, 1961), p. 226. A relative increase in profits is not necessarily the same as an increase in the inequality of income distribution, since the increase may be associated with a corresponding decline of the relative importance of income from rent, and other similar factors. This does not invalidate the conclusion that the ratio of savings to national income is an important function of ratio of profits to national income (which bears a close relation to the inequality of distribution of income, though it is not *just* a function of this inequality). See also Prof. Lewis's interesting discussion of these problems in his 'Some Reflections on Economic Development', *Economic Digest* (Institute of Development Economics, Karachi, Vol. 3, No. 3, Winter 1960), pp. 3–5.

[2] Lewis, *The Theory of Economic Growth*, pp. 225–6.

in institutions for channelling these into productive activities. These will be investigated at a later stage. But an answer to the problem may lie in the actual composition of total savings.

Private savings by Guyanese are relatively high by international standards and averaged about 9 per cent of G.N.P., exclusive of depreciation. As regards household savings and that of local firms in the national income, personal savings are taken as a residual item and this may reduce the reliability of this figure. From information available in Guyana, it appears, however, that quite a considerable sum is being invested overseas by residents and resident firms each year. In considering the possibilities of diverting this annual outflow consideration should be taken of the fact that much of the capital invested externally during the period has not been repatriated and provides a possible source of investible funds to the country if it could be enticed back. A greater degree of political stability with the consequent strong investment climate may provide an answer.

Even if we allow for a substantial error in our estimates—since this is a notoriously difficult figure to arrive at—it still appears that there may be assets worth over $20 million in overseas countries which are the property of Guyanese firms and individuals, who do not come under the category of regular investors. A really small part of these values relate to the really small saver whose savings may be canalized through such institutions as savings banks and credit societies. However, one must note the phenomenal rise in the outflow of savings after 1961, probably on account of the progressively increasing loss of confidence after this date owing to strikes and political and social unrest.[1]

The process of capital formation involves at least three steps: first an increase in the volume of real savings, so that resources can be released for investment purposes. Secondly, the chanelling of savings through finance and credit mechanism, so that investible funds can be collected from a wide range of different sources and claimed by investors; and thirdly, the act of investment itself, by which the resources are used for increasing the capital stock. The first requirement is of fundamental import-

[1] A fuller analysis of the behaviour of savings is given in Chapter VI.

TABLE 6
INVESTMENT AND SAVINGS 1954–64
(Million Guyana dollars)

	1954	1955	1956	1957	1958	1959	1960	1961	1962	1963	1964
1. Gross domestic product	191·7	191·5	207·0	231·6	234·1	239·4	263·5	289·8	307·2	275·5	302·9
2. Gross capital formation	38·4	46·0	48·0	62·6	68·5	56·9	82·4	76·4	55·6	50·9	53·6
3. Gross capital formation as percentage of G.D.P.	20·0%	24·0%	23·2%	27·1%	29·3%	23·8%	31·3%	26·4%	18·1%	18·4%	17·7%
4. Household savings	22·0	14·2	16·5	14·1	12·2	10·8	6·2	19·4	27·7	54·8	19·2
5. Savings of locally owned corporations	1·0	4·5	3·2	7·0	8·1	10·0	3·7	6·2	4·3	1·0	1·4
6. Government savings	3·7	3·9	4·8	4·2	5·2	6·0	10·8	6·3	6·2	3·2	-1·6
7. Total savings as % of G.D.P.	14·0%	11·8%	11·8%	10·9%	10·9%	11·2%	7·8%	11·0%	12·4%	21·4%	6·2%
8. Net investment from abroad	3,809	14,416	15,180	27,701	34,468	21,317	49,567	26,636	6,909	-14,469	—
9. Known private outflow of savings (B)	-6·2	3·6	-5·1	0·2	3·2	-1·4	7·0	-2·5	-8·9	-25·3	N.A.

(B) Line 9 includes flows of migrants' personal effects from 1959 to the end of 1962.

Sources: Quarterly Statistical Digests, June and December, 1964; Central Statistical Bureau, *Analysis of Domestic Product*; Files of the Central Statistical Bureau. O'Loughlin, 'The Economy of British Guiana, 1952–6', loc. cit. Kundu, 'The Economy of British Guiana, 1960–75', loc. cit.

ance if the higher rate of investment is to be achieved without generating inflation. Although the ratio of savings has been high in the country, there still remains the crucial problem of mobilizings avings. But this should not be confused with the monetary financing of investment. The significance of financial institutions lies in their making available the means to utilize savings.[1]

Government savings were relatively low, averaging about 2 per cent of G.D.P. The lack of government spending was not among the factors responsible for the low growth rate of national income. For the ratio of government expenditure on current account rose from 17·4 to 19·0 per cent of G.D.P. in 1961 and to even higher levels from 1962 to the end of 1964. G.D.P. declined while expenditure continued to increase. In addition government development expenditure rose to around 8 per cent of G.D.P. by 1961. These are very high figures by international standards; and if high levels of government spending and investment are a *sine qua non* of economic development, then Guyana ought to be on the road to prosperity.

Despite low G.D.P. growth, one would expect the increase in government expenditures to lead to an increase in the receipts in other sectors, such as transportation, construction, distribution, and also on other expenditures including the wage payments made by these sectors, and the profits arising within these sectors. In turn, the contribution of these sectors to G.D.P. and to national income are made greater by these expenditures. And since the economy is far from being at full employment, these contributions will be real for the greater part and will not merely reflect monetary flows. In addition to this, there are the

---

[1] As one study of the role of financial institutions concludes: 'However poor an economy may be there will be a need for institutions which allow such savings as are currently forthcoming to be invested conveniently and safely, and which ensure that they are channelled into the most useful purposes. The poorer a country is, in fact, the greater is the need for agencies to collect and invest the savings of the broad mass of persons and institutions within its borders. Such agencies will not only permit small amounts of savings to be handled and invested conveniently but will allow the owners of savings to retain liquidity individually but finance long-term investment collectively.' Edward Nevin, *Capital Funds in Underdeveloped Countries* (London, 1961), p. 75. But although the existence of a more developed capital market and financial intermediaries will aid in the collection and distribution of investible funds, they in no way lessen the need for *real* savings. This and other problems connected with the financing of investment in Guyana are discussed in more detail in Chapter VI.

4—E.D.G.

long-run effects of increasing the quantity of productive assets, and the quality of skills and techniques that go hand in hand with these assets. Thus the expenditure made by the government is expected to have both short- and long-run effects on the size of G.D.P. and national income, which will in turn affect the size of government revenues and the level of government expenditures for development and ordinary purposes. The analysis of the structure and composition of public investment given in Chapter VII gives us some idea as to why these cumulative causal chains may not have been operative in the Guyanese context.

In the study of economic growth, interest attaches to the proportion that capital formation constitutes of national product. The larger it is (i.e. the larger the part of current product retained for the use in further production), other conditions being equal, the higher the rate of growth of national product that can be generated. Low capital formation proportions mean low rates of growth of national product, unless capital output ratios decline, i.e. unless more output can be turned out per unit of capital. Assuming that this statement is true, let us examine the behaviour of this aggregate in order to determine whether it was satisfactory, having regard to the future of investment planning in the country. We may examine the composition of capital from at least four angles: the ratio of net to gross capital formation, the industries in which the capital is used, what the capital consists of; these must be distinguished from the actual supply of capital and the sources of capital funds.

Table 6 brought out the encouraging fact that for more than a decade gross capital formation has averaged over 24 per cent of G.D.P. and net capital formation over 18 per cent. Even allowing for the statistical and conceptual difficulties connected with the calculation of the ratio of gross to net investment which lie partly in the knotty problem of calculating replacement costs, the ratios of gross and net capital formation for the economy of Guyana are high by international standards.[1]

---

[1] The crucial role of investment in underdeveloped countries is discussed at some length in *World Economic Survey 1959*. The survey observed that rates of growth attained by individual countries have been closely related to their levels of investment. The higher rates of growth have generally occurred in the countries where the proportion of output allocated to investment has been relatively large.

In a later chapter we examine, among other things, the main sources from which capital formation was financed, but at this stage we could measure in a crude way the relationship between capital formation and output, and indicate broadly the extent to which investment was channelled into the various sectors of the economy.

The gross incremental capital/output ratio can be obtained by dividing gross investment as a percentage of G.D.P. by the average annual rate of growth of G.D.P.[1] If we omit the period 1962–4 on the assumption that there were certain abnormal factors affecting the growth of G.D.P. in this period, with an average investment ratio of 25 per cent for the 1954–61 period and a rate of growth of G.D.P. by 5 per cent, the gross incremental capital output ratio was around 5:1, i.e. for the period 1954 to 1961 an investment ratio of approximately 5 per cent was required to increase output by 1 per cent.[2]

But concentration on the over-all or global capital/output ratio for the entire economy may present misleading results.[3] For this ratio depends on capital/output ratios in the various

Similarly, in countries experiencing low or moderate growth rates, the level of investment has tended to be comparatively small. There are some countries which have grown rapidly despite the moderate proportion of output devoted to investment, and others which have grown slowly, notwithstanding rather high levels of investment, for example Guyana. The fact that the relationship between investment and growth is only moderately close is not, of course, unexpected, for the level of investment is but one of the variables determining economic growth. The main reasons why investment may not have been productive in these countries is discussed at some length: See United Nations, *World Economic Survey 1959* (New York, 1960).

[1] r = the rate of growth of output = $\Delta Y/Y = (\Delta Y/Y)(I/Y)$ where Y is income or product and I is investment. Writing I/Y as $\Sigma I/\Sigma Y$ in order to use all the data used in calculating the ratio, and by transposition we derive

$$\frac{I}{\Delta Y} = \frac{\Sigma I}{\Sigma Y} \times \frac{I}{r},$$

i.e. the average incremental capital output ratio,

$$\frac{I}{\Delta Y} = \frac{I/Y}{\Delta Y/Y} = \frac{\Sigma I}{\Sigma Y/r} = \frac{\Sigma I}{\Sigma Y} \frac{I}{r}.$$

[2] This is high in terms of capital requirements, and in comparison with other development countries where the ratio has seldom exceeded 4. *World Economic Survey*, loc. cit., Ch. 2. However, given the stage of the country in the march towards self-sustaining growth, it may not be unduly high. For a discussion of capital output ratios see G. M. Meier, *Leading Issues in Development Economics* (New York, 1965).

[3] See W. B. Reddaway, *The Development of the Indian Economy* (Allen and Unwin, London, 1962), pp. 206–12.

sectors of the economy with the over-all ratio being an average of the sectoral ratios weighted by the increases in sectoral outputs. Since the over-all ratio will be affected by the changing composition of output and investment among the several sectors, it is essential to analyse the capital/output relationships at the sectoral level. A discussion of sectoral capital/output ratios must await our detailed analysis of investment behaviour in the various sectors, but the factors explaining the high global capital/output ratio may lie in the pattern and division of capital investment between the various sectors of the economy.

Firstly bauxite investment is abnormally capital intensive. Owing to the high degree of mechanization, labour is relatively small. The steady increase in capital accumulation after 1958 in the mining industry was mainly due to heavy investment in manganese mining and the construction of an alumina plant which was completed and commissioned in 1961, with a capacity of 300,000 tons alumina per annum. Investment costs actually amounted to $65 million, and apart from fresh developments in the sugar industry and several minor investments, it was the main contributor in raising the level of direct investments by overseas companies over the level of payments made in respect of such foreign investments. Thus the completion of the alumina plant changed the aggregate investment picture considerably, and is continuing its contribution to net capital formation.

The second factor that led to the rather high global capital/output ratio was that the purpose of much of the investment in machinery in the sugar and rice industries was to reduce employment rather than to increase output. Faced with increasing costs, which have placed the sugar industry at a disadvantage *vis-à-vis* such low-cost producers as Queensland, large-scale mechanization had to be introduced at the inevitable expense, however, of increasing the rate of unemployment in the face of rising population. Mechanization took place mainly in field operations, in such sections as land preparation, tillage, drainage, and transport, in the maintenance of drainage systems and the haulage of loaded punts by tractor.[1] In rice, the substantial

[1] Reubens and Reubens, *Labour displacement in a labour surplus economy; The Sugar Industry of British Guiana.* According to the Report, the number of workers in both field and factory fell substantially, from about 26,300 in 1953 to 20,500 in 1960.

investments that have gone into the various land development schemes have resulted in a shift to mechanized farming, which has enabled more land to be brought under cultivation. As a result aggregate output has been increased considerably, but the average productivity per acre has fallen as more and more marginal lands have been brought into cultivation and employment reduced. Among the other reasons for the high capital/output ratio was the fact that heavy government investment in drainage yielded poor returns, and there was not enough growth of the economy outside bauxite, sugar, and rice. Production for the home market, which is normally below average in capital intensity, did not show the rate of expansion that could have been expected in an economy where exports were expanding rapidly.

The conclusion must be that investment in Guyana has been highly capital intensive both in the private and public sectors. Bauxite is a highly capital-intensive operation; sugar has been continuing with the process of mechanization for the last few years; rice farming has been significantly tractorized (perhaps over-tractorized); public sector investment in drainage and irrigation and land development schemes has also been very capital-intensive. To illustrate, a rough calculation reveals that the capital/output ratio for the mining industry has been over 7, whereas in the manufacturing sector—mostly small-sized, light factories—it has been only about 1·5.

Since capital formation involves the utilization of real resources of the economy in order to increase the size of the future output, it is desirable that the relationship between the capital used up and the output resulting be as low as possible. It is obvious, however, that this relationship will undergo changes over the course of economic development. In the early period, when the stock of capital is being built up on several fronts, the relationship between the capital invested and output will be high. This may be so for two reasons. On the one hand, produc-

As a result output per man at work climbed substantially. In 1953, 100 acres under cane required 27 field workers, in 1960 only 17; in 1953, 1,000 tons of milled sugar needed 24 factory workers, in 1960 only 13. Not only did almost 6,000 persons lose their jobs in this period of rapidly increasing population, but also the nature of the technical improvements was such that seasonal fluctuations in employment were exacerbated.

tion capital will not yield its maximum output right from the outset; a period of adaptation and adjustment is necessary; besides, production capital cannot be expected to yield its full potential in the absence of support from basic social and other overhead capital. Secondly, and in support of this first point, a substantial part of the total fixed capital in the economy must in the initial stages be in the form of social and other overhead capital, and the contribution of this latter to total output in the future is largely indirect.

Thus the factors likely to determine the size of the ratio in the future will depend on the pattern of investment and the nature of specific projects. For example, in the case of ten light-engineering projects considered by the government for possible inclusion in their investment plan, the ratio is about 2·5:1. The data given in Table 7 represent a summary of a few projects on which feasibility studies were carried out by the government with a view to selecting those that qualify for inclusion in the industrial development programme of the country. It is obvious that the capital requirements for these projects are low and that more investment of this nature will reduce the over-all requirements of capital. Similarly, if in the land development schemes

TABLE 7

SUMMARY OF FEASIBILITY STUDIES

Industries	Capital requirement	Labour per factory
Tyres and tubes	910,000	68
Tannery	1,017,500	56
Leather footwear	990,200	190
Canvas boots and shoes	1,192,000	119
Cement packaging	962,000	27
Cellular concrete blocks	3,147,000	179
Plywood	1,604,000	153[a]
Instant coffee	534,600	73
Steel rolling mill	2,799,700	82
Total	13,157,100	947

Source: Feasibility Studies File, Development Secretariat, Georgetown, Guyana.

[a] 153 persons for employment if 1 shift is worked. 287 persons for employment if 2 shifts are worked.

the period of time between initial investment and capacity or maximum output is reduced by greater administrative and organizational efficiency, the ratio, and consequently investment requirements, will come down. On the contrary, if the emphasis on investment is on transport, communications, heavy industry, and other capital-intensive projects, the ratio will go up. The over-all ratio for the whole economy is thus dependent upon the investment programme finally selected.

Now let us look at the composition of capital formation by type of assets, i.e. more generally, the relationship between gross capital formation and real fixed capital formation. The composition of real fixed capital formation in the economy is of significance in any study of investment and economic growth for several reasons. For one thing the import content of the various types of capital assets is likely to vary, and consequently, for those assets for which the import content is high, a claim is lodged against future foreign exchange earnings when the eventual replacement of the asset becomes necessary. The assumption here is that no import substitution takes place in the meantime. There is also the related consideration of whether the capital asset will directly or indirectly earn back its foreign exchange cost, either through increased exports or reduced imports.

Secondly, the composition of capital formation gives some ideas about the directions in which the economy is proceeding. For example, a growing proportion of machinery or equipment in the total indicates some progress towards mechanization and industrialization. This leads to the expectation of increases in output in the short-run future. By contrast, if a growing proportion of the total is comprised of social capital, the expectation is that increases in real output would be some time in coming into fruition. Thirdly, an interesting corollary is the importance of public investment in relation to private investment. The division of capital formation between the public and private sectors and the interrelationships between the two are items of considerable usefulness in determining budgetary, fiscal, and tax policies.

It is evident from Table 8 that the capital formation in mechanical equipment has an extremely high import content. This is corroborated by the fact that average imports of capital

TABLE 8

GROSS CAPITAL FORMATION BY TYPE OF INVESTMENT

Type of investment	(Million Guyana dollars) 1958	1959	1960	1961	1962	1963	1964
Retained imports of machinery	25·7	27·5	45·2	40·4	29·8	22·9	36·1
Domestic production of machinery	2·8	5·4	4·5	3·6	1·8	1·0	1·1
Private building and construction	9·0	8·3	14·1	10·8	10·4	6·4	7·2
Government building and construction	15·8	13·9	9·9	15·6	12·9	8·1	6·9
Capital sunk in plantations and mines	9·6	4·1	5·9	7·0	2·4	2·0	1·5
Fixed capital formation	62·9	52·3	79·6	77·4	57·3	39·9	52·8
Change in stocks	5·0	−1·0	2·8	−1·0	−1·7	11·0	0·8
GROSS CAPITAL FORMATION	67·9	51·3	82·4	76·4	55·6	50·9	53·6

Source: Quarterly Statistical Digest, December 1965.

goods has been running at over 25 per cent of total imports. There have also been rapid increases in both private and public building and construction. Inevitably a rapid increase in the level of fixed capital formation stimulates activity in the construction industry. In Guyana, this may be important since the industry exerts powerful multiplier effects on the economy through the use of large quantities of labour and local building materials. Of late there has been an increase in the importation of building materials mainly for concrete houses, with the result that many of the secondary multiplier effects may not have been present.[1]

Tables 9 and 10 give some statistics on the number of build-

[1] Quarterly Statistical Digest, June 1964; Annual Reports on External Trade. It is necessary to carry out research in the construction of buildings that rely largely on local materials, i.e. timber for construction. The use of cement for this purpose has, as far as possible, to be minimized if investigations into the construction and maintenance costs show that the use of timber is not at all bad economy even in the long run. It is necessary to minimize the use of Greenheart for buildings, and the use of other woods should be popularized. Greenheart is running short, its regeneration takes 120 years, and it is an important article of export, the demand for which is already well established.

ings erected, and additions to buildings, during 1956 and 1964. The number of dwelling houses erected in rural areas in 1956 was of the order of 2,700 and in 1963 this was reduced to slightly over 1,600, but in 1964 had become closer to 2,000.

TABLE 9

HOUSES ERECTED AND ADDITIONS TO EXISTING BUILDINGS
IN AREAS OTHER THAN GEORGETOWN
AND NEW AMSTERDAM—1956–64

Year	Dwelling houses		Dwelling houses and industrial		Industrial buildings		Public buildings	
	Erected	*Added to*	*Erected*	*Added to*	*Erected*	*Added to*	*Erected*	*Added to*
1956	2,699	912	110	124	108	28	18	20
1957	3,134	957	77	115	73	16	48	16
1958	2,455	939	52	114	84	18	49	10
1959	2,152	898	71	94	63	26	32	20
1960	2,150	1,147	88	171	88	22	45	9
1961	2,240	1,303	66	177	98	33	45	10
1962	2,271	2,167	76	153	141	49	51	8
1963	1,630	1,734	57	97	88	36	13	7
1964	1,950	1,565	57	97	62	21	21	9

TABLE 10

NEW BUILDINGS ERECTED IN GEORGETOWN AND
NEW AMSTERDAM—1956–64

Year	New buildings	GEORGETOWN Additions to existing buildings	NEW AMSTERDAM New buildings
1956	101	184	125[a]
1957	77	270	54
1958	92	366	21
1959	167	414	24
1960	125	312	25
1961	122	277	45
1962	98	303	33
1963	45	280	18
1964	56	280	26

Sources: Quarterly Statistical Digests; Colonial Annual Reports on British Guiana.

[a] Includes 104 erected by government.

This high level of activity in the building industry outside Georgetown and New Amsterdam about 1956–7 is partly explained by the erection of certain large-scale housing schemes which were completed soon after that date. The figures on new buildings erected in Georgetown and New Amsterdam show a similar trend. But although the numbers erected serve as a good guide to the level of activity in the construction industry, account has to be taken of the values of these structures. The building cost index is given below. When these figures are

BUILDING COST INDEX (1912 = 100)

1954	360
1955	350
1956	388
1957	403·5
1958	399
1959	392
1960	504
1962	422

Source: Quarterly Statistical Digest, June 1964.

adjusted to bring them in line with estimates of construction costs obtained from building contractors, the upward trend in fixed capital formation contributed by building is reinforced. The rebuilding of property destroyed during the 1962, 1963, and 1964 disturbances should further help to augment this type of investment.

Activity in the construction industry has been one of the significant factors that has promoted the trend towards economic recovery during 1965. Several major construction projects, including blocks of buildings for the Special Service Unit, the Bank of Guyana building, and an extensive road-building programme, were in operation during 1965. The effect of this expansion in construction activity was seen mainly in the higher level of employment among workers in the building trades, and in the greater demand for consumer goods, which in turn kept retail sales buoyant during the year. The impact was also felt in those forest industries that are linked to the supply needs in the construction field; in fact most sawmilling and quarrying firms expected their production to be about 20 per cent better in 1965 than in 1964. Prices for lumber also rose sharply; for instance, the price of Greenheart (and other hardwoods) increased by more than 36 per cent.

Residential construction moved up. By September, 1965, 2,353 houses had been erected or extended in rural areas and localities adjoining Georgetown; this compares with 2,314 houses erected or extended during the same period in the previous year. Most of the construction was in the private sector, as public authorities did little residential construction.

While residential construction in the municipal Georgetown area was rather sluggish during the first half of 1965, building applications approved had increased substantially from 195 during the first half of 1964 to 289 during the corresponding period in 1965. Residential construction activity therefore increased rapidly during the second half of 1965.

Public sector non-residential construction activity has however been the chief factor underlying expansion in the industry. Several blocks of buildings comprising thirty-nine (39) structures were erected for accommodating the Special Service Unit; construction of the Bank of Guyana was pushed ahead; and some 30 miles of coastal roadway were constructed during the year. Public buildings were also rehabilitated, certain government offices were extended or constructed, and plans were prepared for the erection of five large schools in the rural areas.

In order to assist the government in its road-building programme the government of the United States of America agreed to make available to the government of British Guiana US$8·3 million. About US$2·8 million of the amount was an outright grant, and the remaining US$5·5 million, for the Atkinson/McKenzie road, was a loan repayable over 40 years and bearing interest at the rate of 1 per cent per annum over the first 10 years and 2½ per cent per annum during the remaining period. The first instalment will not be due before 10 years (1975). As part of the loan agreement US$1·4 million worth of road-building equipment arrived in the country from the U.S.A. about the middle of 1965.

Construction, like other forms of capital formation in Guyana, has a high import content. Therefore, apart from its effects on the forest industry, expansion in the construction industry would have a substantial impact on the distributive trades. Importation of several items of building materials accordingly increased during the year. It is however anticipated that as the government's drive to encourage greater use of local woods for construction purposes begins to bear fruit, cement imports will not expand as fast.

TABLE 11
IMPORTS OF CERTAIN BUILDING MATERIALS

	Unit	Jan.–Dec. 1964	Jan.–Sept. 1964	Jan.–Sept. 1965
Cement	'000 cwt.	484	250	281
Galvanized and aluminium sheets	'000 cwt.	45	27	60
Window glass	'000 sq. ft.	826	314	458
Nails	'000 cwt.	16	10	8
Paints	'000 lb.	1,955	1,394	1,429

Source: Economic Survey of British Guiana 1965, Ministry of Economic Development, 1966.

Total investment in fixed capital comprises business purchases of machinery and equipment, new construction, and the government's capital expenditures. In 1965, total investment, so defined, rose to $60 million compared with $59·3 million in 1964, an increase of 1·2 per cent. Compared with the gross domestic product at factor cost, fixed investment represented a proportion of about 19 per cent in both 1964 and 1965. A significant trend has been the fall in the ratio of fixed investment to gross domestic product over the last three years. In 1960 this ratio was slightly more than 30 per cent and in 1961 about 27 per cent; but since the latter year this ratio has fallen, reaching the level indicated above.

There were heavy investments in the mining sector, and in transportation, between 1957 and 1960, and large expenditures on land development since 1960. These investments were gestating in 1962 and subsequent years.

At the same time (1962) investments began to decline steeply; no major projects have been undertaken in the private sector since the completion of the alumina plant. This then provides the fundamental explanation for the downward trend of the ratio of investment to Gross Domestic Product, observed in recent years.

In 1960 the private sector was responsible for about 80 per cent of the total investment in fixed capital, but this trend has tended to fluctuate in recent years. In 1963 for instance, the private sector's share in total investment was about 64 per cent. The sector's contribution however rose to more than 83 per cent in 1964 under the influence of substantial investment expenditure in the sugar and bauxite industries coupled with a very much reduced investment expenditure on the part of the government. In 1965, however, government capital expenditure rose sharply, much more so than private investment. The result is that the private sector accounted for about 67 per cent of the investment in 1965.

TABLE 12

INVESTMENT IN THE PUBLIC AND PRIVATE SECTORS

	1960	1961	1962	1963	1964	1965
Total investment $ Mn.	79·6	77·4	59·9	44·8	59·3	60·0
Public sector $ Mn.	16·6	23·3	20·1	12·4	9·9	20·0
Private sector $ Mn.	63·0	54·1	39·8	32·4	49·4	40·0

Source: Economic Survey of British Guiana 1965, Ministry of Economic Development, 1966.

Foreign-owned firms are responsible for the major share of private investment. The bauxite and the sugar companies are very often large investors in fixed capital. For instance, these companies invested about $65 million between 1960 and 1963. Their investment in fixed capital was $18 million in 1964, and reached $24 million in 1965.

Foreign-owned firms together invested approximately $20·5 million in 1964, or 34·6 per cent of a total investment of $59·3 million. The high level of investment by foreign-owned firms increases employment and earnings within the country, and expands Guyana's exports; but they also have significant implications for our external payments in the form of investment income. Available figures indicate that investments by these firms probably reached over $27 million in 1965, an increase of nearly 32 per cent above 1964.

TABLE 13 (a)
INVESTMENT IN THE PRIVATE SECTOR

	1960	1961	1962	1963	1964	1965
Private sector $ Mn.	63·3	54·1	39·8	32·4	49·4	40·0
of which foreign $ Mn.	35·4	20·3	9·3	12·7	20·5	27·1

TABLE 13 (b)
INVESTMENT AND G.D.P. IN BAUXITE AND MANGANESE
MINING

	1957–60	1961	1962	1963	1964	1965[a]
Investment $ Mn.	71·5	12·0	5·5	4·4	11·1	17·0
Net income arising (G.D.P.) $ Mn.	—	32·5	45·9	32·1	49·3	58·1

Source: As per Table 12.
[a] Preliminary.

The figures in the above table demonstrate the fact that following the large investment of approximately $83·5 million between 1957 and 1961, net output arising in the sector increased rapidly except for 1963, when the general strike reduced the scale of operations. In 1961, though some alumina and manganese were being produced, full capacity had not been reached.

Investments in the sugar industry has been fairly constant between 1957 and 1960, and averaged $5·3 million per annum. After declining in 1961 and 1962 investment in the industry rose to $6·8 million in 1964.

TABLE 14
INVESTMENT AND INCOME IN THE SUGAR INDUSTRY

	1957–60	1961	1962	1963	1964	1965
Investment						
Fixed investment $ Mn.	21·5	4·3	2·4	6·6	6·8	7·8
Net output (G.D.P.) $ Mn.	—	50·0	52·2	62·5	44·5	47·1

Fixed investment in the manufacturing sector fell slightly below the 1964 level of $4·6 million for the large firms (with 5 or more employees), that were in existence in 1964. It is clear therefore that so far as 1965 is concerned there has been little expansion in the manufacturing sector. In fact since the figures include purchases of capital for replacement of worn-out assets, net investment or increase of productive capacity in the sector as a whole must be increasing at a relatively slow rate. If capital consumption allowances are taken as a measure of the annual replacement of capital, net investment was $2·4 million in 1964, and less in 1965.

Annual fixed investment in the distribution sector is usually low as distributive firms do not usually employ heavy machinery and plant. Fixed investment in distribution was valued at $1·5 million in 1964 and amounted to $1·6 million in 1965. Most of the investment funds went into the purchase of vehicles and office equipment.

TABLE 15
DISPOSITION OF PRIVATE FIXED INVESTMENT
BY CERTAIN SECTORS 1963–65

	(*In Million Guyana dollars*) 1963		1964		1965	
	Value	Per cent	Value	Per cent	Value	Per cent
Total	*32·4*	*100*	*49·4*	*100*	*40·0*	*100*
Sugar	6·6	20·4	6·8	14·2	7·8	19·5
Manufacturing including power	6·4	19·8	4·6	9·6	4·3	10·8
Mining	4·4	13·6	11·1	23·2	17·0	42·5
Distribution	0·6	1·9	1·5	3·1	1·6	4·0
Transportation and Communication (including Public Utilities)	0·6	1·9	1·4	2·9	2·4	6·0

Investment in the public sector was estimated at $35·5 million for 1965, but actual expenditure was of the order of $20·0 million. This compares with an expenditure of $9·9 million in 1964, and $12·4 million in 1963.

The secondary multiplier effects operate overseas because the greater part of the investment consists of imported capital, and the balance of investment income accruing to Guyanese is low. Variables such as the level of exports and the terms of trade take on added significance in this connection. But there are other difficulties which lie in the quality of co-operant factors, institutions, attitudes, and so on, which have not only affected the productivity of capital, but help to explain why foreign capital has failed to take advantage of investment opportunity in Guyana.

II

THE GROWTH OF POPULATION, EMPLOYMENT AND THE LABOUR FORCE

1. *The Growth of Population*

In this chapter we analyse some of the demographic factors relevant to the economic development of Guyana.

Full employment and the satisfaction of consumer needs are primary ends of economic policy. But full employment must be related to an increasing population.[1] The territorial distribution of the population, its racial composition and the relative size of its age-groups are other demographic factors contributing to the character and pace of economic growth. For example, a population with a high proportion of dependants or old people will need a different sort of investment planning from one in which the actual or potential labour force comprises a relatively high proportion of the total population. In all development countries, even those with a favourable population/natural resources ratio, a rapid increase in population makes investment necessary in order to maintain the standard of living, i.e. to prevent real *per capita* incomes from falling. The economy may have to run in order to remain in the same place. In other words, in Guyana, as in all other retarded countries, the population situation has become one which reflects the over-all *malaise* in the national economy, and must be understood and dealt with as an integral part of the need for an all-round development and transformation of the economy.

[1] Although employment is derived from the growth of product, and is therefore recognized in strict logic as a derivative phenomenon, it is not possible to proceed on that basis today. Removing unemployment and putting the economy on a basis that will result in full employment within some horizon is, therefore, to be accepted as an objective of policy to be reconciled with the objective of increasing output and income. Even if employment may not be accepted as an independent goal, we must still ascertain the population/employment growth relationship obtaining in the country, and its implications for investment.

5—E.D.G.

Different investment and economic plans operate in different orbits of possibilities. In so far as the rate of growth of output is equal to the rate of growth of population, the economy is operating within the *stagnant orbit*. In so far as the growth of output is less than population growth, it is operating within the *retrogressive orbit*; in so far as the growth of output is faster than the growth of population, the economy is operating within the *cumulative growth orbit*. One of the central tasks of investment planning is the initiation of those policies that will result in the country's movement into the cumulative growth orbit.

Data on the enumerated population increase from 1881–1960 are given in Table 1. Acceleration in the growth of population is indicated by the fact that from 1946 to 1960 the population of Guyana increased by about 185,000, i.e. at the annual rate of 12,333 persons. It is estimated that the figure for 1964 stood at 57,000 over that of 1960, a yearly increase of over 14,000 for that

TABLE 1
ENUMERATED POPULATION OF GUYANA 1881–1960[a]

	BOTH SEXES						
	1881	*1891*	*1911*	*1921*	*1931*	*1946*	*1960*
Guyana	252,186	278,328	296,041	297,691	318,312	375,701	560,128
Demerara	159,443	173,898	175,596	173,932	185,184	220,639	338,025
Berbice	47,161	51,176	65,862	68,483	75,919	96,623	141,775
Essequibo	45,582	53,254	54,583	55,276	57,209	58,439	80,328

	Index of Guyana population						
	1881	*1891*	*1911*	*1921*	*1931*	*1946*	*1960*
Guyana	100%	110·37	117·39	118·04	126·22	148·98	222·10
Demerara	100%	109·07	110·13	109·09	116·14	138·38	212·00
Berbice	100%	108·51	139·65	145·21	160·98	204·88	300·62
Essequibo	100%	116·83	119·75	121·27	125·51	128·21	176·23

	Percentage increase of population of Guyana and its three counties						
	BOTH SEXES						
	1881	*1891*	*1891– 1911*	*1911– 1921*	*1921– 1931*	*1931– 1946*	*1946– 1960*
Guyana	—	10·37	6·36	0·56	6·93	18·03	49·09
Demerara	—	9·07	0·98	− ·95	6·47	19·15	53·20
Berbice	—	8·51	28·70	3·98	10·86	27·27	46·73
Essequibo	—	16·83	2·50	1·27	3·50	2·15	37·46

Source: Census Bulletin 1946. Census of Population 1960.

[a] No firm figures exist for the 1960–4 period, but provisional Annual Reports of the Registrar General for these years do not indicate any reverse in the trends noticed prior to 1960.

period.[1] The significance of this rate of growth is clearly perceived when we consider that in 50 years, i.e. between 1881 and 1931, it rose by 66,000, or at a rate of 1,322, a more than ninefold increase in the rate of growth. The slow rate of growth in the 1881–1931 period occurred despite the fact that there was a net immigration of 125,754 persons into the country, i.e. at the annual rate of 2,515 persons, which of course means that but for immigration, there would have been a net decrease of population of nearly 60,000 in the five decades since 1881, or at the annual rate of 1,200.

The year 1931 was the turning point in the record of population growth, and from that year on to 1946 there was an increase of 57,489 or 3,833 every year—more than three times the rate of increase in the preceding five decades. In the next 15 years, 1946 to 1960, there was a much greater acceleration of the rate of growth, and the annual rate of growth was more than tenfold increase over the rate obtained between 1881 and 1931. The annual rate of growth from 1881 to 1960 is set out below:

RATE OF GROWTH OF THE POPULATION OF GUYANA
1881–1960

(Annual per cent)					
1881–90	1891–1910	1911–20	1921–30	1931–45	1946–60
1·04	0·37	0·06	0·69	1·2	3·31

It is obvious that since 1931 and particularly since 1946, the rate of growth of population has become very much faster, and indications are that this rate is, if anything, likely to be exceeded in the next 15 years. Thus not only has a demographic explosion taken place within the country, but if a comparative view is taken of the rate of increase of population with the corresponding rate on other areas, it becomes clear that the rate in Guyana is one of the highest in the world.[2]

[1] Annual Reports of the Registrar General 1960–4, Guyana; Quarterly Statistical Digest, March 1965, Central Statistical Office, Guyana.

[2] As compared with the annual percentage rate of 3·3 in Guyana in 1946–60 the rate in 1950–60 for the world as a whole was 1·8; for South America 2·3; for Africa 2·2; for Asia 1·9; for North America 2·1; for Oceana 2·4; for the Soviet Union 1·7. In South America, though the average rate of increase in 1950–60 was

Table 2 and Figure 1 make it evident that the high rate of natural increase was the outcome of a persistently high birth-

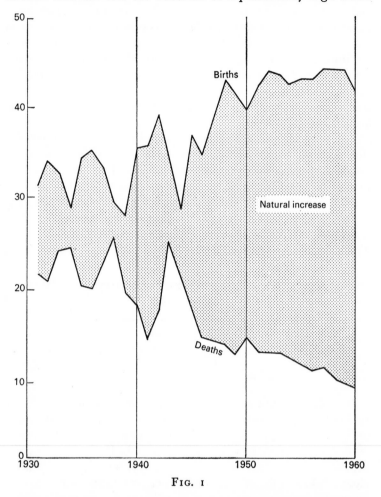

Fig. 1

2·3, there are countries in which the rate for 1953–60 is much higher, e.g. in Brazil the rate was 3·4; in Ecuador 3·7; in Surinam 4·3; and in Venezuela 4·3. There are other development countries in which a rate of increase of population higher than that of Guyana has been attained, e.g. Salvador 3·5; Costa Rica 4·1; Nicaragua 4·1; Ghana 4·4; Singapore 4·6; Burma 4·1; Ceylon 3·6. The rate of growth in Guyana has risen rapidly and is very high, but the fact that in so many countries which are not more highly developed the rate is even higher, shows that a higher rate of growth is attainable, and that a low level of development is no barrier to its being attained. *U.N. Demographic Yearbook, 1961, 1962.*

TABLE 2

NATURAL INCREASE OF THE POPULATION[a] 1931–61

*(Number of births and number of deaths per thousand
of the mean population)*

Year	birth rate	Death rate	Rate of natural increase
1931	31·6	22·0	9·6
1932	34·3	21·2	13·1
1933	32·8	24·6	8·2
1934	29·0	24·9	4·1
1935	34·8	20·9	13·9
1936	35·7	20·7	15·0
1937	33·7	22·1	11·6
1938	29·9	26·0	3·9
1939	28·5	20·0	8·5
1940	35·3	18·8	16·5
1941	36·1	15·9	20·2
1942	39·1	17·6	21·5
1943	34·0	25·1	9·0
1944	29·1	22·3	6·8
1945	37·1	18·2	18·9
1946	35·8	15·5	29·3
1947	39·9	14·6	25·3
1948	43·3	14·2	29·1
1949	42·3	13·3	29·0
1950	40·4	14·6	25·8
1951	42·5	13·5	29·9
1952	44·3	13·5	30·8
1953	44·1	13·3	30·8
1954	42·9	12·4	30·5
1955	43·2	11·9	31·3
1956	43·2	11·2	32·0
1957	44·5	11·6	32·9
1958	44·5	10·2	34·3
1959	44·5	10·0	34·5
1960	42·4	9·5	32·9
1961	40·9	9·1	31·8

Source: West Indian Census 1946, Part D. Census of Population of the Colony of British Guiana (1960), p. XIII. Annual Reports of the Registrar General, Georgetown. Annual Summary for the year 1957 (Georgetown, 1959), p. 59.

[a] Exclusive of Amerindians.

rate combined with a remarkably reduced death-rate. For example, in the years 1957, 1958, and 1959, the crude birth-rate per thousand of population stood at an average of 44·5 per cent, and this was not far from the highest levels observed elsewhere in the world. In contrast, the crude death-rates during the same years were low and still declined at 11·6, 10·2, and 10·0 respectively. Thus the death-rate was reduced from its former levels of 25 or more to the thousand. The resulting differentials upwards of 32 per thousand provides a heavy pressure on the means of support.

Guyana's experience seems to give the lie to the popular theory of 'Demographic Transition' which asserts that the high birth-rates as well as death-rates characteristic of an agrarian low-income country are effected by economic development. The theory can be summarized as follows: the agrarian low-income economy is characterized by high birth- and death-rates —the birth-rates relatively stable, and the death-rates fluctuating in response to varying fortunes. Then as the economy changes its form to a more interdependent and specialized market-dominated economy, the average death-rate declines. It continues to decline under the impact of better organization and improving medical knowledge and care. Somewhat later the birth-rate begins to fall. The two rates pursue a more or less parallel downward course, with the decline in the birth-rate lagging behind. Finally, as further reductions in the death-rate become harder to attain, the birth-rate again approaches equality with the death-rate, and a more gradual rate of growth is re-established, with, however, low risks of mortality and small families as the typical pattern. Mortality rates are now relatively stable from year to year and birth-rates—now responsive to voluntary decisions rather than to deeply embedded customs—may fluctuate from year to year.

The demographic situation and apparent prospects in Guyana give reason for doubting the applicability of the demographic transition as an *exact* description of the likely course of events. The principal reason for doubting the precise applicability of the theory as to *death-rates* is that the death-rate has been markedly reduced without any major reorganization of the economic structure. Without substantially reducing its agrarian structure, the country has so reduced its death-rates that the rate of increase exceeds most of those recorded in the course of the demographic transition in the areas inhabited by Europeans and their descendants. Thus substantial economic improvement may be a sufficient condition for a decline in mortality, but it is not today a necessary condition.[1]

This high rate of growth in itself gives cause for some measure of concern. For the significant feature of population growth as such is that a higher rate of population growth implies a higher level of needed investment to achieve a given *per capita* output, while there is nothing about such a faster growth that generates a greater supply of investible resources. The problem could be illustrated thus. If we assume that technical change is negligible over the short run, and that capital and labour are the only ingredients in output, then an increase of x per cent per annum in population and x per cent per annum in accumulated capital will produce an increase of x per cent per annum in output, i.e., an unaltered *per capita* output. Now we may consider two populations equal, at a given moment, in size, in accumulated capital, and in output. Assume that population A is growing at the rate of 1 per cent per annum, and population B at 3 per cent. If the ratio of capital stock to current annual output is 3 to 1, population A must invest 3 per cent of current output to maintain its *per capita* income, while population B must invest 9 per cent of current output. But under ordinary circumstances the supply of new capital will be no greater in B than in A. There is nothing about faster growth *per se* that will lower consumption and raise savings, at least not by such a large margin.

The implication for Guyana is that with a population growth of about 3 per cent, and a capital output ratio of about 5, real investment of the order of 15 per cent of current output is necessary to maintain *per capita* incomes intact. A rate of investment somewhat higher than this must therefore be necessary to ensure even a meagre growth in real *per capita* incomes. In Guyana, as in most development countries, it is especially difficult to attain adequate levels of investment, and even where adequate levels of investment are achieved, several extraneous variables militate against the productivity of such investments. Added to this is the fact that there is no visible way in which this rapid population growth can evoke a significantly greater

---

[1] The many respects in which the theory of demographic transition may not apply to West Indian populations have been recently analysed. See G. W. Roberts, 'Prospects for Population Growth in the West Indies', *Social and Economic Studies*, Vol. 11, No. 4 (December 1962), pp. 333–50.

flow of investible resources in the country. With the supply of capital as inelastic as it is in the short run at least, this higher rate of population growth would tend to force the diversion of investment to duplicate existing facilities, thus preventing an increase in the capital available for each worker.[1] But this emphasis put on population growth *per se* does not tell us very much. A more fruitful approach may lie in observing the main determinants of such growth Three main influences are usually analysed in the literature, viz. births, deaths, and migration. The effect of each of these on Guyana's population growth will be examined in turn.

The 'demographic gap', i.e. the gap between births and deaths is evidence that mortality reductions were not accompanied by fertility reductions, so that the conquest of disease meant a progressive rise in rates of natural increase The factors which have led to declines in mortality in both developed and development countries are well known and include the development of antibiotics and insecticides, the evolution of effective public health organizations, the invention of suitable low-cost methods of sanitation, and remarkable improvements in the practice of preventive medicine.[2] In Guyana the declining mortality rate reflects especially the enormous improvement in the standard of public health services, both through the general provision of medical care and sanitation, and in the more specific field of the prevention of infectious diseases.[3] Several commentators have emphasized the very effective D.D.T. campaign carried out against malaria, which amounted to its almost com-

---

[1] Prof. Arthur Lewis points out that this is a characteristic feature of West Indian economies where the proliferation of domestic workers and petty traders testifies to their inability to engage in more productive enterprise for lack of capital. W. A. Lewis, 'Industrialisation in the British West Indies', *Caribbean Economic Review*, Vol. 11, No. 1 (May 1950), pp. 1–61.

[2] Kingsley Davis, 'The Amazing Decline of Mortality in Under-developed Areas', *American Economic Review, Papers & Proceedings* (May 1956), pp. 305–18.

[3] G. Giglioli, 'Malaria in British Guiana', *Agricultural Journal of British Guiana*, Vol. 9 (1938), pp. 75–81; and 'Labour, Health and Housing', *Bookers Sugar* (1954), pp. 75–81. A comparison of the malarial phenomenon in British Guiana with its incidence in Ceylon is very illuminating. In Ceylon the malarial mosquito has been wiped out by D.D.T., and deaths fell from 22 to 12 per thousand in the 7 years 1945–52, a fall which took 70 years in England and Wales; in Mauritius a fall from 27 to 15 deaths per thousand, which took 100 years to be achieved in England and Wales, also came about in 7 years. P.E.P., *World Population and Resources* (Distributed by Allen and Unwin, 1960).

plete eradication from the coastal plain. The swampy, water-logged conditions existing on the coastal plains were ideal breeding grounds for the Anopheles Darlingi mosquito—the chief carrier of the disease.[1]

The fluctuations in birth- and death-rates, noticeable before and during the war, are closely correlated with malarial epidemics on the coast. There were serious outbreaks in 1938 and 1943/4, and these were accompanied by high death-rates and low birth-rates (see Figure 1), since malaria lowers the rate of conception, and raises the tendency to abort. The birth-rate in Guyana is among the highest in the world. In 1936–40 it was around 32·6 per thousand; in 1941–5 around 43, in 1956–60 around 44.[2]

Due consideration must be given to the important fact that this population growth reflects the differential growth-rates among ethnic groups, especially that between East Indians and Africans, the two major groups. In the context of the existing state of affairs in the country, this acquires a meaning of its own, and may partly explain the increasing stresses of political and economic life in the country. Table 3 shows that the proportion of East Indians in the total population has increased from 36·62 per cent in 1891 to 40·97 per cent in 1911, and after a slight fall to 40·73 in 1921, it again rose to 43·51 in 1946 and 47·79 in 1960. The proportion of Africans during the same period has fallen from 40·14 in 1891 to 37·40 in 1911, rose to 38·20 in 1921, and 39·06 in 1931, but fell again to 38·17 per cent in 1946 and 32·83 per cent in 1960.

[1] Though the general death-rate in Guyana is low, lower death-rates have been achieved even among the less advanced countries, e.g. 6·7 per thousand in 1961 in Formosa; 6·9 in Trinidad and Tobago; 6·7 in Puerto Rico; 8·1 in Uruguay. The rate of infant mortality in Guyana has also fallen significantly—from 126·4 per thousand in 1936–40 to 111·8 in 1941–5; 83·0 in 1946–50; 76·6 in 1951–5; 62·6 in 1956–9 and 57 in 1960–2. The prevailing rate in Guyana compares favourably with rates in other development countries, but is much higher than the rates in advanced countries which vary in the range of 16 to 30 per thousand. See *U.N. Demographic Yearbooks*.

[2] The rise in the birth-rate since 1936–40 was to some extent due to the increase in the number of women in the reproductive age-group. Higher birth-rates than 42/3 per thousand do exist at present. Ghana had in 1960 a birth-rate of 55, Mali 56, Costa Rica 55·4, Salvador 49·6, and Venezuela also 49·6 (*U.N. Demographic Yearbook 1962*). Though since 1951 the birth-rate in Guyana seems to have stabilized itself at about 42/3 per thousand, conditions are still favourable for a rise in this rate.

These cold figures at least partly explain the percentage increase of East Indians since 1946 which has been 63·88 per cent, and of Africans 28·3 per cent. The birth-rate of the East Indians, which in 1891–1911 was 27·7 per thousand, rose to 40·6 in 1941–5, 46·1 in 1946–50, 49·3 in 1951–5, and 51·1 in 1956–60, while that of Africans fell from 32·1 per thousand in 1891–1911 to 28·4 in 1941–5, rose to 33·4 in 1946–50, 35·3 in 1951–5, and 36·9 in 1956–60. The death-rates of both East Indians and Africans fell during this period; of East Indians 30·4 per thousand in 1891–1911 to 19·6 in 1941–5, 13·9 in 1946–50, 12·1 in 1951–5, and 9·7 in 1956–60. That of Africans fell from 31·4 per thousand in 1891–1911 to 21·1 in 1941–5, 16·7 in 1946–50, 15·0 in 1951–5, and 12·5 in 1956–60. The rate of natural increase of these two major communities has been rising during these periods but that of the East Indians has risen much faster on account of a greater rise in their birth-rate and a greater fall in their death-rate.

The rate of natural increase for the former group was 3·7 per thousand in 1891–1911, and this rose to 21 in 1941–5, 32·2 in 1946–50, 37·2 in 1951–5, and 39·7 in 1956–60; the figures for the latter (Africans) were in 1891–1911 0·7, 7·3 in 1941–5, 16·6 in 1946–50, 20·3 in 1951–5, and 24·5 in 1956–60.[1]

We have so far shown that according to the Census by Race, this century has seen marked differences in the rates of growth in the two major races living in the country. Before 1917, annual increases in population were largely due to immigration. It was not until the 1912–21 decade that the natural increase in the East Indian population became a positive magnitude. The imbalance between the sexes in the immigrant population—among the Indians the average number of females per thousand males arriving on immigrant ships was about 40—resulted in a low reproduction rate, and high mortality rates kept the natural increase in the population extremely low. Large-scale immigration ceased in 1917, but shortly afterwards important changes in mortality and fertility affected population growth. The year 1921 marked the beginning of a sharp fall in mortality rates on account of factors already mentioned, viz. improved medical facilities and sanitation. Whereas the average

[1] Population Censuses, 1946 and 1960.

TABLE 3

POPULATION STRUCTURE BY RACIAL GROUPS

Year	Total	%	Amer-indians	%	Europeans^a	%	E. Indians	%	Chinese	%	Mixed	%	Africans	%	Other races	%
1891	288,328	100	17,463	6·06	16,724	5·81	105,463	36·62	3,714	1·29	29,029	10·08	115,588	40·14	347	
1911	309,041	100	19,901	6·44	14,021	4·54	126,517	40·97	2,622	0·85	30,251	9·80	115,486	37·40	243	
1921	307,391	100	18,850	6·15	12,466	4·06	124,938	40·73	2,722	0·89	30,587	9·97	117,169	38·20	659	
1931	318,312	100	15,727	4·95	10,739	3·38	130,540	41·05	2,951	0·93	33,800	10·63	124,203	39·06	352	
1946	375,701	100	16,322	4·35	11,023	2·93	163,434	43·51	3,567	1·01	37,685	10·03	143,385	38·17	285	
1960	560,406	100	25,450	4·54	3,218	0·57	267,840	47·79	4,074	0·73	67,189	11·99	183,980	32·83	8,655^b	1·54

^a Includes Portuguese. ^b Includes Lebanese, Syrians, others and not stated.

PERCENTAGE INCREASE OF POPULATION ACCORDING TO ETHNIC GROUPS IN GUYANA

Year	Amerindian	Europeans	East Indians	Chinese	Mixed	Africans	Others
1891–1911	13·96	−16·16	19·96	−29·40	4·21	−0·09	−29·97
1911–21	−5·28	−11·09	−1·25	3·81	1·11	1·46	171·19
1921–31	−16·57	−13·85	4·48	8·41	10·50	6·00	−46·59
1931–46	3·78	2·64	25·20	20·87	11·49	15·44	−19·03
1946–60	55·92	−70·81	63·88	14·21	78·29	28·31	3,036·84

Source: Census of Population 1946; Census of Population 1960.

life expectancy in 1920–2 was 33·5 years for men and 35·8 years for women, by 1950–2 it had risen to 53·14 years for men and 56·28 years for women. This rise in the average birth-rate from 1891 onwards was mainly due to the lessening of the imbalance in the sex ratio among more recent immigrants, and within the resident Indian population.[1]

This phenomenal rate of increase of the East Indian element of the population must be put into correct perspective. After the abolition of slavery, labour of the African type was no longer available on a sufficient scale,[2] and the acute shortage of plantation labour that ensued was met by immigration schemes financed jointly by the planters and the colonial government. After experimenting with immigrants from various countries, the planters and the government settled for Indian coolies as being the most suitable. Between 1838 and 1917, 238,960 Indians were imported,[3] more than two-thirds of whom did not return to India. The immigrants were imported under what was known as the 'indenture system', which regulated their recruitment, labour contracts, and living conditions.[4]

It is fairly characteristic of countries undergoing rapid population growth that the percentage of the population in the dependent ages tends to increase.[5] The shift is brought about mainly by the rise in fertility that occurs, though the death-rate, which affects children more than any other group, is of some significance. From 1891 to 1960 while the total population has risen by 94 per cent, that of children (0–14) has risen by 198 per

---

[1] Racial differences in fertility were also noticeable in other Caribbean territories where large-scale indentured immigration occurred. Cf. J. Harewood, 'Population Growth in Trinidad & Tobago in the Twentieth Century', *Social and Economic Studies*, Vol. 12, No. 1 (March 1963), p. 17, and G. W. Roberts, *The Population of Jamaica* (Cambridge, 1957).

[2] The establishment of free Negro villages after emancipation is one of the most remarkable episodes in Guyanese history. See Rawle Farley, 'The Rise of the Peasantry in British Guiana', *Social and Economic Studies*, Vol. 11, No. 4 (1954); also Allan Young, *Approaches to Local Self Government in British Guiana* (Longmans, London, 1958).

[3] D. Nath, *History of Indians in British Guiana* (London, 1950), p. 36.

[4] For a detailed analysis of the indenture system in Guyana see S. Amos, *The Existing Laws of Demerara for the Regulation of Coolie Emigration* (London, 1871); J. Beaumont, *The New Slavery* (London, 1871); J. Rodway, *History of British Guiana*, 3 vols. (Georgetown, 1891–4).

[5] In the high fertility regions of Asia most countries have 35 to 45 per cent of their people under the age of 15. See W. W. Lockwood, *The Economic Development of Japan* (Princeton University Press, 1954), p. 271.

cent. The proportionate increase in the number of children has been rising throughout the period, but since 1931 this difference has become much greater. As compared with the increase of the total population of over 18 per cent in 1931–45, the increase of children was over 40 per cent. The corresponding figures for 1946–60 are 49 and 86 per cent respectively. The proportion of children to total population has on this account greatly increased from 34 per cent in 1921–30 to nearly 38 per cent in 1931–46, and 46 per cent in 1946–60.[1]

Our remarks about the increasing rate of dependency take on a more vivid light in view of the proportion of children to the working population. If we assume that each person of working age is in the labour force, persons in the working age being between 15 and 64, it is interesting to note that while in 1921 less than one-third of the population was under working age, this increased to almost a half in 1960. In 1921 there were almost twice as many people of working age as there were in all other age-groups, so that the average number of dependants was just over one-half. By 1946 the age distribution had changed sufficiently to increase this ratio to three-quarters, while by 1960 each person of working age had to support one full dependant. These figures are an even more correct measure of the increasing burden of dependency due to the growth of population. The implications of this are multidimensional. First, it indicates that the productivity per person in the labour force has had to rise by almost one-third over this period simply in order to maintain *per capita* incomes constant, since an increasingly smaller proportion of the population is actually of working age. Thus an average worker's income of $300 in 1921 would have meant a national average then of $200, while today the corresponding figure would be only $150. We must therefore bear in mind that a large part of each increase in real income that has occurred has been siphoned off into maintaining an even larger proportion of the population out of the labour force, especially since the war.

The fact that the working population has to carry the responsibility of supporting and bringing up an increasing proportion of the total population means that community services such as

[1] Population Censuses.

education and medical services have to be developed much faster in order to keep pace with the population in the lower age-groups. This involves heavy investment in the construction of schools, hospitals, and houses, and of the training of technical personnel, and, in a period of rising standards and expectations, the rise in the rate of investment in these services has to be even higher than the rise in the proportion of children. It is not surprising that government expenditure on social services has been running at an average of 30 per cent of total expenditure for the period, and has been continuously higher than any other category. Of special significance is the contrast between the high level of expenditure on social services and the allocation for economic development, which has been running at an average of a mere 10 per cent of total expenditure.[1]

But within the broader category of social services, cognizance must be taken of the obvious burden paid by the considerable increase in the cost of education that occurs when the school-age population almost doubles, as it did from 1946 to 1960. As expected, more than 70 per cent of public education expenditure has been regularly devoted to primary schools, reflecting in particular the expanding needs of the rapidly growing number of pupils. In the period 1952–61 while expenditure on primary schools *per capita* of population rose by 70 per cent, expenditure *per capita* of pupils enrolled increased by only 34 per cent.[2] In the context of recurrent expenditure the greatest sums have been spent on teachers' salaries which normally claimed between 90 and 95 per cent of all public money that flowed into primary education, i.e. more than 65 per cent of all public educational expenditure. This is an irremovable complex of financial obligations which swelled tremendously under the impact of a rising number of teachers.

The share of primary education in non-recurrent expenditure was even higher than in current expenditure. It amounted to around 85 per cent on an average during the period 1954 to 1961. However, total funds drawn for educational purposes

[1] Estimates Current and Capital as passed by the Legislature.
[2] If we take the cost-of-living index as the basis for price adjustments (which is, in respect of educational expenditure, not a satisfactory yardstick) real increase in expenditure on primary schools per pupil is some 18 per cent over the whole period 1952 to 1961.

TABLE 4

EXPENDITURE ON EDUCATION MET FROM DEVELOPMENT BUDGETS 1954–63 CURRENT PRICES

Year	DEVELOPMENT BUDGET				EXPENDITURE ON EDUCATION[a]	
	Total 1,000	C.D. and W.F. BWI$	1,000 BWI$	Per cent of total budget	1,000 BWI$	Per cent of C.D. and W.F. budget
1954	8,522	3,169	262	2·1	204	6·4
1955	17,522	3,885	288	1·6	281	7·2
1956	20,559	6,124	246	1·2	141	2·3
1957	18,310	5,801	323	1·8	228	3·9
1958	19,881	2,759	306	1·5	117	4·2
1959	18,998	4,594	357	1·9	38	0·8
1960	15,801	4,792	398	2·5	275	5·7
1961	21,660	5,570	723	3·3	459	8·2
1962	18,802[b]	6,407[c]	1,532[b]	8·2[b]	992[c]	15·5[c]
1963	25,339	4,500	886	3·5	120	2·7

Source: British Guiana Report of the Treasurer 1952 to 1963; Development Estimates as passed by the Legislative Council 1962 and 1963, Georgetown.

[a] Expenditure under the responsibility of the Ministry of Education only.   [b] Revised estimate.   [c] Estimate.

from the development budget have been generally low compared with the rising demand. As can be seen from Table 4, the percentage of non-recurrent education expenditure has been fluctuating very much from year to year, reflecting a fringe position for education in the development budget rather than a recognition of its economic importance. If education is expected to pay economic returns then it must be given a share that allows it to respond to economic requirements. The share should at least be in line with the increase in the number of students, and in addition make existing backlogs disappear. In the long-run, this investment is very much worth while, for it is investment in human resources, and in due course is bound to give returns, although it is a slow maturing investment.

Its long gestation period implies that the increase in returns arising from the increase in the size and quality of the population will take place only when the children reach years of discretion, and, it is hoped, begin to make a greater contribution to the total income of the community through investment in community services. But this is a problem in the allocation of scarce, investible resources between the 'social sector' and the 'productive sectors' of the economy, and it has an important time dimension. In the immediate future, investment in child education has to be an 'input' without a corresponding 'output', that is to say, investment without a corresponding flow of goods and services.[1] As children attain the working age, they

---

[1] "Plans for educational expansion pose at every turn problems of choice in the allocation of resources; their reference is consequently economic, notwithstanding the social and pedagogic implications of programmes. In order to choose rationally between alternative expansion plans, the objectives to be reached must first be defined. . . . Every child has an inherent and equal right to education, and it is the duty of governments to implement this in the shortest possible time. While in itself attractive, this approach has serious weaknesses. At best, it tends to over-emphasize education in terms of other pressing needs, . . . in economic terms it neglects the social opportunity cost of educational expansion. It easily becomes emotional and tends to throw all notions of balance to the winds, in favour of developing the primary stage. The alternative approach (which) is economic regards education as a form of investment. . . . Are we concerned primarily with investment in humans as an end in itself—or are we concerned primarily in man as a part of the economic organisation of production and consumption? If the former, there is little chance of rational choice . . . the latter points in a direction which can be of great importance for determining the right amount of education and its optimal distribution between different types of levels of education for development purposes." U. K. Hicks, 'The Economics of Education Expansion in Low Income Countries', *Three Banks Review* (March 1965), pp. 7–8.

will add to the productive resources of the economy if their productivity capacity can be beneficially utilized, i.e. if there is an expanding economy and the increase in outlets for employment keeps pace with the increase in the number of entrants in the working age groups. At present the position is by no means satisfactory, and at the existing rate of growth of the economy, great difficulty is being experienced in making provision for the working population. As will become obvious later in this chapter, this difficulty is greatly exacerbated by the heavy backlog of unemployment in the economy, and this has to be worked off within the shortest possible time.

The need for a balanced educational and economic development will become even more urgent in the future. In the course of accelerating population growth, demand not only for education but also for employment will speedily rise. It has been estimated that by 1975 there will be about 340,000 or 60 per cent more people in Guyana than there were in 1960.[1] More than one-quarter of this increase will add to the age-groups between 5 and 16 years, but more than one-third to those between 16 and 30 years. If these projections are in approximate agreement with future reality this would mean that the present economically unfavourable relation between the number of children and the population of the working age will soon tend to improve again. However, the advantages of such a change will materialize only to the extent that training and employment conditions improve as well, i.e. to the extent that the numerically strong groups of young people who will be entering the labour market find adequate opportunities to develop and utilize their potential skills. The data contained in Table 5 and Figure 2 indicate the enormous expansion that those groups who are in greatest need of post-primary education and vocational training will probably experience.

The problem of dependency becomes even more serious when we consider the low proportion of working women in the total female population—about 13 per cent. This means that only 29 per cent of the population supports 71 per cent, i.e., for every two persons in productive work, there are about seven

[1] See Report of the UNESCO Educational Survey, Mission to Guyana (Georgetown, 1963).

TABLE 5

PROJECTED POPULATION OF GUYANA OF THE AGES 5 TO
UNDER 30 YEARS, 1965, 1970, AND 1975, COMPARED
WITH 1960

Age group (years)	1960	1965	1970	1975	Percentage increase over 1960		
					1965	1970	1975
5 to under 6	19,441	19,960	24,555	27,339	2·7	26·3	40·6
6 to under 12	102,202	113,641	129,760	149,916	11·2	27·0	46·7
12 to under 14	27,052	36,367	37,334	45,182	34·4	38·0	67·0
14 to under 16	24,012	32,532	37,249	41,527	35·5	55·1	72·9
12 to under 16	51,064	68,899	74,583	86,709	34·9	46·1	69·8
5 to under 16	172,707	202,500	228,898	263,964	17·3	32·5	52·8
16 to under 20	40,264	53,961	71,486	74,956	34·0	77·5	86·2
20 to under 25	42,158	51,410	69,120	89,371	21·9	64·0	112·0
25 to under 30	35,962	41,661	50,846	68,419	15·8	41·4	90·3
16 to under 30	118,384	147,032	191,452	232,746	24·2	61·7	96·6

Source: Report of the UNESCO Educational Survey, Mission to Guyana (Georgetown, 1963).

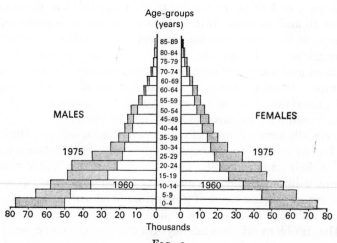

FIG. 2

real dependent persons. This is to some extent due to the progressive reduction of women in the gainfully employed population. The main factors generating this trend will be outlined
later. But if we assume that this will be reversed with further
industrialization, i.e. that more and more women will enter the

employment market, then the number of persons seeking employment will increase even faster than the size of the working population. This will reduce the rate of dependency, add to the proportion of persons contributing to national income, and make a real difference to the productive potential of the country. Besides, it will have other important effects on community life because of the increasing economic independence of women. But this can be realized only if the economy is expanding at a very rapid rate, and employment opportunities are increasing at an even faster rate than the general rate of growth of population.

2. The Distribution of Population

There are three main aspects of the distribution of population in Guyana that will have to be borne in mind in future economic and investment planning. These are: the rural/urban dichotomy; the paucity of cities; and the population density or concentration. The country's population has always remained almost constantly rural in nature.

TABLE 6
POPULATION OF GUYANA CLASSIFIED BY PLACE OF RESIDENCE

Locality or type of area	1946	1960	1965
Urban	27·6	29·0	26·0
Georgetown	25·1	26·5	24·2
New Amsterdam	2·5	2·5	1·8
Rural	72·4	71·0	74·0
All areas	100·0	100·0	100·0

Source: Censuses of Population 1946, 1960; Manpower Survey 1965, Vol. 2.

In the adjoining table the percentage contributions of the urban areas of Georgetown, New Amsterdam, and the rest of the country (which has been classified as rural) are shown for the periods 1946, 1960, and 1965. An important change in the distribution of population which it has been possible to detect is the comparatively recent decline in the total population living in urban areas, although there was a tendency for a small increase during 1946 and 1960. In 1946 the percentage of the total population living in the two urban places was 27·6 per cent, which increased slightly to 29·0 per cent by 1960 but declined to 26 per cent in 1965. Correspondingly rural areas showed a decrease in their contribution from 72·4 per cent in 1946 to 71·0 per cent in 1960, but improved their representation to 74·0 per cent in 1965.

A combination of factors may have been responsible for the trend just noted. Firstly, the increasing relative importance of urban areas between 1946 and 1960 can be explained to some extent by the shifting of population from rural to urban areas. This trend was not however sustained, probably on account of the higher fertility rates in the rural areas, with their predominantly East Indian concentration. The disturbances of recent years could also account in some measure for this change. During this period emigration was relatively high and it seems reasonable to suggest that many more people left from the urban than from the rural areas, since the usual tendency is for the more educated and skilled to play the more important part in any large-scale emigration.

However, notwithstanding the general rural/urban maldistribution, and the fact that the rural bias has been augmented by a few percentage points over the past few years, the growth of population of Georgetown, the main urban area, provides adequate reason for disquiet. The population of Georgetown and its suburban areas has increased from 44,489 in 1871 to 156,000, i.e. by over 300 per cent, and its proportion of the total population from 19 per cent in 1871 to over 25 per cent in 1960. Of the total increase of 103,000 since 1871, the increase since 1931 has been over 71,000 or nearly 70 per cent. Since 1946 the population of this major city has increased by over 60,000, i.e. over 50 per cent of the increase in the urban population in the last 90 years.

Concentration of urban population is accounted for not only by urban economic development, but also to a large extent by the lack of opportunities in the small towns and rural areas.[1]

[1] The disproportionate increase in the population of major urban centres is a world phenomenon which has not been successfully countered by planned action anywhere; but the concentration in one major city, and the general scarcity of

There are other explanatory factors. More provision in the form of 'relief' is being made for the unemployed in the towns. This is partly due to the fact that such development as is taking place in the town itself provides better opportunities for casual employment so that the town has developed a greater number of 'hangers-on' who work for one or two days a week in relatively unremunerative and uneconomic functions. It is also partly due to the spread of education to the rural areas. The people in these areas are becoming dissatisfied, and drift into the city attracted by new opportunites. A corollary of this may be the growing wage gap itself, which, by raising the standard of living of those who have found employment in Georgetown, attracts more and more people to the town.[1]

The result of this tendency is that for a long time there has been high unemployment in Georgetown. This unhealthy trend highlights the need to reorganize the economy. Georgetown is a small city with a disproportionate influence over the national economy. This must be corrected by improving communications, developing other ports, creating centres of counter-attraction, improving the social amenities in the rural areas and generally redistributing the economic opportunities.

It may be a relatively simple matter to plan investment activity in Guyana so as to take care not only of the population explosion, but also its maldistribution. But the racial distribution further complicates the problem. The East Indian element of the population is much more rural in its geographical distri-

cities may be a reflection of slow economic progress. It must, however, be admitted that in terms of the total number of inhabitants Georgetown is a relatively small city as compared with others on the South American Continent, or indeed with other cities of the world. For an account of the role of cities in economic development see B. F. Hoselitz, *Sociological Aspects of Economic Growth* (New York, 1960), especially Chs. 7, 8, and 9.

[1] W. A. Lewis, 'Employment Policy in an Underdeveloped Area', *Social and Economic Studies*, Vol. 7, No. 3 (September 1958), p. 43. Professor Lewis considers that part of the problem is insoluble, and dismisses most of the curative measures proffered from time to time—providing work, drastic measures of imprisonment, or general discouragement, development elsewhere in other towns and rural areas, etc. He concludes, 'if we wish to measure our achievements in development, we must measure them not by the fall of unemployment, but by the increase in employment . . . for we are not likely to do very much to reduce unemployment in the short period of a decade or so'. This is sound, but it does not follow that measures cannot be initiated to reduce unemployment and increase employment simultaneously.

bution than are the other racial groups. The data on the distribution of population reveal that in 1960 about 29 per cent of the population was urban, and of this group only 22 per cent was of East Indian descent, the majority of over 60 per cent being Negro or mixed. The concentration of the East Indians in the subsistence sector and in the sugar estates where they provide cheap labour will have serious implications for the future distribution of investment projects, in the sense that a real conflict may develop between the allocation of projects based on strict economic criteria on the one hand, and those based on 'racial', 'political', and similar 'criteria' on the other. This is a problem of some significance in the Guyanese context where racial tension has gathered tremendous momentum over the last few years.

But the point of more crucial importance in our analysis of the rapid rate of growth of population and its maldistribution is its relation to the *size* of the country. The term *size* is somewhat ambiguous. Guyana is a relatively large country by the standards of other countries in the Commonwealth Caribbean, and is not really small when measured on a world scale. Its area of 83,000 square miles is about the size of England and Wales, and this is colossal when put beside those of Jamaica, Trinidad and Tobago, and Barbados, with areas of 4,411, 1,980, and 183 square miles respectively. The real problem lies in the fact that the narrow coastal strip comprising about 2 per cent of the total land-surface, supports about 90 per cent of the population (see Figure 3). Crowded into an occupied area of about 1,000 square miles, these people give rise to a population density comparable with most of Guyana's West Indian neighbours, and other development countries that have experienced population pressure. In this respect Guyana is an 'overpopulated country.' In many respects the coastlands of Guyana may be termed a 'West Indian Sugar Island', for this pressure on the means of support on the coastal belt can be regarded as a direct result of the development of investment in the sugar plantations by the earlier settlers from the metropolitan country.[1]

Thus we cannot neglect the study of problems connected with population pressure. Firstly, population density must be

[1] On this point see W. L. David, 'Guyana's Earlier Economic Development' *Guyana*, Vol. III (March 1966).

considered in relation to natural resources and technology. Population density cannot be measured simply by taking the number of people per square mile, but depends on a number of factors such as the quality of agricultural land, climate and water supply, the existence of mineral resources, the possibilities of hydro-electric power, and, most important, on the level of productivity and technology. It is possible that the country

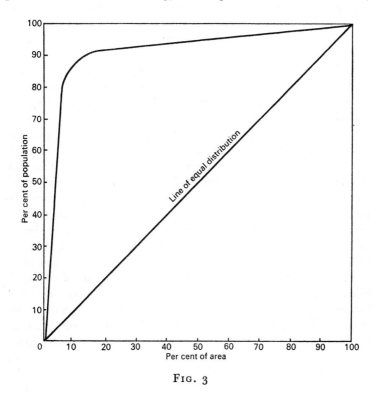

FIG. 3

possesses abundant natural resources of great diversity. If this is so, then the large geographical size would indicate a capacity to support a bigger population. But even if we assume that the supply of capital for development purposes will be more elastic in the foreseeable future, and large-scale techniques and higher levels of efficiency become feasible, provision will still have to be made for the organized transfer of the population from the congested coast to the more sparsely populated areas on newly created settlement regions. Eventually, of course, the vast area in the hinterland will have to be developed, and an internal migration is inevitable. But the problem has more immediate relevance. Because large-scale internal migration consequent upon heavy capital investment will take several years to materialize, more intensive development of certain areas on the coastal plain is required. This will involve detailed and intensive examination of the population distribution and the economic viability of each small unit, together with the formulation of investment plans on the result of such investigations.

But the assumptions of the two sides of the argument call for elucidation. In the case where we are thinking of the total area and resource potential, given the present level and rate of growth of population, an increase in the land-surface utilized would lead to a long-period increase in the average net product per worker. On the other hand where it is assumed that the available resources are somewhat limited at least in the short run, if the population continues to grow at the present rate, this would lead to a long-period decrease in productivity per worker. But in the one case we are assuming that there would be no impact from changes in technology and in the methods of production due to reasons other than the variation in the resource use; that the average resource potentials of the new increments of land is the same as the existing land; that there would not be any added complications arising out of the possibility of new barriers in transport, communications, and like factors, in the general attempt at making the resources economically viable. In the other case, where we think that an increase in the level and rate of growth of population may move it nearer to the required size relative to the resources exploitable in the short run, it is assumed that the increment in the population would be similar qualitatively to that of the existing population.

Although Guyana may be rich in natural resources, in many cases accurate surveys of these resources do not exist, and even where they do, they cannot be readily translated into terms of commercial values because of their inaccessibility. The resources may be economically inaccessible because other co-operant factors of production besides labour are not in adequate supply. A natural resource is valueless when the cost of co-operant resources and the cost of transporting the resources and the products exceed the price the product can command in the best available market. It may be that Guyana's wide network of rivers could be made more navigable to reduce transportation costs. If this happens, and other co-operant factors and the requisite markets exist, then widening of the resource base will take care of the present population explosion and its maldistribution. For the large population size and the low population volume, i.e. the high land/man ratio reveals that the scope for increasing returns and the economies of scale would be greatly enhanced with better distribution of the existing population, or even with a further increase in the level and rate of growth of population. Thus the fast rate of growth of population is not necessarily a hindrance to economic development.

But these arguments seem to suggest that the country's vast potential resources remain unutilized because of the low population volume. It is possible that with the low current income and productivity level, the real problem lies in the need for the accumulation of a large quantity of capital before accelerated rates of income growth and employment can be obtained. A large programme of both intensive and extensive investment would take the form of extending the resources as well as the provision of employment for the overcrowded numbers on the coastal plain. But the implementation of such an investment policy may call for intensive foreign investment, and even large-scale immigration.

The low population volume also has implications as to the extent of specialization and the extent of the market. It has become a popular proposition that the inducement to invest is limited by the size of the market. Although in many cases investment has to be undertaken with the sole aim of providing employment opportunities for the local unemployed, irrespective of commercial motivations to the contrary, it is an established fact that in the majority of cases, the existence of a market of adequate size is a *sine qua non* of both domestic and foreign investment. This proposition is merely a modern variant of Adam Smith's famous dictum that 'the division of labour is limited by the extent of the market'. This means that the utilization of investible resources in the production of goods and services is limited by the small size of the domestic market, an important corollary of which is the lack of domestic purchasing power.

The implication here is that, given the international price and income elasticities of demand for the various goods Guyana may be able to offer, the foreign-trade sector may have to continue to play one of the leading roles in the development process, unless wholesale immigration from the overpopulated West Indian islands helps in the generation of the needed purchasing power. Closer economic integration with the Caribbean or even with Latin America may also have beneficial effects. It may however be argued that the mere lack of purchasing power is not in itself the real problem, in that deficiencies in monetary demand can be remedied by monetary expansion. But this approach may prove equally ineffective. Credit expansion in itself will not stimulate the rate of economic development, since development will still be limited by the lack of certain resources in real rather than in monetary terms. Credit expansion would equally generate little other than a series of inflationary increases in money incomes and prices.[1]

There remains another aspect of the problem. In high-income economies characterized by much lower rates of population growth than in Guyana, a rise in the demand for capital goods suffices to stimulate the whole economy, and eventually to lead to a rise in wages. This is especially so when unemployment of labour and capital is marked. Often a rising population, or more precisely, an increase in the labour force provides the stimulus for such a development. But in Guyana, with a low income-level, it may have to be the increase in savings rather than the increase in effective demand that would be necessary to stimulate the economy. The low effective demand also presents another difficulty. It may be argued that the increased spending of the high-income sector of the country may stimulate the economy. But there is no automatic device whereby mounting numbers of people can assure greater consumption or force up the returns on capital. Large families make it difficult to raise consumption levels. The decreasing mortality in the country means that more children survive, and since they have to be educated, raising consumption levels is not easy, and for

---

[1] See Nevin, *Capital Funds in Underdeveloped Countries*, Ch. 1.

TABLE 7
LABOUR FORCE IN GUYANA CLASSIFIED BY PLACE OF RESIDENCE AND SEX, 1946, 1956, 1960

	1946[a]			1956[b]			1960[c]		
	Both sexes	Male	Female	Both sexes	Male	Female	Both sexes	Male	Female
Colony	147,841	106,517	40,964	164,600	104,100	60,500	174,997	134,130	40,867
Urban									
Georgetown and Environs	38,896	24,499	14,397	49,900	30,500	19,400	52,099	34,348	17,751
New Amsterdam	3,929	2,540	1,389	5,000	2,700	2,300	4,496	2,792	1,704
Rural									
Demerara	51,157	37,510	13,647	54,400	35,900	18,500	54,990	44,636	10,354
Berbice	32,011	24,255	7,756	39,300	25,400	13,900	36,064	30,146	5,918
Essequibo	21,488	17,713	3,775	16,000	9,600	6,400	27,348	22,208	5,140

Sources: Census of Population 1946; Report on Employment, Unemployment and Underemployment, 1956; Census of Population, 1960.
[a] 10 years and over (gainfully employed+S.F.J.). [b] 14 years and over. [c] 10 years and over (working population + other seekers).

questions on the economic situation during the survey week followed the conventional pattern in that those who were in employment were described either as 'worked', of 'in a job but not at work', and those classed as 'unemployed' were those who either wanted or were looking for work during the Survey Week and were *available*. These two combined gave the *week's labour force*, and this definition is consistent with the 1956 Survey.[1] Persons outside the week's labour force were described as either doing house duties, at school, retired, sick or disabled, or in some other condition in which they did not work and did not want to work.

The examination of changes in the labour force presents a complex problem not only because changes in the size of total population are difficult to measure, but also because the age above which persons were considered for inclusion in the labour force was not always constant.[2] But when allowance is made for these factors, and if certain adjustments are made to ensure

TABLE 8

FEMALES AS A PERCENTAGE OF TOTAL LABOUR FORCE, 1946, 1956, 1960

	1946	1956	1960
Colony	27·8	36·8	23·4
Georgetown	37·0	38·9	34·1
New Amsterdam	35·4	46·0	37·9
Demerara	26·7	34·0	18·8
Berbice	24·2	35·4	16·4
Essequibo	17·6	40·0	18·8

Source: Census Reports.

[1] The 1956 Survey defined the labour force as 'All persons engaged during the survey week in any gainful occupation or pursuit in the production of goods or services; or, if not so engaged, were capable of being so and were looking for work or wanted work' (Appendix B, p. 54).

[2] For the 1946 census, the lower limit was set at 10 years, in 1956 it was moved up to 14, and by 1960 it was again lowered to 10. These changes, however, may not be critical as far as interpretation of the figures in Table 10 is concerned, since on examining the 1964 census reports, the number in the labour force in the 10–14 age-group was of the order of only 3,000. A similar evaluation cannot be made for the 1964 census but it is reasonable to expect that participation rates for this age-group is declining, and that its contribution to the labour force in the latter year would have been less.

comparability, the broad conclusions of Table 7 ought not to be materially different from actuality. These figures reveal that the labour force has grown at a much slower rate than the population as a whole, having registered only an 18·7 per cent increase during the period 1946–60 compared with a 49·1 per cent increase for the total population. Withdrawal of females and young persons from the labour force and the fact that the number of females in the labour force remained constant between 1946 and 1960 at about 41,000 is primarily responsible for this difference in growth rates between total population and the labour force.

The above figures give us further cause for concern regarding the comparability between the 1946, 1956, and 1960 investigations. Both the 1946 and 1960 censuses combine to show two unmistakable trends which the 1956 survey does not support. The first of these is that in Georgetown and New Amsterdam (urban areas), females form a significantly higher proportion of the labour force than is the case in rural areas. Secondly, that between the two censuses, females in the rural areas have been withdrawing from the labour force at a faster rate than their counterparts. There are strong reasons for believing that both trends are real. Firstly, the greater need for women in the urban areas to engage in employment would have caused a higher proportion to express a 'desire to work', and therefore to be included in the labour force, although opportunities for employment may not be any greater.[1]

This situation could have been caused by a higher proportion of women in urban areas having to work in order to support 'urban' levels of living. Again, women in urban areas may have a higher state of child dependency in the absence of males than in rural areas, i.e. a higher proportion of urban females may have been left to support children without the assistance of fathers, with the result that a higher proportion would have expressed the desire to work. It is also easy to detect the reasons for the second trend, i.e. that females in the rural areas have been withdrawing from the labour force at a faster rate than their urban counterparts. Since agriculture and industries based on agriculture provide the greater slice of employment

[1] *Manpower Survey 1965*, p. 166.

opportunities in the rural areas, mechanization, the awakening of social conscience to the fact that women should participate less in arduous agricultural occupations, and improvements in the real wage of a large proportion of agricultural workers would be powerful forces at work tending to decrease female participation rates.

These factors may not be present in urban areas because of the absence of large-scale agricultural operations; moreover, large numbers of urban women continue to desire or seek after the relatively few jobs in commerce and manufacturing, thus keeping their participation rates at a high level.[1]

The occupational pattern of the labour force reveals the degree of diversification of the Guyana economy. According to the data given in Table 9 'Primary Occupations' on average account for just around 40 per cent of the labour force, about five-sixths of which category is in rice cultivation and milling, together with sugar cultivation. Mining and quarrying employed very few persons, probably because this activity is capital intensive by its very nature. Manufacturing, including rice milling and sugar processing, provided occupation for over 15 per cent of the labour force, while construction, transport, and communications occupied another 12 per cent, so that these four 'secondary activities' (including some of the labour force in commerce) engaged over one-fourth of the whole labour force. The service activities accounted for over 20 per cent, for this category includes some of the employees listed under 'commerce'. This pattern suggests a considerable departure from the traditional economy, which is overwhelmingly agrarian in occupation.[2] Yet it must be recalled that much of the

---

[1] The figures for 1956 do not support the trends noted above, and the statistics on female participation rates for that year given in Table 9, are very high in comparison with similar calculations for 1946 and 1960. In the 1965 Survey it was difficult to come to any definite conclusions on the reasons for the apparent abnormality in the series, but it could be that differences in methodology and enumerating techniques contributed greatly to a larger number of women being included in the labour force in 1956 than would have been the case if criteria for inclusion were the same as in the two census years. This reinforces the point that in most development countries analyses of time-series information are always plagued by differences caused by changing concepts, techniques of collection, methods of estimation and coverage.

[2] The belief in this hypothesis springs mainly from the acceptance of the thesis set forth by Colin Clark and Allan Fisher to the effect that tertiary production is

TABLE 9

INDUSTRIAL DISTRIBUTION OF EMPLOYED LABOUR FORCE PERCENTAGES

	1946[a]	1956[b]	1960[c]
Agriculture, forestry, hunting, fishing	46·2	39·0	37·0
Mining and quarrying	2·8	3·0	3·8
Manufacturing, including processing of agricultural commodities	15·9	16·0	16·3
Construction	5·0	7·0	8·0
Commerce	8·2	11·0	11·3
Transport, storage, communications	4·2	6·0	4·8
Services	16·9	18·0	18·6
Not stated	0·8	—	0·2
Total	100·0	100·0	100·0

Source: Census of Population 1946. Census of Population 1960. *1956 Report on Employment, Unemployment and Underemployment,* p. 135, adjusted approximately to conform with other data by (a) removing 5,000 sugar and rice-processing workers from Agriculture to Manufacturing, (b) increasing mining workers to 4,000 as suggested on p. 11 of I.L.O. Report.

The share of Agriculture etc. is probably understated in 1956 since the Survey did not cover the Pomeroon Area, the North-West District, and most of the Interior, but it did include Bartica, Mackenzie, and Kwakwani.

[a] April.   [b] September.   [c] April.

of much less importance in pre-industrial societies than in industrialized economies. See Colin Clark, *The Conditions of Economic Progress* (London, 1951) and A. G. B. Fisher, *Economic Progress and Social Security* (London, 1945). Bauer and Yamey have subjected the Clark-Fisher thesis to a thorough criticism based on observations in British West Africa. In brief, they complain that the Clark–Fisher thesis assumes services to have a greater income elasticity than primary and secondary goods and this is not necessarily so, that the occupational specialization in these areas is not sufficiently developed for labour distribution data to be reliable, and the substitution of paid labour for unpaid labour and vice-versa as the economy advances renders very difficult the interpretation of labour force statistics. See P. T. Bauer and B. S. Yamey, 'Economic Progress and Occupational Distribution', *Economic Journal* (December 1951), pp. 741–56. A useful summary of the debate can be found in H. H. Holton, 'Marketing Structure and Economic Development', *The Quarterly Journal of Economics,* Vol. 67, No. 3 (1957), pp. 344–61. The author also examines the behaviour of tertiary production and distribution in Puerto Rico and reaches conclusions similar to those of Bauer and Yamey.

activity under the categories manufacturing, services, and commerce is in those handicrafts, petty trading, domestic service, and public works projects that are not socially valuable production, but rather socially wasteful duplication. The individuals concerned often overcrowd these handicraft and service activities, not so much in pursuit of attractive opportunities there as in flight from the lack of opportunities elsewhere.

This was corroborated by the 1965 investigations which carefully estimated the number of work people in small establishments, i.e. those that have less than 5 paid employees, but any number of unpaid family workers. It is possible to have 6 or 8 persons making some contribution to the running of the business and yet at the same time it is classed as a small establishment if there are less than 5 paid employees. Work in these small establishments makes a substantial contribution to total household income, especially in the rural areas. It became evident that there were a large number of these small business places distributed throughout the country. The average number of persons per establishment was estimated at 1·5, but there is reason to believe that this understates the overcrowding of persons in these establishments, since as already mentioned it is conceivable that some unpaid family workers who were contributing the equivalent of 2 or 3 days' work per week may not have been reported to the enumerators.

An examination of the distribution of these establishments by industry revealed that bakery products and wearing apparel were the chief items found in the manufacturing sector. The wholesale and retail trade of food, was, as expected, important in the distribution sector. In services the most important were restaurants, cafes, bars, and similar establishments. Shopkeepers, shop assistants, tailors and cutters, dressmakers, milliners, motor mechanics, bartenders, and beauticians seem to be the more important occupations in these establishments.

But no examination of small business places will be complete without a consideration of the activity taking place in the markets, distributed throughout the country, as omitting them from the discussion would lead to severe under-representation of both the number of establishments and workers engaged in small business places. The main types of industries found in these places were in manufacturing, wholesale, or retail trade of some kind, with wholesale or retail of food being the most important contributor.[1]

The occupational proportions so far given are broadly correlated with the industrial origin of Gross Domestic Product given in the previous chapter. But when we try to compare these two types of data, we find wide disparities. Mining, with about 3 per cent of the labour force, contributes well over 11 per cent of G.D.P., while manufacturing, with over 12 per cent of the labour force, provided just over 3 per cent of G.D.P. These relationships tend to reaffirm the conclusion that some occupations that account for substantial portions of the labour force are in fact overcrowded and unremunerative rather than attractive and rewarding; the highest-yielding occupations employ very few persons.

Table 10 presents the unemployment figures for the Survey Week ending 20 March 1965. The most striking result that emerges is that the level of unemployment has increased since 1956 from 29,600 to 36,400, and this has caused the percentage of the labour force unemployed to move from 18·0 per cent to 20·9 per cent. The increase in the numbers unemployed is probably even greater than the figures suggest because of the abnormally high proportion which women formed of the labour force in 1956. This increase in unemployment should not be surprising, for it is consistent with the high population growth previously observed, and the doubtful performance of the economy over the past decade or so.

The second important observation is that the rural/urban differentials in the levels of unemployment have changed direction. In 1956 the unemployment rates in urban areas was higher than in rural places, whereas the results of the 1965 Survey indicate that the reverse is now true. The genuine dislike of young persons for agricultural employment, with the result that many remain idle and at the same time live in the hope of finding other kinds of jobs, added to mechanization in certain

[1] The Survey covered the markets in Georgetown, i.e. Kitty, La Penitence, Stabroek, Bourda, and also the New Amsterdam market. Of the slightly over 1,000 establishments found in Georgetown markets, nearly 600 were in wholesale and retail of food, the latter category employing about 2,000 persons out of a total of 2,600. For the New Amsterdam market, the proportion of this industry group was even higher, as 182 of the 208 units enumerated were in this category, with a labour force of 241 out of a total of 269 for this urban area (*Manpower Survey 1965*).

TABLE 10

PERSONS IN THE LABOUR FORCE AND IN UNEMPLOYMENT CLASSIFIED BY PLACE OF RESIDENCE (COUNTIES) AND SEX—1965

Place of residence	Persons in labour force			Persons in unemployment			Percentage unemployed		
	M	F	T	M	F	T	M	F	T
Georgetown	33,570	19,260	52,830	4,770	4,060	8,830	14·2	21·1	16·7
New Amsterdam	2,370	1,590	3,960	420	370	790	17·7	23·3	19·9
McKenzie-Wismar	4,630	1,620	6,250	640	410	1,050	13·8	25·3	16·8
Bartica	1,200	490	1,690	100	140	240	8·3	28·5	14·2
Kwakwani	262	60	322	19	15	34	7·2	25·0	10·5
Matthews Ridge-Port Kaituma	463	60	523	34	21	55	7·3	35·0	10·5
Mabaruma-Morawhanna	270	50	320	55	10	65	20·4	20·0	20·3
Berbice East	24,570	5,240	29,810	4,980	1,400	6,380	20·3	26·7	21·4
Berbice West	6,440	1,750	8,190	1,990	670	2,660	30·9	38·3	32·5
Demerara East	28,090	8,610	36,700	5,900	3,520	9,420	21·0	40·9	25·7
Demerara West	15,070	6,410	21,480	2,520	2,040	4,560	16·7	31·8	21·2
Essequibo Coast	6,870	1,970	8,840	1,550	460	2,010	22·5	23·4	22·7
Essequibo Islands	3,020	690	3,710	220	130	350	7·3	18·3	9·3
	126,825	47,800	174,625	23,198	13,246	36,444	18·3	27·7	20·9

Source: Manpower Survey 1965.

fields, such as sugar and rice, would seem to be the more important factors causing the picture to be reversed. In earlier times rice production was so labour intensive that schools were closed at certain periods so that children could be fully employed at certain stages of the operations.

A third point is that certain areas seem to have severe unemployment. The case of Berbice West with a rate of unemployment of 32·5 per cent is unique. Limited employment opportunities in this area has contributed to the high rate observed. But the main factor is sociological in nature. Many able-bodied persons who might have been engaged in subsistence agriculture in the area have moved to the mining towns of Mackenzie and Kwakwani. This has raised the unemployment rate, because those remaining were still included in the labour force, and they genuinely desired to work although they were not actively engaged. Part of the incomes of those who have migrated flow back to the area and this partly explains how the community exists with such limited opportunities for gainful employment.[1]

The percentage of females unemployed in the various areas are, as expected, higher than the corresponding figures for males. Proper care was taken in the 1965 Survey to ensure that only females who genuinely wanted work were included in the labour force, but the sex differentials in unemployment rates are still large. This seems a common phenomenon in the West Indies. The extent of women's employment outside the household to a large extent reflects the level of economic development that has been reached.[2] With economic development many of the jobs they had been doing inefficiently and with drudgery in the home are transferred to external establishments. Correspondingly women are released from working in the home and are transferred to external establishments including offices, shops, factories, and the professions. The presence of a large number of unemployed women in Guyana reflects not only the lack of employment opportunities, but points to the existence of remnants of the extended family system.

[1] R. T. Smith, *The Negro Family in British Guiana* (London, 1956). The greater part of the research for this study was conducted in villages on Berbice West. It contains an excellent account of the main sociological factors affecting employment and motivating job seekers.

[2] Lewis, *The Theory of Economic Growth*, p. 331.

Another trend of tremendous social and economic significance is the growth of the number of 'inexperienced unemployed'. In 1946, the number of persons in this category
totalled only 1,300. By 1956, this had increased to 10,100, and
the corresponding figure according to the 1960 census was
11,800. The growth of population, the lack of proper employment services,[1] and changes in the age distribution of the
population and the school-leaving age are contributory factors.
There is the additional fact that in former years young persons
leaving school would be drawn into agriculture or other forms
of own-account employment to a greater extent than they are
today, with the result that a higher proportion of them would
have been recorded in particular occupations in previous years.
The developing tendency now for young persons is withdrawal
from, or refusal to enter, agriculture, while at the same time
many of these persons have no particular skill and therefore
remain unemployed for a considerable period. In a later
chapter, light is thrown on the educational training and vocational attainments of the unemployed in this category. But it
must be noticed that the unemployed school-leavers have been
swelling the ranks of the unemployed in the urban areas, to
which they flock in search of 'white-collar' jobs, instead of
returning to the rural sector which they now view with disdain.[2]

Deterioration in employment conditions affect young persons
in the first instance because they lack work experience. With
working possibilities in the family enterprises tending to become
scarcer in the course of technical progess, school-leavers more
than ever before have to look for paid jobs. This kind of employment, although somewhat more expanding than total
employment, has not by any means kept pace with the rapid
rise in the number of aspirants.

The difficulties that young persons encounter in establishing
a foothold in the labour market are a reflection of the limited

[1] See I.L.O. 'The Organisation of Employment Services in Economically
Underdeveloped Countries', *International Labour Review*, Vol. 73, No. 4 (April
1956), pp. 315–33.
[2] This tendency has been noticed in a number of countries especially in Africa.
See A. C. Callaway, 'Unemployment among African School-Leavers', *Journal of
Modern African Studies* (September 1963), pp. 351–71; also I.L.O., 'Unemployed
Youth: An African Symposium', *International Labour Review* (March 1963), pp.
183–205.

elasticity of the present economic structure. As was pointed out earlier, Guyana's economy is still heavily based on a narrow selection of primary products and related tertiary activities, while secondary industry is comparatively undeveloped. As the economy is also limited because of the small population and the moderate level of income, production and marketing are to a large extent monopolistic, giving little inducement for greater diversification of the economic structure. The demands for most consumer goods have been met by imports rather than intensification of local manufacturing and processing. All of the country's major industries, i.e. forestry, sugar, rice, and mining are export industries, with prospects for expansion largely determined by world market conditions.

Although capital investment from national as well as from foreign sources has been considerable, over-all economic development has not been such as to absorb the increasing numbers of workers. Capital requirements for overheads are extremely high in Guyana. Part of the densely settled coastal belt which lies below sea level needs constant protection from floods by a costly system of dykes, canals, and sluices. Road construction is excessively expensive in this swampy area. With such large public investment concentrated on drainage and irrigation schemes, and private investment predominantly attracted by the export sector, changes in economic structure and in employment remain negligible.

It is true that there was a considerable rise in primary production, but because of greater capital intensity, labour demand did not expand to the same extent. In the sugar industry, which is by far the largest single employer, job opportunities have absolutely declined since 1952. A similar development took place in rice milling. Rice production was able to absorb more labour only after a considerable and costly expansion of acreage. However, this has neither reduced prevailing under-employment in rice agriculture nor did it offset losses of employment opportunities in other agricultural branches. In contrast to sugar cultivation, rice cultivation is almost exclusively in the hands of small farmers, whose labour demand in general does not exceed family circles. Mechanization in agriculture did not so much result in spontaneous dismissals as in the renouncing of normal replacements and in restriction of casual labour. Demand for skilled workers has increased but this demand has mostly been satisfied by retraining suitable candidates selected from own personnel. Opportunities for school-leavers to establish a skilled or unskilled position in agriculture have dropped, thus reinforcing the socially motivated aversion to manual labour.

Apart from mining, most non-agricultural activities are heavily concentrated in urban areas, i.e. Georgetown and its environments. New Amsterdam, the second area in Guyana classified as 'urban', is much too small to offer a significant outlet for the heavily growing agricultural-labour surplus even of its immediate hinterland. Many school-leavers looking for paid employment are thus forced into Georgetown, but there, too, job opportunities have not expanded to the same degree as labour supply. With comparatively little investment in manufacturing, labour demand has remained limited in both secondary industries and tertiary activities. In the latter, employment capacity is largely determined by the development in the immediately productive sectors of the economy. While employment for men in manufacturing improved slightly, possibilities for women have declined. In general there has been a distinct shift from agriculture into commerce and the service industries. This is exacerbated by the fact that the occupational composition of the working force is characterized by marked concentrations in a few occupations. Outside agriculture, men are workers in transport and communications, in construction, in metal trades, and in certain private services, while women are service workers or employees in the commercial and professional fields. Again all these occupations are centred on the towns.

In summary, young persons in Guyana at present face the problem of general employment shortage and lack possibilities of social and economic advancement. Prospects for young people in the rural areas have been limited, the drive to urban centres, and the search for white-collar jobs has been intensified. Secondary industry has so far done little to change the traditional dislike for manual work. With insufficient wage differences between skilled and unskilled labour such as prevail in smaller enterprises, there is little stratification in the socio-economic structure at the lower level and consequently little incentive for technical proficiency. In addition, insufficient graduation of skill means inadequate utilization of human resources, excessive production costs even at low wages, limited economic expansion, and restricted employment opportunities at all levels.

Thus the satisfaction of future needs for education resulting from both population increases and rising qualitative requirements will greatly depend upon better employment conditions. But this does not mean that jobs should be provided at all cost, without regard, for instance, to the needs for technical change and mechanization. On the contrary, emphasis must be placed upon improvements in labour productivity if economic stagnation is to be avoided. In general, preference may have to be given to projects promising maximum income rather than maximum employment, for only out of rising income can there be more savings and investments, which in turn will generate more employment and income. However, with present high levels of unemployment and underemployment, the provision of jobs has become a pressing social issue demanding a consideration of more than the mere economic factors.

III

AGRICULTURE AND FORESTS

1. *The Importance of Agriculture*

In this chapter we examine the salient features of agricultural development in order to identify the main factors affecting the investment pattern and coefficients of production. This investigation must necessarily precede any decisions regarding the development strategy within the industry or within the economy as a whole. Although there may still exist some measure of disagreement among economists about the correct balance that ought to exist between agricultural and other forms of industrial growth in the development pattern, there is firm agreement that the agricultural 'revolution' must be complementary to the industrial 'revolution'. We may therefore briefly outline the main reasons why agriculture may be expected to play a strategic role in over-all economic development.[1]

Economic development is characterized by a substantial increase in the demand for agricultural products, and failure to expand food supplies in pace with the growth of demand can seriously impede economic growth. Apart from autonomous changes in demand, which may be of limited significance, the annual rate of increase in the demand for food is a function of the rate of growth of population, *per capita* incomes, and the income elasticity of demand for agricultural products.[2] With this in mind, concern over the growth in the demand for food in Guyana is sharpened by the following considerations. In the

---

[1] There exists a proliferation of literature dealing with the crucial role of agriculture in economic development, but the following present the relevant arguments with notable precision and clarity: Lewis, *The Theory of Economic Growth*, pp. 276–83; B. F. Johnston and J. W. Mellor, 'The Role of Agriculture in Economic Development', *American Economic Review* (Sept. 1961), pp. 566–93. C. Eicher and L. Witt (eds.), *Agriculture in Economic Development* (New York, 1964).

[2] The annual rate of increase in the demand for food is given by the following formula: $D = p + \eta g$, where p and g represent the rate of growth of population and *per capita* income respectively, and η the income elasticity of demand for agricultural products.

first instance, it was noticed that a population growth of over 3 per cent was a characteristic feature of the economy, so that the growth in demand from this factor alone was substantial. That the income elasticity of demand for food was of the order of 0·6 per cent was also revealed.[1] Hence a given rate of increase in *per capita* income had a stronger impact on the demand for agricultural products than one would have expected in an economically developed country.

The situation has been heightened by the high import content in the demand for food. Despite the fact that in aggregate terms the increase in agricultural production has been considerable, it has not been in adequate proportions to raise *per capita* production levels, owing to the stationary, and in some cases the declining yields and the high population growth referred to above. Therefore, imports of food have continued to be a high proportion of total imports, averaging 20 per cent over the years 1959 to 1964, as could be seen from the table below.

TABLE I

FOOD IMPORTS 1959-64

(*Million Guyana Dollars*)

Year	Total imports	Imports of food	Per cent
1959	111	22	20
1960	148	25	17
1961	147	26	18
1962	126	27	21
1963	118	25	21
1964	150	29	19

Source: Annual Reports on External Trade.

If food supplies fail to expand in pace with the growth in demand, the result is likely to be a substantial rise in food prices, leading to political discontent and pressure on wage rates with consequent adverse effects on other factor incomes, investment, and growth.[2] Since cheap starchy foods provide over 60 per cent of the calorie intake in Guyana, there may be a relatively

[1] Cumper, 'West Indian Household Budgets', loc. cit.
[2] See C. N. Vakil and P. R. Brackmanand, *Planning for an Expanding Economy: Accumulation, Employment and Technical Progress in Underdeveloped Countries* (New York, 1956).

limited scope for offsetting a rise in food prices by shifting from more expensive to less starchy foods, and the pressure to resist a reduction in the already low calorie intake may be strong.

Owing to the high import content of food consumption, domestic shortages of food are likely to be offset to some extent by expanded food imports. But since foreign exchange is in short supply, and urgently required for imports of machinery and other requisites for industrial development that cannot be produced domestically, the development of such a tendency cannot be allowed. However, the probability of this arising in Guyana may be low in view of the potential that may exist for increased agricultural productivity in lines other than cheap, staple, starchy foods. But although it is likely that additional food supplies could be obtained by increased domestic output rather than by an increased reliance on enlarged food imports, this could be effected only after a time-lag, so that in the immediate future the outward flow of foreign exchange would continue.

On the more positive side, expansion of exports of agricultural products may be one of the most promising means of increasing income and foreign exchange earnings, particularly in the earlier stages of economic development. The country's erstwhile export experience bears this out. Since an individual country, which accounts for only a small fraction of world exports, faces a fairly elastic demand schedule, substantial expansion of agricultural export production may be a rational policy even though the world supply-demand situation for an individual commodity may be unfavourable.[1] This line of reasoning of course does not belittle the serious disadvantages attached to

---

[1] The greater part of the scepticism that has arisen is a direct consequence of the misrepresentation and misunderstanding of the popular 'Prebisch Thesis' regarding the deterioration of the terms of trade of the developing countries. Most commentators have failed to recognize that this thesis is multifaced in character, that there are at least two Prebisch theses: 'Prebisch I' in *Economic Development for Latin America and its Principal Problems* (United Nations Department of Economic Affairs, 1950), and 'Prebisch II' in Commercial Policy in Underdeveloped Countries, *American Economic Review, Papers and Proceedings*, Vol. xliv (May 1959), pp. 251–73. A careful reading of the first work reveals that Prebisch is much less of an 'autarkist' than his supporters and detractors seem to think, and that he does not rule out expanded agricultural exports as a means of propelling the development ship. See M. J. Flanders, 'Prebisch on Protectionism: An Evaluation', *Economic Journal* (June 1964), pp. 305–26.

any heavy reliance on agricultural exports, especially of a few staple commodities, in which case Guyana's experience is very apposite. We recognize that the longer-run goal of the economy must be that diversification which will lessen its vulnerability by rendering it less dependent than it has been on export proceeds from a few agricultural crops. One of the rewards of a structural transformation of the economy associated with economic growth is the greater flexibility of a diversified economy. Of greater immediate importance, however, is the fact that the introduction of expanded production of export crops can and should play a strategic role in providing an adequate supply of foreign exchange earnings.

Finally, agriculture as a dominant sector in a development country can and should make a net contribution to the capital required for overhead investment and expansion of secondary industry.[1] Net cash incomes of the agricultural population may provide an important stimulus to industrial expansion.[2] In addition, it cannot be overlooked that there may exist the possibility that the labour force for manufacturing and other expanding sectors of the economy may be drawn from the agricultural sector.[3]

According to the 1960 Census of Population, 37 per cent of the working population or 57,790 persons were engaged in agricultural activities. Although no firm figures exist for agricultural employment in 1964 mechanization in sugar and rice

[1] Cf. T. Balogh, 'Agriculture and Economic Development', Oxford Economic Papers (February 1961), pp. 27–42.

[2] W. A. Lewis, Report on the Industrialisation of the Gold Coast (Government Printing Office, Accra, 1953), pp. 1–3.

[3] Much intellectual capital has been invested in models that postulate surplus labour in agriculture as a 'potential investment surplus' available without social cost to the industrial sector. In particular see S. Enke, 'Economic Development with Unlimited and Limited Supplies of Labour', Oxford Economic Papers (June 1962), pp. 158–72; W. A. Lewis, 'Economic Development with Unlimited Supplies of Labour', Manchester School of Economic and Social Studies (May 1954), pp. 139–92; G. Ranis and J. C. H. Fei, 'A Theory of Economic Development', American Economic Review (September 1961), pp. 533–58. The implicit assumption made in these models is that increased industrialization must necessarily lead to a decline of the agricultural sector. We assume that agricultural advance is a concomitant of other forms of industrial development, that large-scale opportunities for additional employment may exist within agriculture, and that the output of the current labour force could be increased by a redistribution of labour with the sector. For a recent exposition of this line of thought see Morton Paglin, 'Surplus Agricultural Labour and Development', American Economic Review (September 1965), pp. 815–34.

almost certainly led to a decline in numbers. This would not be
out of keeping with the tendency noticed in an earlier chapter,
of a percentage decline of numbers employed in this industry
since 1946.[1] Thus while in 1946, 46·2 per cent of the total labour
force was employed in agriculture, by 1956 this figure had fallen
to 39 per cent, with the 1960 figure two percentage points below
this. Although agriculture's share of the national product has
also been substantial, its contribution in this sphere has been
much less spectacular than in the field of employment. Thus
the agricultural sector contributed an average of 29 per cent of
Gross Domestic Product between 1953 and 1964. In 1954 its
share was 30·6 per cent, falling to 28·8, 26·2, and 27·2 per cent
in 1955, 1956, and 1957 respectively. In 1958 the share rose to
28·9 per cent, falling to 27·6 in 1959. Slight gains were recorded
in 1960 and 1961 with figures of 28·3 and 28·2 respectively. By
1963 agriculture's share reached an all time high of 33·9 per
cent, but this was not maintained, for in 1964 it fell to 27·9
per cent. With the exception of minerals, and a few manufactured products, agriculture has accounted for over 60 per cent
of the colony's value of exported domestic produce. This position has been greatly encouraged by the guaranteed markets
for sugar and rice.

General agricultural policy has been directed towards bringing new areas on the coastal belt into cultivation and under
beneficial occupation so as to provide employment for a rapidly
growing population. In addition some attempts have been made
at providing research and extension facilities so as to increase
productivity, as well as developing family-sized farms and a
strong and independent farming community. The efforts of the
central government to achieve these objectives involved heavy
infrastructural works for water control. Hence provision had to
be made for the construction of drainage and irrigation, particularly in the Boerasirie and Tapacuma areas. Because the
greater part of the coastal belt is below sea level, sea-defence
structures were an essential prerequisite to the protection of the
valuable agricultural land in this area.

[1] This tendency is not a result of increased industrialization with any shift of
the labour force from agriculture to industry. It is somewhat a result of mechanization in sugar and rice, followed by increased unemployment in the economy as a
whole.

Investment in agriculture has therefore accounted for a very high proportion of total investment from the government budget. Over the development period 1954 to 1959 expenditure on agriculture amounted to $37·6 million out of a total expenditure of $103·8 million, i.e. about 36 per cent of the total. This figure fell by $1·6 million to $36 million in the development period 1960 to 1964, when there was a total allocated expenditure of $110 million. Of the $36 million devoted to agriculture, approximately $3 million was spent on agriculture proper, some $2 million on land development, $24 million on drainage and irrigation, and the remaining $7 million on river and sea defences. The largest actual expenditure in any one year over the 1960–4 period was $21 million in 1961, of which $8·8 million went to agriculture. Compared with 1954–9 period, expenditure under the heads described was of a similar magnitude and therefore did not represent any marked change in policy. Expenditure in aggregate terms for the two development periods is given in the table below.

TABLE 2

GOVERNMENT INVESTMENT FOR AGRICULTURAL
PURPOSES 1954–64

(*Million Guyana dollars*)

Head	1954–9	1960–4
Agriculture	4·6	3·2
Drainage and irrigation	25·6	23·5
Land development	2·8	2·4
Sea defences	4·6	7·0
Total expenditure	37·6	36·1

Source: Development Estimates.

2. *Rice*

Rice is grown along the flat coastal lands which extend inland from the coast for distances of 10 to 50 miles. It is by far the country's most important food crop. Unlike sugar and bauxite there are no large companies co-ordinating production and marketing, and most of the paddy grown is produced by small peasant cultivators. It has been the fastest-growing sector in aggregate terms over the past five years, and still continues to provide about 12,000 jobs in a situation where the labour force in agriculture has been declining. Its share of Gross Domestic Product has remained at approximately 5 per cent over the period. This is a very small part of national income, and in view of the very large numbers employed, the earnings are shared out very thinly. This shows that the economic significance of rice is extremely small as compared with its political and social significance. It must be noted, however, that not all the total income earned in this sector is distributed as personal income. The industry is a heavy net borrower from other sectors, and much of the expenditure made by the government through grants for drainage and irrigation must be considered invest-ment. The industry would find it almost impossible to service this investment had it not been made in many cases as loans to the industry requiring interest payments. Other industries that benefit directly from the rice industry in that they owe much of their income and employment to the former are: transporta-tion (especially water transportation), importers of machinery, accessories, fuels and bags, and the repair industry, including people who are not growers themselves but who hire out machinery to the growers.

Table 3 sets out data for the acreage and output of paddy and rice for the period 1952–64. It is immediately noticeable that the total acreage brought under cultivation, and the quantities of both paddy and rice produced over this period have been doubled. The aggregate increase in acreage and out-put was the direct result of massive investment by the central government in land-development schemes under the Five Year Development Programme of 1956–60 (later revised to four years 1956–9). This provided for the completion of two main drainage and irrigation schemes, viz., the Courentyne Drain-age and Irrigation Project and the Boerasirie which were already started under the Ten Year Plan for Development and Welfare 1947–56, and the establishment of Land Settlement schemes at Mara and The Garden of Eden. The Courentyne Project, mainly for rice, included the Black Bush Polder and Tapacuma Projects, and by 1961 the former project already provided over 30,000 acres with 27,000 acres allocated to rice cultivation. The Tapacuma project in Stage 1 made available nearly 36,000 acres of land, with over 30,000 acres for rice cultivation; and in Stage II, which is nearing completion, another 15,000 acres will be provided, and it is expected that over 12,000 acres of this area will be devoted to rice cultivation. The Boerasirie Project, which was completed in 1960, yielded approximately 30,000 acres of new land, with 26,400 acres allocated to rice. The Mara scheme provided another 3,870 acres with about 1,400 acres for rice, whereas the Garden of Eden Settlement has provided another 1,200 acres, and of a total of

TABLE 3

ACREAGE AND OUTPUT OF RICE 1952–64

Year	Total acreage	Paddy (tons)	Rice (equivalent tons)	Paddy yield per acre (140-lb. bags net)
(1)	(2)	(3)	(4)	(5)
1952	153,120	129,720	77,832	13·6
1953	134,700	125,062	75,037	14·9
1954	161,453	149,964	89,978	14·9
1955	171,900	148,500	89,100	13·8
1956	136,000	130,833	75,500	15·4
1957	152,500	95,833	57,500	10·1
1958	183,326	167,522	100,519	14·6
1959	195,776	173,459	104,075	14·2
1960	220,207	210,222	126,133	15·3
1961	229,988	206,705	124,023	14·4
1962	269,995	216,540	129,924	12·8
1963	201,145	171,475	102,884	13·6
1964	311,417	259,875	155,926	13·4

Source: Agricultural Statistics of Guyana; Annual Reports of the Rice Marketing Board.

3,500 acres available on the Vergenoegen Land Settlement Scheme, 2,085 acres were made available for rice cultivation.[1] Thus the first revealing feature about investment in rice in Guyana was that the increase in aggregate output was a direct consequence of the extension of the margin of cultivation.[2]

[1] Information received from The Land Settlement Department of the Ministry of Agriculture, Guyana. However, large areas remain unutilized or underutilized for considerable periods of time.

[2] The increase in acreage brought about under land settlement schemes must be contrasted with the other areas under cultivation that have remained comparatively static over the period.

8—E.D.G.

With this massive investment which has taken place in land development schemes in recent years in the coastal areas, the technique of farming has undergone a basic transformation in favour of mechanization which has enabled these large tracts to be quickly brought under cultivation. But this expansion has concealed some basic weaknesses in the situation. In the first place, the cost of this expansion in terms of drainage and irrigation and land settlement schemes has been very heavy in relation to output released so far. The increase in acreage and tractorization has brought down the average productivity per acre. Thus whereas the aggregate output of rice has gone up, output per acre has fallen or failed to keep pace with this increase.

Whereas it is easy to understand low yields per man, it is more difficult to explain low yields per acre under cultivation. A very high density of rural population implies limited 'cultivable' land and capital per man, and therefore low income per head. But if we look at another side we should expect high yields per acre. Other things being equal, the yield per acre should depend on the intensity with which the land is worked. Thus if land and labour were the only two factors, we should expect high yields where there is a high density of labour on the land. Even when we introduce capital into the picture this should not greatly change the conclusion, for much of the agricultural capital is likely to be labour-saving, and labour is already superabundant. Thus if we start with land of equal quality, we should expect high, rather than low, yields in densely populated rural areas.

Although yields per acre for the country have fallen or have remained static in most years, these yields vary throughout the country depending on the soil, drainage and irrigation facilities, and husbandry practices. As can be seen from Table 4, which shows the yields for different rice producing areas, in the Eastern Berbice area for instance, the autumn crop yields are about 11 bags per acre. So is the case with Western Berbice. In Eastern Demerara around the Mahaicony-Abary Rice Development Company, yields vary between 14 and 18 bags per acre. Similar yields are obtained in the West Coast and West Bank Demerara, but rise to about 18 to 19 bags per acre on the Essequibo Coast and Essequibo Islands. Among areas like the

West Coast Berbice where drainage is poor, yields have been fairly static, whereas areas like the West Coast Demerara with good drainage have been growth areas. The yields obtained in some of the main land settlement schemes have also been far from satisfactory, either because of poor drainage conditions or through questionable husbandry practices.

Thus although the average yield of paddy per acre does not seem to have increased significantly, there is a possibility for any attempt at a solution to be based on a regional basis; for there have been no significant decreases in yields except from those natural causes under unseasonable conditions in Essequibo, Leguan, Wakenaam, West Demerara, or the Courentyne coast. Decreases in yield per acre (The Mahaicony-Abary Rice Development Company excepted) in the Mahaicony-Abary area were mainly due to a lack of proper water control and to the outlook of the farmers in the area who tend to maximize profit on volume and not on the application of intensified methods of agriculture for increasing yield. The expansion of acreage under rice has been insignificant in other areas (Land Settlement Schemes excepted), but has been very marked in the Mahaicony-Abary region. Thus the farmer in that area has become more prosperous by taking up more land whilst not increasing yields on his existing cultivation. The yield per acre on his existing cultivation has dropped, and this, together with the expansion of acreage, has shown a reduction of national average yield.

We have been arguing that the outward shift of the extensive margin of cultivation has been accompanied by decreased output per acre, but that this phenomenon was not universal. For it was mainly the completion of land settlement schemes that led to an expansion of acreage, while there was no substantial expansion in other areas. Yield per acre also varied according to the intensity of cultivation and similar factors. But the general impression remains that the major use to which the coastal and riverain areas have been put is rice farming, probably because paddy cultivation does yield some return even though the type of husbandry may not be scientific. A close examination of the various factors that have led to the low returns to investment in rice is therefore necessary.

The first causal factor is the size of the agricultural holdings in

TABLE 4
RICE PRODUCTION DISTRIBUTION

	1965—Spring yield (per acre)	1964—Autumn yield (per acre)	1964—Spring yield (per acre)
Berbice—Eastern			
Orealla—No. 51	7·5	11·3	7·0
Black Bush	7·6	11·8	7·0
Berbice River and West Canje excluding Mara	8·4	11·0	7·0
No. 50 East Canje excluding Black Bush	9·2	16·0	—
Total	7·9	11·3	7·0
Berbice—Western			
L. B. Abary	—	10·7	—
Other areas	4·9	12·3	—
Total	4·9	12·1	—
Demerara—Eastern			
M.A.R.D.S.	11·1	17·0	6·7
Mahaicony and M.A.R.D.S.	7·1	14·4	6·7
Mahaica	6·0	14·1	6·0
Coast and areas mentioned above	6·3	9·7	5·9
East Bank	10·5	14·1	4·5
Total	6·8	14·1	6·6
West Coast Demerara	11·5	16·5	11·0
West Bank Demerara	12·1	15·1	4·6
Total	11·7	16·0	10·4
Essequibo			
Supernam—Adventure Int. Tiger Island	7·1	18·8	7·3
Tapacuma	12·5	18·4	—
Coast and Areas above	12·7	19·2	7·6
Total	12·0	18·6	7·6
Other Islands	7·1	12·0	15·0

Source: Department of Agriculture, Georgetown, Guyana.

general and the rice holdings in particular which have remained small and uneconomic. In 1956, as part of the general Agricultural Census, some information was obtained on the type of farm by size from inquiries conducted by the Co-opera-

TABLE 5

SIZES OF FARMS

(a) *Percentage of operators*

Operating less than	Co-operative Department[a]	Rice Producers' Association[b]	Agriculture Census 1956—only farms less than 50-acres included[b]	Tapacuma Area[a]	Agriculture Department[a]
1 acre	1·5	20·0	5·0	—	21·0
5 acres	23·5	55·0	57·0	38·0	73·5
10 acres	58·5	79·5	87·0	74·5	87·0
15 acres	—	—	—	93·5	—
20 acres	86·5	92·5	98·7	—	93·6
25 acres	—	—	—	96·8	—
50 acres	97·0	97·8	100·0	98·4	97·6
100 acres	99·4	98·7	—	99·3	98·9
150 acres	99·8	99·6	—	99·6	—
200 acres	—	—	—	99·7	—

(b) *Percentage of acres*

In farm size less than	Co-operative Department[a]	Rice Producers' Association[b]	Agriculture Census 1956—only farms less than 50-acres included[b]	Tapacuma Area[a]	Agriculture Department[a]
1 acre	0·1	1·7	0·4	—	1·6
5 acres	6·0	11·0	23·0	5·0	17·0
10 acres	27·0	33·5	61·0	20·0	24·0
15 acres	—	—	—	32·0	—
20 acres	54·0	55·5	91·6	—	37·6
25 acres	—	—	—	38·0	—
50 acres	81·0	64·0	100·0	44·0	54·4
100 acres	92·3	71·7	—	50·0	66·7
150 acres	94·8	86·4	—	53·0	76·6
200 acres	97·3	94·9	—	56·8	81·9

Source: Compiled from information received from the Department of Agriculture and Files of the Department of Land Settlement; Annual Reports of the Guyana Rice Producers' Association.

[a] Mixed farming with rice predominating.   [b] Rice farming.

tive Department, the Rice Producers' Association, the Land Settlement Department, and the Agricultural Department. The Co-operative Department conducted a survey among 45 per cent of the total membership of the Agricultural Thrift and Credit Societies holding 30,467 acres of land and cultivating a variety of crops. The Rice Producers' Association based its results on 234,000 acres under rice, while the Tapacuma statistics supplied by the Land Settlement Department were in respect of 27,378 acres of land under different crops in the Tapacuma area. The Agriculture Department based its investigations on 121, 450 acres of land under a variety of crops. Thus the sample taken was truly representative of the situation in the country as a whole, and although the investigation was carried out in 1956, the information gleaned regarding the type and size of rice farms still obtains. These findings have been summarized in Table 5.

Dealing just with the amount of land held by the farmers or operators we find from the table that according to the five sources mentioned that (a) less than 1 acre of land is held by 1·5 to 21 per cent of the farmers; (b) less than 5 acres of land is held by 23·5 to 73·5 per cent of the farmers, and two of the five sources have 55 and 57 per cent respectively for this category; (c) less than 10 acres of land is held by 58·5 to 87 per cent of the farmers, and four of the sources have between 74·5 and 87 per cent; (d) less than 20 acres is held by 97 to 100 per cent of all the farmers. Thus whichever group of figures is used, it seems an indisputable fact that the large majority of the farmers have very small holdings. At the barest minimum about one-quarter of the farmers have less than 5 acres; but it seems very much more likely that this size of holdings is held by at least 50 per cent of the farmers. At the least 58 per cent of the farmers have less than 10 acres of land and the more likely figure is 75 per cent as shown by four of the five surveys. This means that only 25 per cent of the farmers have holdings of over 10 acres. Of this percentage it seems that about 18 per cent have between 10 to 20 acres while 5 per cent have holdings between 20 to 50 acres, and only 2 per cent of the farmers have holdings larger than 50 acres.

Let us now turn to the percentage of acres in farms of various sizes. (a) Farms of less than 5 acres occupy between 5 to 23 per cent of the total acreage surveyed or an average of about 12 per cent; (b) farms of less than 10 acres occupy between 20 and 61 per cent of the acreage and an average of about 33 per cent; (c) farms of less than 20 acres occupy between 37·6 and 91·6 per cent of the total acreage; two of the four surveys show 54 and 55·5 per cent respectively. The average from the five surveys shows a figure of 56 per cent. The remaining 44 per cent of the total acreage is occupied by farms of 20 acres and over, 11 per cent of this is occupied by farms of between 20 to 30 acres, and on average 33 per cent of the total acreage surveyed is occupied by farms larger than 50 acres. This second set of statistics displays a lower level of correlation than is displayed by the statistics on percentage of operators. Nevertheless, the general picture is quite clear. On average about 50 per cent of all the farmers hold less than 5 acres each and they occupy only 12 per cent of the total acreage; about 75 per cent of all the farmers hold less than 10 acres each and occupy only 33 per cent of the total acreage. On the other hand 5 per cent of the farmers holding between 20 and 30 acres each occupy about 11 per cent of the total acreage while 2 per cent of all the farmers have over 50 acres each and they occupy 33 per cent of the total surveyed.

The statistics on the land tenure system of the Mahaica-Mahaicony-Abary project gives a more extreme picture of in-equality of distribution and a larger percentage of small hold-ings. Most of the land under this scheme was allocated for rice cultivation. About 4·1 per cent of the operators operating less than 5 acres each hold 12 per cent of the total acreage, 22·8 per cent operating less than 10 acres each hold 2·2 per cent of the total acreage, and 36·5 operating less than 15 acres each hold 4·3 per cent of the total acreage. 9·1 per cent of the operators with less than 25 acres each operate 10·2 per cent of the total acreage and 80 per cent of the operators holding less than 50 acres each occupy only 18·8 per cent of the total acreage. On the other hand 10·9 per cent of the operators, holding between 100 to 200 acres, hold 8·5 per cent of the total acreage, and at the top of the pyramid 3·8 per cent of the operators handling over 200 acres each occupy 63·6 per cent of the total acreage surveyed.[1]

---

[1] Calculated from information received from the Departments of Lands and Mines and the Ministry of Agriculture, Georgetown, Guyana.

For completeness, reference must be made to the size of holdings on Land Settlement Schemes. In this case the aim of the Ministry of Agriculture has been the establishment of small-sized family farms with a view to bolstering 'peasant' agriculture. The position in four of these schemes is summarized below.

TABLE 6

SIZE OF HOLDINGS ON LAND SETTLEMENT SCHEMES

Name of scheme	Sizes of farms (acres)	Total
(1) Black Bush Polder	15 (rice) + 2½ vegetables	17½
(2) Mara (a)	15 (rice) + 2½ vegetables	17½
(b)	15 citrus	15
(3) Garden of Eden (a)	7 citrus	7
(b)	25 grass (dairy)	25
(4) Anna Regina	9 (rice)	9

Source: Annual Reports of Land Settlement Department.

But an assumption implicit in our remarks about the un-economic size of farms is that modern agriculture requires large farms. This is not necessarily true. Of course countries with a large population relative to farmland are understandably confronted by strong population pressure against land. This is precisely the pressure that faces many Asian countries, and a contrast with the Guyanese situation may be illuminating.

The nine Asian countries listed in the table have farms that average from 9·5 acres in Thailand and 2·1 acres in Japan, yet the *per capita* agricultural production of the rural population is twice as large in Japan as in Thailand. That difference in the size of farms may not be the clue to productivity is indicated when one compares India with Japan. Although farms are fully two and a half times as large as they are in Japan—5·4 to 2·1 acres respectively, with the cultivable area much higher in the former country, Japanese agriculture obtains higher yields per man, and a considerably higher output per acre than in India. B. F. Johnston,[1] in explaining the striking improvements in

[1] B. F. Johnston, 'Agricultural Development and Economic Transformation: Comparative Study of the Japanese Experience', *Food Research Institute Studies* (November 1962), p. 229.

TABLE 7

FARM SIZE, PRODUCTION PER ACRE, AND PRODUCTION
PER CAPITA OF THE RURAL SECTOR OF NINE ASIAN
COUNTRIES

	Average size of farms	Production per acre	Agri. production *per capita* of rural sector
	Acres	*Dollars*	*Dollars*
Thailand	9·5	42	45
Philippines	8·8	74	72
Burma	7·6	49	79
Cambodia	5·6	48	47
India	5·4	33	39
Pakistan	4·2	55	54
Indonesia	3·3	60	38
Taiwan	3·1	279	114
Japan	2·1	274	102

Source: T. W. Schultz, *Economic Crisis of World Agriculture* (University of Michigan Press, 1965), p. 12.

Japanese agriculture, among other factors identified labour-intensive operations in preparatory tillage and interculture as strategic elements in producing higher yields. Thus the size of farm *per se* does not provide sufficient explanation for its uneconomic nature. Although this may be an important variable, the yield per acre bears some relation to the method and intensity of cultivation and similar factors. Let us therefore look at some of the other factors that have to be considered side by side with the size of holdings.

Of paramount importance in this context is the rapid expansion of mechanization.[1] The substantial investments that have gone into various land development schemes have resulted in a shift to mechanized farming which has enabled new areas to be quickly brought under cultivation. As a result, as noticed above, aggregate output has increased considerably, but the average productivity per acre has fallen as more and more marginal lands have been brought under cultivation and employment

[1] To some extent this increased mechanization was encouraged by the government, by the ease with which farmers could obtain loans from the Guyana Credit Corporation, the lack of stringency in hire purchase agreements, and the duty-free petrol granted by the government.

reduced.[1] As is evident from Table 8, the country's tractor population more than doubled between 1953 and 1964. It is clear that the least tractorized areas like the Essequibo Islands, Essequibo Coast, and West Demerara were those that experienced highest yields, while the highly mechanized areas such as Eastern Berbice, Western Berbice, and the Mahaicony district (excluding the Mahaicony-Abary Rice Development Area) have not shown any significant increases in output per acre. There are several reasons why increased mechanization proved undesirable.

Because other types were not formerly available, the country's tractor fleet contains a high percentage of iron-wheeled and tyre-wheeled machines which are probably not the best for rice. Track-laying crawlers of average power have proved demonstrably more suitable for conditions in Guyana, and greater standardization of the tractor fleet also seems desirable. In some places mechanization has taken place before the drainage standards were high enough to justify it. Many farmers are unfamiliar with the use and maintenance of machinery and large expenses for repairs have resulted.

Rice in Guyana is planted twice a year. There is a spring crop reaped during March and April and an autumn crop reaped in October. Of the two crops, the autumn crop is the more important, accounting for about 92 per cent of the total production of paddy. Between the end of February and the beginning of May, there are only about 40 days during which a tractor of average power must perform all the initial operations of the autumn crop—ploughing, disc harrowing, drag harrowing, and

---

[1] The entire rice cultivation has not been mechanized, however. There are substantial areas of cultivation—Essequibo, Leguan, Wakenaam, and Western Demerara—where mechanization has been introduced for probably 30 per cent of the acreage, and even with this there is partial mechanization, in that tillage may be done by mechanical means but harvesting remains to be done by hand. Private conversation with several farmers revealed that most of them have been forced into mechanization, for although on paper there may be surplus labour, it is difficult to obtain adequate labour on a seasonal basis (except where family labour could be obtained in large quantities) particularly for harvesting. A main explanation for this is that some unemployment is concentrated in the urban areas and there is a natural reluctance of the unemployed in those areas to move to rural areas for seasonal work. Secondly, facilities for accommodation and victualling of migrant labour are either non-existent, extremely limited, or wage rates are too low.

TABLE 8

TRACTOR POPULATION IN THE RICE INDUSTRY BY DISTRICTS 1953–64

Districts	Year 1953	Year 1954	Year 1955	Year 1956	Year 1957	Year 1958	Year 1959	Year 1960	Year 1961	Year 1962	Year 1963	Year 1964	Total 1953–64	
East Berbice	90	107	64	102	120	76	125	361	242	128	215	207	1,837	} 2,338
West Bank Berbice	—	—	—	—	2	—	3	2	6	1	4	8	26	
West Coast Berbice	21	9	18	14	31	58	63	109	55	35	49	13	475	
Mahaicony District	31	24	59	8	21	19	32	49	48	18	45	28	382	} 1,053
Mahaica District	12	7	6	8	16	7	7	24	24	13	18	13	155	
East Coast Demerara	6	12	16	10	15	12	10	41	15	9	43	24	213	
East Bank Demerara	1	—	—	2	4	3	—	3	5	2	4	—	24	
West Bank Demerara	3	2	7	2	1	3	6	12	4	8	19	5	72	
West Coast Demerara	4	9	7	11	13	22	15	37	22	13	34	20	207	
East Bank Essequibo	—	—	1	—	—	2	4	10	2	1	3	5	28	} 582
Leguan	—	3	3	3	5	8	15	37	16	7	12	11	120	
Hogg Island	—	—	—	—	—	—	—	—	1	1	1	—	3	
Fort Island	—	—	—	—	—	—	—	—	2	—	—	—	2	
Wakenaam	—	2	—	5	9	8	15	30	20	4	8	8	109	
Essequibo Coast	2	6	10	6	15	24	23	24	43	19	52	70	294	
Pomeroon	—	3	1	—	1	—	—	5	2	6	4	4	26	
	170	184	192	171	253	242	318	744	507	265	511	416	3,973	

Source : Department of Agriculture.

drilling. Under normal conditions the area that a tractor can work on without night work is thus reduced to 125 acres over this period. Later with a six-foot drawn combine the same tractor can work for about 60 days in harvesting. It can also be used for disc ploughing on the autumn stubble crop for about 20 days. Thus taking transportation into account, effective work totals 700 to 750 hours per tractor. It is generally considered that a tractor does not attain full economic efficiency unless it works over 1,000 hours a year. This under-utilization of machines not only had global import in the colony, but was mainly responsible for some of the larger more mechanized farms experiencing some difficulty in covering running and overhead expenses because of insufficient utilization of machinery, high initial cost, lack of knowledge on use and maintenance, and in other cases poor drainage.

As far as farms of less than 10 acres are concerned, mechanized rice cultivation is virtually impossible, not only in view of the size of the farm, but because it is frequently divided into small plots. In some cases these plots are not in one consolidated holding. An important factor here is that although there has been a considerable increase in the acreage under rice, the direct consequence of this has been an increase in the number of farm units rather than in the size of holdings. In any case the work required on these small plots is well within the capacity of the individual farmer even at the peak periods of transplanting and harvesting.

It has been claimed that while mechanization of farming operations considerably improves the yield per unit of labour, it does not necessarily increase the yield per unit of land. The reason for this dichotomy is the low degree of substitutability between the original factors of production, namely land and labour. The two serve very different purposes in agricultural production: land provides food and water for the plants in addition to providing the necessary space for cultivation, and labour takes care of the necessary movements that plants do not perform themselves. Some capital goods co-operate in these movements, thereby saving labour, while others raise the yield of land by supplying food and water, or by controlling floods, pests, and other natural hazards, or indeed, by improving the quality of the seed itself. Very few capital goods contribute substantially to both groups, though heavy machines for 'deep ploughing' might be an exception[1]. Mechanization failed to increase the yield per unit of land because in the attempt to maximize aggregate output many farmers failed to pay sufficient attention to fertilizers, chemicals, and other farming techniques, which would have improved the productivity on the land.

One of the by-products of mechanization was that the larger farms in Guyana were markedly underworked. The information available is that in a large proportion of districts output per acre declined with farm size, the average yield per acre on large farms being consistently below the yield on small farms.[2] A proposition that seems valid in this connection is that labour input per acre increases as the size of the farms decreases. Associated with the increase in input there is an increase in output per acre, but a probable decrease in output per unit of input.[3] This shows that although there are diminishing returns to input applied to an acre of land, the marginal returns continue to be positive over the range of observation. Thus in Guyana there appears to be an inverse relationship between farm size and the intensity of cultivation. This indicates that higher outputs per acre generally result from higher inputs. The reason for this inverse relationship between farm size and output per acre is seen in the inverse correlation between farm size and inputs per acre. The small farms average higher inputs and outputs than large farms. Despite the structural weaknesses of smaller farms—their fragmentation, lack of credit, and similar factors—they make up for this by intensive application of family labour and more inputs of complementary factors. Conversation with several farmers and an inspection of their farms in two districts in West Coast Berbice carried out by the present writer confirmed that differences in yield per acre seemed to be largely due to dif-

[1] S. R. Sen, in *Proceedings of the Ninth International Conference of Agricultural Economists* (Oxford University Press, 1956), p. 56 and Joan Robinson, *The Accumulation of Capital* (Macmillan, 1965), p. 323.

[2] See C. O'Loughlin, 'The Rice Sector in the Economy of British Guiana', *Social and Economic Studies*, Vol. 7, No. 2 (June 1958).

[3] It has been amply demonstrated on many farms in Guyana that while a small labour force can harvest a given area of paddy in larger than optimum time (say 30 days), the quantity and quality collected will be inferior to a harvest reaped by a larger work force in a 15-day period.

ferences in the use of fixed low-opportunity cost inputs, in particular family labour.[1]

The areas that are better drained and irrigated, where holdings are small so that transplanting of seedlings could be done, have the best yields of paddy per acre. Planting and transplanting the seedlings in rows is a highly labour-intensive activity which pays off in terms of greatly expanded output. Such areas as the Essequibo Islands and Essequibo Coast have shown yields as high as 25 bags per acre. In these two areas over 50 per cent of the crop is sown by transplanting. For example in 1961 the yield for the transplanted crop in the Essequibo Islands was 23 bags per acre as against 16·9 bags per acre when the crop is sown by broadcast methods. When account is taken of the fact that in 1964 the average yield for the country as a whole was 13·4 bags per acre, it would seem that improved yields can be obtained from the more general use of transplanting methods. But this is a form of intensive cultivation that requires a higher percentage of labour inputs, but is also an anathema to any mechanized form of cultivation, which generally favours the broadcasting method of cultivation.[2]

The classic representation of the undesirable effects of increased mechanization, and the accompanying lack of intensive cultivation was witnessed in the results obtained from Land Settlement Schemes, especially in the Black Bush Polder area. This scheme is located in the eastern part of the country between Berbice and Courentyne, and is the largest drainage and

[1] The greater proportion of rice farmers in Guyana are of East Indian extraction, and cultivation practices follow closely the methods brought by their forefathers. It is therefore not surprising that the same problems face Indian agriculture as recently shown in the results of Farm Management Surveys. These were intensive surveys conducted between 1954 and 1957 in six regions of India, samples of farms being selected in two districts of each region. The reports have been published by the Ministry of Agriculture (Government of India) for each of the three years separately for each region. A check made for two years (1955/6 and 1956/7) in the six regions covered revealed that input per acre as well as output per acre increased as the size of farm decreased.

[2] The present writer was very impressed by a small farm in Taymouth Manor on the Essequibo Coast, where of a total of 5·5 acres, 4 acres are planted each crop season, with an average yield of 25 bags per acre (autumn) and 20 bags per acre (spring) with transplantation. In spring 1962, as many as 28 bags per acre were harvested. This small farm amply demonstrates the practical and economic possibilities of the intensification of rice production. In contrast the output of 8 bags per acre obtained at Black Bush Polder on an area three times as big is revealing.

irrigation project carried out for peasant settlement. Table 9 gives the expenditure/revenue account that the government expected to materialize from the scheme, while Table 9 (b) shows what was actually realized for a typical year. A comparison reveals a wide gap between expected and realized income.

TABLE 9 (a)

MINISTERIAL EXPECTATIONS OF EXPENDITURE ON
LAND SETTLEMENT SCHEMES

INCOME

Rice: (a) Autumn crop 15 acres @ 20 bags/acre   300 bags

     (b) Spring crop 7½ acres @ 14 bags/acre   105 bags

                       405 bags @ $7 = $2,835

Legumes 7½ acres @ 400 lb/acre—3,000 lb. @ 14¢   =   420

Kitchen Garden 2¼ acres (¼ acre for house lot) @ $400   =   900

                       $4,155 $4,155

EXPENDITURE   (farm cash operating)

     Rice $1,283

     Legume   188

     Kitchen garden   225

     Rent   300

     Total cash operating $1,996 $1,996

Net income (including family expenses) $2,159

Family expenses   700

Net income (excluding family living expenses) $1,459

Source: Ministry of Agriculture.

The latter table reveals that a typical farmer who cultivated 15 acres in 1961 had sown 6 bags on the first time, 4 on the second, at $10·20 per bag, amounting to $202·00. This farmer's receipts amounted to only $17·00 more than his expenditure. His returns correspond exactly to the Polder's average, and his expenses are nearly the same for all farmers.

Of course, owing to mechanization, the work done was not great, since the farmer set it at about 38 days per year for 15

TABLE 9 (b)

EXPENDITURE AND REVENUE ACCOUNT OF A
TYPICAL RICE FARMER CULTIVATING 15 ACRES
ON BLACK BUSH POLDER

		(BWI$)
1.	10 bags of seed paddy at $10·20 per bag	102·00
2.	Labour costs at $12·00 per acre	180·00
3.	Rent at $17·50 per acre	262·50
4.	Weed killer	6·00
5.	Harvesting 125 bags by reaper-thresher combine at $1·50 per bag	187·50
6.	Transportation of crop to rice mill	20·00
	Total expenditure	758·00

Revenue

1.	125 bags at $6·20 per bag	$775·00
	Net profit	$17·00

Source: Ministry of Agriculture.

acres. These man-days expended brought in a return of only 45 cents each. Thus 38 days per family per year was all the employment the present concept of extensive mechanized farming was able to provide a settler farmer family.[1] As one authoritative commentator averred:

It is the principle itself of this settlement which appears mistaken to the foreign observer. If the purpose is the complete mechanised cultivation of rice, it seems illogical to distribute cultivation plots of 15 acres per family, since they are much too small for this technique. If, on the other hand, the aim is to create small family farms, only a gradually mechanised farming system could be worthwhile, to be adopted as the technical knowledge and necessary capital are accu-

[1] Mechanization was not the only cause for the poor results experienced on Land Settlement Schemes. The authorities seem to have been moved primarily by political considerations, with a dire neglect of the social aspects. The result was an extremely faulty selection of settlers, most of whom were not bona fide farmers, living far away from the holdings and mainly interested in making quick profits. It seems that no study was made of similar schemes in other countries, e.g. the Sudanese Gezira Scheme where problems of a like nature were encountered. See P. F. M. McLoughlin, 'The Sudan's Gezira Scheme: An Economic Profile', *Social and Economic Studies*, Vol. 12, No. 2 (June 1963), pp. 179–99, and literature cited.

mulated. To pay for this mechanisation it is necessary to have a very intensive production with a high yield per acre.[1]

The reluctance to practise intensive methods of husbandry was a characteristic feature not only of land settlement schemes, but also of the larger farms outside the land settlement areas. In the latter case this was reflected in the farmers' reluctance to hire outside labour in sufficient quantities to produce satisfactory yields.[2] The farmer with a relatively large holding has found that he can eke out a moderate income without the trouble of hiring a high percentage of non-family labour (that is, by limiting the labour input), and without the risk of borrowing additional working capital for other inputs associated with intensive cultivation, and therefore he seems to prefer the low effort, low risk, and low output package, to the higher risk, higher profit, higher output combination. A theoretical explanation can be found in terms of the low aspiration model suggested by a famous student of the problem.[3]

The conclusion emerges that mechanization can provide an answer to the problem of low agricultural productivity only if the size of the farms on land settlement schemes and elsewhere is considerably increased. This could be achieved on farms of 100 acres or more. Here assuming that the land is properly drained and irrigated, the objective of economic policy should be to maximize net output per worker rather than output per acre, by enabling each worker to cultivate more acres. This can be attempted on a few farms specially selected.[4] On the other hand mechanical cultivation can be combined with small farming if the machinery is owned by a central agency, which cultivates the land for the farmers in return for a fee while leaving each farmer to plant, weed, and reap on his own

[1] On all this see Rene Dumont, *Planning and Agricultural Development* (Report to the Government of Guyana, F.A.O. Rome, 1963).

[2] Here again a comparison with the Indian case is revealing. For a discussion of this attitude in India see Dipak Majumdar, 'Size of Farm and Productivity: a Problem of Indian Peasant Agriculture', *Economica*, Vol. XXXII (May 1965), pp. 161–73.

[3] See J. W. Mellor, 'The Use and Productivity of Farm Family Labour in the Early Stages of Agricultural Development', *Journal of Farm Economics* (August 1963), pp. 517–34.

[4] These large farms could be operated under co-operative or communal ownership, or by large private entrepreneurs.

account. In this case the optimum size of farm ought to be between 12 and 50 acres.[1]

Mechanization could also be introduced on a selective basis on farms of less than 10 acres with special agricultural equipment suitable to Guyanese conditions.[2]

But even if some degree of selective mechanization is introduced, it cannot be overlooked that Guyanese rice cultivation has a far way to go before arriving at the outer limit of the most labour-intensive production function. We are however bearing in mind the related question of further agricultural diversification, with a consequent shift of the labour force into other forms of agricultural activity. But our immediate argument centres around the underutilization of labour inputs and the possibility of taking up the slack in the rice sector. For although mechanization may increase output per acre or net output per worker depending on the type of mechanization chosen and the size of farms, its contribution to the employment situation is at best negligible. Not only will a more labour-intensive husbandry help to stem the unemployment tide; it will also make a significant contribution to productivity, and stay the shift of the population to the urban areas. It would also entail a shift from the extensive to the intensive margin, as the returns to labour and capital on the intra-marginal land goes up, and improvement in *per capita* incomes realized.

We shall then reverse the tendency in which labour-intensive farming has been replaced by capital-intensive farming, with the result that in order to obtain an additional bag of paddy, inputs of land and capital have been increased, inputs of labour reduced, and a downward shift of marginal lands necessitated. It is obvious that this pattern is out of harmony with the resource endowment of the country. Guyana is chronically short of readily cultivable land, and very deficient in capital, too.

---

[1] If these farms are too small, the machine does most of the work that the farmer could otherwise do himself, and it is cheaper for him to do the operations for himself than to pay for the machine. While if the farm is large enough, there is enough work to justify the farmer having his own machines.

[2] For these small farms animal-drawn and motor mowers may cut rice, which could then be bound by hand. These machines could be bought at not too high a cost by groups of five or six farmers operating adjacent plots. One of the striking features of Japanese agriculture is the extensive use made of small agricultural equipment of this type.

For these reasons resources ought to be utilized in such a way as to economize cultivable land and capital, and where necessary to substitute labour for capital where this would not adversely affect output. This will have the desirable effect of reducing capital requirements and increasing employment.

Thus by skilful investment planning in this sector, increased productivity can be achieved by procuring a better allocation of existing resources, incorporating a better use of land and labour, and improved combinations of enterprises, by allocating scarce resources, especially of capital and technology, at points where they can be most effective. In this way the cost of production will be reduced, paving the way for a higher investment potential in the future without lowering current consumption. In the light of these considerations it still appears possible to discourage ultra-mechanization. The government can achieve this by requesting first that rates of renting combines be equal to their real operating costs. Secondly, the subsidy on agricultural fuel, which enables some families to go to the cinema on their tractors, should be discontinued. Thirdly, a customs duty could be imposed on costly automatic harvesting machines, which have been notorious for creating unemployment by simply reducing the amount of work available without simultaneously increasing output.[1]

Other factors have also adversely affected the returns to investment in rice cultivation, resulting not only in poor yields but also in the quality of the rice produced. These are technical factors which are by no means unique in their application to Guyana, but they nevertheless deserve our close attention. The following factors are conspicuous by their absence from the Guyanese agricultural scene. Besides the total absence or lack of improvement in small agricultural implements and machin-

[1] Lewis, *Theory of Economic Growth*, pp. 129–31. Prof. Lewis considers the justification of mechanization given the relative scarcities of land, labour, and capital. He contends that mechanical cultivation is not economic unless there is a shortage of labour relative to capital, for if labour is superabundant, the main effect of introducing mechanization is to create still more unemployment, at the cost of using up scarce foreign exchange to import the mechanical equipment and its fuel. Although in such a situation the objective of economic policy is to maximize output per acre, and not output per worker, it is more usually the case that hand cultivation is more productive per acre than mechanical cultivation because it is done with greater care. The feasibility of mechanical cultivation also depends on the land and crop, but is doubtful in countries subject to extremes of heat or rainfall.

ery, a gaping need exists for better conservation and use of water, improvement in soil fertility through adequate crop rotations, full use of organic waste and manure, the application of chemical fertilizers, the breeding and multiplication of improved varieties of plant and seed capable of higher yields and resistance to disease and pests, control of plant pests and diseases, the reduction of losses during harvest and post-harvesting operations,[1] and better cultural operations.[2] The improvement of processing and marketing techniques are of equal importance. Most of these improvements to be effected are interdependent or at least closely related.

One factor, which is of crucial significance and to which sufficient attention has not been devoted, is the sowing of indifferent seed. Of the 300,000 acres under rice, only about 10 per cent is sown to pure line seed; another 20 per cent is sown to selected seeds grown by the farmers themselves. The remaining 70 per cent is sown to seeds containing mixed varieties of red rice. The result of sowing indifferent seed is poor germination, a proliferation of red rice and rice of varying grains and sizes, and a high breakage of milled rice. The poor preparation of land made worse by increased tractorization also worked against high yields. Paddy soils must be thoroughly prepared. and a level bed produced under water before the crop is sown. The shallow ploughing of rice fields under dry conditions has led to the reduction of yields as well as the promotion of weeds and red rice. Earlier on we referred to the fact that increased mechanization has led to the replacement of transplanting from nurseries by broadcasting. Transplanting produces higher yields of paddy because it ensures the selection of a single variety of paddy free from weeds and red grains, and also ensures uniform maturity of the plant population. Broadcasting of paddy leads to an uneven field population and makes the control of weeds and red rice virtually impossible. The substitution of broadcasting for transplanting must reduce yields unless

---

[1] *Dumont Report*, pp. 20–6, 36–40, 68–70.

[2] Cf. David Edwards, *Economic Study of Small Farming in Jamaica* (University of the West Indies, Jamaica, 1961). The cultural practices discussed are apposite to the Guyanese context. But caution has to be exercised when emphasizing these variables, for limited incentives rather than backwardness have been instrumental in shaping traditional attitudes. See T. W. Schultz, *Transforming Traditional Agriculture*, Yale University Press, 1964.

there is artificial application of plant food which would offset plant competition where sowings are thick, or produce increased yields per head where sowings are thin.

We have so far considered the main factors on the side of supply that tend to reduce the profitability of investment in rice. The cultural factors referred to above are moulded not only by attitudes and the lack of incentives, but also by the quality of extension services, that is, by the intensity of research carried out into these problems and, the extent to which results have been disseminated among farmers.[1] The practices of poor land preparation and cultivation, questionable cropping and water control, and the inadequate use of waste products and by-products go hand-in-hand with the elementary nature of the local government system.[2] As a framework within which technical services can be provided for the rural community and purposeful direction given to their efforts the local government system is inadequate.

It is therefore not surprising that the net profitability per acre as recorded for most groups was fairly low and for others even negative.[3] The general conclusion is that rice cultivation is in many cases unprofitable, that many farmers manage to produce only because they are continually in debt—borrowing during the period of rice growth, repaying at harvest time, and borrowing again soon after. Thus not only is the average peasant heavily in debt, but the effects of good harvests, which enable him to raise his head above water occasionally, show up rapidly via the multiplier. Those who find rice cultivation profitable are apparently those who combine the function of landlord, miller, shopkeeper, money-lender, and transport contractor.[4] It is not impossible to obtain a fair income by taking a markup

[1] There is a growing awareness of these problems in Guyana. Research is at present being conducted variously by large milling organizations, a large mechanized farm, the Drainage and Irrigation Department, the Rice Marketing Board, and the Rice Producers' Association. Steps are also being taken to ensure that accumulated knowledge and experience are disseminated among the farmers.

[2] The implementation of the Marshall Plan should provide the basis for a solution. See A. H. Marshall, *Report on Local Government in British Guiana*, (Government Printery, Georgetown, May 1955).

[3] See O'Loughlin, 'The Rice Sector in the Economy of British Guiana', loc. cit.

[4] R. T. Smith, 'Ethnic Difference and Peasant Economy in British Guiana', in R. Firth and B. S. Yamey (eds.), *Capital, Saving and Credit in Peasant Societies* (London, 1964), p. 319.

at each stage. But generally speaking, rice as it is presently cultivated in Guyana is a 'poor man's crop'.[1]

We have so far been considering the supply aspects of rice cultivation in Guyana. We will now examine some considerations on the side of demand. Marketing of paddy is left to the farmers, though rice can be sold locally and abroad only through the Rice Marketing Board which was set up by the government in 1922 to encourage production, uniformity of quality and price, and better distribution. The Board has developed into an organization with the main functions of purchasing milled rice and paddy from producers, the stabilization of price through government control of price paid to producers and that charged to consumers, the negotiation of selling prices and quantities of rice with other British Caribbean territories, and the improvement of the export quality of rice.

Table 10 below gives figures for exports of rice between 1953 and 1964. Although home consumption of rice remained almost static over the period, the quantity of rice exported more than doubled, and the value of exports showed a fourfold increase.

Over 90 per cent of these exports went to countries in the Commonwealth Caribbean; all the territories of this area depend completely on imported rice, except Trinidad and Jamaica which grow a certain percentage of their total domestic requirements. The main explanation of this tendency is inherent in contractual arrangements worked out between the government of British Guiana and these territories. The (Guyana) British Rice Marketing Board entered into long-term agreements in 1946 with the Eastern Caribbean Group of British Colonies, including Trinidad, Barbados, the Leeward and Windward Islands to supply the import requirements until the end of 1954. The agreement required the delivery of bulk

[1] The situation is even worse. Rice production is heavily, if indirectly, subsidized. For the benefit of farmers developing their rice lands and improving the drainage and irrigation facilities on their farms, the Drainage and Irrigation Department runs an Agricultural Machinery Hire Pool. Dragline tractor-bulldozers (caterpillar type), centrifugal pumps, and ancillary equipment are employed to provide this service, which is run at a loss. By far the largest item in successive development budgets is on drainage and irrigation mainly for rice cultivation. Nearly half of the development funds is spent on drainage and irrigation, agriculture, and land settlement schemes. Capital expenditure on well-conceived land settlement schemes may be justified, but it is doubtful whether the existing projects lead to the proper utilization of land.

Table 10
RICE EXPORTS 1953-64

Year	Home consumption (tons of rice)	Exports	
		Tons of rice	Value ($'000)
1953	34,700	36,697	4,582
1954	40,462	36,656	9,278
1955	38,750	53,299	12,527
1956	39,330	41,371	9,856
1957	38,607	38,163	9,167
1958	38,719	17,676	4,785
1959	42,567	55,821	13,836
1960	44,708	63,180	15,402
1961	44,357	90,247	22,626
1962	45,407	79,468	20,469
1963	43,968	71,670	20,091
1964	N.A.	77,576	21,847

Source: Annual Reports of the Guyana Rice Marketing Board.
N.A. = not available.

rice of specific grade and quality at fixed prices according to the need of the islands. Later the agreement was extended. In 1954 Guyana entered into a separate agreement with Jamaica to supply full requirements of bulk rice for the period 1955-7. However, in 1956 a new contract—a Regional Rice Agreement —was drawn up between Guyana and all the British Caribbean Islands. Talks for the establishment of the West Indian Federation were then in the offing, and it was felt necessary to ensure that, as far as possible, the rice required for consumption within the region should be met wholly by production within the region.[1]

The contract required that before selling rice to any country outside the contract area, Guyana must fulfil their basic requirements and offer any surplus available. It was also decided to review the supply prices annually at the Rice Conference in consultation with the Rice Marketing Board. These arrangements virtually control the trading of rice in the British Caribbean area up to the present time. Since 1961 small quantities of rice have been exported to Cuba, West Africa, and

[1] Annual Reports of the Rice Conferences.

Eastern Europe. The trends in contractual exports of rice reveal that the three territories, Barbados, Trinidad, and Jamaica, were responsible for the purchase of the greater proportion of exports. But physical quantities exported is not the main variable on the export side. Of more immediate importance not only with respect to the West Indian Market but also in connection with the future possibilities of exports to other countries is the question of quality and price.

In Guyana there is extensive use of mechanical grading by the Rice Marketing Board both for purchases and sales of rice. The grading also differs between local and export markets and the trends in quality purchased are not altogether in keeping with export requirements.[1] The taste for packaged and high-quality rice is quite predominant in the export market, and helps to explain why in recent years the Caribbean Islands have been importing relatively large quantities of high-quality and packaged rice from the U.S.A. and the Netherlands. The data on quality trends show that the greater part of Guyana's production is of parboiled rice, which limits the markets to the Caribbean Islands, although strenuous attempts are being made to increase the production of white rice. The poor quality of the rice obtained is a direct consequence of the questionable husbandry practices analysed in an earlier section, increased mechanization, and inefficient milling, drying, and storage. Attempts to standardize and consolidate these small mills have encountered strong objections from the millers, and governments in the past have capitulated.

The export prices realized in the West Indian markets are about 25 per cent higher than the world price. The contract price has shown a consistent rise since the 1940s and this has been one of the main instruments in the fourfold increase in the value of exports between 1953 and 1964. The price of rice has always been a bone of contention at annual rice conferences, but Guyana still remains a low-cost producer *vis-à-vis* other territories in the Commonwealth Caribbean. This is revealed in Table 11 where a comparison is given of production costs in Guyana, Trinidad, and Jamaica. The cost of production per

[1] For a very authoritative account of this aspect of rice production, see A. Kundu, 'Rice in the British Caribbean islands and British Guiana', *Social and Economic Studies*, Vol. 13, No. 2 (June 1964).

acre for a small farm in Guyana is about $120·00, while the corresponding figures for Trinidad and Jamaica are $189 and $135 respectively.

In recent rice conferences under the Regional Rice Agreement the main point of discussion was the price of rice. As early as in 1956,[1] at the first Rice Conference, it was laid down that the main factors determining price would be: (a) world trends in comparable qualities of rice at the time, (b) the domestic retail price of rice in Guyana, (c) cost of production in the sense of the necessity to maintain remunerative returns to the farmers. Ever since the proceedings of the conference have been marked by vehement arguments between Guyana and the British Caribbean islands about the fixation of price.

An interesting point that arises out of a study of the reports of rice conferences is Guyana's claim that she does not obtain equitable prices for her rice, in view of the possibility of exporting to other neighbouring countries at a much higher rate. In reply the British Caribbean Islands argue that transportation cost from Guyana is much lower than from other countries, and Guyana has a guaranteed market. Although in the past there has been a marked preference for parboiled rice in these markets, of late they have become sceptical of the quality of rice from Guyana. The table below gives comparative costs of rice from Guyana, Thailand, and U.S.A. in the Trinidadian market. Assuming that the rice from all these sources is of the same quality, Guyana has a price advantage. But the rice exported by the U.S.A. and the Far East is of a much better quality than that exported by Guyana. It is a clean, long-grained variety which Guyana can produce only at a higher cost and with great effort.

It seems, however, that if Guyana has to compete in the open market in the future, her ability to dispose of the potential surplus of the expanding rice industry may depend to a considerable extent on the economy of production and the quality of rice. The increase in the cost of production, if taken into account for price fixing, will bring the price of Guyana rice close to that of the United States and Thailand. The possibility of exporting to markets outside the Caribbean area will mean a substantial

[1] *Report of the Rice Conference*, June 1956, § 50c.

TABLE 11

PRODUCTION COST OF PADDY PER ACRE IN GUYANA, TRINIDAD AND JAMAICA

(Dollars)

	GUYANA		TRINIDAD[c]		JAMAICA[d]	
	Small farmer[a]	Large farmer[b]				
Pre-sowing cultivation	25·25	19·05	Labour		Harrowing	18·00
Sowing and transplanting	27·22	6·69	Hired	117·66	Bundling	4·80
Post-sowing cultivation	—	2·22	Family	46·87	Levelling	9·60
Reaping	25·00 }	27·00	Machine ploughing and levelling	6·32	Seed	11·52
Thrashing of crop	14·66	3·60	Transport of crop after harvest	0·79	Fertilizer	21·60
Transport from field to mill	5·40	1·80	Sacks	6·14	Planting	4·80
Drying of paddy	2·70	10·00	Fertilizer	0·10	Reaping	14·40
Rent (basic)	10·00	10·00	Drainage	0·05	Drying	3·60
Maintenance of land	5·40	5·40	Rent and taxes	5·26	Bags	3·00
Drainage and irrigation rates	3·51	3·51	Interest	1·25	Rent	14·40
Miscellaneous transport charges	0·93	0·93	Beating table	0·29	Water	28·80
Total	120·07	81·19	Total	184·73	Total	139·32
Average yield of paddy per acre (lb.)	2,800	1,960		2,200 to 3,000		1,800

Source: Kundu, loc. cit.

[a] Small farmer—all hand labour, rice transplanted.
[b] Larger farmer—fully mechanized, wet cultivation method.
[c] Average for all areas under paddy. For swamp area (Caroni) alone the cost per acre is $167·18 although the yield is at the maximum level (3,000 lb/acre).
[d] Since fertilizer is rarely used and rent and cost of water not always payable, the actual cost comes down to between $105·60 and $120·00 per acre.

TABLE 12

COMPARATIVE COSTS OF RICE FROM GUYANA, U.S.A., AND THAILAND LANDED IN TRINIDAD

Item	(Costs per 100 lb. of rice) Guyana 1st quality 25% parboiled	U.S.A. 20–25% parboiled	Old Thailand 25% parboiled
F.o.b. cost	$10·80 ⎫	US$7·53 ⎫	
Freight	0·75 ⎭	⎬ $12·84	
Insurance	0·05	0·04 ⎭	
Exchange	0·06	5·41	0·06
C.i.f. cost	11·66	12·98	12·90
Import duty	0·24	0·96	0·96
Duty paid landed cost	$11·90	$13·94	$13·86

Source: Guyana Rice Marketing Board.

increase in transportation costs, and although the Guyana Rice Marketing Board is trying hard to improve the quality of the packaged variety of rice in order to share the trade now enjoyed by the United States of America, Belgium, the Netherlands, and countries in the Far East, the danger of ruinous competition still exists. The fact that of late a few West Indian territories have decided to grow more of their own rice by means of more intensive methods of cultivation can offer no comfort to Guyana.

We have noticed that the extension of the cultivable margin and increased mechanization have led to a substantial upsurge of aggregate output, and there are signs that this tendency will continue for some time to come. We must, therefore, assess the possibilities for expanded exports, first in the contracted West Indian markets, and secondly in the world market. The latter avenue will have to be progressively exploited, for the West Indian territories are becoming more and more unwilling to absorb the bulk of Guyana's export potential.[1] On the basis of estimates of the growth of population, price and income

[1] Import substitution in food has become one of the major objectives of development planning in Trinidad and Jamaica. See Government of Trinidad and Tobago, *Draft Second Five Year Plan 1963–67* (Government Printery, Trinidad).

elasticity of demand, the future demand for rice in the West Indian markets works out as follows:

TABLE 13
ESTIMATES OF DEMAND FOR RICE 1965–75

Territory	1965	1970	% rise over 1965	1975	% rise over 1970
(1) Guyana	43,039	49,553	15	57,138	15
(2) Trinidad	45,459	52,794	16	61,079	16
(3) Jamaica	36,400	42,039	15	47,427	13
(4) Leewards Windwards and Barbados	18,061	20,416	13	22,828	12
	142,959	164,802	15	188,472	14

Source: A. Kundu, 'Rice in the British Caribbean Islands and Guyana 1950–75', *Social and Economic Studies*, Vol. 13, No. 2 (June 1964), p. 274.

It will be seen from the table above that demand for rice in the West Indian markets is rising by a little more than 4,000 tons a year. If we exclude Guyana's own domestic market, her traditional markets in the Caribbean are likely to increase by about 3,000 tons a year, a portion of which will be supplied domestically by Trinidad and Jamaica, as their policies of import substitution bear fruit. We must therefore see what other export possibilities are offered.[1]

Although the longer-term outlook for 1970 onwards is for a continued growth in consumption in line with rising population and consumer incomes, and a further expansion of production due to national policies, prospects for world trade are uncertain. National policies in exporting and importing countries are inconsistent. Exporters generally aim at an increase in exportable supplies, while most importers who grow rice hope to achieve

[1] Inefficiency of marketing arrangements, and the question of quality and price rather than the non-availability of markets may be the chief problem especially from two sources of competition in West Indian Markets. The large traditional rice exporters in Asia operate on good soils, little mechanization, but maintain high productivity by using intensive methods and cheap labour, while Guyana can hardly compete with the highly mechanized farming and milling operating in Australia and the United States of America.

self-sufficiency.[1] A key issue here is the lack of any long-term improvement in export revenue. Although instability of export earnings is no serious problem, fluctuations in the exports of different countries largely compensating each other, stagnation of earnings arise from the failure of the volume of trade to sustain its early post-war recovery.[2] From Table 14 it could be seen that the volume of indigenous exports of rice by economic regions increased from 4 million tons in 1948–50 (one-half of the pre-war level) to over 6 million tons in 1956, and since then

TABLE 14

VOLUME AND VALUE OF INDIGENOUS EXPORTS OF RICE
BY ECONOMIC REGIONS

	Average 1934–8	Average 1948–50	Average 1956–	Average 1960–2
	('000 tons)			
Volume				
Developing countries	8,320	3,300	3,960	4,210
Developed countries	240	700	1,410	1,250
Centrally planned countries	—	10	1,070	760
Total	8,560	4,010	6,440	6,220
Value	($ Million)			
Developing countries	278	468	422	428
Developed countries	16	109	191	164
Centrally planned countries	—	—	134	88
Total	294	577	747	680
Unit export value	($ per ton)			
	34	145	116	109

Source: F.A.O. Commodity Review 1964, pp. 29–30.

shipments have shown no significant advance. What is important is that only 4 per cent of the world crop now enters trade compared with 9 per cent in 1934–8. The influences that shape the present poor situation arise from both the supply and demand side, with an increasingly noticeable competition from other grains. The demand situation is dominated by the fact that five-sixths of the world's import markets lies in the develop-

[1] F.A.O. Commodity Review 1962, Special Supplement: *Agricultural Commodities Projections for 1970*, Section 11, p. 8.
[2] F.A.O. Commodity Review 1964, Special Supplement: *Trade in Agricultural Commodities in the U.N. Development Decade*, Vol. 1, Part 2, p. 30.

ing countries. Most of them restrict imports and encourage home production in order to conserve foreign exchange. The entire increase in Latin American demand has been met from local production, and self-sufficiency policies in rice are becoming widespread in West Africa and the Near East. Several other countries have replaced part of their commercial rice imports by other local or foreign food grains. In some cases this reflects a change in dietary patterns, for some governments have been discouraging excessive dependence on rice as a staple food in view of the more ample supplies of other cereals, e.g. wheat and the *non-availability* of cheap rice.[1]

Nevertheless there still exists a considerable unsatisfied demand for rice in world markets, owing to the inability of exporters to fill their contracts for some years.[2] But Guyana has been unable to produce sufficient quantities of the long-grained varieties—'*Indica*'—for which there is an insatiable demand in these markets. Relatively high production costs and poor milling facilities have also militated against Guyana's chances in producing these varieties. The competitive markets in Malaya, Hong Kong, the Arabian Peninsula, and parts of West Africa all require a whole range of qualities which the present Guyanese production complex cannot meet.[3] The free commercial markets in Europe again consume a high quality of rice, but the demand, which has been related to consumer habits rather than price or income, has been stable for several years. In Eastern Europe and the U.S.S.R., which account for between 5 and 10 per cent of total world imports, the possibility of making inroads depends less on pure economic considerations, and more on the ability of the governments to enter into bilateral trade agreements.[4] But the general conclusion seems to evolve that Guyana could probably increase her average revenue by a selective emphasis on the types of rice demanded such as parboiled, long-grained rice in the Far East and a high-grade, clean, packaged rice in Western Europe. The abolition of certain preference duties which at present favour husked

---

[1] The demonstration effect has made significant inroads into Guyanese consuming habits where local consumers show a marked preference for wheat flour and products which are made from wheat over rice and its by-products.

[2] F.A.O. Commodity Review 1964, p. 32.

[3] F.A.O. Commodity Review 1964, p. 32.

[4] Ibid.

brown rice in the interest of inefficient milling may also help the export drive.

It seems that some kind of a commodity agreement ought to be negotiated, both to utilize more fully the productive capacity of low-cost surplus producers, and at the same time to encourage the supply of more rice to deficit areas where demand is left unsatisfied owing to a lack of foreign exchange. This would avoid the dilemma of a set of developing countries being forced to pursue self-sufficiency policies which cut off the export markets of other developing countries like Guyana. Such an arrangement would have as its aim greater confidence in international agreements on both sides of the market. But the initiative should come from rice-exporting and rice-consuming countries,[1] who could without external finance negotiate a multilateral contract type of agreement. Although this may not in itself raise demand, more guaranteed supplies and outlets would create favourable conditions for trade, more certainty, flexibility, and stability.

The government of Guyana and rice producers have shown a curious lack of perception in failing to look into the prospects for development of by-products from rice, e.g. rice bran, rice flour, starch; while rice itself is used in the manufacture of a number of products—beer, bags, and paper. Of these, rice bran seems the only by-product of commercial value.[2] Though long neglected for a number of technical and commercial reasons, rice bran has considerable nutritive value, being rich in fat, protein, and vitamin, and is being increasingly used as a foodstuff for livestock and poultry. It can also provide an important oil, which in its refined form is used in margarine, or as cooking oil, and in its crude form in soap manufacture. Interest in rice bran should be stimulated by the growth of local feed requirements and the greater appreciation of the value of rice by-products as export earners or as substitutes for imported foods or vegetable oils.

In an earlier section we argued that there seems to exist some scope for increasing productivity by more intensive husbandry

---

[1] The Guyana government could be instrumental in initiating moves in this direction.

[2] See 'Rice Bran Utilisation and Trade', *Monthly Bulletin of Agricultural Economics and Statistics* (F.A.O. Rome, January 1964).

and greater labour utilization with consequent alleviation of the unemployment situation. Quality and price competition added to import substitution in the West Indies make the West Indian markets more and more unreliable. Although it is difficult to envisage how world prices will behave in the future, cereal prices will continue to be depressed for many years by the United States Food Policy which gives Asia nearly one billion dollars of food each year. Since Asian populations are growing faster than the output of food in Asia, cereal prices would otherwise be increasing. In ten years the U.S.A. may be growing twice as much food, but the current position makes it unwise to assume that the market for Guyanese rice would have increased in ten years' time. The obvious conclusion is that she must diversify her agriculture in preparation for contingencies that might arise in export markets.

3. *Sugar* [1]

Sugar is the major single support of the economy of Guyana, though relatively less important in 1964 than it was in 1952. According to O'Loughlin's estimates [2] sugar contributed 20 per cent of Gross Domestic Product in 1952, but by 1956 the figure has fallen to 15 per cent. However, the absolute figure for sugar was approximately the same in 1956 as in 1952. This shows that although G.D.P. was rising during the period 1952–6, sugar's contribution remained fairly static. Two sets of accounts are available for the period 1957–60—figures prepared by Kundu, and others by the Statistical Bureau. [3] The percentage contribution of sugar to G.D.P. appears as follows from the two sets of estimates:

	1957	1958	1959	1960
Statistical Bureau	16·6	15·4	13·5	13·7
Kundu	17·9	18·2	17·2	16·9

[1] This section was written before the author became a member of the Commission of Inquiry into the Economics of the Guyana Sugar Industry in 1967. The views expressed are his own.

[2] O'Loughlin, 'The Economy of British Guiana 1952–65', loc. cit., p. 26.

[3] Kundu, 'Interindustry Table', loc. cit., Statistical Bureau Analysis of Gross Domestic Product, op. cit.

Both sets of figures show that sugar's share has been declining but the Statistical Bureaus show that its share has been declining at a faster rate. Our analysis of Gross Domestic Product given in an earlier chapter revealed that the industry's contribution averaged 17 per cent between 1961 and 1964. But these are all estimates in current prices. Even when we take constant price estimates, the situation is not substantially different.

ESTIMATES OF REAL OUTPUT (G $000) (1960 CONSTANT
PRICES)[a]

	1960	1961	1962	1963	1964
Sugar cane	35,200	34,778	34,918	33,968	32,701
Sugar processing	11,100	10,767	10,811	10,523	9,102

[a] Central Statistical Bureau: Analysis of Domestic Product.

It is likely that gross capital formation in the industry has also been rising both in absolute amount and in percentage to G.D.P.[1] This did necessarily arise because of direct undertakings by the sugar industry as such, for whatever form of prosperity characterized the industry during our period of study was partly siphoned off to provide funds, which by way of personal incomes, inter-industry purchases, and taxation have contributed to increased investment in private construction and government projects.

Despite technological labour displacement, the industry still remains one of the major employers of labour in the country. In 1956 sugar companies accounted for 20 per cent of the labour force, but by 1960 this figure had fallen to 15 per cent, the workers remaining in employment having substantially increased their real earnings in sharp contrast to the stagnation

[1] O'Loughlin's estimates for the period 1952 to 1956 showed that investment in sugar ranged from a low 2 per cent of the country's total to a high 23 per cent, but was almost always well below the industry's percentage contribution to G.D.P. There is however good reason for believing that total investment in the industry has continued to increase up to around 1962, if it is considered that some degree of capital formation and accumulation must have accompanied technological change and increased mechanization. But the frustrating secrecy practised by the majority of sugar companies, the fact that certain items of interest to the economist are hidden in consolidated accounts, the inadequacy of costing procedures, all help to explain the limitation of data regarding investment in this propulsive sector.

10—E.D.G.

in real wages during the 1939–49 decade.[1] Between 1948 and 1960, annual money earnings per worker tripled while the cost-of-living index rose by less than 40 per cent. Between 1954 and 1960 average earnings increased by over 85 per cent, the cost-of-living index rising by 11 per cent, leaving real wages about 67 per cent higher in 1960 than in 1954. This is an increase of nearly 9 per cent a year (compound rate) in the purchasing power of the average sugar worker.

The rise resulted not only from increases in basic wage rates but rather from raising the cost-of-living allowance every year from the introduction of bonuses and holiday with pay. Early in 1961 a two-year wage agreement was concluded, bringing into effect a $3-a-day minimum wage for time-workers and consequent increases for piece-workers. The agreement included plans for the introduction of a contributory pension scheme, with substantial provisions for post-service liability being funded by transfers from the Price Stabilisation and Rehabilitation Funds to the Pensions Scheme.[2]

Also covered by the wage agreement was another 'once-for-all' bonus to share the windfall proceeds of the 1960 United States quota with the workers. When in 1963 the world price of sugar reached record peak, the workers shared the fruits of negotiated increases in wages amounting to 15 per cent over the two years 1962 and 1963, and over $500,000 was paid as a special bonus for the 1962 crop.[3] Thus not only are sugar workers one of the highest paid groups of workers in the country, but real wages have shown significant increases. Workers in the industry have maintained a strong position relative to similar categories in other branches of industry. Thus the industry has made a real contribution to the generation of real purchasing power, consumption demand, and, as a corollary, investment demand within the country.

The sugar industry also subsidizes the local consumer through

[1] See Colonial Office, *Report of a Commission of Enquiry into the Sugar Industry of Guyana*, Col. No. 249 (London, 1949), pp. 77 f. and 178.

[2] Annual Reports of the Department of Labour, 1961, 1962.

[3] In 1950 an adult field time worker's average daily earning was $1·18, by 1964 the figure was $4·75. In 1950 a cane cutter's daily earnings were $2·52, in 1964 the figure was $5·88. In October 1954 a mechanical equipment operator earned $3·86 daily, by 1964 it had risen to $10·00 (Annual Reports of the Department of Labour).

the price at which it is required to sell sugar on the local market. This subsidy amounts to over $1 million per annum. The local price of sugar is well below export price levels, not only below the Commonwealth Agreement price, but also below the free market price. For example in 1960, when the average price realized by sugar producers was BWI $178 per ton, the local sales price was $134; as the free market price was $143 per ton in that year, the industry gave up $9 per ton on nearly 20,000 tons sold locally, representing a total sacrifice of almost BWI $180,000.[1] The importance of the subsidy may be gauged from the fact that the average working-class family in Guyana spends about half of its weekly outlay on food items of all kinds. The subsidy will assume a greater and greater significance as population grows.

The actual contribution of the industry to government finance is also substantial. In recent years about 45 per cent of the government revenue from income tax and excise duties was derived from sugar and its by-products. But all income and excise duties provide less than half of the total revenue of the territory, since about two-fifths of the total comes from customs duties and the remainder from a variety of charges. Thus income and excise duties on sugar and by-products contribute roughly 20 per cent of the total revenue of the government. Additional sums are also paid from time to time in indirect taxation—customs duties, bill-of-entry taxes, tonnage, and light dues levied on shipping. These charges altogether come to a somewhat larger percentage of total government revenue than sugar's share of national income.

The industry also makes a significant contribution to the economy and society in many qualitative ways. These cannot be precisely quantified but are nevertheless substantial. The industry's pursuit of improvement in employees' welfare, skills, new technique, efficiency, production, and planning sets useful commercial and industrial standards in the community. We have so far given an indication in broad terms of some of the direct and indirect contributions the sugar industry makes to the economy as a whole. We may now trace the salient features of production and productivity in this sector, in order to ascer-

[1] Guyana Sugar Producers' Association, Special Report 1961.

TABLE 15
ACREAGE AND OUTPUT OF SUGAR 1953–64

Year	AREA		PRODUCTION		INDEX NUMBERS OF COLUMNS 1–4 1953 = 100			
	Planted acres (1)	Reaped acres (2)	Tons of cane ground (3)	Tons of sugar produced (4)	(1A)	(2A)	(3A)	(4A)
1953	79,238	73,198	2,756,291	240,176	100	100	100	100
1954	80,493	79,788	2,745,698	238,922	101·5	109·0	99·6	99·5
1955	80,594	77,500	2,716,949	250,111	101·5	105·8	98·6	104·1
1956	83,263	75,831	2,837,549	263,333	105·1	103·6	103·9	109·6
1957	89,034	83,432	2,962,882	284,973	112·3	113·9	107·5	118·6
1958	90,907	86,988	3,476,275	306,361	114·6	119·0	125·9	127·5
1959	92,569	89,134	3,218,096	284,425	116·5	121·7	116·8	118·0
1960	98,094	96,303	3,737,890	334,441	123·7	131·6	135·6	139·1
1961	107,840	106,303	3,561,677	324,745	136·1	145·2	129·2	133·2
1962	110,334	98,277	3,444,200	326,023	126·6	134·3	124·9	135·7
1963	97,014	95,081	3,416,929	317,137	122·4	129·8	120·3	133·7
1964	95,183	N.A.	3,002,979	258,378	120·1	—	108·9	107·5

Source: Guyana Sugar Producers' Association.

tain the nature of the investment parameter and the future prospects for investment and growth within the industry.

Table 15 presents figures on total production for the period 1953–64. Unlike the experience of other territories in the Commonwealth Caribbean, peasant cane farming contributes an insignificant percentage of the total, sugar estates accounting for about 98 per cent of the country's total production.

The first noticeable tendency is that all the magnitudes showed increases up to 1961/1 and thereafter declined. Acres planted increased by 36 per cent between 1953 and 1961, but by 1964 acreage was back at the 1960 level. Similarly acres reaped increased by 45 per cent between 1953 and 1964, and, as expected, declined thereafter. Tons of cane ground showed a steady increase up to 1960, in which year there was a 35 per cent increase over 1953, and by 1964 production was back at the level reached as far back as 1957. Finally, cane produced after increasing by 39 per cent between 1953 and 1960, showed steady declines until 1964 when the level of production dropped to just over 250,000 tons, which was the tonnage produced in 1955/6. Certain specific factors help to explain this tendency, but it would be misleading to draw any firm conclusions from them. For one thing they fail to bring out the significant increases in production that have taken place in the post-war era. A comparison of the above period with the period 1949 to 1960 should present us with a more realistic picture. Data for the latter period are given in Table 16.

The notable record of growth between 1949 and 1960 reflects the decision by management in the late 1940s to take the risky course of rapid expansion in the hope of obtaining a large share of the market, especially in the quotas to be assigned under the Commonwealth Sugar Agreement which was then in the offing. The number of acres under cane was enlarged by 37 per cent, showing no significant divergence from the 1953–64 figure. But the number of acres reaped rose more rapidly, by 72 per cent, reflecting the tendency to cut younger cane and to reap some acres twice in one year in the drive for greater production. Tons of cane ground increased by almost 86 per cent in response to improved cane types and higher yields per acre, and more efficient transportation to, and efficient use of, factory. The tonnage of sugar produced increased by 92 per cent. This still

TABLE 16

ACREAGE AND OUTPUT OF SUGAR 1949–60

Year	Acres under cane at 31st December. English acres [a] (1)	Acres reaped English acres [a] (2)	Tons of cane ground [b] (3)	Tons of sugar Produced [b] (4)	INDEX NUMBERS OF COLUMNS 1–4 1949 = 100			
					(1A)	(2A)	(3A)	(4A)
1949	68,533	55,945	2,011,627	174,227	100·0	100·0	100·0	100·0
1950	71,472	64,940	2,162,848	196,651	104·3	116·1	107·5	112·0
1951	77,736	67,126	2,453,662	217,306	113·4	120·0	122·0	124·7
1952	80,022	72,787	2,672,493	242,692	116·8	130·1	132·9	139·3
1953	77,163	71,485	2,756,921	240,176	112·6	127·8	137·0	137·8
1954	78,361	78,311	2,745,698	238,922	114·3	140·0	136·5	137·1
1955	78,316	75,928	2,716,949	250,111	114·3	135·7	135·1	143·5
1956	81,012	74,028	2,837,549	263,333	118·2	132·3	141·1	151·1
1957	86,741	81,330	2,962,882	284,973	126·6	145·4	147·3	163·6
1958	87,976	84,788	3,476,275	306,361	128·4	151·6	172·8	175·8
1959	89,825	87,658	3,218,096	284,425	131·6	156·7	160·0	163·2
1960	94,103	96,303 [c]	3,737,890	334,441	137·3	172·1	185·8	191·9

Source: Guyana Sugar Producers' Association Annual Reports.

[a] Estates only. Small farmers had 1,800 to 2,500 acres under cane annually, 1949–60.
[b] Estates' and Farmers' cane. [c] Some acres reaped twice.

higher rate of increase was a result of the higher sucrose content of the cane, steadier supply to the factory, new equipment, larger factories, and a somewhat longer grinding period. On an annual basis, tonnage of sugar grew by over 6 per cent a year (compound rate) between 1949 and 1960, the period of most spectacular growth. The years from 1960 onwards have witnessed a new era in the development of the industry. It is worth examining the main causal factors in some detail.

After 1960 conditions governing production changed somewhat. Early in the year there were depressing signs, but the situation was radically improved later in the year by climatic and political storms elsewhere. Cyclones and droughts in other Commonwealth countries, as well as the rupture between Cuba and the United States of America combined to offer unexpected temporary markets for all the sugar that could be produced. In that year 29,500 tons were exported to the attractively priced United States market. The record crop of 3,737,890 tons of cane and 334,441 tons of sugar produced were really the outcome of efforts to take advantage of these marketing outlets. The weather was also favourable to both the growing and harvesting of cane, with well-distributed rainfall. In the event of the world sugar price falling throughout 1961 and reaching early in 1962 its lowest point since the war—£19 15s. a ton (c.i.f. U.K.)—prospects for 1961 at the beginning of the year were far from satisfactory. There was, however, a happy, shortlived compensation; substantial allocations were renewed on the premium-priced United States market, and the Canadian market became open to Guyana sugar. Thus, although production in 1961 was below the 1960 level, this was in no way due to the lack of markets or effort on the part of the sugar companies.

The weather in 1961 was ill suited to the marketing commitments. Prolonged mid-year rains were responsible for exceptionally poor juices from the early autumn crop, up to 16 tons of cane against the normal 11 tons being necessary to produce an extra ton of sugar. The drop in production to 317,000 tons of sugar in 1963 was mainly due to the 80-day general strike—and were it not for a record autumn crop in that year, that level of production would not have been reached. The further decline of production in 1964 was the consequence of another long, unofficial strike in 1964 which was attended by considerable violence.[1] This made production extremely difficult. A long and severe drought exacerbated these complications. Thus there were at least three sets of factors that militated against increased activity in the sugar industry between 1961 and 1964. The first set of factors was primarily responsible for the decrease in acreage under cane and acres reaped. This period was marred by political and social unrest and a climate of uncertainty about future policy and investment partly brought about by constant threats of nationalization and confiscation by the government that was then in power. Under these circumstances the sugar companies decided that two courses of action were open to them. On the one hand they could succumb to threats and withdraw completely from the country. But this course would have revealed cowardice and bad faith. In the event of a decision to stay on and brave the storm, it was considered that the industry could only maintain its competitive position in world markets, if rationalization with increased efficiency were introduced. The second set of factors operated through inopportune natural conditions such as droughts and poor rainfall. Thirdly, as part of the general unrest, strikes and physical acts of violence to life and property also took a heavy toll.

In view of the various difficulties facing the industry during this period it would not be out of place to examine some of the factors that affect productivity. The relatively high productivity per acre of sugar cane arises from its basic suitability to

[1] Under the condition of near civil war, and the tragic wave of violence that swept the country for six months, nearly 200 people lost their lives. The primitive acts of arson and sabotage on the sugar estates in Berbice and Demerara brought a total loss of nearly $6,000,000 in value (current prices) of the country's sugar exports, not counting lost wages, purchasing power, and government revenue. The situation was aggravated by the unprecedented failure of the winter rains which meant that the 1964 crop had only one-third of the normal rainfall, resulting in reduced yields and quality. It redounds to the sugar companies' credit that they were able to survive these outrages and produced over 250,000 tons of sugar.

The deleterious consequences of these acts of vandalism on the investment climate were very aptly summarized. 'At a time when it was never more important to strengthen and expand the economy, every citizen has a vested interest in condemning actions which can only weaken the country's economic position and diminish public confidence. No less important is the damaging effects on these incidents on Guyana's reputation abroad, and on the Government's declared policy of creating a climate of confidence for investors. Neither existing nor potential investors can be expected to take confidence from the wilful destruction of the assets of the largest industry in the private sector', *Guyana Graphic*, 17 February 1964.

tropical conditions as well as from scientific improvements in the application of capital and labour in cane cultivation. The physical advantages of sugar cane in the tropics can be summarized as follows. The cultivation of sugar cane maintains soil fertility to a remarkable degree; cane resists the ravages of tropical storms far better than any other crop that can be grown in the tropics. The sugar cane bagasse provides the fuel for operating the factories; sugar maintains more labour per acre than any other crop, except bulb-growing and tomato cultivation. Thus while it is possible to use small portions of land more productively in market gardening than in sugar, it is not easy to find in the tropics any other crop that will employ large numbers of workers and extensive acreage with a productivity equal to that of sugar.[1]

But while sugar cane offers great advantages for tropical agriculture in general, there are special problems in Guyana arising from the peculiarities of terrain and climate. The recognition of this is not of recent origin. Thus the first paragraph of James Rodway's *History of British Guiana* (1891) reads as follows:

The story of the Colonies which now form British Guiana is one of plodding perseverance rather than conquest . . . every acre at present in cultivation has been the scene of a struggle with the sea in front and the flood behind. As a result of this arduous labour during two centuries a narrow strip of land along the coast has been rescued from the mangrove swamp and kept under cultivation by an elaborate system of dams and dykes. Scattered along the rivers and creeks lie a thousand abandoned plantations, most of them indistinguishable from the surrounding forest; these represent the failures of the early settlers. At first sight the narrow line of sugar estates seems but a very poor show for such a long struggle with nature, but when all the circumstances are taken into consideration, it is almost a wonder that the colony has not been abandoned altogether.

The twofold problem of sea and floods is still with us; hence the necessity for a system of high and low canals, the low for drainage and the high for transportation and irrigation. Sugar cultivation in Guyana involves special techniques, extra effort,

[1] British West Indies Sugar Association (B.W.I.S.A.), *Sugar in the West Indies and British Guiana*, Handbook, 1958, p. 4.

and more urgent timing than production in most other countries. The unique necessities of water control involves the extensive building of sea walls, digging of canals and ditches, and
of maintaining them. Similarly the heavy soil requires much
preparation, and the superabundance of weeds and pests calls
for intensive tillage and chemical control measures. These local
peculiarities have necessitated heavy overhead investment prior
to and during the cultivation of cane, with consequent high
production costs and the weakening of the competitive position
of sugar produced in the country. Against this background we
may examine the three main indices of efficiency operative
within the industry.

The most commonly used index is that of yields, which can
be subdivided into three categories. Firstly, there is an index of
efficiency at the primary field stage, viz. tons of cane per acre
reaped. Secondly, there is the recovery rate—tons of cane per
ton of sugar—which refers to the secondary or factory stage of
the industry. Thirdly, it is necessary to reduce these two indices
to some common denominator, and thus to integrate both
stages of the industry with another index showing the performance of the industry as a whole. This general index represents the tons of sugar per acre reaped. Table 17 sets out the
behaviour of these indices between 1953 and 1964. The average
yield of cane per acre over the period was 39 tons, Guyana being
the only territory in the Commonwealth Caribbean to have
reached 40 tons per acre in any one year.[1] The heavy rainfall
and high water table make for a heavy growth of cane, but cane
yields per acre have fluctuated well below the 40 ton mark for
most of the period. One of the main reasons for this tendency
is the uncertainty of weather conditions. But while yields are
heavier than in many other countries, the sucrose content is less.

Of the factors that determine the yield of sugar cane, rainfall
is perhaps the most important, though it is the seasonal distribution rather than the annual total that is the deciding factor.
Rainfall must be adequate but not excessive during the growing
period, since too much rain lowers the sucrose content of the
cane. On the other hand, too little rain during the growing
season does not allow the cane to reach maturity, and hence

[1] G. C. Abbott, 'The West Indian Sugar Industry with some Long Term Projections of Supply', *Social and Economic Studies*, Vol. 13, No. 1 (March 1964), p. 7.

TABLE 17
INDICES OF EFFICIENCY IN THE SUGAR INDUSTRY

Year	Average yield of cane per acre	Tons of cane per ton 96° sugar	Tons of 96° sugar per acre[a]
1953	37·7	11·35	3·33
1954	34·4	11·36	3·02
1955	35·1	10·73	3·28
1956	37·4	10·59	3·55
1957	35·5	10·19	3·52
1958	40·0	11·12	3·62
1959	36·1	11·10	3·26
1960	38·8	10·91	3·50
1961	33·5	10·74	3·08
1962	37·1	10·34	3·32
1963	35·9	10·54	3·35
1964	N.A.	11·40	2·78
Average 1953–64	39·2	10·86	3·30

Source: Guyana Sugar Producers' Association.

[a] Dark crystal sugar of 96° polarization.

N.A. = Not available.

maximum sucrose content. The fact that the space of time between wet and dry seasons is relatively short also militates against high sucrose content, for in many instances younger canes have to be harvested. Thus although Guyana with its two wet and dry seasons may be ideal for sugar-cane cultivation, water is as much a problem to the cane farmer as it is an answer to his problem.

It comes as no surprise therefore that it takes about 11 tons of cane to make a ton of sugar in Guyana as against an average of 8 tons for most of the other sugar-producing territories in the Commonwealth Caribbean.[1] But the quality of cane reaped is only of secondary significance with respect to the recovery rate, which is more an index of factory efficiency. Generally speaking the lower the recovery rate, the better is the performance of the factory. Thus a factory that takes 8 tons of cane to make 1 ton of sugar would be considered more efficient than one that takes 10 tons of cane, other things being equal. As an index of efficiency therefore, most factories strive to maintain as low a

[1] Abbott, loc. cit., p. 14.

ratio as possible. The factors that determine the recovery rate may be divided into two broad categories: firstly those that affect the sucrose content of the cane itself, i.e. those that are operative before the canes reach the factory, and secondly those that are operative within the factory itself. We have already expressed some cause for concern over the pre-factory operations, although the short period between the rainy seasons in Guyana make it unlikely that substantial quantities of stale cane can reach the factories.[1] Foremost among the factors operating within the factory is the mechanical efficiency of mills in extracting juice from the canes. This depends on such factors as the age and stage of obsolescence of the mills themselves, their milling rate per hour, the number of mechanical breakdowns and hours out of cane, as well as the length of the grinding season.

With respect to the third index of efficiency—tons of sugar per acre reaped—the average for the period was 3·30 tons. Although it may be possible to reach an over-all ratio of 4 tons of sugar per acre, the climatic conditions in Guyana favour growth rather than sucrose content, and it is doubtful whether very much improvement could be made in this field. Thus given the natural and other peculiarities bedevilling production in Guyana we may conclude that the over-all efficiency has been favourable.

Technological Change

One factor that has had a tremendous impact on efficiency in the industry has been the substantial technical change which has led to a marked and progressive reduction in the labour input per ton. This factor is of crucial importance for the future dimensions of capital intensity in the private sector, and government employment policy for the economy as a whole. It is cost per ton that largely determines the competitive position of Guyana sugar in the commercial export market, and thereby determines the survival of the industry, its ability to pay adequate factor incomes and to make its invaluable contribution to the revenue account of the central government. If unit costs

---

[1] The sucrose content also varies inversely with the length of time the reaped cane stays idle in the field.

in Guyana should rise relative to the cost and prices in Commonwealth Agreement countries and the world market, Guyana's sugar would be priced out of these markets, unless there are substantial profits which can be sacrificed, or large subsidies paid by the rest of the economy to offset the rise in costs. Thus the main object of technical change in the industry is the reduction or restraint of unit costs in the face of wage pressure and other factor-price rises.

The average cost of production per ton in the Commonwealth Caribbean has reached a high figure of $196·80 per ton, while the cost of some other Commonwealth producers varies between BWI$149 and BWI$120 per ton. In 1964 the average cost of production per ton of sugar in Guyana was over BWI$192 as compared with BWI$148 in Australia, Fiji, and Mauritius.[1] When this is set beside the average price Guyana receives for her sugar sales, there is clear evidence that the margin between export sales and costs of production has virtually disappeared. Wage costs per ton of sugar in Guyana and the West Indies are nearly as much as the total cost of producing sugar in Central Africa. In 1964, the average wage cost per ton of sugar in Guyana was $105·60,[2] and in most years wage costs account for an average of 60 to 70 per cent of total unit costs of production.

Guyana's problem arises mainly because the benefaction that she receives from the Commonwealth Sugar Agreement is neither unlimited nor unreciprocated. Although the guarantee given under this agreement has made it possible for participating producers to expand their acreage and modernize factories, the agreed Commonwealth price is not a cost-plus formula which would prop up any producer however inefficient. For although the scheme does incorporate average increases in costs as measured by a factor-price index—covering virtually all the input elements of the member producers, as applied to the 1950 base price—it sets a single uniform price for all participants subject to some small negotiated variations, and thus puts pressure to make improvements on the high-cost producer and on those who get out of line with other producers. Moreover, as

---

[1] Annual Report of the International Sugar Council.
[2] See The British West Indies Sugar Association: Handbook 1964.

approximately one-third of the total Commonwealth exports must still be sold at the low price prevailing in the free market, there is general pressure to hold costs down.

Factors operative in three sets of countries help to explain the predicament facing Guyana. First, the most persistent threat has come from the Australian industry which has introduced a substantial degree of mechanical planting and harvesting in field operations. The second set of countries, mostly in central Africa, which offer a formidable challenge, include those that are in the process of establishing, or have recently established, their own sugar industries. From the outset these countries have equipped their factories and field operations with the most modern techniques and equipment, and are not faced with militant trade union and similar pressures which tend to drive up cost of production in Guyana. The third category of countries includes those that, in the pursuit of self-sufficiency or the possibility of export promotion, are setting up heavily subsidized, well protected, infant industries.

Labour displacement in the sugar industry of Guyana was a direct consequence of mechanization and technological change. Because of the real threat this country faces from low-cost producers, if these labour-saving changes do not tend to reduce costs, then such changes must be regarded as financially unsound and socially undesirable in a labour-surplus economy, whereas if the changes are technically and financially sound then the problem of labour displacement shifts from a question of optimum production technique to a question of social policy. Economic development through time involves an increase in the capital/labour ratio and permits capital deepening. A significant question over which some dispute has arisen in economic discussion, is whether a developing country in its quest for both maximum output and employment should use the technology appropriate to its existing factor proportions, including especially its capital/labour ratio, or whether it should anticipate the relative growth of capital and begin the use of capital-intensive techniques of production before its capital endowment is really suitable for this. In particular the question is whether countries at the early stages of development, with capital scarce and labour abundant, should take advantage of the modern technology developed by advanced countries where capital is abundant and labour scarce, or whether they should develop a technology of their own, or use production methods which are obsolete in countries abroad. The argument is complex. It can include questions of priority, appeals to history, and reference to empirical data and current practice.

Galenson and Leibenstein[1] have argued that capital-intensive industries are more effective producers of savings than labour-intensive, and hence likely to speed development faster despite a possibly lower static level of output. They use a social welfare function in which the aim is to maximize *per capita* income at some time in the distant future rather than to maximize a discounted stream of income over time, and divide income into profits and wages, since the savings from the former may be higher. To maximize total output at some distant future time, they show that the most productive form of investment is not necessarily the one that maximizes income in the near future but the one that leads to the highest savings. Since it is assumed that neither voluntary savings nor taxes can be extracted from wages, the most productive investment will be the one with the highest profit rate per unit of capital invested. The assumption that profits are saved and re-invested leads to the marginal re-investment quotient as a decision rule. This argument in favour of capital-intensive techniques neglects the foreign exchange implications for developing with no domestic capital goods industries and uses a social welfare function in which the starvation of half the population in the near future would be a matter of indifference. The criterion neglects the fact that present income may be more valuable to society or to workers in a particular industry than future income, and the mere promise of a higher income in the future is not sufficient reason for choosing the technique.[2]

[1] W. Galenson and H. Leibenstein, 'Investment Criteria, Productivity and Economic Development', *The Quarterly Journal of Economics* (August 1955), pp. 343–70. Galenson and Leibenstein have been widely criticized for their extreme assumptions.

[2] Cf. F. M. Bator, 'On Capital Productivity, Input Allocation, and Growth', *The Quarterly Journal of Economics* (February 1957), pp. 86–106; O. Eckstein, 'Investment Criteria for Economic Development and the Theory of Intertemporal Welfare Economics', *The Quarterly Journal of Economics* (February 1957), pp. 56–85; and A. O. Hirschman, 'Investment Criteria and Capital Intensity Once Again', *The Quarterly Journal of Economics* (August 1958), pp. 469–71.

Bruton has suggested that the industries that embody external economies are frequently capital intensive. These capital investments must be undertaken before one can take advantage of opportunities for investment in labour-intensive industries. When industries are linked together in complementary interaction, the capital intensity of a single industry is not an appropriate index of its suitability for investment until one has traced through, and imputed to it, its total return, with all the difficulties this involves.[1] This is only mildly persuasive, however, and appears to concede that in industries producing final output, a country should on theoretical grounds adopt the technology appropriate to its factor proportions after subtraction of those considerable lumps of capital needed for the overhead industries. This article further implies that labour productivity is higher in capital-intensive than in labour-intensive industries, and that this is an argument for the former. But this is not true with a competitive market for labour, nor if true, is it relevant. The investment criterion is net capital productivity or gross, if labour is redundant. Thus the proponents of the capital intensity point of view believe that modern technology will lead to rapid growth, and constitute an effective short cut to economic development. But this viewpoint has to be distinguished from the other, which claims that the use of the latest technology fails to produce rapid development and creates no capital for use in other occupations which have been rationed on capital to make possible the capital-intensive investment. In the latter situation the economy should make haste slowly.

Thus A. E. Kahn[2] has suggested that from the addition to output due to investment, the alternative output sacrificed by drawing factors of production from other fields into this one has to be subtracted. Thus the factors are valued at their social opportunity cost, i.e. what they would have produced in other fields had they not been drawn into the investment under question. We would arrive at a different conclusion from the capital-intensive criterion so long as the social opportunity cost

[1] H. J. Bruton, 'Growth Models and Underdeveloped Countries', *Journal of Political Economy* (August 1955), pp. 322–36.
[2] A. E. Kahn, 'Investment Criteria in Development Programs', *The Quarterly Journal of Economics* (February 1951), pp. 38–61.

of labour is positive. When, however, there is large-scale unemployment, the opportunity cost of labour is *nil*, and thus
labour becomes according to this approach costless. Professor
Lewis has also put forward a similar view.

Special care [he argues] has to be taken in those countries which
have a large surplus of unskilled labour, for in such cases money
wages will not reflect the real social cost of using labour. In these
circumstances capital is not productive if it is used to do what labour
could do equally well; given the level of wages such investments may
be highly profitable to capitalists, but they are unprofitable to the
community as a whole since they add to unemployment and not to
output.[1]

In this context it can be argued that since mechanization and
technological change in sugar requires substantial capital investments, and does not always yield incremental productivity
exceeding incremental cost, agricultural equipment may be a
dubious social investment under Guyanese conditions.

Nearer home Professor Lewis has pointed out for Barbados:

It obviously does not make economic sense for the Barbadians to
use their limited foreign exchange reserves to import machinery to
do forms of work on sugar plantations which could just as well be
done by human labour. And yet at the current level of wages it pays
the sugar companies to do so. Their case is that since they produce
for a competitive market they cannot neglect innovations introduced
elsewhere.[2]

The Kahn-Lewis Social Marginal Productivity Criterion also
suffers from drawbacks. In assessing it we should ask what we
are trying to achieve. If the object is the maximization of immediate output, labour should be valued according to its social
opportunity cost and the above criterion seems appropriate. If
however we are interested in the future as well, we have to look
at the rate of growth of income governed by the accumulation
of capital. And there is no reason to believe that the maximum
rate of output would also give us the maximum rate of excess

[1] Lewis, *The Theory of Economic Growth*, p. 386. One notices some changes in
Prof. Lewis's position in his more recent article, 'Unlimited Labour: Further
Notes', *Manchester School of Economic and Social Studies* (January 1958).
[2] W. A. Lewis, 'Employment Policy in an Underdeveloped Area', *Social and
Economic Studies*, Vol. 7, No. 3 (1958), op. cit., p. 50.

of production over consumption, when employment is a variable. Even if the alternative social product is *nil*, the cost of labour will be positive, given the increase in consumption due to the extra employment.

An important element in some of the arguments in favour of modern technology is that abundant labour may not be cheap labour. Two reasons may explain this. Labour may be low in price, but lower in efficiency. Or the price of labour may have been artificially bid up or raised by one or another means. Although it is difficult to make any firm assessment of the efficiency of sugar workers in Guyana in relation to wages, it is nevertheless true that the demonstration effect has extended into the field of social services and collective bargaining, with the consequence that the price of labour, including wages and benefits, is high despite low productivity. Militant trade union pressure in the industry has made labour costs very high, and has discouraged the employment of redundant and seasonally available workers. This could be seen as a part of the drive among the sugar estates for decasualization and ultimate stabilization of the labour force.

The general conclusion that seems to emerge is we cannot resolve the problems connected with the choice of techniques by *a priori* argumentation. This is especially true in the Guyanese context where the sugar industry is a private, foreign-owned concern, and whether or not it is socially desirable to devote scarce capital to labour-displacing purposes in a labour-redundant economy which allegedly contains many opportunities for new labour-absorbing investments turns on this actuality, its ramifications and entailments. Capital could be frequently underpriced or overused in a limited sector, with the result that it is not available for high earning occupations outside. This is usually the case where the capital market is imperfect and split into segments within which the demand and supply for loanable funds yield different rates of return. There is at present no organization to control and reallocate private capital in Guyana, whose capital market is at best rudimentary. If the sugar companies are prevented from investing in modern technology, the most likely result will be to remit accumulated funds to the United Kingdom or failure to draw new capital into Guyana, the net effect of which will be socially harmful. Social and political desirability aside, we may now concentrate on what may be considered the main reason for the introduction of technological change in the sugar industry, viz. the reduction of costs so as to maintain Guyana's competitive position.

In general we cannot assume that every technical change will reduce unit costs. The change will not do so if it entails relatively heavy investment input with consequently heavy annual depreciation and interest charges, if it causes external diseconomies elsewhere, or if it is accompanied by a disproportionate rise in other costs, e.g. wage increases for the remaining work force. Conversely if dollar costs per unit of output do not fall during a period of technical change, the latter is not necessarily to be blamed since all other factors may not have remained constant. We must therefore investigate the trend of actual unit costs, and disaggregate the trend into the behaviors of operating efficiency, capital charges, and factor-cost prices including wages.

The available data on the behaviour of costs is very scanty but Table 18 which summarizes simultaneous trends in total direct costs, routine costs, wage costs per ton, as well as wage rates and earnings per day for the period 1945 to 1960. Total direct costs include all operating costs plus overhead charges, but do not include depreciation, interest charges, and reserves for pension and taxation. It is clear that the total direct cost per ton of sugar rose sharply after the Second World War, but drew approximately level from the middle of the 1950s onwards, despite generally rising factor prices. Wage rates rose throughout this period, piece rates climbing by 6 per cent plus miscellaneous bonuses, while earnings per man-day shot up by as much as 10 per cent on average. These increasing labour costs, which were rising faster than other costs and prices, would have immediately lifted the total costs of production were it not for technological improvements which economized on labour input per ton. Accordingly the wage cost per ton showed a post-war rise until 1954, and has since remained nearly steady or even moved slightly downwards. The annual wage bill paid by the industry has been rising as the wage rates per man-day have increased more sharply than the decline in the total man-days worked. What this shows is that technological advances which have displaced labour in the industry also brought higher incomes to those remaining in jobs, and by increasing their productivity made it possible to pay these higher incomes without a corresponding inflation in the cost of production.

If a comparative analysis is made of the sectors of cultivation, harvesting, and factory processing, there is still closer association of costs per ton with the presence or absence of major technological change. Table 19 presents the sectoral data on routine costs of production per ton for one of the sugar companies for the period 1950 to 1960. Routine costs cover operating costs including bonuses but exclude depreciation, interest

TABLE

COSTS OF PRODUCTION,

	1945	1947	1950	1951	1952	1953
A. Total 'direct' cost per ton of sugar	$77·29	101·28	N.A.	N.A.	N.A.	N.A.
B. Total 'routine' cost per ton of sugar	N.A.	N.A.	93·41	92·27	111·12	108·97
C. Wages paid						
1. Total amount of wages paid ($'000)						
(a) (a) $6,493	9,265					
(b)						
(c)						
2. Earnings per man-day ($)						
3. Wage rates (indices)						
(a) (1953 = 100)						100
(b) (1939 = 100)	120	130	140	150	170	175
D. Total wage-cost per ton of sugar						
(a)	$41·30	55·32				
(b)			$52·77	51·64	59·51	56·68

Source: Reubens and Reubens, *Labour displacement in a Labour-Surplus Economy.*

charges, and all general overhead charges. In the cultivation sector the data shows that the cost per ton did not rise much despite strong trade union pressures. Unit cost actually declined from 1950 to 1953, rose to a new high level between 1954 and 1956, and then declined to a level in 1960 slightly below that of 1950. It is also obvious that wages, which account for half the total cost of cultivation, were the main directors of the cost pattern. Other costs of cultivation have moved less vigorously and show less correlation with total costs of cultivation. Like the Australian case, the cultivation sector was one in which substantial technological change, both mechanical and non-mechanical, took place.

The harvesting sector presents a sharp contrast. Here costs per ton rose steadily, with virtually no interruptions until 1960 when the figure stood at 58 per cent above that of 1950. In this case wages, which account for about 80 per cent of total costs of harvesting, were the sole mover, as the other costs of harvesting showed practically no change over the period. Very little

18
SUGAR INDUSTRY, 1945–60

1954	1955	1956	1957	1958	1959	1960	1961
N.A.	N.A.	140·59	150·04	141·89	148·52	144·20	
117·20	116·50	117·10	118·90	116·95	120·63	114·49	
		$21,082	22,699	22,837	22,074	24,986	
$17,214	18,378	19,361	20,336	22,489	20,616	24,323	
N.A.	2·79	3·06	3·22	3·60	3·63	4·25	
N.A.	107·5	116·6	116·9	122·2	133·6	134·8	
175	182·5	192·5	200·0	210	217·5	225·0	
72·05	73·52	73·52	71·36	73·41	72·48	72·73	
66·68	66·55	68·03	66·19	66·15	69·32	68·39	

N.A. = Not available.

technological change was introduced in harvesting, and there was little rise in productivity per man-day to offset the rise in wages per man-day. The performance in the factories falls between the cultivation and harvesting sectors. The effect of technological changes economizing on labour is seen here chiefly in the modest rise in wage costs per ton. When all the three sectors are aggregated, the figures for routine costs show

TABLE 19
SUGAR PRODUCTION: ROUTINE COSTS[a] WITH BONUSES[b]

(Guyana dollars per ton of sugar)

	1950	1951	1952	1953	1954	1955	1956	1957	1958	1959	1960
Cultivation											
Wages	20·99	18·93	20·79	18·75	24·58	25·64	24·87	21·19	17·49	18·23	17·17
Other	13·26	14·39	15·38	12·96	18·12	18·04	18·92	18·54	16·71	17·05	14·98
Total	34·25	33·32	36·17	31·71	42·70	43·68	43·79	39·73	34·20	35·28	32·15
Harvesting											
Wages	18·44	19·82	23·66	24·25	25·75	25·49	26·85	27·61	30·49	31·88	31·98
Other	4·56	4·28	5·10	4·38	3·94	3·86	3·92	4·56	4·42	4·55	4·50
Total	23·00	24·10	28·76	28·63	29·69	29·35	30·77	32·17	34·91	36·43	36·48
Factory											
Wages	12·80	12·40	14·92	14·76	15·93	14·93	15·45	15·44	15·99	16·17	15·75
Other	19·02	18·83	27·04	27·58	22·97	22·57	20·99	23·92	24·40	23·50	20·73
Total	31·82	31·23	41·96	42·34	38·90	37·50	36·44	39·36	40·39	39·67	36·48

Source: Reubens and Reubens, *Labour Displacement in a Labour-Surplus Economy.*
   [a] Excluding general overhead and special revenue expenditure.   [b] One of the principal sugar companies of Guyana.

that the ability to absorb rises in wages and other prices varied with the degree of relative technical innovation in each sector during the period.

The various elements of costs so far examined exclude depreciation charges and interest on capital invested. If other elements in costs are not taken into account it would be impossible to decide whether the new investments were justified even from the management point of view, but it has been argued that the modernization effort brought small gains to the sugar companies.[1]

We have been examining the main factors that affect the supply side of the industry, but demand considerations are of equal importance. We noted in an earlier chapter that the industry makes a substantial contribution to the country's exports and balance of payments. In view of the small size of the local market, which consumes an average of 20,000 tons of sugar per year or 6 per cent of the value of total output, export markets are of considerable value. Sugar exports account for 45/46 per cent of total exports in most years, though since 1961 there has been a slight decline. This does not represent a fall in the absolute value of sugar exports but arose because of the exports of two new enterprises, manganese and alumina. We have also noticed that the country's favourable terms of trade were to a large extent due to increasing prices under the Commonwealth Sugar Agreement. The prices received from the premium-priced United States market is also consequential in this connection. The importance of sugar to the export sector is such that a drop of about 15 per cent in the value of sugar exports would approximately double the deficit on visible trade.

Four markets are available to Guyana for the sale of its sugar:

(1) The Negotiated Price Quota Market.
(2) The U.S.A. Market.
(3) The Free Market.
(4) The Local Market.

Table 20 summarizes data on the relative importance of each of these markets for the period 1956–65.

[1] See Reubens and Reubens, *Labour Displacement in a Labour Surplus Economy.*

TABLE

MARKETS

	1956			1957			Tons
	Tons	Av. price	Value $	Tons	Av. price	Value $	
N.P.Q.	162,607	183·38	29,819,043	153,181	191·71	29,366,329	154,561
U.S.A.	—	—	—	—			
Free market	80,845	150·64	12,178,455	113,650	195·83	22,255,807	152,455
Local market	19,881	130·91	2,602,610	18,142	135·25	2,453,706	19,355
Total	263,333	169·37	44,600,108	284,973	189·76	54,075,842	306,361

	1961			1962			Tons
	Tons	Av. price	Value $	Tons	Av. price	Value $	
N.P.Q.	166,075	207·25	34,419,585	165,966	211·01	35,020,597	166,019
U.S.A.	80,145	190·78	15,289,985	65,180	182·10	11,809,256	36,158
Free market	57,307	125·85	7,212,340	75,014	119·26	8,946,119	93,440
Local market	21,218	133·81	2,839,228	19,863	130·00	2,582,023	21,520
Total	324,745	184·02	59,761,138	326,023	179·18	58,417,995	317,137

The N.P.Q. market is a result of the Commonwealth Sugar Agreement signed in 1951, and at present running to 31 December 1972. This Agreement was executed by the Minister of Food on behalf of Her Majesty's Government in the United Kingdom and the Sugar Producers' Associations of the following territories:

(a) Australia.
(b) Union of South Africa.
(c) British West Indies (Antigua, Barbados, Guyana, Jamaica, St. Kitts, St. Lucia, and Trinidad).
(d) Mauritius.

Under the Agreement the United Kingdom currently pays the negotiated price for a total of 1,692,500 tons a year from Commonwealth exporters, of which Guyana's basic allocation for 1965 was 181,805 tons. These quantities have shown an increase over recent years, partly to reflect increases in U.K.

20

AND SALES

1958		1959			1960		
Av. price	Value $	Tons	Av. price	Value $	Tons	Av. price	Value $
199·09	30,772,411	159,630	205·70	32,835,890	167,724	202·00	33,880,873
—	—	—	—	—	29,571	201·13	5,947,752
149·38	19,785,225	106,277	138·24	14,692,365	118,668	128·98	15,306,358
131·75	2,550,031	18,518	133·67	2,475,392	18,478	132·86	2,455,050
173·35	53,107,667	284,425	175·81	50,003,647	334,441	172·20	57,590,050

1963		1964			1965		
Av. price	Value $	Tons	Av. price	Value $	Tons	Av. price	Value $
209·26	34,743,136	175,844	208·95	36,742,438	185,520	209·08	38,788,330
232·00	8,388,656	26,232	173·53	4,552,141	29,016	203·40	5,901,874
294·60	27,529,427	31,783	249·88	7,941,920	68,609	113·68	7,799,746
132·68	2,855,274	24,519	131·00	3,212,126	23,000	132·61	3,050,002
231·81	73,516,493	258,378	202·99	52,448,625	306,145	181·42	55,539,952

Source: Guyana Sugar Producers' Association.

consumption and partly because of reallocations of quotas following South Africa's leaving the Commonwealth (and the Commonwealth Sugar Agreement) and because St. Lucia no longer exports sugar.

The total of the negotiated price quotas and the sugar derived from the U.K. beet now represents some 97 per cent of U.K. consumption, and for technical and political reasons another 2 per cent or so has to be reserved for foreign imports. Moreover, U.K. consumption is now virtually static, so that the prospects are negligible for any increase in the total of the negotiated price quotas.

The Agreement provides for the purchase by the United Kingdom government of the quantities of the negotiated price quota annually at a negotiated price 'reasonably remunerative to efficient producers' and stipulates a single price applicable to all Commonwealth exporting territories. The price-fixing method is set out in the Agreement and provides for an index to be compiled of wages and prices of goods and services entering into the costs of production. The basic concept underlying the Agreement was the establishment of a price that would preserve the purchasing power of a sack of sugar in terms of imported goods used in the sugar industry and of imported foodstuffs, clothing, etc., consumed by sugar workers.

The Agreement established a basic price for 1950 of $146·40 per ton, which was accepted as a resonable base by the parties to the Agreement; and provided for annual price negotiations aimed at achieving a new single price to reflect changes in the levels of wages and other cost factors relating to export sugar. In accordance with the provisions of the Agreement the working of the price-fixing system was informally reviewed at the request of the Ministry of Food in 1955 and 1959 and new prices were established. These exercises are termed 'Formula Reviews'. Price movements between the base years—called the Price Index—are determined along the lines of a formula set out in an appendix to the Agreement which measures changes in price, entering into the costs under the three main headings of (1) wages and salaries; (2) supplies; (3) other charges. The negotiated price rose steadily from $160·40 per ton for 1950 to $223·20 for 1964, the average price for 1964 being $208·95, which was just $4·76 above the cost of production.

The industry now has for 60 per cent of its sugar through sales at NPQ prices a guaranteed market at a guaranteed price which is not only reasonably remunerative to the efficient producer but goes some way towards offsetting the loss on the world market.

The sugar arrangements within the U.S.A. are determined by legislation and the government decisions which lay down the proportion of U.S. requirements to be met from domestic production and from imports from various areas, and also lay down the mechanism by which the prices for domestic production and imports are determined.

The U.S. administration is continuously subject to great pressure to grant increased quotas for domestic producers and for overseas countries, particularly Latin-American countries who can argue that they benefit from no protective arrangements elsewhere.

The price of sugar sold to the U.S.A. is currently determined by the relationship between U.S. consumption and the total of the quotas permitted by the administration.

The Free Market

This refers to that part of Guyana's exports that is sold at prices directly related to the free world market price. This portion of Guyana's sugar exports is sold almost entirely in Canada in order to take advantage of the tariff preference granted by Canada to Commonwealth producers (South Africa).

The Canadian market is under great pressure from traditional Commonwealth Sugar Agreement countries (India, Rhodesia, and Swaziland), and from South Africa. Against this competition it is a tough struggle to maintain Guyana's share of it. It should be mentioned that no other market, even if it were accessible to Guyana, provides comparable preference. The price received by Guyana for sales to Canada is the world price plus a part of the Canadian preference, which is $36 per ton. The greater the pressure on the Canadian market, the greater the erosion of the premium that Commonwealth exporters can obtain from Canada by virtue of the preference.

Free quota prices are based on world prices which, as can be seen from Table 21, have been the very opposite of steady. Even with the Canadian preference of $36 per ton this price is below the cost of production.

At no time since the war have the market prospects for sugar

TABLE 21
LONDON DAILY PRICE
(Annual average c.i.f. U.K.)

Year	$ per ton	Index (1966 = 100)
1956	168·00	100
1957	225·50	134
1958	150·62	90
1959	131·09	78
1960	136·70	81
1961	123·26	73
1962	122·83	73
1963	344·16	205
1964	245·35	146

sold in the free market been worse than those confronting the industry today.

In the absence of an effective international sugar agreement there is no indication of any increase in world prices above the present levels. A conference to negotiate such an agreement was held in September 1965, but no decision was reached. Even if and when an agreement is reached, it can only be effective in raising the world price if it achieves a drastic cut in sales on the world market, and this cannot fail to include a cut in sales from Guyana.

Any cut in Guyana total sales would increase the unit costs of production and thus exacerbate the industry's serious losses. It seems, therefore, that the industry cannot look for any relief by way of any substantial improvement in the current low free world market price, and although the cushion arranged under the new Commonwealth Agreement will in some way mitigate the loss that must be anticipated, it will by no means offset it.

The Local Market

Over 22,000 tons of sugar are sold on the local market at government-controlled prices which are considerably less than

TABLE 22

GUYANA SUGAR INDUSTRY: LOCAL SALES OF SUGAR
1956–64

Year	Tons sugar sold	Average production cost per ton ($)	Average sales price per ton ($)	Differ- ence ($)	Total loss on production cost ($)
1956	19,881	158·82	130·91	27·91	554,878·71
1957	18,142	163·95	135·25	28·70	520,675·40
1958	19,355	159·98	131·75	28·23	546,391·65
1959	18,518	164·47	133·67	30·80	570,354·40
1960	18,478	156·67	132·86	23·81	439,961·18
1961	21,218	163·49	133·81	29·68	629,750·24
1962	19,863	154·82	130·00	24·82	492,999·66
1963	21,520	182·07	132·68	49·39	1,062,872·80
1964	24,519	204·19	131·00	73·19	1,794,545·61
	181,494				6,612,429·65

Source: Guyana Sugar Producers' Association.

the cost of producing the sugar. It will be seen from Table 22 that during the period 1956–64 the accumulated loss to the industry through this form of subsidization has amounted to over $6·6 million.

There is no immediate danger of loss of protection in the N.P.Q. market, since the Commonwealth Sugar Agreement is scheduled to run until 1974. Had it not been for such arrangements, Guyana's high-cost producers would have been priced out of world markets a long time ago. The available evidence suggests that the difference between the price Guyana receives under the Commonwealth Sugar Agreement and the free market price exceeds $13 million in most years.[1] There is therefore some degree of warrant for the remark that, without the Commonwealth Sugar Agreement the Guyana's industry's prosperity would vanish; and secondly the subsidy paid by the U.K. consumer to Guyana via a high sugar price is much more important than C.D. & W. gifts.

On the more general front, as noticed earlier, there are basic economic and social forces in Guyana as in most sugar-producing countries of the world, that are compelling industries to introduce labour-saving techniques of production. Underlying the various attempts to regulate the market is the fact that the demand for sugar tends to be inelastic.[2] This type of demand resists efforts to raise total sales volume by generalized price cuts and yet encourages any individual seller to try to increase his share of the market by cutting his own price. Conversely the tendency of demand to be inelastic to rising prices defeats the efforts of any seller to raise his own price, because buyers would switch from high-priced sellers to lower-priced sellers at home and abroad. At the same time supply is quite expansible in response to price rises. But supply does not shrink when prices fall. As this situation has tended towards ruinous competition, with selling prices below costs of production, the industry has obtained various international and internal agreements to provide some shelter from sheer market forces. But cost-price competition persists even within the Commonwealth

[1] *Sugar File*, Central Planning Unit, Georgetown.
[2] For a full and authoritative account of conditions governing the demand for sugar see A. Viton and F. Pignalosa, *Trends and Forces in World Sugar Consumption*, F.A.O. Commodity Series, Bulletin No. 32 (Rome, 1961).

Sugar Agreement. Thus even with stabilization arrangements only the most efficient and low-cost producers could survive.

Clouds hang over sugar in other directions as well.[1] Although the world consumption of sugar may be showing an upward trend, this is not the case with the international demand for traded sugar. The world market is so structured that the large consuming countries pre-empt an increasing share of potential supplies for their own home producers. Since 1934–8 nearly all of the net importing areas have been increasing their self-sufficiency as follows:

TABLE 23

CHANGES IN SELF-SUFFICIENCY OF LARGE CONSUMING COUNTRIES

	1934–8 (%)	1951–5 (%)	1956–60 (%)	1961–2 (%)
European Economic Community	76	94	95	108
United Kingdom	21	30	26	31
Sweden	99	87	82	97
Western Europe	55	70	72	79
Eastern Europe and U.S.S.R.	129	107	99	97
U.S.A.	28	29	29	33

Source: Trade and Development: Vol. III, Commodity Trade (U.N., New York, 1964).

The international demand for sugar is becoming largely a residual demand, and a proportionately declining residual at that. This is perhaps one of the most important structural facts governing the market and therefore the prices at which sugar is sold. It has been argued at the United Nations Trade Conference that maintenance of the pre-war degree of self-sufficiency in Western Europe might have resulted in a sugar market relatively less flooded with supplies than was actually the case in the 1950s. This would have tended to raise the price of all cane sugar exports and would therefore have been of great benefit to the developing countries.[2]

---

[1] Britain's entry into the European Economic Community is likely to have some adverse effects.

[2] Commodity Trade, p. 517.

Thus if we exclude the possibility of the short-run demand for sugar increasing because of factors such as war, expectations of war, political revolutions, there is good reason for believing that there will be no long-run secular increases in demand.

Additional disadvantageous factors are also prevalent. Up to the present time about 18 per cent of the total supplies of sugar (imports plus domestic production) entering the British Market is re-exported to other Commonwealth countries, notably in Africa. Recently, however, sugar production has been intro-duced in several African countries, e.g. Nigeria, Ghana, and the Sudan where it is expected to reach levels sufficient to satisfy domestic requirements, and leave a small surplus for exports.[1] Since Africa is one of the few regions in the world where sugar consumption is growing rapidly, it would appear that these developments are likely to remove one of the most dynamic elements in the United Kingdom demand. There are thus overwhelming reasons for believing that in the world market outside the United Kingdom, Canada, and the United States, Guyana is not a favoured producer. Her competitive position is weak and she has difficulties of access to these markets especially in the European Community. There is a slight possibility of exploiting the Eastern European market, but in this sphere competition from Cuba would be strong. Thus if the over-all world market structure remains unaltered, and provided there are no significant shifts in quota allocations, the long-run rate of growth of world demand is unlikely to be more than 1·5 per cent per annum.[2]

The sugar industry has distinguished itself in Guyana for its efficiency and its ability to make the best use of scarce resources of land and water. In view of the fact that the real limit to the rapid expansion of the industry in the long run is the sluggish-ness of demand, it may be worth considering whether the capacity to use resources efficiently should not be harnessed and put at the disposal of other forms of agrarian activity. For one of the most damaging criticisms levelled against sugar produc-tion in Guyana is that it has always been bedevilled by a plantation mentality.[3] The government intends to persuade the

[1] *Commodity Trade*, p. 517.
[2] F.A.O. Commodity Survey 1963, p. 95.
[3] *Dumont Report*, p. 9.

sugar companies to give assistance with the development of the technical side of peasant cane farming, and thereby dissipate the political clouds that hang over plantation sugar in Guyana.

Peasant Cane Farming

Peasant cane farming contributes only about 2 per cent of total factory capacity in the territory, and contrasts sharply with Trinidad and Jamaica where the contributions are some 35 and 50 per cent respectively. Acreage in Guyana's peasant cane farming has increased from 3,012 acres in 1960 to 3,204 acres in 1963, and thence to 3,481 acres in 1964. An account of the total acreage and production for the period 1960–4 is given below:

TABLE 24

ACREAGE AND PRODUCTION UNDER PEASANT CANE FARMING 1960–4

Year	1960	1961	1962	1963	1964
Farmers (acreage)	3,012	3,219	3,021	3,024	3,481
Production (tons)	9,508	8,164	8,490	9,600	8,606

Source: Annual Reports of the Department of Agriculture.

The argument put forward in government circles is that peasant cane farming may be desirable despite the downward trend in the world market price for sugar; the fact that in both Trinidad and Jamaica peasant cane farming has existed for several years alongside plantation cultivation is taken as evidence that there is much room for participation by Guyanese peasant farmers in such a large section of the agricultural economy.[1] The authorities seem unmindful of the fact that in effecting the shift they are running the risk of lowering yields, but argue that by enlisting the technical support of the sugar

[1] Although it is difficult to defend this move from a strictly economic standpoint, it has grave social and political repercussions, as in Trinidad. Here sugar is being produced at about half the established criterion of efficiency, the chief reason being the high percentage of peasant cultivation and consequent low yields, and it seems possible that substantial economies would result from a reduction in the number of peasants growing cane, a corresponding increase in the number and size of large properties, and a higher over-all efficiency for the island as a whole.

companies they would inculcate a high level of technical super-
vision in order to ensure the observance of good husbandry.
Among the principal constraints on the expansion of scientific
farming on the coast was the fact that the farmers were un-
trained in proper techniques of land preparation, water control,
crop cultivation, and farm management. The framework of
local administration cannot be easily and quickly adjusted so
that the technical services required by the rural economy can
be provided through them. The assumption seems to be that
the severity of these constraints could be mitigated in the short
run if the sugar estates were to be induced on the one hand to
devote more attention to crops other than sugar, and on the
other hand to utilize their equipment and personnel to assist
in the training of farmers,[1] wherever these steps can be undertaken without a decline in the output and technical efficiency
of sugar production.

4. *Livestock*

The livestock sector of Guyanese agriculture deserves special
attention for several important reasons. It ought to play an important role in the quest of diversification of the agricultural
sector, and thus reduce the country's precarious reliance on
sugar and rice.[2] Not only can its development bolster export
earnings, but a significant amount of foreign exchange could
be conserved by the practice of import substitution in this
direction. Finally, although the average calorific consumption
in Guyana averages 2,580 calories per head per day, the *per*

---

[1] The sugar estates will also be expected to release some of the large tracts of
their unused lands for peasant cane farming. Of the 178,000 acres occupied by the
estates, the area under cane averages 95,000 acres. The rest is being used for other
purposes including rice, pastures, coconuts, etc. 3·38 per cent of the total area is
under rice, 15·28 per cent under pastures, 10·6 per cent uncultivated, and 8·85 per
cent leased. Under these four uses the total area involved is 67,800 acres or
38·13 per cent of the plantation area. Thus more than two-thirds of the area under
cane is being used for purposes other than cane production. This means that over
67,000 acres could be released for peasant cane farming with the co-operation of
the sugar companies.

[2] In recommending massive investments in rice under the 1960–4 Development
Programme Berrill drew attention to the need 'to diversify farming away from the
traditional and quick yielders such as rice . . . onto slower providers such as
dairying and beef cattle', *Berrill Report*, p. 10.

capita intake of protein is low, the average intake of animal proteins is 16 grammes per head per day.

Livestock rearing is concentrated in three zones: the coastal belt, the intermediate savannahs, and the hinterland savannahs adjoining Brazil, locally known as the Rupununi. Table 25 below gives an estimate of the total number of livestock between 1953 and 1964. The figures are rather unimpressive considering the size of the country. Except for the cattle in the Rupununi, most of the livestock is concentrated on the coast. Stock raising on the coastal plain is mainly of the 'East Indian' type, the animals being held more or less for tradition's sake

TABLE 25
NUMBER OF LIVESTOCK 1953–64
(*Thousands*)

	1953	1954	1955	1956	1957	1958
Cattle	170	167	—	164	—	172
Pigs	22	22	37	—	—	37
Sheep	41	39	37	—	—	36
Goat	10	13	12	—	—	12
Poultry	423	485	—	110	—	—

	1959	1960	1961	1962	1963	1964
Cattle	175	160	180	220	270	302
Pigs	20	20	40	40	50	66
Sheep	40	40	45⎱	72	⎰54	87
Goat	12	10	15⎰		⎱18	32
Poultry	312	398	1,000	—	1,444	2,560

Source: Agricultural Statistics of Guyana.

and are maintained as a form of savings against the time when an urgent need for cash may arise. In this context numbers count more than productivity and capital more than current income.[1]

Only a few landlords keep large herds, though most of the

[1] The high proportion of East Indian farmers on the coast helps to explain why the 'Hindu sacred cow' might have become a permanent feature of cattle rearing on the coast. For explanation of religious and prestige significance of keeping cattle, see E. T. C. Epstein, *Economic Development and Social Change in South India* (Manchester University Press, 1962).

cattle belong to small farmers, who graze their cattle mainly on rice fields in out-of-crop seasons and on the saline front lands. This form of stock raising produces mainly meat but in such small quantities that there is very little economic incentive to stimulate its development. Furthermore the Guyanese farmer is foremost a crop grower, not a livestock farmer. Thus as soon as a piece of land is drained, he would never dream of establishing an improved pasture, but would immediately turn it into a paddy field. In this situation, the cattle graze on unnutritious grasses and poor pastures, cane tops from sugar estates which can provide an important fodder is buried in the ground, rice bran and molasses are exported, and rice straw, which constitutes the chief cattle fodder in certain countries, is burnt. Recent computations show that in the most favourable parts of the coastal belt, the yield is not more than $20 per acre per year.

The attitude of farmers to sheep, pigs, and other forms of livestock in the coastal area is no different, though with the establishment of a government ham and bacon factory, the government intends to pursue a more enlightened policy in pig production. In livestock products the most important commodities are milk and eggs. The production of milk is increasing, though there has been no decrease in the import of milk products owing to consumer preference for condensed and dried milk. The government is however contemplating the production of condensed and dried milk in its milk-pasteurization plant in the near future. In poultry the production of chicken is expanding rapidly, but imports continue to rise. There seems to be an expanding demand for chicken in the country and expanding production may well replace imports in the future. Average production of eggs in the past few years has been 1,300,000 dozens and imports averaged 19,500 dozens. This output of eggs is not satisfactory; farmers are more interested in producing meat than eggs. Although the present government is determined to embark on a programme of increasing production of pigs poultry and other livestock, there is a significant lack of thought regarding the improvement of cattle for dairy and meat production on the coast.

The following computations are therefore intended to fill the gap in one field. If we assume that the country's population will be over 770,000 by 1970, and set a modest target of one-third of a pint of milk per person per day by 1970, the total intake of milk in that year will be nearly 12,000,000 gallons. The present consumption of one-sixth of a pint per man per day is approximately 4,374,000 gallons, with roughly a half of this quantity produced locally. Thus by 1970, the required increase will be well over 7,000,000 gallons. The setting up of small farmsteads on the coast may go a long way towards solving the problem. In this case a 16-acre farm would be an economic unit, and around 130 acres per year can be absorbed into dairy farming. Although the effect on initial employment may not be substantial, there is a possibility of added employment in the marketing and distribution side. The results of the computations are given in Table 26. An expansion of dairy farming will therefore give the farmer an income higher than he can earn from many of the alternative forms of agriculture pursued in the country.

TABLE 26
REQUIREMENT, INCOME, AND EXPENDITURE (DAIRY CATTLE)

Requirement	Expenditure	$	Income	$
Stock	*Feed* 13,400 lb. @ $7·75		7,200 gal. milk	
12 cows . . . 12 acres	per 100 lb.	1,038	@ $0·60	4,320
2 heifer calves . . .	Grazing 16 acres @ $12		2 fat cows	
1½ acres	per acre	192	@ $140	280
2 yearlings . . .	Labour 300 man days		12 calves	
1½ acres	@ $3·00	900	@ $10·00	120
Total acreage . . .16	2 replacements at cost of			
Feed: 10 cwt.	rearing	324		
per cow per acre	Miscellaneous, minerals	240		
	Total expenditure	2,694	Total annual	4,720
	Total profit	$2,026		
	Profit per acre	$126·25		

There are two possibilities of increasing beef production on the coast, based on two possible systems of rearing cattle. System I embraces farmers who do not merely want to keep grazing animals or rear cattle, but who have a small acreage of grass on their holdings. Under this plan the farmer with government assistance buys one-year-old Friesan steers and sells them fat off grass at two and a half years of age. By that time the steers should weigh 1,200 pounds live and dress out about 58 per cent of 696 pounds of beef. Again, although the employment potential is small, there is much scope for profit. Computations are given below in Table 27.

TABLE 27

PROFITABILITY—BEEF CATTLE (SMALL FARM)

PER YEAR

Cost	$	Income	$
1 steer, 1 year old	120	1 fat steer, 696 lb. beef	
1½ acres grazing	18	@ 34¢ per lb.	236·64
3 man days	9		
Transport	10		
Miscellaneous	5		
Total costs	164	Total income	236·64

Profit $72·64 per year or $48·32 per acre.

Under Plan II the optimal size will be 100-acre cattle farms, with labour requirements of 514 man-days per 100 acres per year. It is reasonable to assume that 2 men working full time would be employed on this type of farm. Under this system the possibilities of beef production are much greater than the first case. A carrying capacity of one adult animal per acre is assumed, and it is therefore estimated that 100 acres would carry 40 breeding cows, 2 bulls, 38 calves, 38 yearlings, and 38 fattening stock. A herd life of 8 years of the breeding cows is assumed. It would therefore be necessary to retain 6 heifers every year as replacement, and to dispose of 5 bull cows. The extra heifers would allow for death or the possibility of one of the replacements not breeding. The calculations in Table 28 would apply in this case. The estimated yield from these 100-acre farms is approximately 230 pounds per acre per annum. About 180 persons would be employed each year, and this expanded production would help to cope with the beef requirements for local consumption and exports.

Alternative possibilities for the development of a beef and dairy industry exist in the intermediate zone just behind the

TABLE 28
PROFITABILITY—BEEF CATTLE (LARGE FARM)
PER YEAR

Expenditure	$	Income	$
Rent	20·00	19 fat steers 696 lb. @ 34¢ per lb.	4,496·16
Grazing 100 acres @ $12·00	1,200·00	13 fat heifers 522 lb. @ 34¢ per lb.	2,307·24
Medicine, minerals, vet, feed	500·00	5 cows 560 lb. @ 30¢	840·00
Total expenditure	3,632·00	Total income	7,643·40

Profit $4,011·40 or $40·11 per acre.

coast. Within this forest area there are grasslands which total several thousand square miles. The largest block, the intermediate savannahs at Ebini show that these savannahs enjoy some technical and economic advantages for the production of beef and dairy products.[1]

The above remarks give us some idea as to how the intermediate savannahs may be developed.

Finally let us look at the third main area of cattle production. The northern and southern Rupununi savannah where cattle is raised covers an area of at least 2 million acres, which feed about 40,000 head of cattle. The population of the Rupununi is about 10,000. There are three types of ranchers in the area: the Amerindians with an estimated 1,600–800 head of cattle of which 4–5,000 are in Annai and 1,200 in Massara and Yacarinta. Secondly there are 12 ranchers each with an average of 900-1,000 head of cattle, and about 50 small ranchers with less than 50 animals each. Thirdly there is the Rupununi Development Corporation with a holding of 2,000 square miles carrying 24,000 head of cattle. The ranching in the Rupununi is characterized by a long dry season, by heavy rains in winter causing extensive floods, and by inherently poor soils giving poor vegetation. The carrying capacity is an average of 10 to 15

---

[1] For an account of a possible investment strategy for beef and dairy products in the area see my *Planning for Economic Development in Guyana* (University of Guyana, 1967).

cattle per acre. In practice grazing is done on only 10 per cent of the land. In recent years the cattle population has been ravaged by rabies and foot-and-mouth disease, and to improve conditions a cattle-breeding station has been established at St. Ignatius two miles south of Lethem. It has been found difficult to improve the botanical composition of the grasses. Fertilizing is too expensive, but there exists some possibility of growing pangola grass for sick animals, of weaning calves at an early stage, castrating young bulls, and spaying females. At present there is over-slaughtering and indiscriminate slaughtering, whereby the farmer kills cows in calf. Management is rudimentary, there is no plan for slaughtering and the weeding out of bad bulls, and the ranching business is regarded as a 'bank book': if money is needed one rounds up some animals for slaughtering. A careful system of input and output is still beyond some farmers.

The present problems facing the area are really a hangover of its organizational and historical development. The settlement of the Rupununi was started in the 1880s. The cattle produced was shipped to Manaoa in Brazil, which was then a rich centre for balata collecting. This practice ceased when the balata boom subsided, as balata was more or less replaced by the rubber produced in Malaya and Indonesia around the First World War. New markets had to be found, and after 1919 a cattle trail was opened up to drive the animals to the Berbice River where they were loaded on ships to Rosignol and thence by train to Georgetown as a substitute for the Manaoa market. The cattle trail, which was only in part passable by heavy motor transport, functioned until 1959 when the government closed it because of escalating costs of upkeep.

Since 1943 and up to 1957 the trade in cattle from the Rupununi was controlled by the Livestock Control Committee. From 1957 when the meat trade was decontrolled, the marketing of Rupununi beef was taken over by Meat Marketing Ltd., a farmers' organization which organizes the slaughtering and sale of cattle. Although this organ has the responsibility of promoting efficiency, increased productivity, and so on in the industry, its achievements have been far from spectacular. The profitability of the industry is extremely low and there still remains much room for improvement in ranching.

In general there exists a case for more intensive methods in Rupununi cattle rearing, with the application of better management techniques. But the soils are reputed for their low fertility, and any attempt to develop these areas further would require large amounts of fertilizer such as lime and nitrogen. It would clearly be unprofitable to use fertilizer on such a large scale unless the cost of marketing and moving the produce would be fairly low in proportion to the value of the product. The problems of transport and communications are particularly difficult in this area. In addition there would be need for the provision of large-scale drainage facilities. In view of this the Rupununi should be accorded a low public investment priority, at least in the short run.

5. *Other Agriculture*

Coconuts: In planted area and value of product, coconuts occupy third place in the country's agricultural production. They are not too important however, as the coconut industry contributes only about 2 per cent of the gross income from agriculture. About 87 per cent of all coconut palms are grown on estates or in small solid plantings; the remainder are found scattered on house lots and along dykes and canals. The total acreage under cultivation showed a slight increase from 31,000 acres in 1953 to 40,000 in 1964, while the number of nuts collected did not show any significant change; the number collected in 1953 was 51,600,000 and in 1964 the figure was 53,026,400.[1] Yields per acre as well as being low, have actually declined over the period. Thus although coconut palms cover large areas, production remains entirely insufficient, and the extremely low yield per acre explains the state of neglect that has characterized the industry throughout its history.[2]

Many of the coconuts are grown on former sugar estates and enjoy the same drainage system. The best plantations are on the coastal sand reefs, but the palm is also found on the heavier coastal clay and riverbank silt, where it requires effective drain-

---

[1] Ministry of Agriculture, Guyana.
[2] In contrast with the situation in Jamaica and British Honduras, Guyana is outside the area regularly devastated by hurricanes, which should make these plantations more interesting.

age to thrive. The health of the palms is extremely poor, and is affected by wilt disease and by the coconut caterpillar which causes considerable defoliation. Standards of cultivation are poor, and only minimum care and attention is given. There is very little weeding and drainage is insufficient. The general economic conditions of the plantations are probably inferior to those in Malaya and other South Asian countries. Yields reflect the conditions of cultivation. A comparison of returns from one of the better plantations in Guyana with corresponding data from Ceylon illustrates the deficiency. From Table 29 it is evident that the average for Guyana as a whole is even lower than the example chosen. The oil content of the local copra is comparable with yields elsewhere, but the low copra content of the nut is not.[1] Coconuts produced other than for domestic use are directed into three or four main avenues—the production of copra, crude oil, margarine, and soap, and the sale of coconut milk for drinking. Exports are negligible since all production is

TABLE 29

COMPARATIVE COCONUT RETURNS OF GUYANA
AND CEYLON[a]

	Guyana plantation	Ceylon in undulating and hilly manured sandy loam
No. of nuts per ton of copra	7,000	4,500–5,500
No. of nuts per tree	50	75–100
No. of palm trees per acre	55	40–50
No. of nuts per acre	2,750	4,000–4,500
Kgs. of copra per acre	390	780–900

[a] International Bank for Reconstruction and Development, *Economic Development of British Guiana*, p. 161.

[1] New plantings which were started under the 1960–4 Development programme are still being carried out. Recent experiments made at the Coconut Palm Station at Port Bouet, Ivory Coast, have shown the great advantage of planting dwarf hybrid varieties with higher yields, a shorter period before bearing, and smaller trees. Experimentation with other types of palms might prove useful. However, experimentation along the Ivory Coast lines would raise the problem of thefts. The addition of nitrogen and potassium in that country tripled yields of the young selected plants and doubled those of the old plantations. Jamaica has also obtained highly successful results by setting up pilot plantations throughout the whole of the eastern part of the island.

needed for local consumption which has continuously increased with the growth of population.

The demand for copra and oil products does not exceed supply.[1] This applies to the world market as a whole, but nearer home in the West Indies the possibility of developing an export market is also negligible. Oil manufacture has been encouraged in most of the countries of the Commonwealth Caribbean, where the coconut palm is widely cultivated. An oil mill and a soap factory were set up in Jamaica in 1932 and a glycerine plant was set up a few years later.[2] Other factories in excess of local requirements were created privately so that by the beginning of the Second World War the total production of the factories was about eight times the demand of the local population.[3] A hurricane in 1944 led to the consolidation of the industry and by 1961 there were only two factories. The capacities of these had however outgrown the local supplies of copra and imports were obtained from Trinidad.[4] Since then coconut production has expanded and the Jamaican market for copra appears to be small,[5] while the demand for externally produced oil is negligible. Self-sufficiency in vegetable oils has also been achieved to some extent in Trinidad, while oil- and soap-manufacturing industries exist in Barbados. The main difference between the West Indian factories and those set up in the producing countries in Asia is that whereas the latter can count on a large and expanding domestic market for their products, the West Indian market for oil and oil products is very limited.

There is, however, more scope for expansion to cater for the home market, to take account of the growing population, and for reasons of import substitution.[6]

---

[1] F.A.O. Commodity Reports: *Fats and Oils*, Rome, Sundry Years.

[2] C. Leubeuscher, *Processing of Colonial Raw Materials* (London, 1951).

[3] *Report on Agriculture in the West Indies*, Col. No. 8182.

[4] The Oils and Fats Agreement regulate the allocation of available copra between territories and fixes the price of copra and manufactured products.

[5] In 1960 Jamaica imported 32·8 tons of copra (*Annual Report of the Government of Jamaica*, 1961). This is equivalent to the produce of 160 acres of Guyana's coconuts.

[6] Because the price of W.I. copra is fixed, the import prices (which include freight charges) is slightly higher than the local price. Local manufacturers of oil therefore prefer to buy locally produced copra. However, the main manufacturer of margarine and soap, Sterling Products, has been forced to rely on imports because of a shortage in the local supply. Thus in addition to importation of copra, imports of oil have been significant. If present local production is not increased,

The production of other crops, viz, coffee, cocoa, corn, citrus, bananas and other fruits, provision crops, fresh vegetables, and so on, has been insignificant. Domestic demand for these commodities is met mainly from imports. In fact these are the commodities on which the diversification of the country's agriculture and the development of its agricultural potential, especially in the brown sands of the intermediate zone, depends.[1] There is increased awareness of this in government circles and the Department of Agriculture is at present experimenting with various types of legumes and vegetables whose export potential is very considerable.

Cocoa is not manufactured in Guyana and processing is carried no further than fermenting and drying of cocoa beans. Leubeuscher[2] has pointed out that the decisive factor influencing the present location of the industries is climate. She argues that in no tropical country has the storage of raw cocoa so far been found practicable for any length of time, and as regards the manufacture of chocolate, storage of the finest product under tropical conditions presents even greater difficulties. She also points out that in Australia the Cadbury-Pascal-Fry Company chose in 1921 to site its factory in Hobart because of the cooler climate in Tasmania, rather than on the Australian mainland, although the former site has disadvantages from an economic point of view. Trinidad is one of the few territories that has set up a plant for manufacturing chocolate for both the domestic market and exports. In view of the above consideration and the fact that cocoa production is highly susceptible to the fluctuation of world market prices, cocoa production in Guyana must be primarily for the local market, and if export possibilities are contemplated, this must take the form of export of the raw material.

In the case of coffee, the average yield per acre in Guyana is 500 pounds, and as there were over 3,000 acres of coffee in the country in 1964, it is capable of producing over 1·5 million

---

and if a 3 per cent annual rate of consumption is projected, in 1970 Guyana would import well over 1,000,000 gallons of edible oil equivalent to over 20,000,000 pounds of copra, or 23,000 acres of land under coconuts. The extension of the area under coconuts or other palms would therefore meet a real internal demand.

[1] *Report of the Guyana Marketing Corporation*, 1965.

[2] *The Processing of Colonial Raw Materials.*

pounds of coffee beans annually, when the whole of the area begins to yield.[1] As green coffee loses about 16 per cent of its weight in the roasting process, the potential yield is well over 1,200,000 pounds of roasted coffee per year. However, very little coffee is consumed locally, and the possibilities of expanding production are not rosy. Short-run demand is highly inelastic and, unlike coffee supply, world coffee consumption does not vary much from year to year.[2] Guyana's producers should therefore concentrate on the home market. No extension of the area is recommended, for any increase in local demand that might arise as a result of increased population could be met by better production practices.

Late in 1965 a 5,000-acres banana pilot project was set in motion with the arrival of 125,000 banana suckers from the Cameroons in a new investment project to be undertaken by Elders and Fyffes. It is expected that this new private foreign investment would help to promote the project by providing one half of the G$3·4 million needed to set the banana industry going, and providing jobs for over 2,500 persons.

In the light of evidence that the cashew nut has a large outlet on dollar markets, its oil being in heavy demand, and since it can grow on poor savannah lands, with about 1,000 tons per year needed to supply a small shelling plant, the government should set up two trial plantations, one intensive with experimental use of fertilizer in quite removed areas along the Berbice River and on the very poor intermediate savannahs, and the other, extensive, without fertilizer, in the Rupununi savannahs. It is hoped that these projects will provide adequate knowledge on which to base the choice of a location for a possible shelling plant in the future.

In the drive for further diversification trials should be started of pineapples, peanuts, and tobacco, and attempts should be made to develop citrus fruits. But all these developments, if trials prove positive, should be organized, planned, and executed around processing plants. Lowering of collection costs would make competition possible, even under slightly unfavourable natural conditions, assuming always that technology is of the highest quality. Peanuts grown on sandy soils would

[1] *Report of the Guyana Marketing Corporation,* 1965.
[2] F.A.O. Commodity Reports.

provide in addition oilcakes, with a high protein content, both for direct human consumption and for animal feed, especially for milch cows, swine, and poultry.

The problem of fisheries has also been neglected for some time. Intensive fish breeding would be technically possible in the lakes, reservoirs, and canals, if the fishing could be properly controlled. The potential for sea fishing, including the very lucrative red-snapper fishing, seems far greater than present production. There still remains a large unsatisfied local demand, and there are possibilities for export promotion. Added to this, cheap fish flour could first supplement the human diet, especially that of children, pregnant and nursing women, and also provide cheap proteins for pigs and poultry.

6. *Forestry*

The forests of Guyana are estimated to cover 70,000 square miles or approximately 84 per cent of the total area, but the contribution of forests to national income has averaged only 3 per cent for the period 1953 to 1964. Its contribution to employment has also been disproportionately small. Only two and a half million acres of forests are under lease and perhaps no more than half of this is under exploitation. Thus the natural forests are very underutilized. For example, in 1960, production from 2,624,474 acres which were under lease was 10,228,324 cubic feet of timber, fuel wood, and wood for charcoal. This is equivalent to 3·89 cubic feet per acre. If all the exploitable forests are considered (13,500 square miles or 8,640,000 acres) average production would be as low as 1·18 cubic feet per acre.[1] Although the forests are the most visible and extensive form of potential wealth that the country possesses, they have not as yet become an important contributor to her economy.

The more intensive local utilization and the finding of profitable outlets for her forest wealth are two main ways in which the government can promote the economic development of the country. In the words of a recent F.A.O. Report:

It is accordingly not difficult to define the forestry problem: how to raise the output and bring the forests' contribution to the country's economy to a level more in keeping with their size. The solution

[1] *Annual Reports* of the Forest Department, Georgetown, 1960, 1961.

is in no way easy, particularly as with a small population and consequently a limited market, any substantial increase in production must depend upon obtaining new and bigger markets overseas for whatever the forests can produce, either in raw or preferably in the manufactured state.[1]

Thus the main problems surrounding the exploitation of Guyana's forests arise because of their physical or economic inaccessibility.

It must be borne in mind that the rather substantial forests of Guyana form only a relatively small part of the tropical and sub-tropical hardwoods of Latin America. Brazil alone has three and a half times more forest area than has Europe. Argentina, Colombia, and Peru together possess about the same area of forests as the United States of America, while Bolivia's forest area is as great as that of Finland and Sweden put together. The fact that the countries of the northern hemisphere referred to above have thriving wood products industries whereas in tropical regions these industries are relatively unimportant is due, in no small measure, to the special and contrasting characteristics between the forests of the former and those in the tropics. The salient features of the forests of Guyana that help to explain why only limited use has been made of them so far are the following. The immense variety of tree species create a highly complex and heterogeneous forest. The forests average 30 to 60 different tree species per acre and 100 to 120 per square mile.[2] This makes the accumulation and marketing of single species difficult and expensive. Secondly, there is a wide variation in intensity as well as physical and chemical qualities of the various species. The physical properties of the trees, unlike similar types in other tropical forests, are of relatively small diameter, and even though possessing high strength qualities, the wood produced by many species is very hard and heavy, thus increasing the difficulty of felling the trees, transporting the logs, and using the timber finally produced.

Another drawback lies in the pattern of highly selective logging practised together with extremely dense stands and this

[1] T. I. Rees, *Forestry Inventory Report to the Government of British Guiana*, Report No. 1762, F.A.O. (Rome, 1962), p. 16.
[2] T. I. Rees, *Forest Inventory Report to the Government of British Guiana*.

has tended to make logging costs high. The high cost of extraction and poor utilization are a direct result of the practice whereby less than half a dozen species were removed in appreciable quantities. This is mainly a result of historical growth of exploitation mainly around the two species of Crabwood and Greenheart which in the earlier days were felled in sufficient quantities to meet the small demand, with the result that both these species are now becoming rare, with progressively increasing costs of production as the search proceeds more inland. This inward movement is also representative of the fact that there has always been a lack of precise knowledge in respect of merchantable volumes of all worthwhile species including Greenheart and Crabwood. This deficiency has contributed to the impossibility of formulating any real or systematic plan for the progressive utilization of the forest resources. These defects became especially severe in the 1960s when large-scale capital investments in this sector were being contemplated. Other problems arise from the lack of storage facilities. Storage timber is attacked by micro-organisms which destroy the cellulose, a difficulty which is germane to the problem of physical inaccessibility reflected in the lack of roads and water transportation, the latter hampered by rapids and water falls.

The 1954–9 Development Programme was intended to take most of these difficulties into account. As a result of the recommendations made by the I.B.R.D. Mission in 1952,[1] a development programme was commenced in 1954, and by 1959 expenditure under the various schemes was as follows:

TABLE 30

PUBLIC EXPENDITURE ON FORESTS 1954–9[a]

Scheme	Expenditure
1. Additional temporary staff	110,000
2. Staff training	20,300
3. Timber appraisals	88,200
4. Improvement of silviculture	125,400
5. Central timber manufacturing plant	288,000
	631,900

[a] Development Estimates as passed by the Legislative Council.

[1] I.B.R.D., *Economic Development of British Guiana.*

The plan for the improvement in silviculture included research work on the natural regeneration of Greenheart, silvicultural operations to improve exploited forests, and the establishment of timber plantations. These operations were hampered by the lack of skilled and trained professional as well as subordinate field staff. It was also found that extensive treatment was useless for the regeneration of Greenheart forests, and since more intensive methods had to be used, costs per unit were consequently higher than had been expected. However, Greenheart was successfully regenerated on a small scale and *Pinus Caribaea* introduced into experimental plantations.

The establishment of the Central Timber Manufacturing Plant was considered to be the most important scheme in the entire forestry development programme. It was to act as a central manufacturing and marketing agency for sawmillers, to guarantee a fair price and cut out middlemen, to popularize as many kinds of timber as possible, to encourage the use of seasoned timber, to establish the practice of grading, and to replace imported softwood (conifers) by the production of local softwood (light hardwood) lumber of comparable quality. The undertaking was beset by innumerable difficulties springing from the fact it was supposed to operate as a quasi-commercial undertaking. It was beset by uncertainty in the supply of lumber, poor quality, high prices, consumer resistance, and numerous and organized frauds. If the 1950s witnessed the recognition of the problem facing this sector, the 1960s brought further investigation into the nature of these problems, with determined attempts at obtaining solutions.[1] The two most important problems from the point of view of economic development lie in the direction of timber trade and the further utilization of Guyanese timber in the development of a viable timber industry and the manufacture of commodities that use timber as a raw material.

[1] By 1964 it had become obvious that the prime need was for a well-planned programme of forest survey, and investigation and research into the most suitable methods of extracting, processing, and marketing forest products. Because of the financial and technical burden of such a programme, it was incorporated into an application for assistance from the U.N. Special Fund. These arrangements have now been finalized, but between 1961 and 1964 technical assistance was obtained from the F.A.O. of the U.N. on various measures including forest inventory, marketing, and utilization of wood and wood products.

The average value of timber exports for the period 1952–61 was $3,825,000 while the average value of imports was $3,679,000, and an adverse balance of trade was registered for most years in this sector. Table 31 shows imports and exports of wood products for the year 1961, which has been selected because it highlights the adverse balance of trade in the sector, and because it gives ample proof of the unsatisfactory state of the wood and wood products industry in Guyana. In only one year a favourable balance of $414,414 in 1960 was converted into an unfavourable balance of $76,723. The reasons for the small margin of exports over imports on average must be examined in detail.

In the past, exports of piling, sawn timber, and hewn timber have been almost exclusively of Greenheart which is relatively limited in quantity, and species other than Greenheart, which are relatively numerous, have hardly been touched either for export or local use. It is believed that Greenheart was first exported from Guyana in about 1770 since which time it has become one of the well-known timbers in the world. The value of Greenheart exports has been rising steadily until 1958 when it reached a figure of $3,276,500. Greenheart is indeed the goose that lays the golden export egg. This is further demonstrated in Table 32 below which shows the f.o.b. export value of Greenheart and other timbers exported for the years 1955–61. It also shows that very nearly all the export eggs were in one basket.

It could be argued that as the export value of Greenheart is so high, everything should be done to export every cubic foot possible. But what militates against this is that Greenheart is the most commonly used of all timbers within Guyana itself, and many thousands of tons annually are used quite unnecessarily within the country. This is proved in Table 33 which shows the production of round timber from government forests. It will be seen that the production of Greenheart in round was 67,184 tons of 50 cubic feet converted to 85,525 tons of 50 cubic feet according to Hoppus measure. If we deduct from this 8,937 tons for piling, and 4,399 tons of hewn because these items are exported in the round (hewn being counted as round for technical reasons), this leaves 72,189 tons round. Assuming that 3,000 tons of this is required for essential wharf construction

13—E.D.G.

TABLE 31

IMPORTS AND EXPORTS (DOMESTIC PRODUCE ONLY) OF WOOD AND WOOD PRODUCTS FOR THE YEAR 1961

Kind of produce	Unit	IMPORTS		EXPORTS	
		Quantity	Value $	Quantity	Value $
Fuelwood	Tons weight	1	281	1,316	9,524
Charcoal	„	×	103	4,738	236,500
Sawlog and veneer logs (non-conifer)	Tons of 50 cu. ft.	7,083	81,111	2,408	54,414
Piling (non-conifers)	„	—	—	6,512	472,386
Poles and posts (non-conifer)	„	(a) 142	2,110	3,117	254,459
Sleepers	„	—	—	153	11,894
Sawn timber (conifer)	„	1,458	215,244	—	—
Sawn timber (non-conifer)	„	×	152	9,185	1,617,858
Hewn timber (non-conifer)	„	—	—	5,731	586,258
Hewn timber (conifer)	„	—	—	—	—
Veneer sheets	„	8	7,800	—	—
Plywood	„	474	109,991	—	—
Fibreboards	„	946	124,847	312	53,606
Particle board and other reconstituted wood	—	—	22,698	(b)	2,542
Boxes, cases, etc.	—	—	589	(b)	40
Cooperage	—	—	439,834	(c)	4,050
Builders' woodwork (doors, etc. and shingles)	—	—	9,096	(c)	27,896
Other wood manufacturers	—	—	46,481	(d)	1,667

	Tons weight			
Newsprint paper	1,134	377,295	—	—
Other paper and paperboard	" 2,572	890,809	—	—
Articles made of paper and paperboard	" 2,255	1,639,794 (e)	1	1,651
Wood furniture and fixtures	—	189,010	—	2,103
Matches	—	2,160	—	45,834
Total all items	—	4,159,405	—	3,382,682
Prefabricated buildings	—	601,062	—	—
Metal furniture	—	933,861	—	16

BALANCE OF TRADE   Imports $4,159,405
Exports $3,382,682

$ 776,723 Excess of *Imports* over Exports.

Source: Annual Account Relating to External Trade 1961, Department of Customs and Excise, Georgetown. × Quantity too small to record; (a) Not known, probably conifer from Canada or U.S.A.; (b) probably all local made particle board; (c) Not known; (d) of which $27,840 was shingles; (e) made locally from imported material presumably.

TABLE 32
EXPORT VALUE OF GREENHEART AND OTHER TIMBERS 1955–61
(Figures in thousands of dollars)

Kind of produce		1955	1956	1957	1958	1959	1960	1961
Piling	Greenheart	553·2	704·8	634·7	496·1	447·7	680·2	471·3
	Others	2·7	—	10·6	—	13·1	4·0	1·0
Sawn timber	Greenheart	1,359·9	1,351·9	1,488·3	1,714·6	1,822·4	1,940·5	1,513·3
	Others	101·8	133·3	156·7	138·3	146·8	133·4	116·4
Hewn timber	Greenheart	749·3	778·8	878·4	1,065·8	671·6	450·0	586·2
	Others	5·7	16·6	14·8	—	7·4	—	—
Total	Greenheart	2,648·4	2,834·6	3,001·4	3,276·5	2,941·7	3,070·7	2,570·8
	Others	110·2	149·9	182·1	138·3	167·3	137·4	117·4
Total Greenheart and others		2,758·6	2,984·5	3,183·5	3,414·8	3,109·0	3,208·1	2,688·2
Percent of Greenheart to total		96·0	94·9	94·3	95·9	94·6	95·7	95·6

Source: Annual Accounts relating to External Trade.

and repair within Guyana, this leaves 69,189 tons. 38,373 tons was consumed locally. Out of this 12,000 tons could have been exported. The important point here is that if this additional timber had remained in the forest it would have been available later, for *accessible* Greenheart is running out and supplies may be exhausted in about fifteen years from now. Thus the sooner the local consumer begins economizing on this species the better, for by using it quite unnecessarily now, he is merely hastening the day when there will not be any for export.[1]

Another noticeable tendency in the balance of trade is the import of what may be termed unnecessary items. In 1960 these included $287,076 of sawn conifer timber, $99,301 of plywood, $143,711 of fibreboards, $7,047 of particle board and other reconstituted wood, $190,866 of wood furniture and fixtures, $3,750 of boxes etc., $15,011 of builders' woodwork and $4,101 of other wood manufactures, a total of $700,943. There were also imports of unnecessary items of metal such as metal furniture and prefabricated metal houses totalling $1,352,841. The suggestion is not that all the unnecessary items could or should be replaced by locally grown wood, but it is considered that a considerable proportion of each item could be so replaced by the most suitable local substitutes.[2]

It has been argued that one of the chief obstacles to the local utilization of many tropical species is their lack of concentration, and the lack of availability in large enough quantities. This argument is valid only if it is intended to utilize individual timber species, but it is possible to utilize mixed tropical hardwoods by grouping species with similar characteristics, but these groupings should not be proposed without adequate knowledge of the timbers concerned.[3] Experience combined with research will show modifications in the grouping and will eventually show which groups are sufficiently homogeneous and comprise timbers of such a character as will be suitable for general utility purposes. The demand for new species is based

[1] C. O. Flemmich, *Report to the Government of British Guiana on the Marketing of Wood and Wood Products, with particular reference to the Export Timber*, F.A.O. Report No. 1737 (Rome, 1963), pp. 13, 32–3, 48.
[2] A detailed account of the possibilities for import substitution is given in the *Flemmich Report*, pp. 13–31.
[3] See B. J. Rendle, *Co-operative Research in the Development of the Empire's Timber Resources*, H.M. Forestry Commission Report 1947, C.M.N.D. 1947.

TABLE 33

PRODUCTION OF HARDWOOD TIMBER FROM GOVERNMENT FORESTS (LOGS, SPLITWOOD, AND ROUNDWOOD)

(Figures in tons of 50 cubic feet Hoppus measure)

No.	Kind of hardwood timber	Volume to nearest 2 tons (100 cu. ft.) Hoppus measure						
		1955	1956	1957	1958	1959	1960	1961
1	Greenheart	62,164	66,094	69,454	67,422	69,720	67,184	72,178
2	Crabwood	16,576	15,348	8,252	6,452	7,746	8,580	8,564
3	Mora	5,642	9,302	10,352	10,502	7,478	6,774	6,142
4	Wallaba	2,082	2,618	6,332	5,860	5,094	5,466	6,410
5	Dalli	2,706	2,332	2,238	1,786	2,498	3,294	1,968
6	Kereti	2,636	2,162	2,206	2,612	2,056	2,966	2,522
7	Purpleheart	1,018	956	1,542	1,116	1,278	1,946	1,566
8	Kabukalli	2,208	1,820	1,734	1,954	1,572	1,728	1,686
9	Kurokai	3,208	2,214	1,472	1,434	972	1,104	1,216
10	Kirikaua	490	760	2,422	2,092	830	1,086	2,094
11	Simarupa	1,210	856	1,036	576	512	974	762
12	Karahoro	252	506	×	688	×	818	1,202
13	Tauroniro	660	834	894	878	744	754	1,090
14	Duka	482	422	×	556	434	736	918
15	Silverballi	274	×	364	424	410	368	400
16	Locust	722	368	450	294	×	352	334
17	Futui	244	×	×	×	×	294	352
18	Bulletwood	252	380	300	490	302	286	×

19 Dukali	x	x	x	x	x	260	x
20 Red Cedar	270	418	x	x	x	x	284
21 Kurahara	848	x	x	x	x	x	x
22 Manniballi	546	292	436	398	x	x	x
23 Determa	358	x	x	x	x	x	x
24 White Cedar	258	x	x	256	x	x	284
25 Manni	x	564	502	284	x	x	x
Total all species *except* Greenheart[a]	44,994	49,894	45,500	42,966	35,232	40,056	40,322
Total all species	107,158	115,988	114,954	110,388	104,492	107,240	112,500
% Greenheart to total	58%	56·9%	60·4%	61·1%	66·4%	62·7%	64·1%

Source: Annual Reports of the Forest Department.

[a] Those named above plus those not named because the production of them was less than 12,000 cu. ft. (240 tons per year).

x Volume not shown because less than 12,000 cu. ft. (240 tons) per year, but their volume is included in the figure for 'total all species except Greenheart'.

on availability and the state of the economy. In Trinidad, where the economy has expanded rapidly, and where there is no particular high quality timber, almost all species are utilized. There is nothing inherent in the quality of tropical timbers therefore that should limit the intensity of utilization. The initiative should be taken by the government in its building programme of schools, hospitals, houses, and so on. This is important for two reasons.

Firstly, effective demand should be comparatively unaffected by fluctuations in price, and secondly the control of species used and exploited rests in the hands of the government. If instructions were issued to the relevant government departments insisting on the purchase of species other than Greenheart whenever possible, a more economic exploitation of forests would result.

Local consumption of timber bears no relation to price fluctuations and *per capita* income levels. *Per capita* consumption of timber in Guyana has been running at an average of 9·7 cubic feet for the period under review. But considering the country's forest potential, and the fact already mentioned of high imports of wood products and metal furniture, this average *per capita* consumption is very low. For example, in 1960 Trinidad's *per capita* consumption of sawn and industrial wood was 16·7 cubic feet, Jamaica 4·7, and Barbados 9·5.[1] Thus not only is there much scope for increased *per capita* consumption locally, but the further processing of these woods for export. In the natural forests of Guyana there are many beautifully textured and figured woods, which may have considerable potential for the manufacture of plywood.[2] Woods of this character are becoming relatively scarce and the prices of decorative

---

[1] *Yearbook of Forest Products Statistics 1959–60*, F.A.O. (Rome, 1961).

[2] An F.A.O./U.N.T.A.D. team from Yugoslavia in a report to the government of British Guiana suggested that there are excellent possibilities for the manufacture of veneer and plywood from local woods. D. Orescanin, S. Stankovic, V. Jelovac, and E. Hamberger, *Draft Report to the Government of British Guiana on Forest Inventory Development*, Ministry of Economic Affairs (Georgetown, 1965). However, seeing that in the past there have been conflicting reports on the suitability of local species, consideration should be given to a detailed feasibility study including all aspects of the problem—markets, raw materials, fuel and power, transport, technical suitability of locally produced veneers and plywood, production costs, site location. Consideration should also be given to the feasibility of

veneers and plywoods are high on the world market. A veneer and plywood plant would utilize such native species as Dalli, Crabwood, Silverballi, Red Cedar, Purpleheart, and others. This could be the first step towards the manufacture of integrated wood products.[1]

In the field of export promotion the Guyanese may try, as an initial gesture, to exploit the West Indian market. The West Indian islands are overpopulated and land hungry. The natural forest areas that they possess are, with the possible exceptions of Trinidad and Dominica and St. Lucia mainly of a protective nature, and are generally unproductive. Both Trinidad and Jamaica have afforestation schemes, but the returns they will receive when these schemes come to fruition will provide only a small amount of the timber and timber products that they will need.[2] At present their imports are mainly of coniferous timber from outside the area. Thus progress should be made in the substitution of net Caribbean softwood imports by Caribbean hardwood production. There is no intrinsic technical reason why Guyana's light and medium density hardwoods should not replace coniferous timber in these islands.

In recent years much attention has been given to the possibility of pulp and paper products. This has become necessary not only for reasons of import substitution on account of the high import figure of paper and paper products, but also because of the possibility of export promotion in this field.[3] Research on the possibilities of using tropical hardwood including species from Guyana for pulp and paper was commenced some thirty-five years ago.[4] There has been much discussion concerning the influence of wood structure on pulp

manufacturing a construction grade of plywood from some of the lighter species and from the Caribbean Pine material.

[1] *Report to the Government of British Guiana on Wood Utilisation in British Guiana* by J. A. Doyle, Head of the Wood Utilization and Anatomy Section at the Canadian Forest Products Laboratory, Ministry of Economic Affairs (Georgetown, 1965), pp. 4–5. Doyle also suggested that a small Forest Products Laboratory should be established.

[2] See M. N. Gallant, *Report to the Caribbean Commission on Forestry and the Timber Trade in the Caribbean Area*, F.A.O. Report No. 1060 (Rome, 1959).

[3] See *The Role of Forest Industries in the Attack on Economic Underdevelopment*, F.A.O. (Rome, 1962).

[4] P. Le Caheux, *Report to the Caribbean Commission on a Preliminary Pulp and Paper Survey*, F.A.O. Report No. 477 (Rome, 1956).

making and the quality of the product, and it was once generally held that tropical hardwoods were unsuitable for paper because of the shortness of their fibres. The reason for this preference for long fibres is probably historical and traditional. However, it must be noted that the world paper industry has developed from the use of rags with very long threads. After the last world war, however, when Sweden was short of long-fibred softwood, short-fibred birch was used on a large scale. Frankel,[1] a wood industrialist has stated that from the practical point of view the pulp maker is not concerned whether the fibre he gets from wood is of this or that type. Though it would influence the layout of the mill, and might influence their process and even the economics of their process, they must work with the raw material available. Rendle[2] has also averred that any statement about wood properties in relation to pulp quality is subject to qualification because so much depends on the way the wood is processed and on the end product that is required.

Finally, in the words of an F.A.O. Report:[3]

Research in British Guiana has shown that mixtures of hardwoods in the proportions in which they are found in the forests, give good pulp which can be used as a raw material to produce every grade of paper except those requiring high strength. A test of 56 commercial and non-commercial species from the tropical forests of Surinam showed that only one species was unsuitable for pulping and that mixtures of species from the wet as well as from the dry forests have good paper qualities. Twenty-one Amazon species have been tested in mixtures with successful results.

Thus it is clear that there are no technical reasons why pulp and paper cannot be manufactured from Guyana species. The remaining problems are mainly economic and environmental, and these two can be solved in the future through trial and experiment.[4]

[1] T. H. Frankel, 'Development of the Wood-Pulp Industry', Supplement to *Forestry* (Oxford University Press, 1960).

[2] B. J. Rendle, 'Anatomical Criteria for Industrial Use', Supplement to *Forestry* (Oxford University Press, 1961).

[3] *Pulp and Paper Prospects in Latin America*, F.A.O. (Rome, 1955), p. 20.

[4] The F.A.O./U.N.T.A.D. Team have confirmed this finding, but it was stated that no firm investment projects should be undertaken without a more detailed forest inventory and further research and experimentation. In the short run the

Interesting results have also been achieved in the experimental growing of Caribbean Pine, a non-indigenous species, although details of cost of commercially growing the species are not available. Despite the fact that most of the planting has taken place during the past eight years indications are that commercial pulpwood could be produced on a 15-year rotation with yields of from 3 to 4 cords per acre per year on suitable sites. This is an exceptional rate of growing, making the species potentially attractive as a source of pulpwood as well as for lumber and plywood. However, its ultimate suitability for pulpwood in Guyana will depend on the cost of growing, harvesting, and delivering it to a specific pulpmill site. These data should be available in a few years when the present plantations reach commercial size.

Bamboo may also have commercial value as a pulping raw material which could be grown commercially in Guyana. In other countries, notably India, Pakistan, Japan, and Burma, bamboo is extensively used.[1] In recent years modern pulp and paper plants utilizing 100 per cent bamboo have been established in Taiwan and Pakistan. It is reported that in tropical countries with a climate similar to that of Guyana, that bamboo when planted from seed can be harvested at the end of the sixth year and every three years thereafter. Silviculture experiments have indicated that a three-year rotation is generally the most satisfactory, and that yields of from 3 to 4 tons of dry fibre per acre per year are often obtained. In conclusion, on account of the great potential value of the pulp and paper industry detailed consideration should be given to the conducting of a feasibility study on the economic possibilities of producing pulp and paper from native species, Caribbean Pine and bamboo plantations or combinations of all these.

team considers that there exists a possibility of utilizing rice straw, sugar cane bagasse, and waste paper as raw materials for the paper industry. See Orescanin (et al.) *Report to the Government of British Guiana on Forest Inventory Development*, pp. 16–60.

[1] F.A.O. *Raw materials for More Paper*, F.A.O. (Rome, 1953).

IV

MINING

1. *Introduction*

The mineral resources of Guyana are not yet fully assessed. Heavy tropical rain forest has made mapping very difficult and the mantle of residual sands and clays resulting from conditions of deep tropical weathering obscures outcrops, so that surface observation is limited. The result is that although much of the interior has been reconnoitred by official geologists and geologists of mining companies, no intensive systematic geological exploration for development as a whole has yet been possible. The chief economic minerals of Guyana are bauxite, manganese, diamonds, and gold. Other mineral prospects include columbite, radioactive minerals, chrome ore (merumite), iron ore (laterites), natural gas, and petroleum. We begin our analysis of the mining sector by a brief discussion of the minerals other than bauxite. Bauxite has made the most significant contribution to the economy, and the greater part of this chapter will be devoted to it.

Diamonds

The first recorded discovery of diamonds in Guyana was in 1897 [1] but production did not commence before 1900 when some 4,891 stones weighing 740 carats were recovered. The geographical distribution of diamond placers in Guyana shows that the largest and the most valuable deposits are situated at the base of, and fanning outwards from, the Roraima mountains which are occupied by sandstones and conglomerates. The most interesting feature of diamond production in Guyana is that it has depended, along with about 80 per cent of gold production, solely on surface-washing manual methods by thousands

---

[1] *Annual Report of British Guiana*, 1923.

of small-scale operators or 'porknockers', scattered throughout the Potaro, Mazaruni, Cuyuni, and Rupununi drainages.

During the twenty years following the discovery of diamonds, production fluctuated to a very great extent, rising to a peak in 1923 when 1,141,423 stones weighing 214,474 carats were recovered.[1] After that, production declined steadily to only 15,442 carats in 1945 when it rose again to an average of 30,000 carats per year for the next twelve years. In 1959 production doubled owing to the discovery of deposits in the beds of the Kurupung and Ekreku Rivers above the escarpment level. This development led to a rush to prospect the upper reaches of other rivers and spectacular results were obtained from diving methods so that production rose still higher in 1960 and 1961, the value of production for the latter year being an all-time record for the local industry (see Table 1).

Attempts have been made in recent years by company ventures such as the Diamond Mining Corporation Ltd., Diamonds and Metals Exploration Company Inc., and the San Franciso Metals Company Limited, to use mechanical methods for the recovery of diamonds, but these methods have proved unsuccessful mainly because of boulders and buried timber and the consolidated nature of the gravels. Diving for diamonds has been recently introduced from Brazil, and this has become a very popular method of working river-bed deposits.

Gold

Gold occurs in alluvial deposits almost throughout the area of the crystalline basement in the northern part of Guyana and in a few areas in the southern part of the country. This mineral was first mined in Guyana in 1884 when 250 ounces were recorded. Production fluctuated over the years, but by 1938 it had reached 41,919 ounces.[2] Since then output has remained between 15,000 and 25,000 ounces per year. As with diamonds, production is carried out mainly by small-scale producers. The closing down of dredging operations by the B.G. Consolidated Goldfields Company Limited in 1958 was a serious blow to the goldmining industry as since 1950 that company has been responsible for nearly 80 per cent of total production.

---

[1] *Annual Report of British Guiana*, 1923.   [2] *British Guiana Blue Book*, 1938.

Other Minerals

Some production of columbite and tantalite took place between 1950 and 1953 but ceased with the fall in prices when the United States government stopped the stockpiling of strategic minerals from non-domestic sources. The Guyana shield is a promising area for radioactive minerals. Several uranium localities have been discovered but either the mineralization is too sparse or the uranium is present in refractory mineral. The wide extent of the dolerite rocks of the Younger Basic Intrusives in Guyana leads to the expectation that economic concentrations of the chromium-nickel-platinum metals may be found. Chromium is promising and is found in the form of a mixture of minerals called *merumite*. Repeated prospection has failed to find an economic deposit but a fresh campaign based on detailed geological mapping with geophysical and geochemical prospection is being planned by the Geological Survey Department.

Guyana has large reserves of low-grade aluminous and ferruginous material in the form of the laterites which cap many parts of the old plantation surface. The tonnage available is extremely high but the laterites are of low grade especially for iron, and are virtually inaccessible. These laterites have been considered as low-grade bauxites and the high alumina content renders them refractory to normal iron-smelting processes. The future of these deposits from the point of view of the development of iron ore lies in the development of a process for separating both iron and alumina, and research along these lines has already been started.

Traces of pitch and inspissated oil have been found at various times on the coasts of the North West and Pomeroon districts. The indications are that oil may be discovered on the Continental Shelf and since 1958 a subsidiary of the Standard Oil Company of California has been carrying out a marine seismic survey over the offshore areas. These operations are still in progress, and they have recently been supplemented by drilling on a small scale. Many other minerals than those mentioned above could be developed in Guyana if the demand is sufficient and the cost of production can be made competitive with imported materials.

The mineral 'breakthrough' for Guyana, although based upon many years of hard work, may perhaps be dated to 1962. At that time when the first comprehensive technical surveys of the country were begun, all that could have been expressed was the view that the country was well mineralized because of the widespread distribution of alluvial gold. The operative theory in this case was that where gold is, mineralization has occurred. But for two reasons there are no sub-surface mines currently operating in the country. In the first place, as mentioned earlier there has been the difficulty of pinpointing mineralization under the thick cover of tropically covered weathered rock. Fresh rock may be buried as much as 200 feet beneath this obscuring blanket, and virtually every indication of mineralization that elsewhere might be apparent has been removed. The sole exception is gold, which is resistant to decomposition.

The second reason concerns diamonds which have given many sizeable fortunes, and which still promise to be profitable to many more. But while diamond prospecting has kept the country's vast interior alive, it has also diverted the 'pork-nockers' of Guyana from gold. Had this not been the case, gold operations would have been pursued with more industry, and this might well have led to important finds, and so attracted big concerns. It is against this background that Guyana has been able to obtain financial and technical assistance and launch current explorations which have achieved some success. But the results of these new drives will not become evident for some time to come. We must therefore proceed to a consideration in more detail of the growth of the mining sector in the period under review with special emphasis inevitably being given to the bauxite-alumina-aluminium complex.

Mining is the second largest propulsive sector of the economy after sugar. In this sector the most important industries are bauxite and manganese mining and the manufacture of alumina. We saw that there is also some mining of gold and diamonds, but this is not carried out to any significant degree. Tables 1 and 2 show the trends in the quantity and value of mining operations for the various mineral products, and the importance of bauxite in relation to other minerals.

Between 1954 and 1964 the average annual rate of growth in money terms of the mining and quarrying industries was 8 per cent. Most of this growth occurred during 1961 and 1962 when an alumina plant began operations. Table 3 shows the trends

TABLE 1
QUANTITY OF MINERAL PRODUCTION

Year	Bauxite[a] ('000 long tons)	Alumina ('000 tons)	Manganese ('000 long tons)	Diamonds ('000 metric carats)	Gold ('000 troy oz.)
1954	2,310	Nil	Nil	30	27
1955	2,435	Nil	Nil	33	24
1956	2,481	Nil	Nil	30	16
1957	2,202	Nil	Nil	29	17
1958	1,586	Nil	Nil	33	19
1959	1,674	Nil	Nil	62	3
1960	2,471	Nil	123	101	2
1961	2,374	120	212	113	2
1962	3,036	277	271	100	2
1963	2,343	222	140	100	3
1964	2,468	292	117	107	2

Source: Annual Accounts Relating to External Trade.

[a] Including bauxite which is converted to alumina.

TABLE 2
VALUE OF MINERAL EXPORTS[a]
(Million Guyana dollars)

Year	Bauxite	Alumina	Manganese	Diamonds	Gold
1954	23	Nil	Nil	1·2	0·9
1955	25	Nil	Nil	1·3	0·8
1956	29	Nil	Nil	1·3	0·4
1957	30	Nil	Nil	1·4	0·5
1958	21	Nil	Nil	1·4	0·6
1959	25	Nil	Nil	3·0	[b]
1960	29	Nil	2·2	4·8	[b]
1961	28	12	5·4	5·1	[b]
1962	31	23	6·7	3·7	[b]
1963	29	22	5·7	—	[b]
1964	30	27	4·0	4·5	[b]

Source: As per Table 1.

[a] These values include the cost of transportation and other services as well as the value attributable to mining operations.

[b] Less than $100,000.

TABLE 3

GROSS DOMESTIC PRODUCT ORIGINATING
IN MINING AND QUARRYING[a]

(*Thousand dollars*)

| Year | Without adjustment of price changes | | |
	Value	% of G.D.P.	1960 constant prices
1954	24,517	13%	Not available
1960	29,059	11%	29,059
1961	37,330	13%	36,476
1962	49,945	16%	45,969
1963	35,205	13%	38,291
1964	53,280	17%	47,611

[a] Central Statistical Bureau, *Analysis of Domestic Product.*

in Gross Domestic Product originating in mining and quarry-ing.

A contrast with the Jamaican mining industry is revealing. In 1952 bauxite was being produced only in insignificant quantities in Jamaica, while by 1962 output had grown to over 7·6 million tons. On one estimate, the direct and indirect effects of the industry's expansion accounted for at least 20 per cent of the growth of total real domestic product that took place between 1950 and 1960.[1] There are several significant reasons why the mining and especially the bauxite complex has not made a more striking contribution to the economic development of Guyana, and these will become obvious later in this chapter.

2. *Bauxite*

The dispassionate analysis of the main variables and parameters operating in this sector is impeded by certain statistical encumbrances. Until quite recently, there was no legal provision compelling companies to provide statistical data on their reserves, production, prices, and general contributions to the government and the economy. Such statistical data as are available to the government are received at irregular intervals

[1] C. O'Loughlin, 'Long-Term Growth of the Economy of Jamaica', *Social and Economic Studies*, Vol. 12, No. 3 (Sept. 1963), pp. 246–82.

on a purely voluntary basis. Some of the statistical data incorporated in the available statistical records are indirectly arrived at from customs and tax returns. Furthermore, owing to lack of personnel, such statistical work as is done is usually slow, often incomplete, and in most cases unevaluated. Since 1964 the companies have been obliged in theory to supply the Government with details of their costs and local outlays, but whatever information is supplied is confidential and therefore not available to the public. The research worker in consequence finds it extremely difficult to disentangle the activities and contributions of the bauxite companies.

The most glaring statistical lacunae exist in the field of investment, but a clear enough picture emerges by piecing together information from various sources of varying degrees of reliability. The bauxite enterprise is the most capitalized complex in the economy. The high capital bias compared with the rest of the economy is marked particularly in the early years when the capital increments to other sectors were relatively low. A further illustration of the high capital bias of this sector is given in Table 4 which shows capital formation originating within this sector in 1959. We saw in an earlier chapter that capital formation accounted for an average of 24 per cent of Gross Domestic Product between 1954 and 1963. There was a marked acceleration in the rate of total capital formation in the years after 1957, and this rise was mainly the result of heavy investment in manganese mining and alumina plant and, to a lesser extent, the sugar industry, and not to increase in government development expenditure.

The high capital formation noticeable in the industry after 1959 was the result of developments in which the economies of scale began to have a major effect. The most important development after 1959 was the construction of the alumina plant by the Demerara Bauxite Company (locally known as DEMBA). In 1956 DEMBA began to construct an alumina plant at Mackenzie to process some of their bauxite production locally. The plant was completed and commissioned in May 1961, with a present capacity of 300,000 tons of alumina per annum. Originally DEMBA intended to complete the work in two and a half years, but owing to the business recession in 1957, the project was slowed down. In construction work a labour force

TABLE 4

GROSS DOMESTIC FIXED CAPITAL FORMATION AS PER-
CENTAGE OF GROSS DOMESTIC PRODUCT 1959

Sector	Per cent		
	Total	Land and building	Plant and machinery
Agriculture	2·61	0·59	2·02
Livestock, etc.	0·08	−0·10	0·18
Mining	124·49	10·63	113·86
Food processing	34·23	0·64	33·55
Chemicals	0·79	0·20	0·99
Engineering	24·65	13·38	11·27
Other manufacturing	−22·23	5·94	−28·17
Fuel and Power	2·48	—	2·48
Distribution	11·70	7·61	4·09
Transport and Communication (non-government only)	3·93	1·50	2·43
Banking and Insurance	1·54	1·30	0·23
Professions	5·31	4·66	0·65
Rent of dwelling	25·61	25·61	—
Government	64·48	55·62	8·86
Household (private housing as percentage of total household income)	4·60	4·60	—

Source: A. Kundu, 'Inter-Industry Table'.

of 1,800 was engaged of which 1,700 were Guyanese. Prior to going ahead with the scheme, the company signed an agreement with the Guyana government whereby in appreciation of the company's readiness to extend the scope of their operations in Guyana, special concessions were granted in terms of revenue and the duration of bauxite leases. Investment costs amounted to G$65 million of which G$8 million was spent on housing and township, leaving G$57 million for plant premises and installations, representing roughly $160 million per annual ton capacity of alumina. Capital expenditure per annual ton capacity is in fair agreement with that of North American plants in general where investment costs of plants of the same order of magnitude processing trihydrate gibbsite vary from US$110 to US$150 per annual ton capacity.

It must be emphasized, however, that only a small share of

the value of capital purchases in bauxite and alumina has accrued in the form of income shares in Guyana. In the case of the item Land and Building in Table 4, only in the construction of buildings is income created. This income arises in the form of wages to building labour and profits to contractors, as well as the derived income that accrues to producing factors in the form of local raw materials used (e.g. timber). Small amounts of income are also created from the elements of exploration, research, and land development in this item. In the case of Plant and Machinery Equipment all income created arises from transportation and installation of plant, but this income constitutes a minor share, usually under 30 per cent of the final value of the item.

The nature of the open-pit mining made it unlikely that bauxite mining would ever employ large numbers of labourers, and the production of alumina, a continuous chemical process, also has a low labour/capital ratio. In Chapter 2 we noticed that mining and quarrying accounted for 2·8 per cent of the total labour force in 1946. In 1956 the corresponding figure was 3·0 per cent, and by 1960 this figure showed only a slight increase when it stood at 3·8 per cent. In terms of numbers, while in 1964 4,136 persons were employed, by 1960 the figure increased to over 6,000. For the bauxite industry alone current employment is estimated to be 3,900, excluding 800 men employed temporarily in construction activities. Average employment in the bauxite industry decreased from 2,600 in 1954 to 1,800 in 1959, but increased to 2,300 in 1960, 3,300 in 1961, 3,360 in 1962, and 3,700 in 1963.[1] In the field of employment we may again draw an interesting contrast with the Jamaican-mining industry: Table 5 shows the number of persons employed in the bauxite and alumina enterprises in the latter country. Although the bauxite complex in Guyana employs more labour than its Jamaican counterpart, the Jamaican companies are engaged in non-mining activities which are labour intensive. Their agricultural undertakings employ as many people as their mining and related operations. In Guyana, the bauxite companies do not engage in any extra-mining activities.

[1] Annual Reports of the Department of Labour.

TABLE 5

PERSONS EMPLOYED IN BAUXITE AND ALUMINA
ENTERPRISES IN JAMAICA[a]

Categories	1958	1959	1960
Mining and related activities	2,565	3,105	2,990
Construction	2,098	669	69
Agriculture and other	2,178	2,119	1,577
Prospecting	—	—	47
Total	6,841	5,893	4,683

[a] *Economic Survey 1962*, Central Planning Unit, Jamaica.

Although the companies in Guyana have not had any great effect numerically on the labour force, their influence has been greater than the numbers employed would suggest. The highly mechanized nature of the mining and alumina operations has made it necessary for the companies to train labour, and a nucleus of trained workers has been created. The advantages associated with external economies are noticeable in this context. The question of external economies affects costs and often has an important bearing on policies of location. Alumina extraction, while not employing a large labour force, does require a limited number of highly trained technicians and these skills are not readily found in sufficient quantity and quality in Guyana. Guyana has little tradition in industrial skills, apart from those acquired in the sugar industry, and employers have in general paid too little attention to training their workers. But the bauxite companies have shown that with adequate preparation for the job, and good prospects for continued high earning power, the performance of Guyanese labour was encouraging.[1]

Fundamentally, the importance of trying to retain foreign enterprises in development countries does not spring merely from the capital they may bring in, but also the technical skills and knowledge they build up for long periods in the context of

[1] Similar considerations have been found to apply to workers in the mining enterprise of Jamaica. R. L. Aaronson, 'Labour Commitment among Jamaican Bauxite Workers', *Social and Economic Studies*, Vol. 10, No. 2 (June 1961); and Ella Campbell, 'Industrial Training Methods and Techniques', *Social and Economic Studies*, Vol. 2, No. 1 (1953).

local conditions. Skills and knowledge, available in well-articulated form and fitted into a going economic concern, are less easily replaceable than capital funds which may be obtainable from other sources. If properly tapped, therefore, the 'educative effect' on Guyana may be much greater than the many technical aid programmes using a fresh group of 'foreign experts' who have no local knowledge. But the mines (and this is true of the sugar plantations as well) cannot function as leading sectors, diffusing modern technology and skills in Guyana, unless they are allowed to continue their policy of replacing traditional cheap labour by a new pattern of higher wages and higher productivity. But this requires heavy additional investments on their part both in material and human capital, and these enterprises are naturally unwilling to undertake these investments unless they can be reasonably sure of reaping the fruits in the long run. Unfortunately, however, the Guyanese investment climate [1] has been unfavourable for many years, and this sense of security and the inducement to wait for the fruits of a long-term policy was precisely what was not available to foreign-owned enterprises.

In Guyana, both economic nationalism and insecure, unstable political and social conditions have caused uncertainty and lack of confidence. Although the insecurity that springs from the inherent instability of primary export production may not have had much causative force in this context, the constant threat of nationalization, and lack of conditions necessary for the pursuit of long-term policies may have prevented the foreign-owned mining companies from making a fuller contribution to the economy.[2]

If the high degree of capital intensity has prevented the bauxite companies from making a marked contribution in the field of employment, the wage rates paid in bauxite and alumina are much higher, and in most cases have grown much faster than the rates paid to similar categories of workers in

[1] The salient factors governing the investment climate have been well documented. For example, Charles Wolf and Sidney Sufrin, *Capital Formation and Foreign Investment in the Underdeveloped areas* (Syracuse University Press, 1958), Ch. 4.

[2] It is expected that the advent of the more politically stable era after 1964 will increase the enterprises' contribution to material and human investment in Guyana.

other sectors, both public and private. The workers through their unions have always pressed for rates of pay that bear a favourable relationship to the earnings of bauxite and alumina workers in Canada and the United States, with increasing emphasis in wage negotiations on the companies' ability to pay. The high wage structure operating in the bauxite complex has influenced wage negotiations in other sectors, for it is probable that it has led in turn to pressure for higher wages in other industries, and has been in part responsible for maintaining the share of wages in the Gross Domestic Product.

The stimulating effect of the spending of bauxite and alumina workers on retail trade in the mining areas is noticeable; unfortunately no firm information is available on their consumption patterns. But interviews carried out by the present writer among employees at DEMBA revealed that apart from house purchase most of their surplus income was absorbed by the purchase of imported durable consumer goods. The high rate of earnings enjoyed by the labour force in bauxite and alumina is also an important source of revenue to the government through income and indirect taxes. But a more significant contribution in this sphere accrues from company taxation. This will be considered at a later stage when we consider the pricing policy operating in the industry.

(a) *Production.* Firstly, we may outline Guyana's position among the major world producers. A breakdown of output by producing countries in Table 6, as well as an indication of the share of the major bauxite-producing countries in total world output as given in Table 7 show Guyana's relative position. As a result of the rapid increase in the demand for aluminium, world bauxite production rose continuously from 8·3 million tons in 1950 to 30 million tons in 1962, an average rate of increase of 11 per cent a year. The rise in demand for bauxite since 1949 is largely due to the expansion of the industry, but also to the stockpiling policy of the United States government. It is estimated that the bauxite equivalent of the totals of bauxite, alumina, and aluminium held in various United States stockpiles in 1962 amounted to some 22 million tons.[1] This special demand was almost entirely met by producers in the

---

[1] United States Bureau of Mines, *Mineral Yearbooks.*

western hemisphere, particularly by Jamaica, Surinam, and Guyana.

Guyana was the world's third largest contributor to world consumption in 1940–56, but with many new bauxite-producing countries entering the field, lost a great deal of ground since, and became the world's fourth contributor to world

TABLE 6
WORLD PRODUCTION OF BAUXITE BY COUNTRIES
(Long tons thousands)

Producing country	1955	1956	1957	1958	1959	1960	1961	1962
Ghana	116	138	185	207	148	224	193	29●
Jamaica	2,645	3,142	4,596	5,722	5,126	5,745	6,663	7,00●
Guyana	2,435	2,481	2,202	1,586	1,674	2,477	2,374	2,40●
India	90	99	108	166	215	377	468	56●
Malaya	222	264	326	262	382	452	410	30●
Pakistan	1	3	3	2	2	1	1	●
Sarawak	—	—	—	136	207	285	253	25●
Australia	8	10	8	7	15	71	26	2●
Austria	19	22	22	23	24	26	18	1●
France	1,470	1,439	1,663	1,801	1,729	2,006	2,148	2,14●
Germany (Fed.)	4	5	5	4	4	4	4	
Greece	492	689	820	843	904	935	1,280	1,28●
Hungary	1,221	879	893	1,032	942	1,170	1,327	1,47●
Italy	322	271	257	294	290	313	318	29●
Roumania	36	51	60	72	70	87	87	9●
Spain	6	7	8	8	8	3	5	●
U.S.S.R.	2,030	2,190	2,410	2,710	2,950	3,450	4,000	4,00●
Yugoslavia	779	867	874	721	802	1,009	1,213	1,26●
Guinea	485	444	360	325	296	1,356	1,739	1,73●
Mozambique	3	4	5	5	4	5	5	●
Dom. Republic	—	—	—	—	759	678	722	1,06●
Haiti	125	125	263	280	255	268	263	35●
United States	1,788	1,744	1,416	1,311	1,700	1,998	1,228	1,36●
Brazil	44	69	63	69	95	119	140	14●
Surinam	3,074	3,430	3,324	2,941	3,376	3,400	3,351	3,27●
China	20	40	80	150	300	350	400	35●
Indonesia	260	299	238	338	381	389	413	47●
World total	17,700	18,700	20,200	21,000	22,700	27,200	29,000	30,00●

Source: U.S. Bureau of Mines, *Mineral Yearbooks.*

consumption in latter years, dropping from a 17·7 per cent peak in the decade 1940–9 to 8 per cent in 1962. Guyana's position was lost because of the steadily growing quota of Jamaica, which has become the world's greatest producer.

TABLE 7

SHARE OF PERCENTAGES OF MAJOR BAUXITE-PRODUCING
COUNTRIES IN WORLD TOTAL PRODUCTION

Producing country	1955	1956	1957	1958	1959	1960	1961	1962
Jamaica	14·3	16·7	22·8	27·3	22·6	21·1	22·9	23·3
Surinam	17·4	18·3	16·4	14·0	14·8	12·5	11·6	10·9
Guyana	13·7	13·3	10·9	7·5	7·4	9·1	8·2	8·0
United States	10·1	9·3	7·0	6·2	7·5	7·3	4·2	4·6
France	8·3	7·7	8·2	8·6	7·6	7·3	7·4	7·1
Guinea	2·7	2·4	1·8	1·6	1·3	5·0	6·0	5·8
U.S.S.R.	11·5	11·7	11·9	12·9	13·0	12·7	14·0	13·3
Hungary	6·9	4·7	4·4	4·9	4·2	4·3	4·6	4·9
Total	84·9	84·1	83·4	83·0	78·4	79·3	78·9	77·9

Bauxite production commenced in the territory in 1917, the
year when the Demerara Bauxite Company[1] began working
their first mine at Mackenzie sixty-five miles up the Demerara
River from Georgetown, and has characteristically followed the
trend in world production. The production figures for the
period 1953–63 are given in Table 8, while a comparison of the
growth rates of world bauxite production and that of Guyana is
given in Table 9. It is obvious that after 1953 aggregate production rose steadily for in that year the Reynolds Metal
Company started production at Kwakwani up the Berbice
River. But the 1958–9 recession had its repercussions, in that
bauxite production declined by some 20 per cent in Guyana,
whereas the figures for world bauxite production show a slight
rise for the same period. The reason for this is that Guyana with
a comparatively modest commitment of bauxite exports to the
United States participated less in the stockpiling programme of

[1] DEMBA is a subsidiary of Aluminium Ltd., (ALCAN) Group of Companies,
one of the leading aluminium producers in the world. DEMBA was the sole producer until 1946 when the American Cyanamid Co. started production at
Kwakwani through its subsidiary Berbice Co. Ltd. In 1953 the Berbice Co. sold
its assets in Guyana to the Reynolds Metals Co. of Richmond Virginia, who
maintained production and opened new mines within recent years. DEMBA,
under agreement with the British and Colonial Bauxite Co. Ltd. provided management and technical services to the Plantation Bauxite Co., for operating the mine
at Christianburg, opposite to Mackenzie, but operations were shortlived owing to
uneconomic production, and the mine is now lying idle; the ore reserves were
acquired by DEMBA for future use. Thus bauxite mining is at present being conducted by DEMBA and the Reynolds Metals Company.

MINING

TABLE 8

BAUXITE PRODUCTION IN GUYANA 1953–64

(On washed and dried basis)

(*In long tons*)

Year	Name of operating company				Total
	Demba	Berbice	Planta-tion	Reynolds	
1953	2,013,995	54,960	43,120	—	2,112,075
1954	1,917,203	—	—	167,365	2,084,568
1955	1,974,628	—	—	190,840	2,165,468
1956	1,911,163	—	—	214,161	2,125,324
1957	1,704,815	—	—	306,815	2,011,630
1958	1,397,340	—	—	188,539	1,585,879
1959	1,511,077	—	—	163,339	1,674,416
1960	2,231,940	—	—	239,250	2,471,190
1961	1,982,650	—	—	390,965	2,373,615
1962	2,246,089	—	—	472,908	2,718,997
1963	2,074,790	—	—	267,499	2,342,289

Source: Reports of Lands and Mines Dept., Guyana.

Note: The figures in this table in respect of total production do not always agree with those given in Table 6, because of the different methods of computation used by the American authorities and those in Guyana.

TABLE 9

GROWTH RATE OF BAUXITE PRODUCTION OF WORLD AND GUYANA

(*Thousand tons; 1951 Output = 100*)

Year	World		Guyana	
1951	11,000	100	2,002	100
1956	18,700	170	2,125	107
1958	21,000	191	1,586	79
1959	22,700	206	1,674	84
1960	27,200	247	2,471	125
1961	29,000	264	2,374	118
1962	29,600	267	2,719	135

the United States than producers from other areas of the world. The drop in 1963 production was due to the 80-day general strike. Without this, production would probably have reached the 2·8 million ton mark. On the other hand as could be seen from Table 9, the growth rate of all output from Guyana lags far behind that of the world in general.

However, bauxite in Guyana differs from other world sources, excepting the new discoveries in eastern Australia, in its relatively high average degree of purity. The account in Table 10 shows the compositional range for the major producers in the world.

The value of the ore lies in its alumina content. The other constituent shown in Table 10 are impurities. For example, for each unit of silica present, approximately 1·1 units of alumina and 1·2 units of soda ash are lost in processing. Up to 8 per cent of silica is tolerated in the most commonly known process, of manufacturing alumina, the 'Bayer Process', and ore with 12–13 per cent silica and up to 15 per cent is converted by what is known as the 'Combination Process'. Iron oxide is objectionable as a diluent in the 'Bayer Process'. Guyanese bauxite averages 50–61 per cent alumina, 3–12 per cent silica, and about 3 per cent iron.[1] This high-grade bauxite is specially adaptable for the abrasive and refractory grades, after beneficiating and calcining. The Demerara Bauxite Company has steadily increased its output from the world's largest bauxite calcining plant situated at Mackenzie. As far back as 1938 the company installed calcining facilities for the manufacture of refractory and abrasive grades of bauxite.[2] Up to 1945 such shipments averaged 10,000 tons per annum. In 1946 production of calcined bauxite was 33,000 tons rising steadily to 1952 when 145,000 tons were exported. Exports of this valuable grade of bauxite has continued to increase, and in 1964 it was 469,000 tons.

---

[1] The economic importance of Guyana's deposits is somewhat reduced by their occurrence deep below the surface soil, thus necessitating the use of expensive and heavy machinery. By contrast the Jamaican deposits are much more accessible, for they occur in the form of surface deposits which can be reached by removing only about 9 inches of overburden. See V. A. Zans, 'The Bauxite Resources of Jamaica and their Development', *Colonial Geology and Mineral Resources*, Vol. 3, No. 4 (1952), pp. 307–30.

[2] Calcined bauxite is a mineral product formed by a process of calcining selected grades. The calcination process involves heating bauxite to a very high temperature, causing the chemically combined water in the bauxite to be driven off. At the same time chemical and mineralogical changes take place in the ore resulting in the formation of a mineral product quite different in character and properties from the original bauxite. DEMBA sells calcined bauxite to the refractory and

A further stage in the processing of bauxite beyond drying and calcining was undertaken in 1961 with the installation of the alumina plant at Mackenzie.[1] In recent times there has developed a growing tendency to site alumina plants as near to the bauxite mines as possible. This is especially the case where the aluminium-reduction plant processing the alumina is located a considerable distance from the mining base from which the bauxite for the manufacture of the alumina is obtained. For example, a considerable part of the alumina used by North American smelters is produced in conjunction with bauxite operations in Jamaica, Surinam, and Guyana. By long-distance

TABLE 10

COMPOSITIONAL RANGE OF ORE FOR SOME MAJOR WORLD PRODUCERS[a]

Constituent (%)	Guyana	Jamaica	Haiti	U.S.A.	Surinam	Brazil	West Africa	Australia
Water	24–31	23–29	24	29–30	30	28–33	23–30	22–28
Silica	2–12	14	3·4	2–5	2–15	1–7	1–5	5–8
Titania	2–4	2–3	2·8	2–3	2	1–2	1–4	4–6
Iron oxide	1–10	20–30	22	11–21	5–15	1–7	5–20	3–8
Alumina	50–62	48–52	47	45–50	50–63	59–65	48–60	40–51

[a] Compiled from United States Bureau and Mines, *Mineral Facts and Problems*, 1956 and 1960.

shipping of alumina instead of bauxite, considerable economies may be derived in bulk shipping costs. Integration of bauxite with alumina production also permits the elimination of drying the ore at the mine plant. There is also a further economic benefit especially with bauxite from tropical countries where the mechanically combined water content of the ore is usually high.[2]

abrasive industries, which require the hard, heat-resistant, and stable product which is calcined bauxite.

[1] For an account of technological conversion of bauxite to alumina and alumina to aluminium, see H. D. Huggins, *Aluminium in Changing Communities* (André Deutsch in association with the Institute of Social and Economic Research, University of the West Indies, 1965), pp. 156–71.

[2] Huggins, *Aluminium in Changing Communities*, pp. 28–56; also R. A. Abu-El-Haj, *Pre-Investment Data for the Aluminium Industry* (United Nations Secretariat, 1963).

(b) *Exports*. Though aluminium is the most abundant metallic element in the earth's crust, yet most of its ore (bauxite) is mined outside the aluminium-producing countries, because the weathering conditions that form bauxite from the alumina-bearing materials, e.g. clays, rarely coincide with the cheap hydro-electric potentialities and with the socio-economic conditions necessary for huge capital investment in the same country. Since a great majority of the bauxite mining operations are owned by the big aluminium-producing companies, the bauxite trade is mostly based on long-term contracts and it occurs in a few well-defined flows. The chief flows are (1) from the Caribbean countries and the Guianas to the United States and Canada; (2) from West Africa to Europe; (3) from South East Asia to Japan; (4) from certain European producers (France, Greece, Hungary, Yugoslavia) to European consumers, Germany, U.S.S.R., and Italy. The direction of bauxite trade is strongly influenced by the fact that the transportation costs are relatively high compared to the low value of the ore, and because of this imports and exports tend to find the nearest markets. Furthermore, as already noticed, there is a strong tendency to raise the proportion of ore processed into alumina in the mining country before exportation, a procedure which halves the transportation costs.

Official external trade statistics in Guyana feature only calcined and 'other' bauxite, the first comprising abrasive and refractory grade ores and the second metallurgical and chemical grades. A breakdown according to the latter, while made available by the companies, was not in complete harmony with official figures. We have therefore been constrained to base our analysis mainly on official estimates. A summary of exports for the period 1953 and 1964 in tonnages is given in Table 11 below.

Exports of calcined bauxite have gone up by 90 per cent over the 12 years under review. Exports of dry bauxite on the other hand, declined from 1955 onwards. The reasons for this are manifold. Calcined bauxite from Guyana has met with little competition on the world markets, and the Demerara Bauxite Company pursues a vigorous policy of finding new markets for abrasive and refractory bauxite. In fact the number of countries to which calcined bauxite is exported increased from 10 in

1953 to 25 in 1963.[1] Under these circumstances, the export of
calcined bauxite has proved highly profitable. The position
with regard to dried bauxite, however, is a different one. As the
most easily accessible deposits were mined out, ore became more
difficult to extract. Guyana has benefited to a minor extent from
the United States government buying for stockpile and barter,
but ALCAN has mined a growing proportion of its ore requirements in Jamaica, since it started alumina production there.
The rate of increase in bauxite reports slowed down the world
over quite sharply between 1950 and 1959, partly because of a
slackening of the rate of growth of aluminium production in
Canada and the United States, and partly because of the rise in
the proportion of alumina exports from some of the bauxite-
producing countries. In 1960, however, demand for aluminium
recovered in Canada and West Germany, and owing to the
stepping up of United States purchases, total world exports of

TABLE II

BAUXITE AND ALUMINA EXPORT OF GUYANA
1953–64

Year	Calcined		Other		Alumina ('000 tons)
	'000 tons	1953 = 100	'000 tons	1953 = 100	
1953	244·9	100	1,867·2	100	—
1954	209·3	85	1,916·2	102	—
1955	252·3	103	1,916·9	102	—
1956	317·9	130	1,789·8	96	—
1957	287·1	117	1,734·1	93	—
1958	195·6	80	1,168·6	63	—
1959	272·3	111	1,242·4	67	—
1960	307·0	125	1,788·0	96	—
1961	370·8	151	1,235·6	67	120·2
1962	366·6	150	1,502·2	81	215·0
1963	358·4	146	945·7	51	216·0
1964	469·0	190	838·6	44	245·0

Source: Years 1953–61: *Annual Accounts Relating to External Trade*, Dept. of
Customs and Excise, Georgetown, Guyana.
Years 1962, 1963, 1964: Data Supplied by DEMBA and Reynolds.
Also: *Economic Survey of Guyana, 1966.*

[1] *Annual Accounts Relating to External Trade.*

bauxite rose by some 17 per cent,[1] and exports from Guyana took advantage of the favourable conditions.

Despite this growing demand for bauxite and alumina in world markets, Guyana's exports continued to fall after 1961 because of political and social unrest and wild-cat strikes over the country as a whole. Although exports showed a marked recovery in 1964, the decline in 1963 was a direct result of the racial and political disturbances and the 80-day general strike. It is hoped that by reaching independence and political stability, the trend in exportation will increase again in accordance with the growing world demand for bauxite and alumina.

Exports of alumina in the second year of the plant's operation were nearly up to the level of the originally planned capacity of 240,000 tons, and following the general strike in the second half of 1963, the alumina plant was operating at full capacity of 300,000 tons per annum. This accounts for the substantial increase in exports in 1964. The number of countries to which alumina was exported steadily increased from 2 in 1961 to 5 countries in the years to follow. While about half of the alumina exported went to Canada, the other half was shipped to Norway, Switzerland, Sweden, and the United States. The low costs of alumina production, coupled with the tax holidays granted by the government and the very favourable prices received renders alumina production and exports profitable to DEMBA.

While there are two companies mining bauxite in Guyana, only one—the Demerara Bauxite Company (Canadian) converts its bauxite into alumina within the country. The other company—Reynolds (American) does not even produce any calcined, abrasive or refractory grades of ore; they merely dry the bauxite before exporting it to alumina-reduction plants in the United States. Several factors help to explain the different behaviour of the Canadian and American companies. In the first place there is the problem of transportation. Over two tons of bauxite are required to produce a ton of alumina. The reduction of bauxite to alumina at the source of the ore therefore results in a reduction of shipping costs by about two-fifths. As Canada is much further away from Guyana than the ports in

---

[1] United States Bureau of Mines, *Mineral Yearbooks*.

the United States, transportation costs would naturally be of greater concern to Canadian than to American producers. But there are also other considerations which tended to tilt the balance in favour of the export of crude bauxite rather than alumina to the United States.

During the Second World War the United States government had erected national plants for carrying out the various stages of aluminium smelting to as to augment the supplies needed for the war effort. After the war the government was reluctant to sell these plants to the giant Aluminium Company of America against which it had brought an unsuccessful anti-trust action in 1937.[1] Instead the government sought to promote competition by helping Reynolds Metals Co. and the Kaiser Aluminium and Chemical Corporation to establish themselves as integrated units by leasing to them most of the government's plants on very favourable terms. Subsequently, Reynolds and Kaiser purchased these plants at a fraction of their original costs, financing the acquisition by loans obtained from the government.[2] With these initial advantages, it has been profitable for the companies to ship the crude bauxite to the United States, rather than to establish plants in Guyana, for reducing it to alumina. Furthermore for a long time, the American tariff fell more heavily upon alumina than upon crude bauxite, and the subsequent suspension of the duty has not brought about any change in the pattern of production.[3]

Throughout the years bauxite exports represented an average of 29 per cent of the total value of exports. The position of alumina and bauxite exports related to the sum total of Guyana's exports is demonstrated in Table 12. There was a slight downward trend in the rate of bauxite exports to the total value of exports up to 1961, the year when alumina operations

[1] John V. Krutilla, 'Aluminium, A Dilemma for Anti-Trust Aims', *Southern Economic Journal*, Vol. XXII, No. 2 (1955).

[2] 'Aluminium—Tremendous Growth', *Quarterly Review Rotterdamsche Bank*, Rotterdam (May 1953), p. 22.

[3] Under the United States Tariff Act of 1930 crude bauxite and alumina were dutiable at the rate of 50 cents and 5 dollars per ton respectively. The duty on crude bauxite was suspended for two years in the first instance under P.L. 499 of July 1954, and for further two-year periods up to 15 July 1964. Similarly, the duty of alumina entering the United States was suspended in 1956 under the terms of Public Law 725. United States Bureau of Mines, *Minerals Markets Reports*, MMS, No. 2683, 1957.

TABLE 12

BALANCE OF VISIBLE TRADE AND THE VALUE OF BAUXITE AND ALUMINA EXPORTS 1953–64

(Million Guyana dollars)

	1953	1954	1955	1956	1957	1958	1959	1960	1961	1962	1963	1964
1. Exports (total)	83·1	85·4	90·5	94·6	108·1	97·2	103·5	127·3	148·9	164·2	174·8	162·8
2. Imports (total)	72·0	80·0	94·5	99·9	118·5	110·6	110·6	147·6	147·0	126·3	118·5	149·8
3. Balance	+11·1	+5·4	−4·0	−5·3	−10·4	−9·2	−7·1	−20·3	+1·9	+37·9	+56·3	+13·0
4. Dried bauxite	15·3	16·2	16·2	18·2	19·6	13·4	14·7	17·9	14·2	17·0	10·5	9·3
5. Calcined bauxite	8·2	7·1	8·6	11·1	9·9	7·2	10·1	11·6	14·3	14·1	15·2	20·9
6. Alumina	—	—	—	—	—	—	—	—	12·1	22·7	22·3	26·7
7. Total of 4, 5, 6	23·5	23·3	24·8	29·3	29·5	20·6	24·8	29·5	40·6	53·8	48·0	56·9

Source: Annual Reports on External Trade.

were commenced, whereupon both the value of total exports and the rate of bauxite and alumina exports in the country's total exports have gone up.

The commencement of alumina operations, in addition to causing a steep rise in the over-all value of exports has also significantly improved the country's balance of payments. Apart from certain developments in the sugar industry and a few other minor investments, it was the main contributor in raising the figure of direct investments of overseas companies over the level of payments made in respect of such foreign investments as shown in Table 13. It is significant that before 1957 the balance of investment income, i.e. the transfers to foreign investors, was substantially higher than direct investment of overseas capital in the country. In 1953 for instance, overseas companies invested BWI$5 million, i.e. double the amount that was transferred in interest, instalment payments, and so on to non-resident investors. The situation was similar in the following years up to 1957 when DEMBA began the con-

TABLE 13

YEARLY BALANCES OF INVESTMENT INCOME
AND DIRECT OVERSEAS INVESTMENTS BETWEEN
1953–60

(Plus: receipts   Minus: payments)

(*Thousand B.W.I. dollars*)

Year	Balance of investment income	Direct investment of overseas companies	$\dfrac{A \times 100}{B}$
	A	B	C
1953	− 10,234	+ 5,028	202
1954	− 9,874	+ 6,885	144
1955	− 9,367	+ 5,267	178
1956	− 11,101	+ 6,753	164
1957	− 18,079	+ 28,900	63
1958	− 14,598	+ 28,000	52
1959	− 17,733	+ 22,000	80
1960	− 22,352	+ 34,800	64

Source: *Quarterly Statistical Digest*, June 1962.

struction of its alumina plant. As shown by column C of Table 13, from that year on, investment of foreign capital was substantially higher than the transfer of funds to non-residents in respect of such investments.

(c) *Transportation*. The question of transportation deserves consideration because not only has it prevented the potential growth of the bauxite enterprise but also it will be one of the main controlling variables in the future development of the bauxite-alumina complex. It was certainly proffered as one of the main reasons for the delay in the establishment of an alumina plant in the country. In this context not only is the wastage of time disadvantageous, but transportation costs comprise nearly a half of the total cost of metal produced in Guyana. All bauxite destined for Canada or the United States is transshipped at Chaguaramas Bay in Trinidad, 375 miles from Georgetown. Chaguaramas is a well-sheltered, windfree bay, providing bunkering facilities for bauxite boats, and the stockpiling of the metallurgical-grade ore during the winter months when the Saguenay River, through which such shipments are to enter Canada, is frozen and unnavigable for five months of the year. Owing to the poor navigability of the Demerara River, and the difficulties presented to navigation by the Demerara entrance bar, 8,000-ton carriers cannot be loaded at Mackenzie to capacity but have to depart for Chaguaramas Bay with cargoes limited to 4,000–5,000 tons. Arriving there, cargoes are completed from the available stockpiles and despatched to Port Alfred on the Saguenay River. In the case of the Reynolds Metals Company, the ore is shipped from Everton on the Berbice River to Port of Spain and thence to Mobile or Corpus Christi, both on the Gulf of Mexico.

It is obvious that cheaper prices would be possible if transhipment costs and harbour dues in Trinidad could be eliminated and direct shipment made from the loading point to the finish. If we assume that the Georgetown bar and the Demerara River channel were able to permit navigation of ships of 30-foot draft (8,000 tons bauxite) to Mackenzie, the saving would be the difference between the cost of shuttling bauxite to Trinidad, and the cost of deepening and keeping clear the bar and channel. If the river were not dredged, and the bauxite were topped off from an installation in Georgetown harbour, the saving would be the difference between shuttling to Trinidad and shuttling to Georgetown. Should the Georgetown bar and harbour be dredged only to 25 feet, the saving would be the difference in the cost of dredging and keeping clear the bar and channel and the cost of shuttling less bauxite to Trinidad. The first alternative would necessitate dredging not only the Georgetown bar, but also the bars in the Demerara River channel to enable ships to take a full load of bauxite from Mackenzie direct to destination without having to deviate to Trinidad. This situation would be the ideal one because it would reduce freight rates in a substantial manner, and the transhipment centre at Trinidad could be abolished. It would, however, be necessary to organize a stockpiling centre somewhere in the system either at Mackenzie or Georgetown. It would clearly be attractive for Guyana to have a port that the standard ships of the world could use with a full load. The costs of maintaining such facilities would nullify the benefits as far as general cargo is concerned because of it low volume, but a different case can be made out in respect of the large-volume cargoes of sugar and bauxite, and the increasing volume of trade as industrialization proceeds.

No firm computations exist on the costs of dredging and maintaining the Demerara River channel bars or the George-

	(US $ per ton)
Distance in travelling time by deviation to Trinidad This difference in travelling time direct from Georgetown to Canada or through Trinidad is about half a day in navigation and one to two days loading bauxite in Trinidad, corresponding to about 7 per cent of the duration of a round voyage using the direct route from Mackenzie to Trinidad (the difference in fuel for deviating to Trinidad is not taken into account, being not substantial on such a long voyage)	0·50
Freight for shuttling bauxite to Trinidad This freight is calculated on completing cargo which is about 50 per cent of full load	1·25
Transhipment costs at Trinidad On completing cargo only which is about 50 per cent of full load	0·63
Port dues, pilotage, and agency at Trinidad For ships coming both shuttling and completing cargo	0·20
Total benefit per ton of metal grade bauxite	$2·58

town bar, but we may calculate the actual expenses incurred in the necessity for ships to call at Trinidad on their way to complete their bauxite cargo. The computations are based on elements available for a ship of 10,000 tons loading capacity. Only metal grade bauxite should be considered in full measure in these calculations; other qualities of bauxite and alumina are forwarded in smaller quantities by smaller and special ships for which the present condition of navigation is more or less suitable. For the calcined and miscellaneous grades of bauxite, the benefit is calculated at 30 per cent of US$ per ton and 20 per cent for alumina. On this basis the benefit derived from deepening the bar and Demerara River channels to 30 feet would be as follows.

		(US$ per ton)
1,500,000 tons metal grade bauxite @ $2·58 per ton		3,870,000
520,000 tons calcined and miscellaneous grade bauxite @ 77¢ per ton		400,400
220,000 tons alumina @ 52¢ per ton		114,400
2,240,000 tons	Total benefits	$4,384,800

Dividing the total benefit of US$4,384,000 by 2,240,000 tons of different grades of bauxite that are exported results in an average benefit of US$1·96 per ton.

If the Demerara estuary bar and Georgetown harbour were to be deepened to 30 feet only without deepening the river bars to Mackenzie, the benefit would be smaller:

		(US$ per ton)
Difference in travelling time by deviating to Trinidad		0·50
Freight for shuttling bauxite to Trinidad		1·25
	Total	1·75
Less freight for shuttling bauxite to Georgetown		0·25
Total freight per ton for metal grade bauxite		$1·50

On this basis the benefit derived from deepening the Demerara estuary bar and Georgetown harbour to 30 feet would be:

		(US$ per ton)
1,500,000 tons metal grade bauxite @ $1·50 per ton		2,250,000
520,000 tons calcined and miscellaneous grade bauxite @ 45¢ per ton		234,000
220,000 tons alumina @ 30¢ per ton		66,000
2,240,000		$2,550,000

Dividing the total benefit of US$2,550,000 by 2,240,000 tons of different grades of bauxite that are exported results in an average benefit of US$1·14 per ton. If they were to be deepened to 25 feet only the benefit could presumably be about 50 per cent or 57 cents per ton.[1]

These calculations do not take into account the added traffic that would ensue by diverting bauxite exported via the Berbice River to the Demerara River. Since it has been considered uneconomical and extremely difficult to dredge the Berbice River,[2] a railway line linking Kwakwani via Ituni would serve to transport bauxite from the Reynolds Metal Co. at Kwakwani to some suitable point at the Mackenzie area. It is also expected that further economies will be gained when aluminium smelters are installed in the Mackenzie area, with a consequent increase in export tonnage.

(d) *Power.* The electrolytic smelting of alumina into aluminium requires enormous quantities of very cheap power, but although many investigations have been made into the possibility of harnessing Guyana's hydro-electric potential, no firm decision has yet been taken.[3] In recent years three investigations have been carried out into this problem. In 1957 there was a large-scale investigation on behalf of the Demerara Bauxite Company, carried out by another subsidiary of ALCAN.[4] Its results were not encouraging, but this cannot be considered conclusive for several reasons. In the first place it was carried out with a view to providing power for bauxite and alumina rather than aluminium, and since load factors differ for differ-

---

[1] These computations are based on information supplied by the Demerara Bauxite Co. and the Reynolds Metals Co. Also see B. J. Smodlaka, *Report on Transport and Communications in British Guyana* (Georgetown, 1964).

[2] Delft Hydraulics Laboratory, *Demerara Coastal Investigations*, 1962.

[3] It can be argued that cheap power is potentially available in Guyana as it is abundantly so in Surinam whose rivers have similar hydrological regimes as those in Guyana. ALCOA's Brokopondo Project in Surinam comprises a hydro-electric power station, an alumina plant, and a smelter of 60,000 tons aluminium yearly capacity. The Brokopondo Project will yield power at a cost of 0·3 cents (3 mills per unit), which is certainly cheap enough for aluminium smelting. The Brokopondo project, moreover, is on the Surinam River, which like the Demerara is not the largest river in the territory. Other rivers in Surinam, such as the Marowinje, have much larger power potentials. *Facts and Figures about Surinam* (Surinam Government Information Service, Sept. 1964).

[4] *Hydro-electric Investigations—Demerara River*, Aluminium Laboratories Ltd., Montreal, Canada.

ent products, the latter possibility cannot be said to have been examined in detail. Secondly, the project was considered a hydro-electric one; the possibility of thermal backup was not investigated. It can be said that the possibility of thermal back-up might make an integrated power system more economical. Thirdly, it was an investigation on the Demerara River only, which is not necessarily the most suitable river for electric power.

More recently, two dispassionate surveys carried out by United Nations Technical Assistance experts have re-empha-sized the country's hydro-electric potential.[1] In particular John B. Snethlage has recommended that the best sites are at the Tiboku Falls and the upper Mazaruni area, which are only 90 miles and 140 miles respectively (transmission distance) from Mackenzie. The close integration of the bauxite-alumina-aluminium industry has severely circumscribed action by the government in this regard, but it remains to be seen whether co-operation between the government and the companies will bring in its wake development along these lines.

(e) *Pricing and taxation.* Since practically all bauxite pro-duced in Guyana is exported the pricing of bauxite is of great significance in the present-day economy and in the future development of Guyana. The question of 'fair pricing' of bauxite has been the subject of considerable debate in nearly all development countries producing this ore, because there is no open market price for bauxite in the world. One of the main features of the aluminium industry is the strong concentration of capital. A few mammoth concerns, mainly North American, while controlling most of the aluminium metal production of the western world, own nearly all the bauxite mines and alumina plants as well. This pattern is even more pronounced in the Caribbean where the large majority of bauxite ore processed by these concerns are located.

As the mines are in most cases controlled by big alumina and aluminium combines, prices usually reflect inter-company transfers and are to a large extent governed by other considera-

[1] J. B. Snethlage, *Report on the Hydroelectric Development Possibilities of the Rivers of British Guiana* (United Nations Technical Assistance Bureau, 1961); G. D. Sauer, *Report on the Development of Water Resources in British Guiana*, (United Nations Technical Assistance Bureau, 1962).

tions than those determining open market prices. Here, the usual pricing mechanism of open markets, such as competition among buyers and sellers and bargaining between buyers and sellers are often replaced by pricing practises which can be manipulated to distort company income for tax assessment purposes and create re-partition of profits for tax purposes between the parent company in an industrially developed and its subsidiary in a development country. Governments of bauxite-producing countries, are greatly interested in bauxite pricing because it represents, one of the most important sources of government revenue. However, if they have insufficient knowledge of the activities of mining companies, government agencies may have no means of influencing such pricing practices. Therefore, the view that individual efforts by each of the Caribbean governments in obtaining a fair price would be less effective than collective bargaining, appears to be perfectly justified. For this reason collective action by interested governments in the Caribbean appears highly desirable, to establish the principles of a common inter-Caribbean bauxite aluminium policy, and also to promote an exchange of information and collective measures that would ensure a fair bauxite-pricing practice as a basis of adequate taxation.[1]

To arrive at the nearest approach of what may be considered a world market price of bauxite, it is usual to work out average per-unit prices from official external trade accounts. Although figures obtained from external trade statistics are sometimes arbitrary and do not always take into account such differences as exist in the chemical or mineralogical composition of ore, they usually serve as useful guides for approximating prices prevailing in different countries of the world.

Table 14 is a summary of average f.o.b. prices of crude and dried bauxite exported by the major producing countries in 1960 on the one hand and average c.i.f. prices arrived at during the same year by some of the importing countries on the other. Canada and the United States whose imports are valued on a f.o.b. basis are not listed among the importing countries, but prices applicable to these countries are discussed later. It will

---

[1] For a fuller elucidation see N. Girvan, *The Caribbean Bauxite Industry*, Studies in Regional Economic Integration, Vol. 2, No. 4 (University of the West Indies, 1967).

TABLE 14
EXPORT AND IMPORT PRICES OF BAUXITE
(Per long ton)

Countries	Destination	US$	Note
Export (f.o.b.)			
From	*To*		
Ghana		7·0	
Jamaica		7·3	
Guyana	U.S.	8·1	(On dry basis, 9·5)
		5·9	(On dry basis)
Malaya	Japan	5·6	
	Australia	5·9	
Sarawak	Japan	6·2	
	Taiwan (Formosa)	7·0	
France		7·0	
	Federal Germany	7·9	
	U.K. and Italy	6·2	
Guinea	Canada	6·5	
Dom. Republic	U.S.	10·5	(On dry basis, 12·6)
Haiti	U.S.	7·6	(On dry basis, 9·0)
Surinam	U.S.	7·6	
	Canada	6·5	
Yugoslavia	Federal Germany	6·7	
	Italy	6·2	
Export (c.i.f.)			
To	*From*		
United Kingdom	France	9·8	
	Greece	10·6	
	Ghana	13·7	
Federal Germany	France	9·8	
	Yugoslavia	10·2	
	Greece	10·6	
	Guinea	11·7	
	Ghana	12·0	
Italy	Yugoslavia	7·6	
Japan	India, Malaya	10·6	
	Sarawak	10·9	

Source: S. Bracewell, *Bauxite, Alumina and Aluminium* (H.M.S.O., London, 1962).

readily be seen that of all the major bauxite-producing countries, the average export price of Guyana is the lowest. This is significant in that the bauxite produced in Guyana, with a remarkably low silica and ferric oxide content, is of a superior grade. Moreover, export prices are calculated in Guyana on a dry equivalent in contrast to the majority of the other exporting countries where the figures represent crude ore. Thus it seems that although Guyana is one of the largest contributors to bauxite exports in the world, prices compared to other major exporting countries are kept unreasonably low for the simple reason that the operating companies owned by non-residents in the country have no interest in adopting a different price basis. It was explained earlier that the bauxite mines in Guyana are operated by two companies: the Demerara Bauxite Company, a subsidiary of Aluminium Ltd., of Canadian interests, and the Reynolds Metals Company, with their base in the United States. Evidently, the low margin of profits reported by the Reynolds Metals Company in all their returns to the Guyana government, due to low pricing, is a safeguard to achieve higher profits coupled with higher taxation for alumina and smelter operations in the United States. As for DEMBA, though a limited company registered in Guyana, there is reason to believe that a similar pricing policy is maintained to further the interests of the parent company. In fact there can hardly be found another explanation why a company owned by non-residents should apply such discriminatingly low prices for a highly graded commodity unless such an attitude was governed by the interests of their parent company.

As Table 15 shows, the price of domestic bauxite in the United States rose from US $5·36 in 1939 to US $12·77 in 1961, an increase of 138 per cent, although the average grade of domestic ore declined sharply during the same period. In contradistinction, the average price of bauxite imported into the United States, compared to the 1939 price, was on the decline up to 1956 when price trends changed largely owing to the growth of imports from Jamaica, Haiti, and the Dominican Republic, with higher price levels than that of Guyana. The main reason why bauxite prices have gone up within the last few years in all countries of the Caribbean except Guyana may be largely attributed to the fact that there is a law in the United States whereby certain corporate income tax concessions are granted to companies operating in other countries of the hemisphere through what are called Western Hemisphere Corporations. Such corporations have to pay the United States only 25 per cent corporate income tax instead of the usual 52 per cent.

Apparently, under such circumstances, higher bauxite prices and the intensification of operations in these areas coincide with the interests of the major aluminium producers in the United States. Consequently for the first time in the history of these countries, bauxite prices began to rise substantially despite advances in technology and decrease in production costs. While most of the Caribbean territories benefited from this trend, Guyana did not.

A comparison of domestic and imported bauxite in the

TABLE 15

BAUXITE PRICE TRENDS IN THE UNITED STATES

Year	U.S. AVERAGE PRICE OF BAUXITE				Price
	Domestically produced (dried)		Imported f.o.b.		
	US$ (long ton)	1939 = 100	US$ (long ton)	1939 = 100	Ratio $\frac{C}{A}$
	(a)	(b)	(c)	(d)	E
1939	5·36	100	7·24	100	135
1940	5·51	103	6·82	94	124
1941	5·63	105	6·69	92	119
1942	5·05	94	6·73	93	133
1943	6·10	114	7·03	97	115
1944	5·59	104	6·93	96	124
1945	5·93	110	7·15	99	121
1946	6·98	130	7·00	97	100
1947	7·67	143	6·42	89	84
1948	7·50	140	6·20	86	83
1949	7·58	141	5·99	83	79
1950	7·66	143	6·20	86	81
1951	7·71	144	6·31	87	82
1952	8·54	159	6·64	92	78
1953	9·82	183	6·75	93	69
1954	11·82	221	6·90	95	58
1955	9·65	180	7·03	97	73
1956	9·68	181	7·85	108	81
1957	10·83	202	8·58	119	79
1958	10·88	203	8·86	122	81
1959	11·17	208	9·03	125	81
1960	12·09	225	8·93	123	73
1961	12·77	238	9·65	133	76
1962	12·26	228	11·54	159	76

Source: U.S. Bureau of Mines, *Mineral Yearbooks*.

United States will demonstrate that while the price ratio (the average price of imported bauxite in relation to that of domestic ore) continuously declined from 1939 to 1954 when the price of imported bauxite was 42 per cent less than that of domestic ore, in 1939 the import price was actually 35 per cent higher than that of the domestic ore, thus the price ratio declined by 57 per cent within this period. In 1961 the average price of import bauxite was 24 per cent less than that of domestic ore, representing a price ratio 44 per cent less than that of the last year before the Second World War. From a comparison of prices of bauxite imported into the United States from different countries of the Caribbean as per Table 16, it appears that the import price of Guyana bauxite is by far the lowest and that countries like Jamaica and Surinam achieved a substantial rise in bauxite prices within the last five to seven years. In 1961, in the United States, the price of ore from Surinam was 29 per cent, from Jamaica 31 per cent, from Haiti 30 per cent, and from the Dominican Republic 82 per cent higher than that from Guyana.

The low price level of bauxite from Guyana is also manifest from the fact that stockpiling and barter arrangements with the Federal Government of the United States were concluded generally at a higher price than that of usual inter-company transfers. It is commonly believed that the United States government over the years 1948 to 1959 has in most instances paid more for Surinam and Guyana ore purchased for stockpile than the price used by Reynolds and DEMBA for inter-company transactions. The reason for this is obvious. When the bauxite-producing companies are selling bauxite to the United States government they are usually not threatened by competition, and thus are more interested in obtaining the highest price possible than in avoiding local taxation by low-level prices.

Average prices of dry bauxite shipped from Guyana to North American destinations based on official external trade accounts are to be found in Table 17. It will be observed that bauxite prices have not changed substantially from 1953 to 1956. From that time on export prices went up by about 40 per cent. A peak was reached in 1959 by shipments to Canada and in 1961 to the United States. It should also be noted that f.o.b. prices arrived at from external trade statistics of Guyana are 10 to 14 per cent lower than f.o.b. prices obtained from the United

TABLE 16

AVERAGE F.O.B. PRICE OF BAUXITE IMPORTED INTO THE UNITED STATES

(per long ton)

Country of origin		1953	1954	1955	1956	1957	1958	1959	1960	1961	1962
Guyana	US$	5·72	6·78	6·75	6·81	6·92	6·99	6·99	6·85	7·24	9·16
	1953 = 100	100	119	118	119	121	122	122	119	126	160
Surinam	US$	6·51	6·62	6·75	6·77	7·84	7·85	8·04	7·72	9·32	9·86
Surinam	1953 = 100	100	102	104	104	120	121	124	119	143	151
Guyana=	100	114	98	100	99	113	112	115	113	129	108
Jamaica	US$	7·44	7·34	7·30	9·12	9·28	9·44	9·51	9·48	9·47	12·58
Jamaica	1953 = 100	100	99	98	123	125	127	128	127	127	169
Guyana =	100	130	108	108	134	134	135	136	138	131	137
Haiti	US$	—	—	—	—	9·05	8·71	8·72	8·90	9·41	9·39
Haiti, Guyana =	100	—	—	—	—	131	125	125	130	130	103
Dominican Republic	US$	—	—	—	—	—	—	12·73	12·59	13·21	12·38
		—	—	—	—	—	—	182	184	182	135

Source: U.S. Bureau of Mines, *Mineral Yearbooks.*

TABLE 17

F.O.B. EXPORT PRICES OF DRY BAUXITE IN GUYANA

Destination		1953	1954	1955	1956	1957	1958	1959	1960	1961
Canada	BWI$	8·17	8·39	8·32	10·31	11·66	11·59	12·24	9·93	10·86
	US$	4·77	4·89	4·85	6·01	6·80	6·76	7·14	5·79	6·33
	1953 = 100	100	103	102	126	143	142	150	122	133
United States	BWI$	8·47	8·57	9·12	9·32	10·02	10·83	10·44	10·21	12·26
	US$	4·94	5·00	5·32	5·44	5·84	6·32	6·09	5·96	7·15
	1953 = 100	100	101	108	110	118	128	123	121	145
Total	BWI$	8·21	8·43	8·45	10·16	11·29	11·46	11·81	10·03	11·49
	US$	4·79	4·92	4·93	5·93	6·59	6·68	6·89	5·85	6·70
	1953 = 100	100	103	103	124	138	140	144	122	140

Source: *Guyana Annual Accounts relating to External Trade.*
Note: About 95 per cent of total exports is directed to Canada and the United States of America.

States customs returns for the same shipments. Comparing Jamaica or Surinam bauxite prices in Table 16 with those available from external trade statistics in Guyana, it appears that in 1961, the average Jamaican and Surinam price was 30 per cent and 32 per cent higher respectively than Guyana for the same year.

Bauxite price trends in Guyana also lag behind those of primary aluminium on the major world market. The price of primary aluminium, in the United Kingdom rose from £74 per long ton in 1946 to £186 per long ton in 1959, i.e. by 151 per cent.[1] From Table 18 it can be seen that the increase in the United States was from 14 cents per pound in 1948 to 25 cents in 1961, an increase of over 70 per cent.

TABLE 18

AVERAGE PRICE OF PRIMARY ALUMINIUM INGOT
ON THE NEW YORK MARKET 1948–61

Year	Monthly average price in cents per pound
1948	14·7
1949	16·0
1950	16·6
1951	18·0
1952	18·4
1953	19·7
1954	20·2
1955	21·9
1956	24·0
1957	25·4
1958	24·8
1959	24·7
1960	26·0
1961	25·5

Source: United States Department of Commerce, *Business Statistics 1961*, p. 160.

The bauxite industry differs from all other productive activities carried out in Guyana by the fact that the proportion of capital to labour employed is extremely high. There is little prospect that bauxite mining will employ any really large

[1] *Metal Statistics*, Metallgesellschaft, A.G., Frankfurt.

number of Guyanese workers; but since it employs so much capital, it can be expected to earn rather large profits in Guyana, and to be in consequence a rather prolific source of taxable capacity. The industry's wage bill is small relative to output, and the relatively high profits tend to be exported. Given these conditions, tax rates should be set at such a level to enable the country to ensure a reasonable return from what is, in effect, a wasting asset. Tax policy should also be used as an instrument for encouraging as much local processing of bauxite as possible. A generous remission of royalties on bauxite processed into alumina is repayed many times over by the increase in taxable capacity which results from the processing. And if the lower royalty rate fails to encourage processing no revenue is lost.

Revenue derived directly by the government from mining falls into three main categories: (a) rentals and royalties, (b) import and export duties, and (c) income tax. In the case of exploration for bauxite and other base minerals a rent of 1 cent per acre per year with no upward escalation is charged. The royalty on ore processed within the territory is 2 cents per ton compared with 25 cents per ton on bauxite exported in the raw state. This differential of 23 cents per ton between the royalty on crude bauxite and bauxite processed into alumina although very high did not encourage the American Company (Reynolds) to process their bauxite in Guyana in view of the advantages of low capital costs in America. The companies also pay corporate income tax of 45 per cent, and export duties of 45 cents per long ton.[1]

In view of the lack of a market price for bauxite, and the consequent difficulty of arriving at a 'true' profit residual, the

[1] *Annual Reports of the Department of Inland Revenue.* The royalty and export duty are paid on long dry tons. The law in fact does not stipulate whether the unit of account should be dry or wet tons. As dried bauxite may be from 5–25 per cent lighter than wet ore (the average for Guyana nearer 20–30 per cent), the correct interpretation of the law is important and should be clarified. In Jamaica, under the 1957 Agreement, the royalty is 4s. (95 cents, B.W.I.) per long dry ton for tonnage up to 1 million long dry tons, 3s. per long dry ton if the tonnage exceeds 1 million long dry tons, but does not exceed 2 million long dry tons; it is further reduced to 2s. for amounts in excess of 2 million tons only. Half the royalty, however, varies with the price of aluminium ingot. It does not appear that an export duty is levied in Jamaica. In Guyana royalty of 10 cents for exclusive permissions issued before July 1947, and 25 cents per long dry ton and export duty (45 cents per long dry ton) make a total of 55 cents and 70 cents per long dry ton.

Guyana government has always complained that the combined income tax, royalty rates, and export duties were much too low to bring it the revenue in keeping with the scale and nature of the operations involved. Therefore in 1962, the government appointed a Select Committee to deal with bauxite pricing policies and to examine various proposals for a tax agreement with the Reynolds Metal Company.

The Committee suggested a base price formula which should move in sympathy with the market price of aluminium ingots in the United States.[1] Although fluctuations in the world market price of aluminium metal may be influenced a great deal by the producers themselves, with a considerable part of the metal production being disposed of as an end product as far as these major producers are concerned, such price trends seem to take the variables of a competitive market more realistically into account than the pricing of bauxite where, in the absence of an open market, a fair price is more difficult to assess. A formula whereby the pricing of ore would be linked to that of the aluminium metal would have the distinct advantage that by a fixed ratio the share of bauxite and smelter operations in relation to the total profits of the major concerns would be established, thereby providing a fair basis for taxation.

On the other hand, it does not appear expedient to relate the basic price of bauxite to variations in the pricing of steel, the main competitor of aluminium, as recommended by the Committee. It has now been a policy with the major aluminium producers of the world for many years past to keep aluminium metal prices at a comparatively stable level so as to permit aluminium to compete with, and to be used as a substitute for, other metals or materials. Accordingly, with fresh advances in mining and processing technologies, the major producers of the world were not affected by the impact of price fluctuations characteristic of other metals, and in line with this policy aluminium prices rose at a much slower rate than those of other metals. For example, between 1939 and 1960 in the United kingdom the average steel price increased by 300 per cent and

[1] A similar provision was made in the 1957 Jamaican Agreement, whereby the revenue from bauxite was made partially dependent on the price of aluminium ingot by an escalator clause, by which one-half of the combined royalty and income-tax rate was fixed while the other half was to vary in response to changes in the price of aluminium ingots.

16—E.D.G.

that of copper by 400 per cent while the price of aluminium only doubled. In fact trends in the price of steel and other metals are determined and influenced by factors entirely different from those applying to aluminium. Therefore, it does not seem desirable to tie up bauxite pricing with any such factors.

The main idea of the Committee's recommendations is to assure for Guyana nearly equal total levies to those assured for the government of Jamaica under the New Jamaica Agreement or for the Surinam government under the Brokopondo Agreement. Taking into consideration that the rate of income tax is lower in Surinam than in Guyana (30 per cent as against 45 per cent), and that the government levies too are different, the Committee recommended to apply as an equivalent to the BWI$19·00 Surinam price, a bauxite price of $14·00 which is about 14 per cent higher than the actual average export price of metallurgical-grade bauxite exported by the Demerara Bauxite Company in 1963 (BWI$11·85), and about 17 per cent higher than the estimated export price of Reynolds in 1963, (BWI$12·00). The taxation system recommended by the Committee is expected to bring sizeable financial benefits to the government. However, firm decision is yet to emerge as regards the most lucrative or feasible taxation structure for the bauxite enterprises in Guyana.

(f) *Long-term development prospects.* The long-term outlook for the bauxite complex in Guyana depends both upon the general prospects of alumina and aluminium products industry in the world market and on policies pursued by the government. The growth potential of the industry seems favourable. Demand has been increasing rapidly, and consumption of aluminium in all its forms has grown at about 9 per cent per annum despite the recent emergence of keener competition from plastics, fibreglass, and stainless steel. Experience of the last few years has made it clear that because of its inherent qualities and economic attractions, aluminium should be considered a product of the future which has not yet reached a point where expansion follows closely the trend of the expanding world economy. This makes the forecasting of the demand for aluminium even more difficult. The consumption of the metal is growing, both through traditional outlets and in new end-uses. For obvious reasons it is more difficult to estimate growth trends dependent on end-uses, since these depend in turn on such factors as the actual progress achieved in technology, the effort spent in promotion, and the price of the metal in relation to other competitive materials. Through all these factors, growth in demand is intimately interrelated with growth in supply, as was learnt from the experience of the wartime economy when expansion of productive capacities in aluminium attracted new outlets by improvements in technology, cuts in production costs, and a well-conceived promotion programme.

Therefore trends in future demand should be calculated carefully but realistically at a growth rate higher than that of the existing pattern of consumption, but probably not higher than that arrived at by simple extrapolation of past trends, i.e. allowance should always be made for the significant development in end-uses. This is supported by the fact that the new applications of aluminium in different fields of industry continue to grow at a rapid rate in the United States among other countries in spite of the already high level of consumption. In other countries, especially in Western Europe, the possibilities are even greater. The rapid industrialization of the socialist countries too will result in a substantial rise in aluminium demand, and projections of aluminium consumption for these countries therefore envisage a much higher rate of growth than the general development of industrial production. There can be little doubt that the industrialization process of less developed countries would result in a substantial increase in their own aluminium consumption, and this will probably produce a higher growth rate than that of the more industrialized countries.[1] Thus the over-all demand prospects for bauxite, alumina, aluminium, and related products are very encouraging.[2] It must, however, be noted that the expansion of the world industry has been accompanied by the setting up of additional refining facilities in many countries, with the result that capacity has been growing faster than demand. The current position is that aluminium plants in most parts of the world are working

[1] *Per capita* consumption of aluminium products in development countries is only 1·3 pounds compared with 9·1 pounds in Western Europe and 28·1 pounds in the United States of America.

[2] See United Nations, *Perspective Demand for Non-Agricultural Commodities* (United Nations Secretariat, May 1962); K. A. Bohr, *The Prospects for Aluminium*, I.B.R.D.

at approximately 85 per cent of capacity while new plants are being planned for, or being constructed, in Ghana, Venezuela, Argentina, Australia, and a number of other countries.

It is therefore very likely that aluminium companies will prefer to move further toward fuller and more efficient utilization of available capacity as a means of improving their profits. With this shift in emphasis from volume towards efficiency, the companies' policies are becoming geared to putting the plants nearer full capacity and old plants are being modified to enable them to adjust quickly to new peak demand, while avoiding the construction of entirely new plants. ALCAN are operating further below capacity than the average for the industry as a whole. All this may well mean that before Guyana can get a smelter, she may have to wait until the next drive towards the expansion of capacity begins. In this respect her neighbours Surinam and Venezuela have been more diligent.[1]

Guyana's bargaining position, however, is not altogether weak. She is the third largest producer of bauxite for the North American market, and her reserves place her third in the Western Hemisphere. Besides, her ore is of a relatively high degree of purity. This is an important advantage both for the production of alumina, for sweetening United States low-grade ore, and for the manufacture of refractories and abrasives. There is no doubt that these advantages can be fully exploited if the bauxite ore were to be converted into alumina and aluminium within the country. To bring this about Guyana would need foreign partners with finance and technical knowledge. The government would have, then, an opportunity for direct participation through a share in the equity capital.

---

[1] The need for a more integrated Caribbean Bauxite policy becomes very obvious is this regard. See Girvan, op. cit.

V

FOREIGN TRADE AND PAYMENTS

1. *The Importance of Trade*

In previous chapters we hinted at the important influence exercised by external trade upon the development of some of the more influential sectors of the economy. In the present chapter we extend the analysis a stage further by tracing the nature and extent of the connection between foreign trade and the development of the economy as a whole. In particular, we shall be concerned with changes in the structure and direction of trade and the implications for future development.

Both exports and imports increased appreciably during the period under review. The growth of these variables at current prices is shown in Table 1 below. Total merchandise exports at current prices increased from an average of $85 million in 1953/4 to nearly $163 million in 1963/4, representing an average annual increase of about 9 per cent. On the other hand, imports showed an average rate of annual increase of about 8 per cent, rising from nearly $80 million in 1953/4 to over $149 million in 1964. Thus the growth of exports tended to outpace the growth in imports, but only to a marginal degree. Unfortunately no constant price indices exist for the growth of these variables, but it may be expected that when corrections are made for price increases the above figures will be reduced. However, there is no reason to believe that the tendency of the growth of exports to outstrip slightly that of imports will reverse itself.

Before attempting a more rigorous analysis of the behaviour of the strategic variables in the foreign trade sector, we may give some indication of the importance of foreign trade in the Guyanese economy. Throughout the period under review a close similarity is revealed in the movements and direction of change of trade and Gross National Product. The periods of

TABLE 1

MERCHANDISE EXPORTS AND IMPORTS
(CURRENT PRICES)

(*Thousand dollars; 1954 = 100*)

Year	Exports	Index	Imports	Index
1954	85,404	100	79,970	100
1955	90,533	106	94,518	118
1956	94,592	111	99,877	125
1957	108,086	127	118,470	148
1958	97,228	114	116,026	145
1959	103,520	121	110,620	138
1960	127,312	148	147,599	184
1961	148,863	174	147,001	183
1962	164,187	192	126,277	158
1963	174,825	204	118,511	148
1964	162,816	191	149,781	187

Source: Annual Accounts Relating to External Trade.
The figures for exports exclude sugar preference certificates.

stagnation, rapid growth, and settling down of this variable were matched by similar movements in trade. The results of a multiple correlation analysis carried out between Gross National Product and the main components of foreign trade reveals how important trade is to the economy. A summary is given in the table below.

TABLE 2

CORRELATION BETWEEN G.N.P. AND MAIN COMPONENTS
OF FOREIGN TRADE

(1) Variables	(2) Correlation coefficients	(3) Regression equations
1. G.N.P./Exports (X)	0·935	$Y = 96386·12 + 1·115734X$
2. G.N.P./Imports (M)	0·866	$Y = 77962·18 + 1·252265M$
3. Exports/Imports	0·780	
4. G.N.P./Exports, Imports	0·921	$Y = 74827·63 + 7905X + 0·5051M$

The simple correlation coefficient of 0·935 between G.N.P. (dependent variable) and exports (independent variable) was significant at the 1 per cent level, while all the other results were significant at the 5 per cent level. As a further check of these results and those of other correlations carried out later in this chapter, a double log function of the form $\log Y = \log A + b \log X$ was employed, but this did not alter the conclusions.

Another rough indication of the importance of trade in the Guyanese economy is gained by expressing both exports and the value of retained imports as a percentage of gross domestic product. This exercise reveals that between 1953 and 1964 both imports and exports constituted around 50 per cent. This is also a measure of the degree of openness characterizing the economy.[1]

The relative importance of trade in the Guyanese economy is in part related to the nature of its historical development as a plantation economy geared to the export trade and relying on imports for the greater part of its supply of manufactured goods.[2] Unlike the Trinidad and Jamaican cases, recent years have not seen any significant diversification of the resource base, so the reliance on imports to furnish such things as raw materials and capital equipment was only part of a secular trend rather than a demand for raw materials for new industries. The continual increase in income has increased the demand for a wide range of manufactured goods which cannot yet be produced, or never will be produced locally. As imports grew, more and more strenuous efforts had to be made to increase the value of exports so as to meet external obligations.

The heavy reliance on foreign trade makes the country very susceptible to fluctuations in the level of activity within the borders of its principal trading partners. It can be categorized as a dependent economy in that external transactions account for a relatively large part of the social income and it is too small a consumer of the world's exports to have much influence upon

[1] Guyana is not unique in this regard. For example in Trinidad and Jamaica imports accounted for an average of 40 per cent and 34 per cent respectively of G.D.P. over the period. The lower figures for these territories reflect their attempts at setting up their own light manufacturing industries, with a consequent reduction in the import leakage. The corresponding import figures for the U.S.A., the United Kingdom, and Canada were 4, 25, and 23 per cent respectively in 1963. *International Financial Statistics*, 1964.

[2] The salient features regarding the growth of the traditional 'Export Economy' have been admirably summarized by Prof. Myint. See H. Myint, *The Economics of Developing Countries* (London, 1964), Chs. 2–4.

the countries that provide its principal markets.[1] Given the small contribution that the country's demand makes to total world exports, the territory is in fact a price taker. While this characteristic has induced little internal instability, it is highly responsible for the failure of the standard of living to increase.

2. *Exports*

We saw that during the period under review both exports and imports accounted for an average of 50 per cent of Gross Domestic Product. We also noticed that the value of domestic exports nearly doubled between 1953 and 1964. Not only were exports virtually the only autonomous source of income growth, but the export sector was the dynamic centre of the whole economy. But when the composition of domestic exports over the period is examined, it is discovered that the increase has been almost entirely due to the dominance of a few items, while other commodities have shown relative stagnation. From Tables 3 (a) and 3 (b), which present the value and percentage contributions respectively of the main items of domestic exports, it can be observed that the governing dynamic of the economy is provided by three main groups of products, viz, sugar and its by-products, bauxite and alumina, and rice, with a very insignificant contribution made by the timber industry. The country has from time to time also exported small quantities of coffee, oil (coconut), and ground provisions to other countries in the Commonwealth Caribbean, but in small quantities which are statistically insignificant.

Thus sugar and its by-products have accounted for an average of 50 per cent of the total value of exports, the contribution of bauxite and alumina averaged 30 per cent, while that of rice amounted to 9 per cent. In earlier chapters we discussed the main factors governing the demand-and-supply coefficients of

---

[1] In the literature on monetary and development problems, the terms 'dependent economies', 'dependent systems', 'export economies', have all been used interchangeably and not always in such a way that the meaning attached to these terms was quite clear. A concise and useful discussion of the semantics of these terms can be found in the following study: H. M. A. Onitiri, 'Nigeria's Balance of Payments and Economic Policy 1946–1960' (Unpublished PH.D. Thesis, London, 1963), pp. 129–36.

TABLE 3 (a)

VALUE OF THE PRINCIPAL ITEMS OF DOMESTIC EXPORTS

(*Million Guyana dollars*)

	1954	1955	1956	1957	1958	1959	1960	1961	1962	1963	1964
Sugar	41·9	40·3	41·6	53·6	54·7	46·4	57·5	56·8	59·3	73·6	53·9
Molasses	1·2	1·0	0·9	2·0	2·6	2·3	2·7	2·7	3·0	5·7	4·0
Rum	2·3	3·2	3·8	3·3	3·5	3·5	3·0	3·1	3·2	3·1	3·3
Rice	9·3	12·5	9·9	9·2	4·9	13·8	15·4	22·6	20·5	20·1	21·8
Bauxite	23·0	24·8	29·3	20·6	24·8	29·5	28·5	31·1	28·6	28·6	30·2
Alumina	—	—	—	—	—	—	—	12·1	22·7	22·3	26·7
Manganese	—	—	—	—	—	—	2·2	5·4	6·7	N.A.	
Gold and diamonds	2·1	2·1	1·7	1·9	2·0	3·0	4·8	5·1	4·0	3·6	4·5
Timber	—	—	—	—	3·6	3·3	3·5	3·0	3·0	2·5	2·6

TABLE 3 (b)

SHARES OF MAJOR EXPORTS IN TOTAL DOMESTIC EXPORTS

(*percentage*)

	1954	1955	1956	1957	1958	1959	1960	1961	1962	1963	1964
Sugar, rum, and molasses	52	52	53	54	63	51	50	42	40	42	38
Bauxite and alumina	25	29	34	27	21	24	24	27	32	29	35
Rice	11	14	11	9	5	13	11	15	13	12	13
Others	11	5	2	10	11	12	15	16	15	17	14
Total	100	100	100	100	100	100	100	100	100	100	100

Source: Annual Accounts Relating to External Trade.

these commodities. But a striking feature of the growth of exports has been the significant contribution made by the new exports of alumina after 1961, the year that marked the commencement of export of this valuable item. Thus even if one is struck by the high percentage contribution of exports to Gross Domestic Product, the relative paucity of items that enter export must give rise to concern regarding the territory's vulnerability in the event of changes of attitudes of its main foreign customers.

In addition, it was decided to obtain a separate index of the relative importance of these three main items of domestic exports, and the results of the multiple correlation analysis given below confirm our earlier findings.

REGRESSION OF G.N.P. OF MAIN ITEMS OF DOMESTIC
EXPORTS

Variables	Correlation coefficients
G.N.P./Exports of sugar	0·903
G.N.P./Exports of bauxite	0·758
G.N.P./Exports of rice	0·737
G.N.P./Exports of sugar and bauxite	0·834
G.N.P./Exports of three main items	0·897

We referred earlier to the possibility of Guyana suffering from a high degree of instability because of the lack of control over the factors determining her income. It has been suggested that the ratios of exports, investment, and government expenditure are characteristically different in developing and developed countries.[1] The importance of the relative ratios is that since domestic investment and government expenditure are subject to national control, while exports are not, a high ratio of exports to national income means that the country has little control over the course of its income. The level of exports depends on incomes abroad and inventory policy, and only to a limited extent on what takes place at home. It has been further argued that in developing countries, the ratio of exports to

[1] H. C. Wallich, 'Underdeveloped Countries and the International Monetary Mechanism', in *Money, Trade and Economic Growth* (Macmillan, New York, 1951), pp. 15–32.

total income (X/Y) tends to be higher than either the ratio of investment to income (I/Y) or the ratio of government expenditure to income (G/Y). The table below, which compares these ratios for the Guyanese economy, shows that although the government expenditure and investment have been high in comparison with developing countries generally, the ratio of exports to income has in most years been twice as high as the other two ratios.

TABLE 4

RELATIVE SIZES OF EXPORTS (X), INVESTMENT (I)
AND GOVERNMENT SPENDING (G) AS
PROPORTION OF INCOME (Y)

Year	X/Y	I/Y	G/Y
1954	45	20	17
1955	47	24	20
1956	46	23	19
1957	47	27	18
1958	42	29	19
1959	43	24	18
1960	48	31	19
1961	52	26	19
1962	53	20	20
1963	63	17	22
1964	52	21	21

Source: Compiled from *Quarterly Statistical Digests*, Sundry Years.

However, the hypothesis discussed above is subject to qualification. For when a comparison is made with other countries (Table 5), it turns out that there are both developed and developing countries in each of the four categories. But even if doubts are cast on quantitative differences, the qualitative ones may be more significant. An exporter of primary products like Guyana has a poorly developed capital market and a relatively under-developed domestic sector. When exports rise, two consequences follow. The profitability of exports makes further investment in the sector possible, so that investment rises; and the undeveloped state of the capital market means that the

TABLE 5
RELATIVE SIZES OF EXPORTS (X), INVESTMENT (I), AND GOVERNMENT SPENDING (G) AS A PROPORTION OF INCOME (Y) 1960

Country	X/Y	Country	X/Y
$X > I+G$		$X > I$ and $X > G$ (*continued*)	
Luxembourg	103	Great Britain	24
Trinidad and Tobago	94	Honduras (1957)	24
Puerto Rico	58	Guatemala	22
Netherlands	57	Portugal	20
Belgian Congo	52	Egypt (1956)	19
Cyprus	51	Nigeria (1957)	18
Denmark	41	Mexico	17
Cuba	40	Chile	14
Panama	38	Philippines	14
Ceylon	36		
Eire	33	$X > I$ or $X > G$	
Ghana	32	Iceland	37
Tanganyika	29	Peru (1957)	31
Morocco	27	Finland	30
Belgium	23	Canada	25
		Burma	23
$X > I$ and $X > G$		Australia	19
Norway	52	Italy	18
Rhodesia and Nyasaland	47	Japan	16
Venezuela	41		
South Africa	38	$X < I$ and $X < G$	
Jamaica	34	France	17
Switzerland	34	Israel	14
Austria	32	Greece	13
Costa Rica	32	India (1956)	7
Germany	31	United States	6
New Zealand	30	Spain (1957)	6
Ecuador	24		

Source: United Nations, *Yearbook of National Accounts Statistics*, 1961.

government is not well placed to borrow for expenditure, with the consequence that government expenditure waits on revenue. As the value of exports rises government tax revenue increases. This would normally have a stabilizing effect, but the government may have many projects waiting, and responds to added tax receipts by enlarging expenditure. In consequence both investment and government expenditure depend on exports in contrast to the situation in a developed economy, where they may be larger and are independent.[1]

3. *Imports*

One way of gauging the importance of trade in the economy and the role it has played in the economic development of the territory is by examining the relationship between trade and the individual demand components, i.e., consumption, capital formation, and exports. One procedure in this analysis is the derivation of the import content of final demand consumption, capital formation, and exports. Such a measure yields the importance of imports to the economy, and will be carried out at a later stage. However, on the more general level we may indicate the importance of imports by correlating import changes with the individual demand components referred to above. As expected, there is a high degree of correlation between imports and these variables, as an examination of the correlation coefficients reveals.

TABLE 6

Variables	Correlation coefficients	Regression equations
Imports/Consumption (X_1)	0·923	$Y = -24161·17 + 798·58X_1$
Imports/Capital formation (X_2)	0·904	$Y = 25215·84 + 1·5031X_2$
Imports/Exports (X_3)	0·780	$Y = 42680·73 + 0·6437X_3$
Imports/All components	0·946	$Y = 8766·18 + 96·42X_1$
		$+ 1·1459X_2 + 0·18517X_3$

All these results were significant at the 5 per cent level.

Tables 7 (a) and 7 (b) present data on the value and percentage contributions respectively of the broad categories of imports. A significant feature of the data is that imports of food were responsible for an average of 20 per cent of the total value of imports over the period. This is revealing in a country whose potential for agricultural development cannot be exaggerated. The high percentage of total imports absorbed by manufac-

---

[1] There is some offset to this instability, however, in the fact that Guyana has a high propensity to import and therefore a low internal multiplier, which may contribute to stability.

TABLE 7 (a)

VALUE OF TOTAL IMPORTS BY COMMODITY SECTIONS 1953-64

(Thousand B.W.I. dollars, c.i.f.)

	1953	1954	1955	1956	1957	1958	1959	1960	1961	1962	1963	1964
1. Food	16,035	18,068	19,706	20,600	21,626	22,069	22,147	24,755	25,751	26,956	24,578	28,680
2. Beverages and tobacco	1,927	2,099	2,293	2,086	2,173	1,899	1,688	2,118	2,377	1,620	1,591	1,732
3. Crude materials exc. fuels	587	634	564	594	953	742	805	919	811	808	557	792
4. Mineral fuel lubricant and materials	5,991	6,524	7,620	8,399	9,423	8,357	9,168	11,183	12,927	13,080	12,032	14,486
5. Animal and vegetable oil and fats	809	603	537	692	1,182	1,445	1,386	1,802	1,370	570	1,275	1,180
6. Chemicals	4,787	6,019	7,254	8,333	8,982	9,266	9,018	10,246	13,434	13,021	16,839	16,460
7. Manufactured goods by materials	17,003	19,592	25,460	25,554	32,853	32,134	28,996	36,086	33,250	27,778	24,898	32,776
8. Machinery transport equipment	14,293	17,773	20,665	23,043	28,243	28,544	26,357	44,899	41,936	30,390	24,388	38,427
9. Miscellaneous manufactures	7,475	8,509	10,332	10,446	12,935	11,442	10,904	15,092	14,555	11,633	11,009	14,822
10. Miscellaneous transactions	279	376	418	391	537	519	532	499	589	621	438	437

TABLE 7 (b)

PERCENTAGE CONTRIBUTION OF CATEGORIES OF IMPORTS

	1953	1954	1955	1956	1957	1958	1959	1960	1961	1962	1963	1964
1. Food	22·2	22·5	20·7	20·5	18·2	19·0	20·0	16·8	17·6	21·3	20·8	19·2
2. Beverages and tobacco	2·7	2·6	2·4	2·1	1·8	1·6	1·5	1·4	1·6	1·8	1·3	1·2
3. Crude materials inedible excl. fuels	0·8	0·8	0·6	0·6	0·8	0·6	0·7	0·6	0·6	0·6	0·5	0·6
4. Mineral fuel lubricant and materials	8·3	8·1	8·1	8·4	8·0	7·2	8·3	7·6	8·8	10·2	10·2	9·6
5. Animal and vegetable oil and fats	1·0	0·8	0·6	0·7	1·0	1·2	1·3	1·2	0·9	0·2	1·1	1·2
6. Chemicals	6·6	7·5	7·7	8·3	7·5	8·0	8·1	6·9	9·1	10·2	14·2	10·9
7. Manufactured goods by materials	23·6	24·4	26·8	25·5	27·5	27·6	26·1	24·5	22·6	22·0	21·1	21·8
8. Machinery transport equipment	24·0	22·2	21·8	23·0	23·8	24·5	23·7	30·4	28·5	24·1	21·1	25·6
9. Miscellaneous manufactures	10·4	10·6	10·9	10·5	10·9	9·8	9·8	10·2	9·9	9·2	9·3	9·6
10. Miscellaneous transactions	0·4	0·5	0·4	0·4	0·5	0·5	0·5	0·4	0·4	0·3	0·4	0·3
	100·0	100·0	100·0	100·0	100·0	100·0	100·0	100·0	100·0	100·0	100·0	100·0

Source: Annual Accounts Relating to External Trade; Quarterly Digests of Statistics.

tured goods and machinery and transport equipment is also evident. Imports of manufactures accounted for an average of over 30 per cent of total imports, while in most years machinery and transport equipment were responsible for over 23 per cent of the total. This is to be expected, for while production for the domestic market tends to put a brake on the importation of certain classes of goods, the relative shift from consumption to investment which characterizes the early stage of development tends to increase the demand for such imports, mainly because in developing countries the import content of investment goods tends to be higher than that of consumption goods. This was reflected in the years between 1957 and 1961 when there were heavy imports of machinery for the construction of the alumina plant at Mackenzie, and the expansion of the bauxite and manganese industries.

It would seem that the increasing trend in the value of imports was a result more of an increase in the volume of imports than in the prices of the main categories.[1]

We noticed at the beginning of this chapter that although the value of exports nearly doubled between 1953 and 1964, imports showed a more or less proportionate increase, so that over the years net foreign earnings have been insignificant. This not only reveals the need for export stimulation and promotion in a wider range of commodities, but also a closer examination of the import structure of the territory in order to ascertain what changes are possible in the field of import substitution [2] and related avenues so as to increase the potential size of the foreign exchange component.

4. Terms of Trade

The terms of trade are very important economic indicators in a country such as Guyana in which foreign trade accounts for a

---

[1] See *Indices of External Trade of Guyana* (Statistical Bureau, 1966).

[2] There is a growing realization of the limitations on, and adverse consequences of, the policy of fostering development through import substitution on a national basis. The *indiscriminate* pursuit of import substitution in a small market and from a rudimentary base of industrial skill and organizing ability tends to produce enormous inefficiency and waste. For balanced amplifications of this argument see H. G. Johnson, *The World Economy at Crossroads* (Oxford, 1965), Ch. 5, and E.C.L.A., 'The Growth and Decline of Import Substitution in Brazil', *Economic Bulletin for Latin America*, Vol. IX, No. 1 (March 1964), pp. 1–60.

relatively large portion of the social income. The relevant data on the movement of the terms of trade are given in Table 8 below.

TABLE 8

TERMS OF TRADE

Year	(1) Export price index	(2) Export value index	(3) Import price index	(4) Commodity terms of trade Col. (1) ÷ Col. (3)	(5) Income terms of trade Col. (2) ÷ Col. (3)
1953	97	85	95	102	89
1954	95	90	93	102	97
1955	94	96	96	98	100
1956	100	100	100	100	100
1957	113	115	101	112	101
1958	105	103	99	106	104
1959	105	109	95	111	115
1960	103	133	95	108	140
1961	—	—	—	112	—
1962	—	—	—	115	—

Source: *Quarterly Statistical Digest* (June 1964).

We may consider the commodity or net barter terms of trade which is the ratio of the export price index to the import price index. The movement of this index was very favourable during the greater part of the period between 1953 and 1962. This has been due to a combination of favourable price movements for agricultural and mining commodities, which accounted for the overwhelming proportion of Guyana's exports, and the relative constancy of the import price index.

Thus although the major generating factors in the economy are externally dependent, this has fortunately not been compounded by a situation of external price flexibility. The comparative stability and favourable nature of export prices is principally due to the marketing arrangements of the country's export products. These marketing arrangements have been examined in detail in the earlier chapters dealing with sugar, rice, and bauxite. But, as we also saw, sugar prices are partially stabilized by the existence of the Commonwealth Sugar Agreement. We have also seen that the bauxite industry is vertically integrated with the parent companies in Canada and the United States, and inter-company transactions insulate the industry against price fluctuations. Rice, the other main export commodity, is sold to the Caribbean area, Cuba, and Eastern Europe under state agreements. The comparative stability of export prices has also contributed to the relative stability of internal incomes. In doing so, it has helped to make internal expenditure, and hence prices, relatively stable, thus helping to explain the fact that the consumer price index for Guyana (1956 = 100) stood at 104·5 in 1961, and 111 in 1964.[1] The absence of significant internal price rises is in part due to the high average and marginal propensity to import, as well as the small economic size of the country in relation to the rest of the world, measured in terms of national income. By this is meant that increases in domestic income are quickly leaked abroad in the form of imports.

Favourable commodity terms of trade operate to the advantage of the country by promoting the growth in real income. In turn it tends to increase the real import capacity. However the income terms of trade or capacity to import is probably a better indicator of the performance of the economy.[2] The income terms of trade is the index of the value of exports divided by the index of the price for imports, and shows the imports obtainable for the exports actually sent out.[3] From column 5 of Table 8, it can be observed that the trend in the income terms of trade was steadily upwards throughout the period. In 1960,

---

[1] *Quarterly Digest of Statistics* (December 1964), p. 33.

[2] For an amplification of the view that the income terms of trade is of more relevance than the commodity terms of trade for policy decisions in developing countries see T. Morgan, 'The Long Run Terms of Trade between Agriculture and Manufacturing', *Economic Development and Cultural Change*, Vol. VIII, No. 1 (Oct. 1959), p. 20.

[3] Or alternatively, the income terms of trade weights the commodity terms of trade in proportion to shifts in the volume of exports. The two statements are algebraically identical. The income terms of trade are by definition

$$\frac{P_{x_i}}{P_{x_0}} \frac{Q_{x_i}}{Q_{x_0}} \frac{1}{P_{m_i}/P_{m_0}}$$

Where P is price, Q is quantity, x stands for exports, m for imports, i for the given year, and o for the base year, the formula can be presented instead as

$$\frac{P_{x_i}/P_{x_0}}{P_{m_i}/P_{m_0}} \frac{Q_{x_i}}{Q_{m_0}}$$

for example the economy's capacity to import was 40 per cent above the 1956 level and over 50 per cent above the 1953 level.

But arguments based on the direction of the terms of trade must be treated with some caution. They may not be an index of any marked changes of factor productivity in the economy. The point could be illustrated thus. Divide the total labour force of the economy into two parts; L_h which is the labour force devoted to home industry, and L_x which is that part of the labour force devoted to producing for export. Let P_h be the physical productivity of labour in home industry, and P_x the physical productivity of labour producing for export. Then let T_x be the physical term of trade, that is, the amount of real imports obtainable per unit of real exports. $L_h P_h$ then is the real product of domestic industry, and $L_x P_x T_x$ is the real domestic product of the export industry. The *per capita* income of the whole society can then be expressed by the following equation:

$$\Upsilon = \frac{L_h P_h + L_x P_x T_x}{L_h + L_x}$$

This equation brings out the main factors in the long-run rise in *per capita* incomes, and shows that there are roughly three ways in which *per capita* income can rise. Firstly, we can have a rise in T_x the terms of trade. Secondly, if $T_x P_x$ is greater than P_h a shift in the labour force out of home industries into export industries will increase *per capita* income. Thirdly, an increase in either P_h or P_x or both will increase *per capita* income. However, it is clear that the only hope for a long-run increase in *per capita* income is the third method. An increase in the terms of trade may increase *per capita* incomes for a while, and this seems to have been the case in Guyana. But this is something that cannot go on indefinitely, and it is a movement that is all too likely to reverse itself. A shift from low-income industries to high-income export industries or vice versa can also raise *per capita* incomes for a while, but this is a phenomenon that is fairly short lived, for as the shift goes on, the marginal incomes in the two sectors of the economy soon tend to equality. The only hope for sub-stantial and *sustained* rise in *per capita* income is a rise in the productivity of the labour force in one or both sectors of the economy.

A further qualification lies in the possible effects on the

distribution of income including the remission abroad on earnings on foreign investments and for immigrant labour services. The following account of outflow of profits shows that such surpluses may sometimes account for a very high proportion of the total value of exports, so that the question of the proportion in which export earnings are shared may be as important for local people as the terms of trade. The regression of outflow of profits on exports yielded a very high and significant correlation coefficient of 0·935 showing that exports are responsible for well over 80 per cent of the variation in profits. But the point of real importance in this connection is that the terms of trade that relate to the trade of a particular country may be quite different from the terms of trade of the nationals of that country. In cases like those of Guyana where foreign enterprises play the dominant role in the national economy, it may be useful to make a

OUTFLOW OF PROFITS

(Thousand Guyana dollars)

1954	11,015	1957	19,327	1960	22,380
1955	10,608	1958	15,781	1961	21,557
1956	12,497	1959	16,546	1962	34,110

Source: *Quarterly Statistical Digest* (June 1964 and December 1964).
Note: These profits relate to direct investment only. Depreciation is not subtracted for investment. Some of the differences between 1956 and 1957 are probably due to different methods of obtaining data.

distinction between the terms of trade of the country as a geographical entity, which we may call the 'domestic' or 'territorial' terms of trade, and the terms of trade of the nationals of that country, which may be referred to as the 'national' terms of trade.[1] It is not unlikely that changes in the two terms of trade may diverge widely, although tremendous difficulties may be encountered in attempts at measuring the latter.

[1] Professor Myint makes a similar but slightly different distinction between the internal and external terms of trade and also lists several important qualifications to heavy reliance on favourable movements of the terms of trade. See H. Myint, 'The Gains From International Trade and Backward Countries', *The Review of Economic Studies*, Vol. XXII (2), No. 58 (1954–5), pp. 131–3.

5. *The Direction of Trade*

For obvious reasons the British Commonwealth in general and the United Kingdom in particular have traditionally been Guyana's most important trading partners. Table 9 shows the percentage distribution of domestic exports by country of destination, while Table 10 shows the distribution of imports by country of origin. In 1954 the United Kingdom took 36·9 per cent of the territory's exports, and supplied 47 per cent of its imports. However, by 1964, exports to the United Kingdom accounted for only 20·5 per cent of total exports, while imports declined to 33·4 per cent. This points to a relative decline in our trade with the United Kingdom over the period, and over the period 1954 to 1964 exports to the United Kingdom averaged 32·4 per cent of total exports, while imports from this country averaged 41 per cent of the total. Nevertheless, in terms of volume the United Kingdom still remains our principal trading partner.

On the other hand, in the case of exports the relative shares of the United States of America and Canada changed from 8·4 per cent and 38·9 per cent respectively in 1954 to 16 per cent and 30 per cent respectively in 1964. During the same period imports from the United States increased from 13·6 per cent to 22·5 per cent, while that from Canada decreased from 10·2 per cent to 9 per cent. Thus on average between 1954 and 1964, the United States supplied 17·7 per cent of our total imports and took 14 per cent of our exports, while the corresponding figures for Canada were 8·4 per cent and 30·9 per cent respectively. It seems therefore that the decline in the relative position of the United Kingdom has been accompanied by the United States gaining ground as a supplier of imports and as an outlet for Guyana's exports. Not only has the relative position of the United Kingdom been gradually eroded, but her position in terms of the absolute level of Guyanese exports and imports have not shown any marked signs of improvement.

The data in Table 11 show that exports to the United Kingdom stood at $31 million in 1954, reached a high level of $46 million in 1958, declined again in 1959 to $43 million, and then rose again to $47 million in 1960. By 1964, it stood at $33 million, a figure just above the 1954 level. On the other hand,

TABLE 9

VALUE OF EXPORTS TO INDIVIDUAL COUNTRIES AS A PERCENTAGE OF TOTAL EXPORTS

Year	U.S.A.	Canada	U.K.	Barbados	Jamaica	Trinidad	Cuba	Netherlands	Other
1954	8·4	38·9	36·9	2·5	3·2	5·9	—	0·7	3·5
1955	8·8	35·6	35·7	3·1	4·6	6·6	—	1·3	4·3
1956	11·0	39·9	32·2	2·5	3·2	5·5	—	1·3	4·4
1957	7·3	37·1	40·1	1·8	3·2	4·4	—	0·5	5·6
1958	6·1	31·6	48·0	1·3	2·9	4·9	—	0·6	4·9
1959	8·7	27·4	41·2	2·2	4·0	7·5	—	0·6	8·4
1960	16·4	24·8	37·2	2·0	4·5	7·5	—	0·6	7·0
1961	23·3	25·7	24·6	1·7	3·0	6·2	5·4	1·3	8·8
1962	21·3	27·1	23·5	1·7	2·8	5·9	3·1	1·5	13·1
1964	16·1	30·0	20·5	1·8	2·5	8·9	2·6	1·5	15·1
(1954–64 ex-cluding 1963)	14·0	30·9	32·4	2·0	3·3	6·5	1·6	1·0	8·3

Source: Calculated from *Annual Accounts Relating to External Trade.*

TABLE 10

VALUE OF IMPORTS FROM INDIVIDUAL COUNTRIES AS PERCENTAGE OF TOTAL IMPORTS

Year	U.S.A.	Canada	U.K.	Barbados	Jamaica	Trinidad	Netherlands	Other
1954	13·6	10·2	47·0	0·7	0·1	9·5	4·7	14·2
1955	12·9	6·3	47·7	0·5	0·1	9·5	5·6	17·4
1956	12·9	8·7	44·6	0·5	0·1	10·0	5·2	18·0
1957	17·7	8·6	44·1	0·3	0·2	9·3	4·7	15·1
1958	16·0	7·4	46·1	0·2	0·2	9·5	4·9	15·7
1959	13·7	7·2	45·1	0·3	0·2	10·0	4·8	18·7
1960	19·8	10·5	30·1	0·2	0·2	0·3	9·4	16·3
1961	19·5	7·1	38·4	0·3	0·3	10·3	4·4	19·7
1962	22·9	7·4	35·3	0·2	0·3	12·3	4·7	16·9
1964	22·5	9·0	33·4	0·2	0·4	11·0	4·6	18·9
(1954–64 excluding 1963)	17·7	8·4	41·3	0·3	0·2	10·0	4·8	17·3

Source: Calculated from *Annual Accounts Relating to External Trade.*

TABLE II

TOTAL VALUE OF EXPORTS BY COUNTRIES

(Million Guyana dollars)

Year	Total	U.S.A.	Canada	U.K.	Barbados	Jamaica	Trinidad	Cuba	Netherlands
1954	85·4	7·2	33·2	31·5	2·1	2·7	5·0	a	0·6
1955	90·5	8·0	32·2	32·4	2·8	4·1	6·0	a	1·1
1956	94·6	10·4	37·8	30·4	2·4	3·0	5·1	a	1·2
1957	108·1	7·9	40·1	43·3	1·9	3·4	5·8	a	0·5
1958	97·2	5·9	30·7	46·7	1·2	2·9	4·7	a	0·5
1959	103·5	9·0	28·4	42·6	2·3	4·1	7·8	a	0·6
1960	126·8	20·8	31·5	47·2	2·6	5·7	9·5	a	0·7
1961	148·3	34·6	38·2	36·4	2·5	4·4	9·2	8·0	1·9
1962	163·7	34·9	44·4	38·5	2·8	4·6	9·7	5·1	2·5
1963	174·8	25·2	58·9	41·1	2·8	4·4	14·8	N.A.	2·7
1964	162·8	26·2	48·8	33·4	2·9	4·1	14·1	5·8	2·5

Source: Annual Accounts Relating to External Trade.
a Negligible.

TABLE 12

TOTAL VALUE OF IMPORTS BY COUNTRIES

(*Million Guyana dollars*)

Year	Total	U.S.A.	Canada	U.K.	Barbados	Jamaica	Trinidad	Netherlands
1954	80·2	10·9	8·1	37·7	0·6	a	6·8	3·8
1955	94·8	12·2	5·9	45·2	0·6	a	9·0	5·3
1956	100·1	13·0	8·7	44·7	0·6	0·1	10·0	5·2
1957	118·9	21·0	10·2	52·4	0·3	0·3	11·1	5·6
1958	116·4	18·6	8·6	53·7	0·3	0·2	11·0	5·7
1959	111·0	15·2	9·0	50·1	0·3	0·3	11·1	5·3
1960	147·6	29·1	15·6	57·6	0·3	0·4	13·8	6·4
1961	147·0	28·6	10·4	56·4	0·4	0·3	15·1	6·5
1962	126·3	29·0	9·4	44·6	0·3	0·4	15·6	6·0
1963	117·8	24·5	9·6	39·5	0·5	0·5	14·2	6·0
1964	149·8	33·8	13·5	50·0	0·4	0·7	16·3	6·9

Source: Annual Accounts Relating to External Trade.

a Negligible under $100,000.

exports to the United States increased from around $7 million
in 1954 to over $26 million in 1964, an increase of nearly 400
per cent. Exports to Canada also increased over this period,
rising from $33 million in 1954 to $49 million in 1964. Details
of changes in the absolute value of imports from these sources
are given in Table 12. The value of imports from the United
Kingdom fluctuated very widely over the period, rising from
$38 million in 1954 to $50 million in 1964. As noticed earlier,
imports from Canada and the U.S.A. increased steadily over
the period, from $8 million and $11 million respectively in 1954
to $13 million and $34 million respectively in 1964. Attention
should also be paid to the increasing value of our trade with the
Commonwealth Caribbean, and especially with Trinidad,
which has been selling more and more manufactured goods to
Guyana. The possibilities for increasing inter-unit trade in the
Commonwealth will be explored in a later section.

6. *Balance of Payments*

Before proceeding to an analysis of the main variables in the
country's payments sector, it is worthwhile clearing up a few
terminological and conceptual issues. The terms 'favourable'
and 'unfavourable' are frequently used to describe a country's
foreign balance, and they can be said to have validity in
describing a country with a managed currency, since it is
possible for such a country to find itself in a position where it is
unable to meet its foreign obligations. In such a case a devaluation of the currency may become necessary. However, for
some time now the view has been widely held that the terms do
not have the same meaning when used to describe a country
with a dependent currency. Thus Greaves claimed that a
colony cannot have a balance of payments problem as that
term is commonly understood.[1]

Under the Sterling Exchange Standard, which was in opera-

---

[1] Ida Greaves, *Colonial Monetary Conditions* (H.M.S.O., London, 1953). Greaves
supports her claim that a country cannot have a balance of payments problem by
asserting that if a colony is unable to meet its external obligations, it is because of a
lack of money—of income in internal currency—not because of a lack of foreign
exchange. For support of this claim, see A. Hazlewood, 'Economics of Colonial
Monetary Arrangements', *Social and Economic Studies*, Vol. 3, Nos. 3 and 4 (1954).

tion in Guyana until 1960, the territory was obliged by law to provide 100 per cent sterling assets as backing for the currency. The monetary system was then an extension of the monetary system of the United Kingdom and there was no question of a balance of payments problem arising since sterling could always be secured by tendering local currency, and through sterling other currencies could be purchased. In December 1954 a modified system was introduced. Currency Boards were to be empowered to purchase limited amounts of the securities of their local territories, but this recommendation was not implemented in Guyana until 1960, and even in that case the modification was only a marginal one. However, it could be claimed that from 1960 onwards the possibility of a balance of payments problem existed in the sense that the country could find itself short of sterling to meet its external obligations.

But even before this modification was introduced, it was not correct to argue that the sterling exchange standard necessarily involves the currency supply in a mechanical and inflexible relationship with the balance of payments. If it were true to argue, for example, that a surplus on the balance of payments of a country on the sterling exchange standard automatically involved expansion in the monetary supply, and vice versa, a serious problem would obviously arise. At a time of surplus on the balance of payments the internal pressure on resources is particularly high, and the danger of inflation is especially great. If in such circumstances an expansion automatically occurred, in the currency issue, some additional stimulus to this inflationary pressure would undoubtedly be given. Similarly, if a country is running an import deficit, there will naturally be deflationary influence at work in the economy; a contraction of the currency issue at such a time would give additional impetus to this downward pressure.

In fact, the connection between the issue of sterling exchange currency and the balance of payments is by no means wholly automatic and mechanical, primarily because the total volume of credit in most countries operating this system can be influenced by the banking system as well as the currency authorities. Although a surplus on the balance of payments would be one factor operating towards an increase in the issue of currency, the operations of the banking system can be such as to offset this tendency wholly or partly. Thus even in an independent monetary economy a balance of payments problem is not defined as occurring when the foreign exchange reserves are exhausted, for a balance of payments problem can exist even before this stage. All that the traditional arguments amount to is that a colony's external reserves will only be exhausted when all domestic cash balances are exhausted. But the process by which this occurs results in decreasing activity, incomes, and employment, and it is in these ways that a balance of payments problem may manifest itself.

Thus a balance of payments problem exists for a colony when its external reserves are falling. External reserves here would have to include all the monetary assets available to the community—the foreign assets held by commercial banks and private and public institutions. Secondly, when the level of activity, incomes, and employment are decreasing so as to force the community to import only what it can afford, and also to free reserves for export promotion. Thirdly, the level of trade restrictions is raised with the intention of preventing or correcting difficulties in trade and payments with the rest of the world. Therefore, unless meaningful assumptions are made about the levels of activity, employment, and the level of trade restrictions, and a proper definition of external reserves is given, no meaningful conception of the balance of payments problem can be arrived at.[1]

However, the fact remains that, on balance, dependent monetary economies like Guyana have not experienced severe balance of payments problems, and this for the following reasons. Firstly, the foreign trade multiplier has worked towards equilibrium in the balance of payments. A change in exports leads to a multiple expansion in money national income. This expansion depends on the size of leakages in the economy, i.e. the marginal propensities to import and save. Because in Guyana the marginal propensity to import is high, and the

---

[1] See C. Y. Thomas, 'The Balance of Payments and Money Supplies of a Colonial Monetary Economy', *Social and Economic Studies*, Vol. 12, No. 1 (March 1963), pp. 27–36. One of the main results of the functioning of the colonial type of monetary system in Guyana has been that the balance of payments problem has expressed itself in terms of income stagnation and unemployment rather than inflation and pressure towards devaluation.

marginal propensity to save probably small, the greater has been the tendency for balance of payments equilibrium to be preserved. Thus, given positive savings and no autonomous shifts in the schedules of investment and government expenditure, the foreign trade multiplier will of itself be sufficient to ensure equilibrium. The other vital factor is that the economy has largely been a price taker so that the domestic cost/price ratios were not likely for long to be out of line with the rest of the world. We saw that export prices are determined largely by international demand and supply, the same holding true of imports. And since the external sector has been responsible for the greater part of social income, domestic cost/price ratios were roughly in line with the foreign sector. This factor becomes more important the greater the substitutability of production and consumption patterns between the foreign and domestic sectors, and is true of any open economy.

Though for the period under review the balance of payments may not have had the same implications for Guyana as it would for an independent monetary system, nevertheless the accounting identities are useful as tools of analysis because they shed light on trends in the movement of certain variables which are important indicators of the behaviour of the economy, and will assume a more crucial importance now that the country has become an independent nation with responsibility for the management of its own financial affairs.

The balance of payments on current account for the years 1953 to 1964 are set out in Table 13. We have already considered the factors influencing the level of exports and imports. Throughout the period the territory incurred relatively sizeable deficits in respect of its merchandise trade. In 1953, when a surplus of nearly $12 million was recorded, this was to a large extent due to a reduction in the level of imports in that year. In 1954, the surplus of 1953 was halved, for although the level of exports continued an upward trend imports were rising faster. In 1955 there was a big shift in imports which seemed to represent an autonomous movement in the whole import schedule. The balance of trade swung into deficit, where it remained until 1960, when the highest deficit of the period— nearly $20 million—was recorded. From 1961 to 1964 the balance of merchandise trade was in surplus and this amounted

TABLE

BALANCE OF PAYMENTS

(*Thousand Guyana*

Year	1953	1954	1955	1956	1957
1. Exports f.o.b.	83,899	85,404	90,533	94,592	108,086
2. Imports c.i.f.	71,987	79,970	94,518	99,877	118,470
3. Balance of visible trade	+11,912	+5,434	−3,985	−5,285	−10,384
4. Foreign travel	150	150	200	250	−1,629
5. Transportation	446	359	289	881	−2,320
6. Investment income	−11,119	−10,929	−10,492	−12,051	−16,711
7. Transfers, subscriptions, etc.	785	750	2,528	1,041	1,004
8. Balance on current account	524	−4,864	−15,541	−16,130	−30,974

Source: Annual Accounts Relating to External Trade. Quarterly Statistical Digests.

to $2·2 million in 1961, $37·3 million in 1962, $54·2 million in 1963, and $18·3 million in 1964. Prices of rice and sugar were particularly good during these years, but the period was also one of low investment, and therefore an artificially depressed level of imports. Consumption too was relatively low from 1962 to 1964. With the recovery of the economy and a return of business and political stability and normal levels of activity, imports of capital equipment increased, the process of rebuilding inventories was started, and public and private consumption boomed.

The account for foreign travel after showing small net gains between 1952 and 1956 went into deficit in 1957, and has shown a continuous rise since then. Receipts on foreign travel account represent expenditure by foreigners visiting Guyana for goods, hotel accommodation, entertainment, and transportation within the country. Payments include similar expenditure abroad by Guyanese residents. The growing deficit on this account is mainly explained by the fact that the tourist industry is virtually non-existent in Guyana, unlike the situation in Trinidad and Jamaica which have flourishing tourist industries.[1]

[1] For example, expenditure on foreign travel by Jamaican residents stood at £2·6 million in 1961, but during that year foreigners spent £14·6 million in the country, so that a positive balance of £12 million emerged. See *Balance of Payments of Jamaica*, 1961, Dept. of Statistics, Jamaica. The value added by the Jamaican tourist industry now amounts to around £20 million annually.

13
CURRENT ACCOUNT

dollars)

1958	1959	1960	1961	1962	1963	1964
97,228	103,520	128,224	149,544	164,020	172,863	169,369
116,026	110,620	147,869	147,370	126,675	118,685	151,074
−18,798	−7,100	−19,645	+2,174	+37,345	+54,178	+18,295
−1,585	−1,925	−2,364	−2,012	−1,509	−1,616	−3,950
−5,015	−3,046	−4,731	−5,047	−1,107	+657	−640
−13,587	−17,431	−23,609	−23,246	−36,993	−28,476	−29,776
1,239	252	3,767	7,011	6,161	3,345	5,574
−39,082	−28,534	−44,723	−19,638	+8,994	+26,357	+11,695

Economic Survey of Guyana 1966.

The large deficits in the transport account in the years after 1957 is a reflection of the paucity of international transport facilities owned and operated by Guyanese. The investment account reflects a large and growing deficit and in most years has been the main variable responsible for the large deficit on current account. Payments on this account represent interest, profit, and dividend after tax, of foreign-owned concerns resident in Guyana, as well as interest paid abroad by Guyanese-owned private companies. Interest on Public Debt and on private capital payable overseas is also part of the payments in respect of investment income. On the receipts side the item covers income earned abroad by Guyanese-owned companies and by the government on investments in foreign securities, including sinking funds, Post Office Savings Bank, Sugar Funds and Trust Funds. Thus although the public sector did not contribute much to the outflow of investment income abroad, it did export some capital and therefore reduced the proportion of import capacity that could be used for consumption and capital formation. The export of capital was largely in the form of building up of the country's currency reserves and to provide backing for the note issue which by law contained only a negligible proportion of domestic securities.

An indication of the trend in payments and receipts on the investment income account is gained from the data in Table 14.

Between 1952 and 1962 payments on this account amounted to $203 million, of which only $41 million was in respect of interest on the public debt. The rest accrues to foreign holders of private investment in Guyana. This component of investment amounted to $162 million between 1952 and 1962. In 1962 it stood at $31 million or nearly four times what it was in 1952. The increasing outflow of investment income bears a direct relation to the heavy inflow of foreign capital during the period, particularly into mining and the sugar industry. On the receipts

TABLE 14
RECEIPTS, PAYMENTS ON INVESTMENT ACCOUNT AND INTEREST ON PUBLIC DEBT
(*Thousand B.W.I. dollars*)

Year	Receipts	Payments	Interest on Public Debt.
(1)	(2)	(3)	(4)
1952	1,044	9,517	946
1953	1,122	12,321	945
1954	1,141	12,070	1,900
1955	1,241	11,733	1,992
1956	1,396	13,447	2,601
1957	1,840	18,551	3,624
1958	2,068	15,655	4,159
1959	2,041	19,472	4,387
1960	2,261	25,870	5,951
1961	2,253	25,499	6,590
1962	1,739	38,732	7,938

Sources: Quarterly Statistical Digest. Statistical Bureau, *Analysis of Domestic Products.*

side interest and dividends earned by the government on foreign investments amounted to $81 million between 1952 and 1962, which was far less than the outflow of payments in 1964. From Table 15 it can be seen that in relation to the size of the Gross Domestic Product the net outflow of investment income is relatively small, amounting to an average of 7 per cent between 1954 and 1962. But its significance is better understood if it is expressed as a percentage of net capital formation. Between 1954 and 1962, the net outflow of investment income amounted to approximately 34 per cent of the value of net investment. This ranged from a low level of 18 per cent in 1958 to as much as 73 per cent in 1962. The relative size of the outflow can be diminished only to the extent that foreign capital becomes less important as a component of capital formation. But this is compatible with continuing growth of real output only to the extent that domestic savings increase appreciably relative to national income, or by the government taking more steps to participate in the gains from foreign investment by promoting more joint investment ventures.

TABLE 15

GROSS DOMESTIC PRODUCT, NET INVESTMENT,
AND OUTFLOW OF INVESTMENT INCOME

Year	G.D.P.	Net invest- ment	Net outflow of investment income	Col. (4) as % of Col. (2) av.	Col. (4) as % of Col. (3) av.
(1)	(2)	(3)	(4)	(5)	(6)
1954	191,652	29,968	10,929	6	46
1955	191,540	47,378	10,492	6	22
1956	206,894	46,619	12,051	6	26
1957	231,561	58,994	16,771	6	28
1958	234,102	73,568	13,587	6	18
1959	239,427	69,924	17,431	7	25
1960	263,487	74,954	23,609	9	31
1961	289,785	71,540	23,246	8	33
1962	307,181	50,107	36,993	12	73

Sources: Quarterly Statistical Digests. Statistical Bureau, *Analysis of Domestic Product.*

Payments on the transfer account (Table 13) include remittances to foreign countries by migrants to Guyana, pensions from the government and contributions by the Guyana government to other governments. Receipts include remittances from emigrants mainly in the United Kingdom, the United States, and Canada as well as official grants from overseas governments and international organizations. An important element in this account has been the local expenditure by United Kingdom forces stationed in the country. This account grew from a small deficit of $760,000 in 1952 to a surplus of $6 million in 1962. The favourable situation after 1960 was to a large extent due to increased emigration to the United Kingdom after that year, for unlike that of a country such as Jamaica emigration to foreign countries of Guyana nationals has always been numerically insignificant.

Thus the sizeable deficits on the balance of merchandise trade experienced for most years, the large amounts that have to be remitted abroad in the form of transportation costs, payment for insurance, and the net outflow of investment income, have all contributed to the country's experience of sizeable deficits on current account for most of the period reviewed.

7. *Trade Balance with Principal Trading Partners*

We saw in an earlier section that there was a total decline in Guyana's trade with the United Kingdom, but that the rate of decline of exports was faster than that of imports in this case. We also noticed the increasing importance of the territory's trade with the United States of America. Lack of detailed information prevents a detailed breakdown of all the items in the current account by trading area—an exercise which would shed further light on the structural changes of Guyana's trading relationships. However, the information contained in Table 16 indicates how Guyana fared, in trade with the principal currency and trading areas.

Guyana had a deficit with the Sterling Area for the greater part of the period under consideration. In 1955 it stood at $15 million, but, after a small surplus in 1962, rose to over $17 million in 1964. The deficit with the United Kingdom is the instrumental variable in this regard. The country has been experiencing a continuing deficit with Trinidad, small surpluses with Barbados, Jamaica, and the other islands and this has been responsible for turning the aggregate flow of trade with the Commonwealth Caribbean in Guyana's favour. But this has not been high enough to counteract the growing deficits with the United Kingdom.

Throughout the period, this territory maintained sizeable surpluses with the Dollar Area. Although total imports from this area have shown increases for most years, exports showed signs of increasing at a faster rate, especially in the years after 1959. The main reason for this lay in Guyana's ability to sell larger quantities of calcined bauxite for the abrasive and re-

TABLE 16

EXPORTS, IMPORTS, AND VISIBLE TRADE BALANCE WITH PRINCIPAL TRADING AND CURRENCY AREAS

(*Million Guyana dollars*)

Trading or currency area	1955	1956	1957	1958	1959	1960	1961	1962	1963	1964
Sterling area										
Imports	62·6	61·5	70·7	71·9	68·0	79·5	79·1	67·6	61·7	74·7
Exports	47·6	43·1	56·4	56·5	59·1	68·3	55·1	58·6	65·0	57·5
Trade balance	−15·0	−18·4	−14·3	−15·4	−8·9	−11·2	−24·0	−9·0	+3·3	−17·2
Dollar area										
Imports	18·2	21·6	31·3	27·3	24·5	44·7	41·9	39·4	35·7	48·5
Exports	40·2	48·2	48·3	37·0	39·3	52·3	73·5	83·3	85·4	76·6
Trade balance	22·0	26·6	17·0	9·7	14·8	7·6	31·6	43·9	49·7	28·1
O.E.C.D. countries and dependencies										
Imports	10·7	13·5	12·9	12·6	13·5	15·2	18·4	13·7	13·8	18·2
Exports	2·3	2·9	2·2	3·0	3·6	3·9	8·9	17·3	15·7	20·0
Trade balance	−8·4	−10·6	−10·7	−9·6	−9·9	−11·3	−9·5	3·6	1·9	1·8
Rest of the World										
Imports	3·3	3·8	4·1	4·5	4·9	8·1	7·7	8·3	7·3	8·4
Exports	0·7	0·8	1·5	0·9	1·9	2·5	10·8	2·5	8·6	8·6
Trade balance	−2·6	−3·0	−2·6	−3·6	−3·0	−5·6	−3·1	−5·8	−1·3	−0·2

Source: Annual Accounts Relating to External Trade.

fractory industries to Canada, and the rewarding premiums gained from alumina exports. After 1960 we were also able to sell small quantities of sugar on the premium-priced United States Market.

It can also be observed that for most of the period the country had deficits with the O.E.C.D. countries and the rest of the world,[1] so that on average Guyana has deficits with the majority of her trading partners. This is to a large extent due to the high elasticity of demand for the manufactured and related goods that the country has to import, and the rather low income elasticity of demand for foodstuffs and raw materials which form the greater part of her exports, although this tendency has been counteracted to some extent by the preferential markets in which the territory sells most of her exports. It is also a reflection of the narrow reproduction structure of the economy. It is evident that Guyana must at some time take steps to increase her exports to the United Kingdom and the United States of America, as well as increasing the total number of her trading partners. The other side of the coin points to decreasing the volume of inessential imports from these areas.

8. *Capital Account*

The cumulative deficit on current account for the period 1953 to 1964 was financed by capital inflows that arose either through an increase in the net holdings of foreigners in Guyana through loans and direct investment or as a result of assets held abroad by Guyanese residents. Unfortunately the necessary data that would enable us to trace these capital flows in detail do not exist. The data presented in Table 17, which covers the short period between 1960 and 1964, are therefore intended merely to give an indication of the main capital flows. In this section our intention is merely to relate these flows to the behaviour of the balance of payments. In the next chapter other elements of capital flows are dealt with in greater detail.

Thus long-term capital flows were the principal balancing items making up the current account deficiencies. These flows tended to have considerable variations because of the lumpy

---

[1] Excluding the Dollar Area.

TABLE 17
CAPITAL ACCOUNT
(Thousand Guyana dollars)

Item	1960	1961	1962	1963	1964
Net long-term private capital inflow[a]	+32,363	+10,381	−853	+8,797	+8,255
Net short-term private capital inflow	—	−539	−2,454	+734	+3,318
Net investment loans received by central government	+7,412	+7,267	−10,521	+5,437	+2,496
Currency surplus account with the Currency Board[b]	+2,235	+399	−316	−109	−92
Total net capital transactions (Inflow+, Outflow—)	+42,010	+17,508	+6,898	+14,859	+14,161
Unidentified capital transactions including error (Inflow+, Outflow−)	+2,392	+4,052	−6,856	−15,086	+4,555
Capital deficit (+) or surplus (−)	+321	−1,922	−9,036	−26,130	−7,021
Total of changes in foreign reserves[c] (7–8)	+321	−1,922	−9,036	−26,130	−7,021
(a) Government foreign assets[d]	−3,456	−143	+4,823	−5,294	+741
(b) Currency in circulation	−3,850	−2,603	−6,308	−6,384	−1,517
(c) Commercial banks	+7,368	+546	−10,100	−13,809	−6,282
(d) Post Office Savings Bank	+259	+278	+2,549	−643	+37
Total investment and capital financing (18+19+20)	+44,723	+19,638	−8,994	−26,357	+11,695

Source: *Economic Survey of Guyana 1966.*
Capital Inflow and reduction in Foreign Reserves (+)
Capital Outflow and increase in Foreign Reserves (−)
[a] Includes foreign direct investment in Guyana net contribution to Sugar Funds.
[b] In 1960 and 1961 includes investment of the Currency Board. In 1965 includes recovery of government debentures issued against Currency Board Notes.
[c] Financing the Capital Deficit or absorbing the Capital Surplus.
[d] Includes Joint Consolidated Funds, and investment on account of Sinking Funds, Sugar Industry Special Funds, and Trust and Miscellaneous Funds.

character of investments and the character of Exchequer Loans. The net outflow of investment income which was mainly responsible for the sizeable deficits on current account for most years was matched by a massive inflow of direct investment capital. Most of this capital represents the net investments by foreign-owned companies operating in Guyana. These amounts have fluctuated tremendously through the years, being highest in the years 1960 and 1961 when the alumina plant was being constructed and lowest in 1962 and 1963—years marked by political and social unrest. Another major source of financing was the net inflows arising from loans to the central government. These were mainly Exchequer Loans from the United Kingdom. The net capital inflow in respect of loans to the central government increased from approximately $7 million in 1960 and 1961 to $10·5 million in 1962 but declined thereafter.

The commercial banks' holdings of external assets, that is, their deposits with head offices abroad, are most important. The level of this holding tends to fluctuate directly with the general trend of the country's external transactions, current as well as capital. The balance increased in years when there were surpluses or small deficits on the current account accompanied by fairly large inflows of private capital and public sector loans. These increases in the foreign balances were approximately $9·0 million in 1962, $29·0 million in 1963, and $11·7 million in 1964. In fact, these external assets have been part of the country's external reserves which have been utilized to a large extent to finance the net international payments of the country, on account of current and non-monetary capital transactions.

9. Trade with the Caribbean

We learnt from our analysis of exports that the number of commodities exported from Guyana is extremely limited, and that the concentration of such trade is very high. Thus strenuous efforts will have to be made in the field of export promotion and stimulation. While the drive to conquer extensive new markets must proceed, the immediate goal should be the exploration of markets in the neighbouring Caribbean and Latin American countries. It would take us too far afield to discuss what particular form of economic association is the most suitable for the expansion of trade in the area, i.e. close economic integration in the form of a common market, a free trade area, or some looser form of economic association.[1] The theoretical implications of closer economic integration have been given summary

[1] On this see W. L. David: 'Carifta and the Question of Closer Caribbean Unity' (University of Guyana (Mimeo), 1967).

treatment in the literature.[1] The idea is also fraught with practical, political, social, and economic difficulties, and these have been considered elsewhere.[2] Our aim therefore is the limited one of an examination of the extent and nature of inter-unit trade with a view to ascertaining how this could be re-organized in the interest of trade expansion.[3]

We noticed in an earlier section that Guyana's trade with the main Commonwealth Caribbean countries of Trinidad and Tobago, Jamaica, and Barbados is significant. But her main exports to this region comprise rice, wood, and wood products. Between 1954 and 1964 Guyanese exports to Trinidad accounted for an average of 6·5 per cent of total exports, while the latter country was responsible for an average 10 per cent of the total value of commodities imported into Guyana. Thus, apart from the main trading partners (the United Kingdom, the United States of America, and Canada), Trinidad is the territory's most significant trading partner. In fact the country imports more commodities from Trinidad than it does, say, from Canada. Jamaica and Barbados take an average of 3·3 per cent respectively of the country's exports, but very minute quantities of imports are taken from these two territories. This suggests that in one respect the basis for promoting inter-regional trade already exists.

But the more important point is that inter-regional trade plays only a secondary and minor role in the total commerce of the region, involving just a few territories and a small number of commodities. Trinidad and Tobago and Guyana are the only main territories in the area that dispose of more than 10 per cent of their exports in the Caribbean market. This is shown in

[1] See 'Symposium on the Report of the Trade and Tariffs Commission', *Social and Economic Studies*, Vol. 9, No. 1 (1960); also *Studies in Regional Integration* (University of the West Indies, 1967).

[2] These factors include the inward-looking nationalism in the individual territories, the non-complementarity of their economies, difficulties in communication, commitment, and so on. For a full discussion of these and related issues see W. L. David, 'Common Markets in Developing Countries', *The Guyana Graphic*, 6, 7, and 8 September 1965 (Georgetown); also W. L. David 'Carifta and the Question of Closer Caribbean Unity', *Guyana Graphic*, 7, 8, 10, 13, 14, 17, and 19 April 1967 (Georgetown).

[3] For a very detailed and authoritative treatment of this matter see H. Brewster and C. Y. Thomas, *The Dynamics of West Indian Economic Integration, Studies in Regional Integration*, Vol. I (U.W.I., 1967).

Table 18. A greater all-round expansion in this regard could bring Guyana sizeable benefits.

However, a close examination of the currents of inter-regional trade reveals a high degree of commodity concentra-

TABLE 18

COMMONWEALTH CARIBBEAN: SHARE OF INTER-REGIONAL TRADE IN TOTAL TRADE

Territory	Year	Exports	Imports
American Group			
Puerto Rico	1962	0·8	1·5
British Commonwealth Group			
Barbados	1961	19·7	13·7
British Guiana (Guyana)	1961	16·1	11·2
British Honduras	1961	7·4	6·4
Grenada	1959	2·7	18·0
Jamaica	1962	3·8	9·1
St. Lucia	1959	12·7	16·4
St. Vincent	1959	21·8	13·8
Trinidad and Tobago	1962	12·6	2·7
French Group			
Guadeloupe	1960	0·3	7·0
Martinique	1960	1·8	8·1
Dutch Group			
Netherlands Antilles	1961	1·8	0·7
Surinam	1960	4·6	0·7

Sources: Official Trade Reports of Individual Territories. Caribbean Organisation, Annual Report, 1962, Puerto Rico, 1963.

tion in this trade. The data in Table 19 show that trade is dominated by three commodities—petroleum, rice, and ferti-lizers—whose combined share of the total value of trade was nearly 80 per cent. The fact that Trinidad and Tobago and Guyana together supplied over 80 per cent of the exports which moved between the six countries shown in the table reinforces the conclusion that at least from Guyana's point of view, the basis for further export promotion in the area already exists. Thus the country can take advantage of the low level of inter-regional trade in goods by trying to export commodities other than rice to the area. Her chances are enhanced by the fact that

TABLE 19

TRADE BETWEEN SIX CARIBBEAN ECONOMIES, 1961

(*Thousand U.S. dollars*)

Exporter \ Importer	Puerto Rico	Jamaica	Trinidad and Tobago	Guyana	British Honduras	Barbados	Total
NETWORK OF TRADE							
Puerto Rico	—	231·0	513·1	199·5	1·3	127·7	1,072·6
Jamaica	83·1	—	1,189·7	196·4	727·3	204·4	2,400·9
Trinidad and Tobago	253·4	7,988·7	—	6,302·7	260·0	3,681·7	18,486·5
Guyana	8·5	2,553·4	5,347·7	—	2·5	1,443·9	9,356·0
British Honduras	125·2	457·1	3·1	2·1	—	1·8	589·3
Barbados	11·3	59·0	762·9	327·4	5·0	—	1,165·6
Total	481·5	11,289·2	7,816·5	7,028·1	996·1	5,459·5	33,070·9

MAIN COMMODITIES

Commodity	Territory of origin	Thousand U.S. dollars	Percentage of total trade
Petroleum	Trinidad and Tobago	15,956·5	48·2
Rice	Guyana	7,344·3	22·2
Fertilizers	Trinidad and Tobago	2,370·8	7·2
Total of three commodities		25,671·6	77·6

Source: A. McIntyre, *Aspects of Development and Trade in the Commonwealth Caribbean* (Economic Commission for Latin America March, 1965).

TABLE 20

WORLD EXPORTS OF SELECTED PRODUCTS TO MAIN TERRITORIES IN THE CARIBBEAN 1962

(*Thousand U.S. dollars*)

Selected products	Jamaica	Trinidad and Tobago	Barbados	Guyana	Surinam	Netherlands Antilles	French Antilles[a]	Others[b]	Total
Meat (fresh)	1,143	2,409	251	—	126	1,995	696	847	7,467
Wheat flour	3,766	7,463	731	2,593	155	1,000	4,935	2,392	23,035
Paints	786	1,071	182	471	355	861	501	635	4,862
Cotton fabrics	6,076	3,813	746	1,183	1,088	886	1,973	1,251	17,016
Glassware	600	336	212	118	—	369	513	633	2,781
Metal containers	755	1,461	—	172	—	874	558	349	4,169
Nails, bolts, etc.	279	344	—	130	—	210	213	162	1,338
Hand tools	663	1,224	—	192	185	171	236	312	2,983
Housewares of metal	859	936	225	223	100	238	847	228	3,656
Furniture	932	1,140	171	383	184	914	1,934	783	6,741
Handbags	236	120	—	100	—	259	385	—	1,100
Clothes	1,885	2,274	1,179	392	409	7,693	4,135	597	18,564
Footwear	1,075	3,740	615	1,229	1,213	1,967	2,450	832	13,121

Source : United Nations, *Commodity Trade Statistics, 1962.*
[a] Guadeloupe and Martinique.   [b] British Honduras, Windward, and Leeward Islands.

OXFORD UNIVERSITY PRESS send with

compliments a review copy of

THE ECONOMIC DEVELOPMENT OF GUYANA
1953 - 1964
by Wilfred L. David.

PRICE in   70/- net
United Kingdom:

NO REVIEW should appear before publication
of the book on: 4 September, 1969

THE SOURCE of the book should be stated
as follows:

   Clarendon Press : Oxford University Press

———————

The publishers would be grateful for a clipping
of your review, which should be sent to them at

ELY HOUSE,
37 DOVER STREET, LONDON W1

the area as a whole has by no means exhausted the possibilities for regional import substitution in respect of a wide range of foodstuffs and manufactures. Table 20 lists some of these possibilities on the basis of world exports to the area in 1962.

The table shows that the Commonwealth Caribbean together with the French and Dutch Caribbean territories spent $7·5 million (f.o.b.) on meat, $23 million on wheat flour, nearly $8 million on metal containers and housewares of metal, and $6·7 million on furniture. These are all areas in which Guyana ought to make sizeable inroads into the Caribbean market. The schemes for agricultural development outlined in Chapter III, if implemented, should enable her to supply the area's total requirements of meat and substitutes for wheat flour. Her source endowment in wood and metal should also give her a comparative advantage with regard to the manufacture of furniture and a wide range of metal products. Thus any scheme of regional integration will assist Guyana in developing exports of resource-based products, including wood and forestry products, jewellery and precious stones, aluminium and simple metal manufactures such as houseware and containers. She could also benefit from the participation in 'regional industries'. These regional industries will be those comprising one or more plants, having access to the whole Caribbean market in order to operate under reasonably economic and competitive conditions even at minimum capacity. Such a scheme would avoid the waste of scarce resources in the area, and at the same time to achieve an adequate balance between the participating countries with respect to industrial location.[1]

[1] See A. McIntyre, 'Aspects of Development and Trade in the Commonwealth Caribbean', E.C.L.A. 1965. Also A. McIntyre, 'De-Colonisation and Trade Policy in the West Indies', Paper presented to the Second Conference of Caribbean Scholars, April, 1964.

VI

THE FINANCING OF ECONOMIC DEVELOPMENT

1. *The Composition of Investment and Savings*

The process of economic development inevitably involves an increase in the share of the national product that is withheld from consumption and devoted to investment. In the early stages of development it is likely that foreign capital will make a substantial contribution to the growth process by supplementing the low level of savings generated by low income levels. But the process is likely to be self-sustaining only if the increased income generated with the aid of foreign capital leads to a substantial increase in domestic savings, which, in turn, lessens the dependence on foreign sources of capital.

We saw earlier in Chapter I that capital formation accounted for a substantial proportion of domestic product during the period under review. In 1954 it stood at $38·4 million or 20 per cent of Gross Domestic Product. By 1960 it had more than doubled to $82·4 million or 31·3 per cent of Gross Domestic Product, and although there was an absolute decline of gross capital formation after 1960, nevertheless it constituted an average of 24 per cent of Gross Domestic Product between 1954 and 1963. This chapter is intended to carry a stage further the analysis of investment given in Chapter I, and is concerned with throwing light on the sources from which economic development was financed and the factors influencing the changes in the level of the flow of funds from different sources.

A convenient way to start the exposition is to show the breakdown of net investment between domestic and foreign sources. This is done in Table 1. An examination of the data reveals the important role of foreign capital during the period under review. The estimated net inflow of foreign capital between 1954 and 1962 amounted to $524 million representing 53 per cent of net investment. In the years between 1958 and 1961 when the alumina plant was being established, the contribution of foreign capital was in excess of 60 per cent of the total. It rose to a peak of 64 per cent in 1959/60 but thereafter declined to 48 per cent in 1962. The decline in the foreign component of investment was probably due to the unfavourable investment climate which characterized the economy in the years after 1961, which were marked by an inordinate amount of political and social unrest.

The inflow of foreign capital that Guyana experienced is related to the trend in the balance of payments on current account analysed in the previous chapter. We recall that the foreign balance tended to deteriorate throughout most of the period mainly because the rise in exports was not sufficient to offset the increasing trend in imports. The available evidence suggests that the capital inflow was largely conditioned by the state of export markets, particularly those connected with sugar and bauxite and alumina. In addition to these forms of direct investment, foreign capital also flowed in through the medium of loans in the public and private sectors. The extent of public borrowing, for which the data is more readily available, will be indicated when we deal with sources of government finance.

It should however be borne in mind that the data in Table 1 are estimates of *net inflow*, that is, the difference between capital inflows and outflows. In many years a portion of domestic savings have leaked abroad due to the combined operations of the commercial banks, the government, and monetary authorities. Furthermore the undistributed profits of overseas companies are treated in the national accounts as an inflow of capital, and these are sometimes ploughed back into the economy.

In the case of the government and the monetary authorities, a portion of the outflow of capital arose out of the statutory obligations regarding investment in securities in the United Kingdom and the Colonies and of large proportions of sinking funds, deposits of the Post Office Savings Bank, and the backing for the currency under the Sterling Exchange System. The commercial banks operating in Guyana are branches of international banks with head offices in the United Kingdom and Canada, and a portion of the funds deposited with them tends to be exported if investment opportunities are more profitable in foreign countries.

The importance of foreign capital should not be allowed, however, to obscure the growth of domestic savings which has accompanied the rise in the real incomes of the community. It accounted for an average of 46 per cent of net investment between 1954 and 1962. Another indication of the increasing importance of domestic savings is the fact that as a proportion

TABLE 1

FOREIGN AND DOMESTIC COMPONENTS OF NET INVESTMENT

(*Thousand Guyana dollars*)

Year	Net investment	Net domestic savings	%	Net capital inflow	%
1954	29,968	20,588	69	9,380	31
1955	47,378	26,224	55	21,154	45
1956	46,619	19,423	42	27,196	58
1957	58,994	25,492	43	33,502	57
1958	73,568	28,805	39	44,763	61
1959	69,924	25,335	36	44,589	64
1960	76,954	27,587	36	49,367	64
1961	71,450	29,295	41	42,155	59
1962	50,107	25,868	52	24,239	48

Source: Central Statistical Bureau, *Analysis of Domestic Product. Quarterly Digests of Statistics.*

of national product, it accounted for an average of 11·6 per cent over this period, as can be seen from Table 2.

The growth of domestic savings will be considered with reference to the growth of three components, i.e. corporate savings, personal savings, and government savings. The grouping of the sources of investment into these broad categories is to some extent arbitrary in that decisions to consume or save that are taken in each of these sectors have repercussions on savings behaviour in the other sectors. For example, the dividend policy of companies may affect savings behaviour in the household sector. Similarly a change in tax policy may affect savings

TABLE 2

NET DOMESTIC SAVINGS AS A PERCENTAGE OF
GROSS NATIONAL PRODUCT

Year (1)	Net domestic savings (2)	Gross national product (3)	Col. (2) as % of Col. (3) (4)
1954	20,588	181,778	12·3
1955	26,224	182,173	14·4
1956	19,423	195,793	9·9
1957	25,492	216,941	11·3
1958	28,805	222,901	12·9
1959	25,335	228,007	11·1
1960	27,587	239,878	11·1
1961	29,295	266,539	10·9
1962	25,868	269,493	9·5

Source: Central Statistical Bureau, *Analysis of Domestic Product. Quarterly Statistical Digests.*

behaviour in all three sectors.[1] Nevertheless, analysis by these three broad categories of savings is a convenient way of looking at the behaviour of net domestic savings. This approach also enables us to disentangle the diverse factors that have been responsible for shaping savings behaviour.

A breakdown of domestic savings into the three components mentioned above is given in Table 3. In most countries in the recent past, the government and the corporate sector have been responsible for the overwhelming proportion of domestic savings, with personal savings making only a small contribution.[2] Guyana has been an exception to this rule. Throughout the period the government and the savings of locally owned corporations accounted for an average of 50 per cent of total net domestic savings, with personal savings contributing the other half. Although personal savings behaved in a volatile manner, its contribution remained relatively high throughout the period

[1] For empirical support see J. Meyer and E. Kuh, *The Investment Decision* (Harvard University Press, 1957), and 'Topics in Economic Theory', *American Economic Review, Papers and Proceedings*, Vol. LIII, No. 7 (May 1963), pp. 237–74.

[2] For example, throughout the period 1951–61, the government surplus and undistributed profits of local corporations accounted for more than 80 per cent of the total net domestic savings in Jamaica. See *National Accounts, Income and Expenditure* (Department of Statistics, Jamaica).

1954–63. But this picture may not present a realistic image of the behaviour of personal savings; and its growth may be much better assessed by expressing the annual figure as a percentage of household incomes. This is carried out in Table 4.

TABLE 3

COMPONENTS OF NET DOMESTIC SAVINGS

(*Million Guyana dollars*)

Year	Total	Personal savings	%	Govern- ment savings	%	Savings of locally owned corpora- tions	%
1954	20·6	15·8	76·8	3·7	18·1	1·0	5·1
1955	26·2	17·8	67·8	3·9	10·4	4·5	21·8
1956	19·4	11·5	59·1	4·8	24·5	3·2	16·4
1957	25·5	14·3	56·2	4·2	16·5	7·0	27·3
1958	28·8	15·5	53·7	5·2	18·2	8·1	28·1
1959	25·3	9·3	36·9	6·0	23·8	10·0	39·3
1960	27·6	13·2	44·1	10·8	38·7	3·7	17·2
1961	29·3	16·9	57·5	6·3	21·4	6·2	21·1
1962	25·9	15·3	59·2	6·2	24·2	4·3	16·6
1963	16·3	5·2	31·7	7·1	43·9	4·0	24·4

Source: As per Table 2.
Note: Although every attempt has been made to take account of leakages, the figure for personal savings remain unduly high relative to the other components of domestic savings. This highlights the tremendous statistical difficulties encountered in measuring this aggregate, and casts doubts on the procedure followed in Guyana where saving is considered a residual item after personal consumption expenditure has been deducted from household net incomes.

In 1954 personal savings amounted to 13·7 per cent of house-hold net incomes. In 1955, the figure was 8·9 per cent, but by 1963 it had risen again to 14 per cent. The difference between the figures in Tables 3 and 4 should however be noticed. The former figures are net, i.e. they take into account the inflow/outflow of savings over these years, while in the latter case such leakages are not accounted for. This difference does not unduly disturb the picture.

The data on personal savings lack refinement and the margin of error is likely to be high. For example, the substantial

TABLE 4
GROSS PERSONAL SAVINGS 1954–63
(Million Guyana dollars)

Year	Personal disposable income (1)	Personal consumption expenditure (2)	Col. (2) as % of Col. (1) (3)	Savings of persons (gross) (4)	Col. (4) as % of Col. (1) (5)
1954	165·9	143·7	86·3	22·0	13·7
1955	160·5	164·2	91·1	14·2	8·9
1956	175·0	158·5	90·5	16·5	9·5
1957	181·5	167·4	92·3	14·1	7·7
1958	184·4	172·1	93·4	12·2	6·6
1959	189·0	178·1	94·3	10·8	5·7
1960	208·1	201·9	97·0	6·2	3·0
1961	228·9	207·5	90·7	19·4	9·3
1962	230·3	206·0	89·5	24·3	10·5
1963	207·1	206·0	89·5	30·4	14·7

Sources: As per Table 2.

changes from 1960, and the very high figures for 1962 and 1963 in an atmosphere of low confidence need explanation. One also wonders where these high savings are reflected. Guyana in 1960 had just recovered from the effect of a mild recession in 1958 and 1959, but imports of consumer goods increased significantly in that year, as illustrated in Table 5. Imports generally increased by $36·6 million—all S.I.T.C. sections recording increases.

It would appear therefore that consumption increased rather significantly in 1960, and this made sizeable inroads into potential savings. In estimating household income for 1959 we may take comparative figures for the two most important sectors, viz, *mining* and *sugar*.

(Guyana dollars)

	1959	1960	1961
Wages and salaries	31,594	38,331	44,824

These were in fact the main growth sectors in the period. While these figures are incomplete, it will be observed that the increase in the c.i.f. value of *imported consumer goods* was at a high level compared with the increase in income in the sectors that were responsible for a substantial part of the increase in total income between 1959 and 1960. However, it should be pointed out that if there was a significant increase in inventories of consumer items in 1960 and 1959, this amount would have been reflected in consumption. This is a shortcoming in the consumption figures which can be remedied only when better figures of stocks in the distributive sectors are available.

TABLE 5

IMPORTS OF MAIN CONSUMER ITEMS

1959 AND 1960

(*Million dollars, c.i.f.*)

Items	1959	1960	Increase
Food	22·1	24·8	2·7
Beverage and tobacco	1·7	2·1	0·4
Textiles	9·1	13·2	4·1
Motor cars	1·8	2·5	0·7
Ready-made clothing	1·9	2·7	0·8
Footwear	2·5	3·1	0·6
Furniture	0·9	1·3	0·4
Refrigerators	0·5	0·8	0·3
	40·5	50·5	10·0

Sources: As per Table 2.

Further the years 1961 and 1962 were bad years of confidence. Savings in the banks—commercial and Post Office Savings—which had been increasing at the rate of about $3 million to $4 million annually showed a decrease rather than an increase of $0·8 million in 1961. The position improved slightly in 1962 after Exchange control. In 1962 savings in the Post Office Savings Bank decreased by $3·5 million and in the commercial banks increased by $5·5 million, an over-all increase of $2·0 million. It is significant, however, that over-all savings in the banks increased by $10·5 million in 1963. Insurance premiums paid to eleven of the important companies operating in the country and representing probably 95 per cent or higher of the total payments were as follows.

TABLE 6

INSURANCE PREMIUMS

(*Million Guyana dollars*)

1960	6·5
1961	6·9
1962	6·2
1963	5·8

The savings in Bank Deposits and Insurance Premiums together were as follows:

1960	9·6
1961	6·1
1962	8·3
1963	16·7

Source: Statistical Bureau, *Analysis of Domestic Product.*

The figure of $6 million given for savings in 1960 viewed against the partial figure of $9·6 million appears to be low. As remarked before, this could be because there was a running-up of inventories of consumer items in 1960. On the other hand, bank loans and advances changed from $22·3 million in 1959 to $32·8 million in 1960, an increase of $10·5 million. In 1961, there was a drop in this figure to $29·4 million—a decrease of $3·4 million. The unusually high level of bank loans and advances in 1960 seems to be consistent with the increased spending of consumers. Much of this spending on durable consumer goods and even travel, was probably financed out of bank loans and advances, rather than savings. Similarly, small businesses were probably financing their capital formation out of borrowing. In other circumstances, e.g. in 1961, when credit was tighter, these concerns would have been forced to save more or to utilize existing savings. As it was, however, such spending and its financing from borrowing or hire purchase would have made bank savings go up, but in the accounts the surplus of personal income over personal expenditure would be depressed. It is probably significant too that demand deposits increased by $2·5 million in 1960 and declined by $3·8 million in 1961. There was also the practical disappearance of savings in the banks in 1961 and 1962—a time when it is alleged that money was leaving the country in large quantities. Exchange control was extended and became complete in 1961.

Under these circumstances a surplus of personal income over expenditure would not show up in the balance of financial institutions. Even after the Exchange Control Amendment Ordinance was passed, no one pretended that money was not still leaving the country. Hoarding was also probably prevalent. Statistics were not however able to show these trends or to show any funds which may have left the country through the banking system or by less refined means of redemptions in Trinidad after 1962, but the issue of notes by the Currency Board in this period is significant. Details of currency in circulation between 1958 and 1963 are given in Table 7 below. The figures underlined demonstrate a tendency to hold cash outside the banking system.

TABLE 7
CURRENCY IN CIRCULATION 1958–63

	1958	1959	1960	1961	1962	1963
Notes	22·3	22·9	26·7	29·2	35·5	41·8
Coins	0·8	0·9	0·9	1·0	1·1	1·1
Demonetized notes	0·3	0·2	0·2	0·2	0·2	0·2
	23·4	24·0	27·8	30·4	36·8	43·1
of which:						
Commercial banks	5·9	4·3	5·2	6·4	5·0	6·4
Treasury and other govt. depts.	0·8	0·8	0·7	0·2	1·0	1·2
Other (residual)	16·7	18·9	21·9	23·8	30·8	35·5
Change in other holdings	—	+2·2	+2·2	+1·9	+6·8	+4·7

Source: Annual Report of the Accountant General; Annual Reports of the Treasurer.

Finally, it should be pointed out that a substantial part of household income is income from farms and incorporated enterprises. Any capital formation by these enterprises would be financed, if not from borrowing, then from savings. The following are the c.i.f. value of agricultural machinery (ploughs, combines, tractors), imported during 1959–61.

(*Thousand Guyana dollars*)

	1959	*1960*	*1961*
Combines etc.	1,861·0	3,676·7	3,705·4

After duty and mark-up have been added, these values would probably have increased by 50 per cent. This machinery is mainly for rice farming in which unincorporated enterprises

TABLE 8

KNOWN PRIVATE INFLOW/OUTFLOW OF SAVINGS[a]

(*Thousand dollars*)[a]

1954	−6,171
1955	3,581
1956	−5,057
1957	247
1958	3,243
1959	−1,278
1960	7,062
1961	−2,041
1962	−8,606

Source: Annual Reports of the Treasurer. Central Statistical Office, *Analysis of Domestic Product.*

[a] The figures for this item were arrived at by using three items in the capital account of the balance of payments for the aggregate, viz., *Other Long-Term Private Investment, Other Short-Term Private Investment,* and *Commercial Banks' Assets and Liabilities* with/to banks abroad. If the net change in these quantities is a credit, the amount represents an inflow of claims, and vice versa. *Other Long-Term Private Investment,* for the greater part, comprises the statutory contributions by the sugar companies to certain sugar funds held locally, changes in foreign securities held by the Post Office Savings Bank, local insurance companies, the Sugar Funds, a few miscellaneous funds, and the current liabilities and assets of the resident foreign-owned firms. The figures on Securities can be regarded as satisfactory because they are derived from the list of security holdings published by the insurance companies concerned, the government, and the Post Office Savings Bank. Current liabilities and assets since 1962 were reported to the Statistical Bureau by firms whose figures could be accepted. *Short-Term Liabilities and Assets* are mainly changes in the holding of currency which are based on the reports of the Currency Board and the banks. Commercial banks' liabilities are reported by the two commercial banks and are considered reliable. The *Known Private Inflow of Savings* is thus a term for the aggregate of the items indicated. Not all the items can be regarded as savings in the true sense of the term, though the contributions to the Sugar Fund could be regarded as a saving, as could the changes in the holdings of currency issues. The total certainly represents a net movement of funds, and shows the vast potentially investible resources that leave the country.

dominate. It therefore becomes obvious that the purchase of this mechanical equipment had to be financed from *household savings* if not from borrowing. In 1960, hire-purchase credit was much extended, and the same was true of bank credit. In 1961, however, credit was restricted, and purchases were probably financed out of crop income, i.e. from savings.

The 1963 savings figure was obtained from income less consumption. Consumption was low during the strike period owing to the unavailability of imports and the closing of many stores. Some evidence to support this increase in savings is available from the accounts of the commercial banks given in some detail above. Also involved in the high savings for 1963 was the payment of a $6 million bonus by the sugar companies for services rendered by the workers in 1963. Since this counted as 1963 income, and could not possibly have been spent in 1963, it gets included in savings, although this is 'forced' saving.

The difficulties encountered in respect of accounting for private savings are further compounded by the fact that a large proportion of these savings leaks abroad annually. Table 8 gives an account of this element of savings.

2. *Corporate Savings*

We recall from Table 3 that the savings of locally owned companies amounted to slightly over $1 million or 5 per cent of domestic savings in 1954. With the exception of the year 1956, this figure grew to a record height of nearly $10 million in 1959, or 39·3 per cent of total domestic savings. By 1963 the figure had declined to $4 million, or 24·4 per cent of total savings. Like the other components of total domestic savings the savings of locally owned companies fluctuated widely over the period,[1] and accounted for an average of 22 per cent of total domestic savings.

The poor contribution made by local companies to domestic savings reflects the relatively undeveloped state of the capital market in Guyana, and the gaping 'enterprise gap'. It was not until 1956 for instance that the first local public company was

---

[1] This volatility is a reflection of the fluctuating nature of the national economy referred to in Chapter I.

established in the country, and between then and 1961 a total of 120 were formed with a total share capital of $19·81 million.[1]

Most of these companies are small and their issues are negotiated by solicitors and accountants, and in almost all cases their sales of securities were concentrated in 'friends' and 'family'. This illustrates the point that there is no formal market for new issues, and none of the major financial institutions has displayed any initiative in underwriting the issues of these companies. Thus to a large extent, the development of enterprise awaits the development of a viable capital market, but the development of the latter has been hampered by the prevailing form of organization. The dominant organizations of enterprise are the foreign-owned companies which dominate the present industrial life. A total of 108 of these companies were registered between 1945 and 1962, and as all their capital issues were raised abroad, they are probably of no real importance in a statement of the financial assets and liabilities of the territory. The other organizations are negotiated by solicitors and accounts, and one-man family enterprises.

But perhaps the main reason for the existence of the enterprise gap is the lack of government leadership in this regard.[2] It could be argued that the 'local' private sector in Guyana has not been permitted to play its full part in the development process over the years because the government failed to take the responsibility of initiating, co-ordinating, encouraging, and assisting the total efforts of the many segments to make a significant contribution by developing an adequate financial infrastructure, or creating a favourable political and economic climate for the promoting of new industry, and providing a wide range of assistance to existing industry. The creation of a proper climate is an elusive factor which may require some years to develop to an acceptable level, but it nevertheless remains true that enough progress was not made during the period under review in granting the requisite concessions to small investors and towards the development of a more friendly and secure environment for the potential promotion of industry.[3]

[1] Annual Reports of Guyana (British Guiana).
[2] Cf. D. F. H. Black, *The Industrial Development of British Guiana*, and *The Development of Small Scale Industry* (Ministry of Economic Affairs, Georgetown, 1965).
[3] However, a step was taken in this direction in 1963 by the setting up of the

3. Government Savings

We referred earlier to the poor contribution to domestic savings made by the government component in relative terms. Between 1954 and 1963, it amounted to an average of 24 per cent of total domestic savings. Although this may be a very high figure for a small developing country, it is low in relation to the country's development needs, and to the contributions made by other components of domestic savings.

The figures for government savings given in Table 3 include as savings the following items, among others, which are included in the annual estimates on current expenditure: the surplus on current account, additions to sinking funds, repayments of loans (capital portion only), purchases of 'capital equipment', such as motor vehicles, counted as current in the estimates, and savings of local authorities.[1]

But the instrumental component of government savings is the government surplus, which is determined by the level of government expenditure on current goods and services in relation to revenue. Government revenue increased from \$29·9 million in 1952 to \$67·6 million in 1964, i.e. a more than two-fold increase. However, this was not sufficient to match the faster rate of growth of recurrent expenditure which rose from \$28·5 million in 1952 to \$68·1 million in 1964, so that in most years the government was unable to transfer a sizeable surplus

Guyana Industrial Development Corporation with the very broad functions of carrying out industrial development and promotion. It is rather surprising that this vital institution should have come so late in the country's industrial history, as a recommendation for its establishment was made as far back as 1946. See *British Guiana Ten Year Development Plan, 1947–56*, laid before the Legislative Council in 1947–8.

[1] As in the case of personal savings, an explanation has to be given for the situation in 1961 and 1962. The following factors, therefore, help to explain why government savings remained constant at \$6 million while the current surplus of the central government was decreasing from \$3 million to \$2·4 million. In the first place, \$1·8 million of this amount included in the 1962 accounts for revision of salaries was counted by the statistician as being expenditure for 1961. This accounts for \$3·6 million out of the \$5·4 million difference between the Treasury figures of 1961 and 1962, i.e. the 1961 surplus decreases by \$1·8 million, and the 1962 deficit decreases by \$1·8 million. The other problem arose because the statistician allocated income taxes to the year the income is earned, rather than to the year the tax is collected. Therefore the 1962 income tax increase shows up in 1962 rather than in 1963. The Statistical Bureau's income tax figure was \$24 million compared with the Treasury's \$21·5 million.

to its capital account. An indication of the small size of the revenue surplus for most years is given in Table 9, for although the ratio of government revenue to domestic product is on average high, the ratio of expenditure to domestic product is also high.

TABLE 9

GOVERNMENT REVENUE AND CURRENT EXPENDITURE

	Revenue[a]	Revenue as % of G.D.P.	Expenditure (Mn. G$)[a]	Expenditure as % of G.D.P.	Revenue surplus (Mn. G$)
1954	35·0	18·3	33·4	17·4	1·7
1955	41·2	21·5	38·8	20·2	2·5
1956	40·6	19·6	38·9	18·8	1·6
1957	44·3	19·1	41·7	18·0	2·7
1958	47·6	20·3	45·1	19·3	2·5
1959	47·4	19·8	44·1	18·4	3·3
1960	54·5	20·7	48·9	18·6	5·5
1961	58·0	20·0	54·9	19·0	3·0
1962	57·4	18·7	59·9	19·5	−2·5
1963	61·7	22·7	59·2	21·8	2·4
1964	64·9	20·9	65·4	21·0	−0·4

Sources: Estimates Current and Capital. Annual Reports of the Treasurer. Annual Reports of the Accountant General.

[a] Post Office and Telecommunications revenue deducted from both revenue and expenditure.

Thus an interesting feature of the revenue account of the country is that such revenue accounted for an average of 20 per cent of gross domestic product between 1954 and 1964. This is very encouraging for an economically small developing country such as Guyana. In an attempt to find a plausible explanation of this tendency, a regression analysis was carried out between government revenue shares and its two main determinants— *per capita* incomes and the 'openness' of the economy. The generalization has often been made that government revenue shares increase with *per capita* income (Y/N), taken as a determinant of development.[1] But since the chief source of revenue in the territory is the foreign trade sector, two indicators of

[1] U. Tun Wai, 'Taxation Problems and Policies of Underdeveloped Countries', *International Monetary Fund Staff Papers*, Vol. IX, No. 3 (Nov. 1962), pp. 428–45.

'openness' were used as alternatives to *per capita* incomes (Y/N) as an independent variable, viz. (M/Y), the ratio of imports to income, and (T/Y), the ratio of exports plus imports to income. The results of this exercise are summarized below.

TABLE 10

CORRELATION BETWEEN GOVERNMENT REVENUE SHARES AND THE OPENNESS OF THE GUYANESE ECONOMY

Variables (1)	Correlation coefficients (2)	Test of significance (%) (3)
1. $(R/Y)/(M/Y)$	0·635	5
2. $(R/Y)/(T/Y)$	0·743	5
3. $(R/Y)/(Y/N)$	0·537	5

The conclusion emerges that revenue shares are more closely related to the degree of openness of the economy than to the level of *per capita* income. Such a result is expected in a country such as Guyana where the foreign trade sector is responsbile for the greater part of the social income, and where *per capita* incomes are strongly influenced by the behaviour of the main variables in the foreign trade sector. This result was confirmed by a highly significant correlation coefficient of 0·758 between foreign trade taxes as a share of total government revenue and 'openness'.

In Table 11 tax revenue is expressed as a percentage of Gross Domestic Product. There was a slight change between 1952 and 1964 in the share of national product absorbed by taxation. In 1962, the share was 15·8 per cent of Gross Domestic Product, and by 1964 it had increased to 18·1 per cent. No general or formal criteria exist with regard to the proportion of national income the government should aim at appropriating through taxation, and even if such criteria exist, they need not be applicable without reservation to the conditions obtaining in individual economies. Nevertheless, recognizing the strategic importance of an adequate flow of tax revenues and the inadequacy of their own revenues, the governments of many developing countries have sought to increase the proportion of national income collected in taxes. Thus the United Nations Fiscal Experts have suggested: 'Underdeveloped countries are under no illusion that they can, or should, push their tax ratios of 10 to 15 per cent of national income to the 30 or 40 per cent levels reached in . . . advanced countries.'[1] On the more specific level, Professor Arthur Lewis has suggested that there is no fundamental reason why the government of any country should not raise 20 per cent of the national income by taxes.[2]

TABLE 11

TAX REVENUE AS PERCENTAGE OF G.D.P.

(*Million Guyana dollars*)

Year	Gross domestic product	Tax revenue	Tax revenue as % of G.D.P.
1952	158·6	25·1	15·8
1953	175·8	27·7	15·8
1954	191·7	31·0	16·2
1955	191·5	35·8	18·7
1956	207·0	35·4	17·1
1957	231·6	39·2	16·9
1958	234·1	42·3	18·1
1959	239·4	41·5	17·3
1960	263·5	47·8	18·1
1961	289·8	51·2	17·7
1962	307·2	49·9	16·2
1963	271·8	53·6	19·7
1964	310·9	57·9	18·1

Source: *Annual Reports of the Treasurer;* Estimates Current and Capital.

These suggestions raise many important issues, but the one that appears most relevant in the context of Guyana is the possibility that the government, in aiming for a higher share of national income, may increase its taxation not at the expense of consumption but of capital formation in the private sector, so that in the final analysis total investment does not increase. In this regard, tax policy faces a basic dilemma in its role as an

[1] *U.N. Taxes and Fiscal Policy in Underdeveloped Countries* (United Nations, New York, 1954), p. 6.
[2] W. A. Lewis, 'Economic Problems of Development', in *Restless Nations* (Council of World Tensions, George Allen and Unwin Ltd., 1962), p. 84.

instrument of capital formation for economic development. On the one hand, high levels of taxation are necessary to finance that part of the development process that falls in the government sphere and to mobilize for investment the private resources that might otherwise be dissipated. On the other hand, the lower the taxes the greater will be the inducement to private investors, per unit of net incomes, to take the risk associated with investment in agricultural and industrial development. The dilemma is worsened by the fact that these taxes, which are most effective in capturing a large share of the gains from economic development for further capital formation, are the ones most likely to affect the returns from private investment. For it is the taxes that vary directly and rise progressively with the size of income that are most effective in absorbing the gains from development, and are generally preferred on equity grounds; yet these are precisely the ones that are likely to offset marginal effort and risk-taking. One way out of this dilemma may be to combine high rates of taxation in general with preferential treatment for categories of desired developmental activity, and penalty taxes or rates on undesirable economic activities. To implement such a policy requires careful economic analysis and planning, skilful structuring of taxes, ruling out political favouritism, and competent tax administration.

This basic dilemma has particular relevance to the situation in Guyana, a country which already collects the near 20 per cent of national income in taxation suggested by Professor Lewis. Yet, as we have emphasized, sufficient revenue has not been generated to meet the growing expenditure burden. There are several probable explanations for the existence of such a state of affairs. The first of these concerns the very nature of the tax structure. Traditionally government revenue has depended heavily on three sources of taxation, viz, customs duties, excise duties, and income tax. In 1952 these three sources of revenue accounted for 68 per cent of the total revenue of the central government. By 1964 their combined share had increased to over 80 per cent of the total. The share of revenue from income taxes averaged 33 per cent between 1952 and 1964 while customs and excise duties contributed an average of 46 per cent of total revenue over this period. We saw that there was a highly significant correlation coefficient between foreign trade taxes as a share of total government revenue and the openness of the economy.

But the significant contribution made to the super-buoyancy of revenue conceals the rapid rise in the yield of income tax in the post-war years. Indeed, if a comparison is made with the pre-war period, a rise in the importance of income tax is discovered, with a simultaneous decline in the weight of taxes on commodities. In 1938, income taxes yielded only 10 per cent of government revenue, the tax rate being about one twentieth of taxable income. By 1958 it was yielding over 38 per cent of government revenue, the tax rate being about a quarter of taxable income. The other side of the picture is the decline in the relative importance of commodity taxes. In 1938 commodity taxes provided 60 per cent of government revenue, mostly from import duties, which averaged about 28 per cent of the value of imports.[1] By 1958 commodity taxes provided only 45 per cent of government revenue, and the average rate of import duties had dropped to 14 per cent.[2] It was hoped that the introduction of P.A.Y.E. in 1962 would have increased the percentage contribution of income taxes, but it has failed to have any marked effect to date. Although the increasing emphasis given to income taxes in the 1950s was somewhat a reflection of economic development and rising *per capita* incomes, its potential contribution has been reduced by the small economic size of the country and the small number of potential contributors. But however one looks at the tax structure, it remains evident that too few taxes have for too long carried the burden of current and capital expenditure.

The problem may be best analysed against the massive investment programme the government undertook after 1956. From 1956 to 1959 the public investment programme ran at an average level of $19·3 million which was about 9 per cent of Gross Domestic Product.[3] The planned rate for 1960–4 was $22·1 beginning with $25 million in 1960 and trailing off to $19 million in 1964.[4] Whether this planned rate was too high or too

[1] O. A. Spencer, *Memorandum on the Financial Position of British Guiana, 1920–1946* (Georgetown, 1946).
[2] Annual Report of the Department of Inland Revenue.
[3] Development Estimates, 1964.
[4] Ibid.

low cannot be answered at this stage. However, the sluggish rate of economic growth of about 3 per cent seems *prima facie* evidence that it was too low, though the programme was drawn up on the assumption that the real rate of growth of G.D.P. had recently been, and would continue to be, at 6 per cent irrespective of the size and allocation of public investment. But the important point in this context is that the low level of the actual programme constituted a sufficiently heavy burden on the economy that the government felt itself unable to finance more than a fraction of the planned expenditure. During 1955–9 only $10 million was raised from revenue surpluses, out of a total expenditure programme of about $100 million. For 1960–4, it was planned to raise $15 million from revenue surpluses, and $10 million from local borrowings in order to finance a total of $110 million. Of the balance $23 million was to be in outright grants from the British Government, and about $38 million in the form of Exchequer Loans. It was hoped that the gap of $23 million would be filled by international grants and loans and by underspending.[1]

At the beginning of the programme, the announced reluctance to tax adequately was even more marked in practice, for the first year began with a revenue surplus of only $1·1 million, merely a third of what had been planned. It soon became evident that taxes would have to be raised to provide a higher surplus, especially as the international grants and loans were not forthcoming.[2] The shortfall in financial resources was largely due to inability to attract external financing either from the International Bank or other international agencies such as the United Nations, although finance from the United Kingdom

[1] Sessional Paper No. 5/1959. Berrill had allowed for a 10 per cent slippage, but a comparison of the estimates on the plan indicate that in 1956–9, the rate of slippage was 15·4; in 1960–1, on the basis of actual expenditures, the slippage rate had risen to about 20 per cent. In order to make up the losses for the first two years, the government had originally proposed to accelerate the expenditure rate to $31·6 million, but owing to the lack of financial resources, it was necessary to cut the figure back to $20·5 million early in 1962.

[2] The factors surrounding the impossibility of obtaining external aid have been adequately summarized in the *Report of a Commission of Enquiry into Disturbances in British Guiana in February 1962*, Col. No. 354 (H.M.S.O. London, 1962), pp. 11–14. A useful account of American reactions is found in Arthur M. Schlesinger, Jr., *A Thousand Days: John F. Kennedy in the White House* (André Deutsch, 1965), pp. 665–9.

was forthcoming. For example, of the $13·4 million expected from external agencies, only $0·2 million was actually obtained. We have already referred to the fact that over 75 per cent of the programme was expected to come from external sources. The heavy reliance on external aid was due to the unwillingness to place heavy and progressive tax burdens on the residents of the country. Prior to 1962 tax revisions, the tax burden on local, individual residents was estimated at being 23

TABLE 12

PROGRESS OF THE DEVELOPMENT PROGRAMME

1960–64

(*Million B.W.I. dollars*)

		1960	1961	1962	1963	1964	Total
1. Original development plan estimates		24·8	22·7	23·7	20·4	18·9	110·5
2. Revised to take account of under-estimation and increased cost of material and labour		—	—	—	—	—	135·0
3. Development estimates	1960	24·7	—	—	—	—	—
4. Budget speech revision	1960	22·1	—	—	—	—	—
5. Actual expenditure	1960	15·8	—	—	—	—	—
6. Development estimates	1961	—	24·0	—	—	—	—
7. Revised estimates, 1961, incl. supplementary votes	1961	—	31·6	—	—	—	—
8. Actual expenditure	1961	—	21·6	—	—	—	—
9. Development estimates	1962	—	—	31·6	—	—	—
10. Budget speech revision	1962	—	—	20·0	—	—	—
11. Actual expenditure	1962	—	—	18·8	—	—	—
12. Development estimates	1963	—	—	—	25·5	—	—
13. Budget speech revision	1963	—	—	—	17·6	—	—
14. Actual expenditure	1963	—	—	—	12·3	—	—
15. Development estimates	1964	—	—	—	—	20·7	—
16. Budget speech revision	1964	—	—	—	—	13·7	—
17. Actual expenditure	1964	—	—	—	—	8·5	—
18. Actual expenditure	1960–64	15·8	21·6	18·8	12·3	8·5	77·0

Sources: Development Programme 1960–64, Sessional Paper No. 5/1959. Development Estimates 1960, 1963, 1964. Budget Speech 1960, Sessional Paper No. 2/1960. Budget Speech 1961/62, Sessional Paper No. 2/1962. Budget Speech 1962/63, Sessional Paper No. 8/1962. Budget Speech 1963, Sessional Paper No. 2/1963. Budget Speech 1964, Sessional Paper No. 4/1964. Budget Speech 1965, Sessional Paper No. 2/1965. K. C. Jacobs, *British Guiana, Report on the Financial Situation*, Col. No. 358 (H.M.S.O. 1964). Statement by the Government of British Guiana on the Jacobs Report and on the insolvency allegations by the Secretary of State for the Colonies, Sessional Paper 1/1964.

per cent of household (personal) income and 19 per cent of G.N.P., with comparable rates in the United States of America of 29 per cent and 6 per cent, Puerto Rico 15 per cent and 12 per cent respectively. The rates are even lower for other Latin American countries. In addition revenue from taxes on expatriate companies amounted to another 4 per cent of G.N.P. But despite the relatively heavy tax burden, it was impossible for the country to generate significant surpluses in the recurrent budget for development purposes.

Thus after its election to office in August 1961, the Jagan government in its first budget courageously attempted to increase substantially the locally raised funds for development to a level above that envisaged by the original programme. These were the revenue proposals of Mr. Nicholas Kaldor and will be analysed later. As it turned out, the new revenue proposals were withdrawn, and others proved administratively difficult to implement. Thus in the years 1962–4, Guyana had chronic difficulties with her development programme, mainly caused by the financial stringency, and certain practical problems of implementation. Table 12 provides a report on the development programme, from which can be observed a recurrent pattern of high initial estimates, lower revised estimates (except in 1961 following the boom of 1960), and actual expenditure at yet a lower level.

We have been arguing that despite the relatively heavy tax burden and the high ratio of revenue to domestic product, it has been impossible for the Guyana government to generate significant surpluses in the recurrent budget for development purposes. We also suggested that this was to a certain extent reflected in the inelasticity of the tax structure. But there are two other essential reasons why this has arisen. The first concerns the inordinate cost of sea defences, the second concerns subsidies, the bulk cost of which is included in the recurrent budget.

Over the period 1945 to 1964, the government spent about $120 million on development schemes. Of this expenditure, some $100 million was financed by borrowing internally and externally, as a result of which the public debt rose from $19 million to $134 million, and public debt charges from $1 million to $10 million. $135 million—more than the total financed by

borrowing—were spent on the renewal and expansion of the
capital of revenue earning public undertakings, i.e. drainage
and irrigation, land settlement, marketing, the railways,
steamer and air transport services, in fact nearly all the public
or semi-public undertakings in the country. These undertakings
not only do not recoup their capital costs in the form of interest
and depreciation, but do not usually cover their operating costs.
As a result the taxpayer must meet some $13 million in annual
losses of public undertakings, as Table 13 shows. The estimates
given in the table are based on the historical cost of the capital
engaged in the undertakings, allowing interest at the rate of

TABLE 13

ANNUAL LOSSES ON PUBLIC UNDERTAKINGS

(*Million dollars*)

	Capital engaged[a]	Operating loss[b]	Interest[c]	Depreciation[d]	Total loss[e]
Agriculture					
Drainage and irrigation	60·0	0·3	3·3	0·9	4·5
Land Settlement	6·0	0·3	0·3	0·1	0·7
Marketing	2·0	0·7	0·1	0·1	0·9
Transport and Communications					
Road Services	0·3	0·16	0·02	0·04	0·22
Railways	8·0	1·2	0·4	0·2	1·8
Steamers	12·0	1·2	0·7	0·2	2·1
Airways, airstrips	3·0	0·3	0·2	0·1	0·6
Posts	4·0	0·1	0·2	0·1	0·4
Telecommunications	11·0	−0·3	0·6	0·3	0·6
Other Services					
Credit	14·7	—	0·3	—	0·3
Housing	10·0	0·1	0·6	0·3	1·0
Timber seasoning, etc.	0·5	—	0·03	0·02	0·05
Total	131·5	4·06	6·75	2·36	13·17

Sources: Annual Estimates Current and Capital as passed by the Legislative Assembly, Sundry Years.

[a] Based on historical cost, estimated from capital expenditure over period 1945–64.
[b] As per 1965 Estimates.
[c] At average rate (5½%) of interest on Public Debt at end of 1964.
[d] Allowing that sums put aside annually for replacements, etc., earn interest at 5½%.

20—E.D.G.

5½ per cent, which is well below the prevailing market rate. Moreover, the operating costs are strongly based on the 1965 estimates which under-provide for a full year's labour costs with full staff at the revised rates of wages and salaries, so that the true deficits are certainly understated.

While therefore, the government was able to find revenue and grant finance sufficient to cover all its non-revenue-earning development projects, and incurred no debt that could not earn its keep, it nevertheless finds itself burdened with the operating losses and debt charges incurred in respect of public undertakings which are supposed to be financially self-supporting. We saw that these losses and subsidies now account for over $13 million annually. The paramount need for removing the losses of public undertakings becomes evident.[1]

The major subsidy arises in the drainage and irrigation sector. Some $60 million have been spent by the government in the last twenty years to improve water control on the coastlands. This service is now administered by the government through statutory boards—the Drainage and Irrigation Board and two Water Conservancy Boards. The operation and maintenance costs of these works are met from rates levied by these boards on proprietors in respect of the land benefited. These rates are subsidized by the government, include no charge for interest on the capital sunk by the government in flood control and drainage and irrigation works, and make very little contribution to reserves for replacements, and do not (as in the case of Drainage and Irrigation Board) meet administrative costs. In 1965, with the estimates certainly understating the case, the operational and maintenance costs (excluding sums reserved for replacements) of these works amounted to $1·4 million including $0·1 million for the maintenance of works outside the declared drainage and irrigation areas. The administrative expenses met from the Department's votes amounted to $0·1 million; revenue from rates levied on operators including the government and local authorities in respect of benefited lands held by them amounted to $1·2 million. The deficit before capital charges was therefore of the order of $0·3 million.

[1] On this see the author's 'The Question of Subsidies', *Guyana Graphic*, 5 March 1967.

Interest and depreciation amounted to $4·2 million. Table 14 shows how the government met all of this.

The government therefore subsidizes drainage and irrigation on the coastlands to the extent of 80 per cent ($4·5 million) annually of its cost. The gross rates levied by the Drainage and Irrigation Board and the Conservancy Boards on other urban lands and sugar estates average $6·20 per acre. These rates vary widely between different drainage and irrigation areas, ranging

TABLE 14

DRAINAGE AND IRRIGATION EXPENDITURE AND
MEANS OF FINANCE

Expenditure	$ Mn.	Revenue	$ Mn.
Maintenance and operation of Conservancies and drainage and irrigation works[a]	1·4	Rates met by proprietors and local authorities	0·6
		Rates on government lands	0·6[d]
Administrative overheads	0·1	Rates met by government subsidy	0·4[e]
Depreciation[b]	0·9	Unrecouped by costs ulti-	
Interest at 5½% on $60 Mn.[c]	3·3	mately met by the government	4·1
Total	5·7		5·7

Source: Compiled from Estimates, Current and Capital, as passed by the Legislative Assembly, 1965.

[a] Expenses of Drainage and Irrigation and Conservancy Boards including $0·1 Mn. for maintenance of drainage and irrigation works in other than declared areas.

[b] Based on department's estimates of required level of reserves and replacements.

[c] See notes to Table 13, page 283 (*supra*).

[d] As voted under 39 (35–37–39) and 26 (30–38) of 1965 estimates.

[e] As voted under 39 (36) of 1965 estimates.

from under $1 to over $30 per acre. The subsidized rates average about $4·50 per acre; heavier subsidies are granted to bring down the very high rates, sometimes to very low levels, e.g. $0·44, but the annual subsidy is 20 per cent of the rate. To cover costs completely, including capital costs, the subsidized rates would have to be increased by 400 per cent on average, i.e. $22·50 an acre. Judging by the level of some of the subsidized rates (sometimes as high as $9·0 an acre) and the smallness of the charge in relation to the return per acre from crops, there seems to be no reason why the present subsidized rate of $4·50 per acre should not be doubled, completely wiping out the rate subsidy and making nearly full provisions for replacements. However this would still leave the government carrying the heavy interest subsidy.[1]

Closely connected with the predicament of the drainage and irrigation complex, are the financial difficulties facing local authorities. For example in 1962 the financial position of the local authorities was as follows: revenue from all sources excluding loans and government contribution towards drainage and irrigation rates totalled $1,543,000, while expenditure totalled $1,432,000. The rates collectible amounted to $1,192,000, but the amount collected totalled $845,000 i.e. arrears totalled $347,000 for that year. Government loans outstanding at the end of 1962 were $461,000, while further loans totalling $40,000 were sanctioned in the same year.[2] The degree of government subsidy to the local authorities is fully brought out when we include the government contribution to the payment of drainage and irrigation rates, and miscellaneous payments made in respect of rural water supply and roads.

It is the view in government circles that the local authorities should pay their way as far as possible, and that their incomes should be augmented by charges made to individuals to cover costs of supplying water, roads, and similar services. The implementation of the East African graduated personal income

---

[1] The entire matter needs special examination (1) to determine what is the best form of organization for administering drainage and irrigation works; it seems that there should be a single authority for the entire coastlands and that it would be best organized as a public corporation; (2) to determine what rates should be levied. It seems that the rate should be uniform throughout the coastland for land of the same quality carrying crops requiring the same amounts of water facilities, i.e. the rates should vary only with acreage, quality of land, and the amount of water facilities required; (3) to determine how, and to what extent, it is practicable to recover the full costs of the water control works; and (4) to determine the financial relationship between the administering organization and the government, e.g. it seems that some figure should be ascribed to the value of the assets (water control works) vested in the administering authority with a corresponding liability to the government in interest-bearing debentures—any subsidy from the government being completely open. These are among some of the suggestions put forward by the present writer in a general study made of the problem of subsidies in 1965. See W. L. David, *Criteria for Securing the Operational Efficiency and Financial Balance of Public Undertakings in Guyana* (Central Planning Unit, Georgetown, September, 1965).

[2] Report of the Local Government Department, 1962.

tax[1] operated on a local basis, and the introduction of a land tax could also provide useful funds in this connection. Although it is desirable that the government should advance loans to meet capital expenditure, there is no reason why recurrent costs should not be met by the local authorities. The quick implementation of the Marshall Plan on local government could bring sizeable benefits, for the author offers useful guidelines to assist the local authorities in their task of efficient financial management.[2]

In particular, it is suggested that the government will pay rates on its property in preference to the loose arrangement of allocating small grants towards the operating expenses of some local authorities. Local authorities are expected to pass on to consumers wherever possible the charges for rural services. Further, they should levy both a drainage rate and a general rate, the latter based on the assessed value of land and building. By these means it is hoped that they can provide themselves with working balances and appropriate reserves, so that the assistance of the central government will become less necessary. This would necessitate a modernizing of the valuation system. At present the valuation of property is carried out in an approximate and haphazard manner by carpenters, farmers, and others of similar standing appointed as appraisers by the existing local authorities. Such a method has naturally resulted in uneven and sometimes inequitable assessments. A fair and uniform system of valuation for rating purposes is now essential.

An increasing proportion of central government funds is spent every year in subsidizing the losses of the railways. The capital engaged in the undertaking appears to be of the order of $8 million (at historical cost), involving an interest charge of 5 per cent of $0·44 million and a depreciation charge (2 per cent) of $0·16 million. The operating deficit is $1·16 million as per 1965 estimates, so that the total deficit is of the order of $1·76 million per annum, more than the revenue of $1·35 million estimated for 1965. The rates and fares on the railways were last revised in 1952. Since then, with large increases in labour costs, operating expenses have increased by a third in

---

[1] For details, see U. K. Hicks, *Development from Below* (Oxford, 1961) and *New Sources of Local Revenue*, Report of a Working Party (Allen & Unwin, 1956).

[2] Marshall, *Report on Local Government in British Guiana*.

spite of the improvements in the economy of the operation of the services. In 1962, there were recommendations for increased fares and rates, but this would not add more than 15 per cent to revenue. However, the deficit of 130 per cent of revenue justified a much heavier increase. The question is to what extent charges could be raised without defeating their own purpose by diverting traffic from the railways to the road. This was the case when fares were last increased, when passenger traffic fell by 20 per cent. However, if improvements in the services can be effected, i.e. modest improvements in accommodation, a few fast trains, simultaneously with any increase in fares, it should be possible to raise rates and fares immediately by at least a third without undue repercussions. However, this would still leave a huge subsidy of some 70 per cent of the revenue.[1]

In Chapter III we gave some indication of the degree of wastage which has taken place on land settlement schemes. Over $6 million has been sunk into these schemes in the past few years. These undertakings earn revenue of $0·75 million and involve expenditure of $1·01 million. A rough idea of the burden on the central government is given if we include capital charges—$0·33 million for interest, $0·1 million for depreciation, and $0·25 million for certain miscellaneous expenditures of the land development department. Thus an annual loss of around $1·0 million is incurred, that is, the revenue recoups less than 50 per cent of the expenditure. The rents are low in relation to those charged by private proprietors, and appear to offer scope for substantial increases.

The analysis of the method of financing overhead capital formation so far carried out reveals that the government was constrained to make a small and declining contribution from its own savings. This is a feature of many developing countries. It was partly due to the pressure of rising current expenditure on administration and social services which has accompanied economic growth and absorbed most of the increased tax revenues. The contribution to the finance of irrigation, transport, and other public investments made from the surplus earnings of these undertakings themselves has fallen to negligible pro-

[1] For a further discussion of Railway finance see Chapter VII, Section 3(b).

portions. To some extent, this has been largely the result of an unwillingness to raise charges for public utility services despite rising costs. There are some general reasons for this. In an inflationary situation, the prices of public services are the easiest to hold down, and in any case public undertakings are rarely very quick to adjust to rapidly changing cost conditions. In Guyana there is a very strong prejudice against the use of the price system and profit-making. This may be merely a question of words, but it may also stem from the association of profit-making with the activity of foreign business interests during the colonial era. Charges for transport, power, and water in some instances, have been deliberately kept down with the aim of inducing industries and peasants to increase output. The relative ease with which the country was able to obtain finance for overhead development from Colonial, Development, and Welfare Grants also made it unnecessary for the government to adjust charges for public services to ensure surpluses for reinvestment.

However, it must be emphasized, and past experience makes it clear, that there must be an appreciation of the reality of the capital costs and a clear statement of the true net costs of public undertakings if there is to be any disposition to operate them to cover their costs. To this end, it is necessary that where public undertakings, in the form of corporations or likewise, are set up, any capital provided by the government should carry a fair interest charge, i.e. a market rate of interest on a market valuation of property. Even where a public corporation is not set up and the undertaking is operated as a department of the government, the estimates and accounts for the undertaking should be arranged to show in a one-line vote the true net cost or net revenue, if any, of the undertaking, including capital costs and other hidden costs.[1]

---

[1] With the setting up of the Electricity Corporation, the first principle has been accepted by the government. Public corporations are required to keep fully costed accounts of their operations and pay the government a fair market rate of interest for the use of any capital the government supplies. With regard to the second principle, this was the case with the marketing schemes before the Guyana Marketing Corporation was set up. The expenditure on these schemes was shown as a one-line vote in the expenditure estimates, reflecting the true net cost, including interest and depreciation of the operation, with contra-revenue items in the revenue estimates for the interest and depreciation charges, and for general

Thus by the end of 1961 Guyana was faced with a situation of a chronic revenue/expenditure imbalance in which the internal resources were extremely small and wholly inadequate to meet the needs of the development programme. Foreign aid was not forthcoming as expected. The growing suspicion that Dr. Jagan's failure to arouse international sympathy was due to his ultra-socialist leanings made the commercial classes of Guyana apprehensive of the country's future and their own prospects. They began to look elsewhere for opportunities to set up and expand their business. Thus a flight of capital was started. At first this was gradual, but soon more and more financiers were transferring funds and assets to other countries. In addition to these difficulties the government was faced with the immediate need for $15 million for certain extra-ordinary expenses, and to meet increases in the cost of certain services. The government had agreed to increase the salaries of civil servants,[1] and for this an additional $3·5 million was required. There was also need for the repayment of certain loans, and $1·5 million for extra expenditure on sea defences, maintenance of roads, and improvements to the aerodrome, all of which were long overdue.

It was in this not too propitious atmosphere that Mr. Kaldor was invited to propose means of reform of the tax structure of Guyana. These proposals formed the basis of the new budget proposals of 1962.[2] These proposals were thus intended to serve both immediate needs and also the long-term purpose of securing through progressive taxation, a more equitable distribution of wealth and income. The *immediate* needs were concerned with the precarious state of Guyana's international reserves, and the absence of financial reserves at the disposal of the Government; they were also concerned with the urgent need to increase the resources available to economic development.

charges, i.e. for services financed by the votes of other departments. It seems that the same should be done for the Post Office, Transport and Harbours, and Drainage and Irrigation Departments.

[1] Based on the recommendations of the Guillebaud Commission of 1961. See *Report of the Commission to Review Wages, Salaries and Conditions of Service in the Public Service, British Guiana, 1961* (Government Printery, Georgetown, 1961).

[2] N. Kaldor, *Proposals for a Reform of Taxation of British Guiana* (Ministry of Finance, Georgetown, December, 1961). A close reading of this report and the Budget speech of 1962 reveals that the proposals were fully accepted and endorsed by the government of the day. See Sessional Paper No. 2/1962.

The long term need was to increase the effectiveness of the tax instrument in securing to the people of Guyana a fair share of the surpluses generated in the economy, and to ensure that the wealthier individuals in the economy contributed an appropriate share of the public burden.[1]

Firstly, because of the precarious state of the country's international reserves which had fallen by some $16 million between 1959 and 1961, it was considered necessary to impose some further restriction on imports and increased duties were imposed on a wider range of goods.[2] The increased duties were expected to add 17 per cent to the c.i.f. value of the imports but, according to budgetary calculations, the average retail price should not rise by more than 10 per cent.

The most sweeping proposals were however to be found in the field of income taxes, firstly in regard to business profits. Working on the assumption that foreign companies that were mainly branches or subsidiaries of companies abroad could understate their true profits through the over-invoicing of imports and the under-invoicing of exports, in so far as their transactions were conducted with associated companies, it was proposed that the profits for the year of a company operating in Guyana, with headquarters overseas, should be deemed to be not less than that proportion of total consolidated profit of the whole group of the associated companies (including both the resident and non-resident companies), that the turnover of that company as shown in its accounts bears to the consolidated turnover of the whole group of associated companies. It seems that the idea behind this provision was to increase the taxable

[1] Kaldor, op. cit., Introduction.
[2] The less essential goods on which duties were concentrated included alcoholic drinks, tobacco, concentrates for non-alcoholic drinks, tea, motor spirit, perfumery, cosmetics, dress fabrics, footwear, glassware, chinaware, jewellery, radios, refrigerators and other household electrical appliances, and motor cars; and the items for which adequate substitutes could be provided from local production including meat, fish, butter, milk (excluding condensed milk and milk-based infant foods), cheese, fruit, fruit juices, jams, coffee, confectionery, prepared paints, toilet soap, paper bags, and some varieties of clothing. This seems a sensible list in view of the need for import substitution, but the primary function of the import levies was revenue earning, and no mention was made of the protective element to encourage the local manufacture of these products or adequate substitutes. In any case, in his broadcast of February 1962 the Premier announced the removal of duties on most of these commodities, and the imported commodities on which taxes remained were motor cars, spirits, tobacco, coffee extracts and concentrates.

capacity of expatriate companies, mainly in the bauxite and sugar, that are vertically and horizontally integrated with companies in other countries, and which present difficulties as far as taxation of their profits is concerned. From our observations of the pricing structure of bauxite given in an earlier chapter, we saw that there was difficulty in ascertaining the nature of their true profits because of the low price reported for their sales of bauxite. In this case there might have been adequate justification for the introduction of this tax. But it is rather risky to generalize these arguments.

The following extra provisions were also to apply to companies. A minimum income tax payment was to be based on the assumed income of 2 per cent of turnover in the case of mining, manufacturing, or other mercantile business, even where loss occurs, but adjustable against future profits. Secondly, restriction of provisions regarding trade losses would allow only the indefinite carry forward of loss from the same source but disallow the set-off of loss against other income in the same year. Thirdly, removal of the previous tax concessions for new enterprises, and the introduction of a new provision, under which such new enterprises as were primarily concerned with mining, manufacturing, or processing activities, would be allowed to write off 70 per cent of any capital expenditure incurred during the first five years of their operations in Guyana as a charge on their current profit. Fourthly, there was to be a reduction of initial allowances for non-tax holiday companies from 40 per cent to 20 per cent. There was also to be a disallowance of entertainment expenditure, and the allowance on expenditure on advertising was to be limited to one quarter of 1 per cent of turnover, which was to exclude general or 'prestige' advertising. Finally, the expense of any excessive change in respect of directors' emoluments was to be disallowed.[1]

It is perhaps fair to comment that these measures would have

---

[1] In the 1965 Budget proposals the minimum income 'turnover' tax was removed. It was also decided to allow depreciation and initial allowances on all buildings used for business purposes. Advertising and entertainment were restored as proper expenses for income tax purposes if proved by the production of vouchers to be reasonably and necessarily incurred for the purpose of the business (Sessional Paper No. 2/1965).

increased the taxable capacity of the business sector, although it is difficult to envisage what the probable disincentive effects on capital formation in this sector would have been. It could also be argued that agricultural industry should have been included in the provision for the minimum income tax. But the crucial objection lies in the disincentive effect of this tax on the development of small-scale industry, most of which is in the retail trade. The margin of net profit on many staple foodstuffs is below 2 per cent and enterprises in whose turnover sales such items figure largely were faced with a perpetual loss in meeting such a levy; also there could be no future profits from such items from which losses could be recouped in subsequent years. The incidence of the tax produced some genuine and indisputable cases of gross hardship which resulted in the failure and closing down of many small enterprises. This was perhaps justifiable in the case of inefficient small businesses, but it was rather paradoxical in a situation where small enterprises were in need of government guidance and encouragement.

In the field of personal income tax, there were certain reductions in personal allowances, and P.A.Y.E. was to be introduced as soon as possible. But the most controversial tax in this package was the scheme for compulsory savings which was to be administered in close relationship with the administration of income tax. The rate of contribution was to be 5 per cent of the total income of wage and salary earners, and 10 per cent of all other incomes. Individuals whose total income was less than $1,200 a year were to be exempted from the obligation to make a contribution, and in the case of the self-employed the 10 per cent rate was only applicable to persons whose incomes were in excess of $5,000; in the range of $1,000–$5,000 the rate was to be 5 per cent, just as in the case of employees. Contributors were to be given government bonds registered in their names and not transferable but repayable at the end of 7 years tax-free at 3·75 per cent. Any bonds not encashed at maturity continued to earn interest at the higher rate of 4 per cent per annum compounded annually. The bonds were to be repayable when a person died, or, in the case of expatriate persons, when they left the country permanently. They were also to be repayable upon retirement, provided the holder attained the age of 60, in five annual instalments. Interest accruing up to the date of repayment was payable in all such cases. Certain lottery features were incorporated in the scheme, and an additional proposal that one-third of any contribution could be withdrawn at the end of three years with appropriate changes in the interest charged.

This scheme violated one of the major tenets for satisfactory income taxation, i.e. the voluntary compliance on the part of tax-payers. The roots of a tradition of voluntary compliance with tax laws are not easy to trace, but it is evident that such a spirit does not grow overnight. A long period of popular education and efficient and equitable administration of those taxes that can actually be enforced seems necessary to establish firmly the habit of the fiscal responsibilities of citizenship. Adoption of elaborate measures that will not be uniformly applied delays improvement in tax-payer morale. Finally, the political conditions for development of income taxes into a major source of revenue, like the spirit of voluntary compliance, are intangible and difficult to explain; but it may be suggested that these conditions were unfavourable in Guyana at the time when these tax proposals were introduced.

The final set of taxes to be introduced included a triumvirate on capital gains, net property, and gifts.[1] Under this scheme, capital gains came under taxation under ordinary rates, the maximum rate being set at 45 per cent. There was an annual property tax in existence prior to 1962, but it was simply one on net worth, viz. the value of the assets of the individual less his liabilities. Assets for the purpose of this tax were redefined to include 'the same classes of property as will be subject to the capital gains tax plus cash and bank deposits'.[2] The valuation of the assets was to be their book value, i.e. 'the cost of acquisition of each asset plus any subsequent expenditure on its improvement'. The rate schedule proposed ranged from nothing to the first $50,000 worth of property to 1 per cent per annum on property valued at $500,000 and over. Companies were to be taxed at the flat rate of 1 per cent of their assets,

---

[1] These taxes were of similar nature to those recommended for India, Ceylon, Ghana, and Turkey. Mr. Kaldor gave a full defence of these taxes in his report. For fuller discussion see N. Kaldor, *Indian Tax Reform* (Ministry of Finance, Government of India, June 1956), also 'The Problem of Tax Reform', in his *Essays on Economic Policy*, Vol. 1 (Gerald Duckworth & Co. Ltd., 1964), pp. 203–93.

[2] Budget Speech 1962, Sessional Paper No. 2/1962, p. 3.

'written down but excluding allowances'. The gift tax was levied on the donor, and the taxpayer's position was the same whether the gifts were *inter vivos* transfers or bequests on death, whether the gifts were capital gifts or income gifts.

It is evident that more caution should have been exercised in the introduction of these taxes, not only because of their novelty, but also because of the unpleasant aftermaths following their introduction in other countries. In fact the measures did not treat realistically the dilemma that confronts taxation for capital formation on the one hand and taxation for reducing the inequitable distribution of income on the other. The hidden assumption of wide variations in the levels of income in Guyana was probably misjudged. A budget in any country rarely commands universal agreement. But it is rare for a developing area to produce a budget over which indigenous attitudes have been split so acrimoniously as in the case of Guyana. In view of the situation of near bankruptcy facing the territory in 1961, and the urgent need for the reform of the tax structure, many of the fiscal measures were perhaps quite sensible. But in the final analysis, explanation of the budget's explosive reception must lie as much in the controversial political intentions of the government and the consequent deep-rooted fears that have been generated over a decade, and in the association of Mr. Nicholas Kaldor in search of fertile ground for his long-held views on the financial approach in developing areas, as in the nature of the budgetary proposals themselves.

The initiation of the process of development requires a very intelligent husbanding of resources and greater sacrifices on the part of citizens. But textbook recognition of this necessity does not necessarily mean popular recognition, much less acceptance of the sacrifices required for progress in many emergent territories.

4. *The Burden of Indebtedness*

One of the points stressed in this chapter is that over the years the government surplus on current account has proved insufficient to finance its development expenditure. From Table 16 it can be observed that the revenue surplus financed only 13 per cent of development expenditure between 1954 and

1964. Under the circumstances the government had to resort to extensive borrowing mostly on overseas markets. Over this period over $47 million was obtained in the form of grants mostly from Colonial Development and Welfare sources, while loans accounted for over $111 million. Grants were responsible for financing around 26 per cent of the development effort, while loans accounted for an average of 61 per cent.

TABLE 15

DEVELOPMENT EXPENDITURE, SOURCES OF FUNDS, AND PUBLIC DEBT

(*Million Guyana dollars*)

Year	Develop- ment expendi- ture	Method of finance			% of total financed by		
		Revenue surplus	Grants	Loans	Revenue surplus	Grants	Loans
1954	8·6	1·6	3·2	3·9	18·4	36·7	44·9
1955	17·5	2·6	3·9	10·0	15·1	22·9	62·0
1956	20·6	4·2	6·1	10·3	20·3	29·8	49·9
1957	18·3	5·1	5·8	7·4	27·9	31·7	40·4
1958	19·9	2·5	2·8	14·6	12·7	13·8	73·5
1959	19·0	3·3	4·6	11·1	17·1	24·2	57·7
1960	15·8	3·0	4·8	8·1	18·7	30·3	51·0
1961	21·7	2·5	5·6	13·6	11·6	25·7	62·7
1962	19·4	1·9	4·7	12·8	10·1	24·0	65·9
1963	12·0	−2·7	2·6	12·0	—	21·7	78·3
1964	9·7	0·2	2·9[a]	6·6	2·0	29·9	68·1
Total 1954–64	182·4	23·8	47·0	111·3	13·1	25·9	1·0

Sources: Estimates, Current and Capital.
[a] Excluding $624,000 Special Grant for the Special Service Unit.

In most years since 1952 the ratio of net real flows from abroad (loans plus grants) to gross domestic capital formation has been over 30 per cent, and the ratio of net inflow to net domestic capital formation has averaged 40 per cent. Between 1957 and 1960 the ratio of net borrowing abroad to net domestic capital formation reached an average of 45 per cent. However, it is not enough to consider real flows alone. We are also concerned with the total foreign liability the economy has to incur in order to undertake a given investment programme. As it has turned out in the past, the gross long-term financial liabilities incurred by the economy fell below 40 per cent of net domestic capital formation in one year only between 1952 and

1964. It reached 118 per cent in 1959, and averaged nearly 90 per cent between 1957 and 1961.

A concomitant of the heavy borrowing of the government has been the sizeable growth in the Public Debt. In 1954 it stood at $34·9 million, and grew steadily until in 1964 it stood at $134 million, showing nearly a fourfold increase. Of the total outstanding debt of $134 million in 1964, the external debt amounted to $105 million. About $30 million of this external debt represented loans obtained from the United Kingdom Exchequer, and is repayable in equated annuities. The remainder of the external debt, together with all the internal debt is backed by sinking fund investment. The internal debt represents long-term loans obtained by the government to finance its post-war development and expenditure. No attempt has ever been made by the government to affect either directly or indirectly the price of the securities after issue and there is literally no trading in these internal claims against the government. During the period the government's internal issues of long-term debt were the major financial securities available in the rudimentary organization of the capital market in Guyana. A large part of the internal debt was absorbed by three semi-governmental intermediaries—the Currency Board, the Post Office Savings Bank, and Special Funds.[1]

The overwhelming majority of the remainder is held by insurance companies. Private individuals' holding of the debt is probably negligible and the turnover of the debt is virtually non-existent. The semi-governmental authorities hold all their

---

[1] The Special Funds are associated with the sugar industry, and are concerned with fiscal problems since they are really accumulated through the imposition of a compulsory levy on the exports of sugar. The three funds in existence were created in 1947 under the provisions of Chapter 248 of the Laws of British Guiana. They include (a) the *Rehabilitation Fund*, i.e., a fund which would provide for investments in replacements, improvements, or additions to existing plant or machinery in a factory; and the extension, renovation, or reconstruction of any existing building with the object of increasing the efficiency of production, but does not include normal maintenance. (b) *The Price Stabilisation Fund:* essentially the Fund is there to stabilize the export earnings of the sugar industry (and hence the income of sugar workers) if there should be any significant variation in sugar prices. (c) *The Labour Welfare Fund:* this is a fund to provide loans to sugar workers for improving their living conditions, mainly in the field of housing, the provision of pure water supply, etc. These funds are all administered by the Financial Secretary as Statutory Trustee, with the exception of the Workers' Loan Account, under the Welfare Fund.

298 FINANCING OF ECONOMIC DEVELOPMENT

debt firmly, and so do the insurance companies. Financing of capital expenditure in this way means that, broadly speaking, the government debt issue process, in the absence of any debt management process, is 'neutral' as regards the internal income/expenditure ratio, if it is assumed that the resources obtained by the government would have found their way into investment in any event. This is a reasonable assumption as regards the Guyana government's internal debt, and the only probable effect therefore was to divert capital resources from other sectors to the government. If, however, the funds obtained would not have been otherwise employed, then the internal issue of the debt may have had an anti-deflationary effect on the internal economy.

Finally, let us consider whether the increase in the country's international indebtedness has been matched by its capacity to meet its external obligations. While numerous non-economic factors may influence the *willingness* to service the debt from time to time, the debt-servicing *capacity* of the country is of crucial importance.[1] This capacity cannot be divorced from the general problem of economic growth particularly in a low-income country. This is so because reconciliation of competing claims on resources is easier when total resources are growing than in a stationary economy. As long as the incidence of debt service falls on a part of the increment of *per capita* income, it is impossible for consumption and nationally financed investment to rise *pari passu* with service payments. And if the rate of increase of real incomes and savings remaining available after the claims on foreign capital have been met is reasonably high, if growth occurs in a continuous fashion, and if its benefits are widespread, it can also be argued that debt service payments will also behave smoothly. In this case the opportunity cost of fulfilling external obligations is less obvious, and presumably less burdensome, than in a situation in which service payments impinge upon existing living standards and employment levels. It can therefore be argued that the continuing growth in *per capita* production and the underlying process of rapid accumulation of productive capital is the basic long-run condition for debt-servicing capacity.

[1] Cf. D. Avramovic, *Economic Growth and External Debt* (Johns Hopkins Press, Baltimore, 1966).

There is a close relationship in theory and in practice between the long-term growth in income and internal savings on the one hand, and the capacity to transfer externally a part of domestic income and savings on the other. A sustained growth in income is dependent on growth in savings, and the growth in savings is dependent on the growth in income. Similarly a sustained growth in income cannot be achieved unless the foreign trade sector of the economy develops fast enough to provide external earnings needed to satisfy growing import requirements. Thus the change in debt-servicing capacity over time requires an examination of the economy in the fields of income, savings, and foreign trade.

On the surface it seems that there has been no slippage in the country's capacity to service the debt in that although payment in the form of interest has shown a more than fivefold increase between 1952 and 1964, this has been matched by countervailing increases in *per capita* incomes, export earnings, and domestic savings. But this capacity to service the debt conceals certain other features of the situation. The most important is the fact that the substantial increase of the debt in absolute terms over the period has meant an increase in the 'burden' of the debt whether measured by expressing the debt as a percentage of Gross Domestic Product or calculating the percentage of annual recurrent revenue that the servicing of the debt involves. In absolute terms whereas in 1954 the public debt represented 18·2 per cent of Gross Domestic Product, by 1964 this had more than doubled to 43·1 per cent. Charges on the debt, while representing a low 0·89 per cent of Gross Domestic Product in 1954, were absorbing 3·30 per cent in 1964. Also while these charges were absorbing 5·3 per cent of annual recurrent revenue in 1954, by 1964 they were absorbing 15·1 per cent. These 'crude' measures of burden not only indicate that public borrowing is running ahead of the capacity of the economy to sustain it, but also brings out very clearly certain structural weaknesses of the economy of Guyana.

For although incomes, export earnings, and savings have been rising in absolute terms, their real growth rates have been far from satisfactory. We saw in the previous chapter that increased export earnings are constantly eroded by the growing import bill so that in most years the balance of merchandise trade was in deficit; and although both savings and capital formation have been rising, their potential impact in the generation of increased incomes has been reduced by the rising rate of population growth and unemployment. The chronic financial instability which characterized the economy in the years after 1961 has also compounded these difficulties. It is also feared that this problem will take on added dimensions now that Guyana is an independent nation, with expanded commitments in the field of investment and overseas commitments.

5. *Conclusion*

Thus far we have been dealing with the growth of domestic savings in both the private and public sectors and the contribution of foreign capital to total investment in the economy. But the study of how investment was financed would be incomplete without a consideration of how the net savings of the economy are channelled into productive investment. This involves the study of the functioning of what may be called the capital or money market of Guyana. If by a capital market is meant, 'An organized market in which transactions in existing stocks and shares take place and through which in combination with special institutions dealing there it is possible to raise new capital by the offer of stocks and shares to the public',[1] then no such market exists in Guyana. However, if the definition is not stringently applied, an elementary organization of some sort can be said to exist.

Rigidities in the local capital market are a common feature of developing countries, and Guyana is no exception to this rule. As a consequence capital funds are frequently channelled into forms of expenditure that would not be given priority in a rational scheme of resource allocation. Savings in Guyana tend to be institutional in nature, i.e. they go into savings accounts, insurance companies, one building society, and a Government Savings Bank—the trading in stocks being vir-

[1] For an authoritative study of the monetary sector of the Guyanese Economy, see C. Y. Thomas, *Monetary and Financial Arrangements in a Dependent Monetary Economy* (University of the West Indies, 1965), and 'The Transfer Process: Theory and Experience in a Developing Economy', *Social and Economic Studies*, Vol. 15, No. 2 (June 1966).

tually non-existent. In such a situation the commercial banks and other financial intermediaries have traditionally stood at the centre of the rudimentary capital market in that they provide the main link between saver and investor. But while providing valuable service by providing credit for those sectors of the economy that could offer adequate security, they could not by the very nature of their operations provide a type of credit which tends to be scarce in developing countries, and which has to be provided if development is not to be retarded. This gap has been bridged to a certain extent by the setting up of the Guyana Credit Corporation in 1953, which together with Co-operative Credit Societies assists in sponsoring agricultural and other credit, but there is much to be desired in the functioning of these organs of credit.

The failure of the economy to make the best use of its potential savings for investment in domestic development, and the consequent excessive dependence on foreign capital are in some measure due to the weakness of the financial system. The economy has not been well served by the existing financial institutions despite their diversity particularly because there are few organized interrelationships between the institutions. A properly functioning money market is yet to become a reality. The absence of such a market is mainly due to the fact that there was no central bank to supervise the working of the system as a whole, to demarcate the specialized roles of the different types of intermediaries, and to permit healthy intercourse between them.

In the field of currency, the basing of the system on the Sterling Exchange Standard involved making the Guyanese dollar a foreign asset on account of the backing arrangements, the operation of a fixed exchange rate restricted the ability of the economy to control the propensity to import, and reduced its capacity to promote forced savings by creating money. In the field of banking the degree of freedom granted to the commercial banks and other financial intermediaries also encouraged the holding of foreign rather than local assets via balances due from banks abroad, and permitted the misallocation of retained savings between competing investment possibilities in so far as the intermediaries were free to determine the disposition of credit and its cost. The freedom accorded the intermediaries also affected the savings rate in so far as the granting of loans to the import trade increased consumption opportunities and consequently the long-run propensity to import. In the public sphere, the regulations relating to the Post Office Savings Bank and other government schemes of regular savings such as Pension and Provident Funds together with other arrangements for the holding of Treasury Funds also required inordinately large holdings of foreign assets.

Whatever the cause, the fact is that there is not the variety of local assets necessary for the financial institutions to make any significant reductions in the proportion of foreign assets to total assets that they hold. Thus even if the commercial banks were less inclined to hold their surplus balances with their head offices, and respond more willingly to national development needs, and even if the Currency Board, the Post Office Savings Bank, and the various Pension and Provident Funds were not legally bound to hold foreign securities, it would be difficult to mobilize domestic savings for domestic investment unless intermediaries which could provide suitable paper were established. It is in this connection that the establishment of the Central Bank late in 1965 is expected to lead to the development of an adequate and flexible financial infrastructure.[1]

The present government of the country seems conscious of the need to improve financial institutions and relationships so as to mobilize for development purposes such savings as already exist and to encourage their expansion. While household savings can be expected to increase in absolute terms, if *per capita* incomes continue to rise, it is not likely to increase relative to disposable income if the present 'demonstration effect' consumption pattern persists, and it is unlikely that it will change

[1] The answer to the problem of increasing home savings and harnessing them to development lies in creating an effective financial infrastructure. Broadly, a financial infrastructure comprises four elements, each of which can become a source of additional savings. These four elements are firstly, the currency, secondly a central bank, thirdly an effective commercial banking system, including savings institutions, and fourthly, a foundation for the growth of developed monetary institutions, including a market for short-term funds and a stock exchange. Cf. Nevin, *Capital Funds in Under-developed Countries*.

During the first year of operation the Bank of Guyana has shown some imaginativeness in fulfilling its role as a Central Bank and as the main architect in the construction of a financial infrastructure in Guyana. See *Bank of Guyana Annual Report*, 1966.

to any appreciable degree in the near future. Again if domestic savings are to increase then the impetus will have to come from the public sector. This is also applicable to savings in the corporate sector. An increase in savings in the public sector can be achieved without reducing expenditure on current services only to the extent that losses and subsidies to public undertakings are cut, and tax rates are fixed in such a way that an increased share of national income accrues to the government as development proceeds. But the experience of the days following Kaldor and the 1962 Budget shows that this can be a very delicate operation requiring very accurate data on matters such as the distribution of income and expenditure patterns of different income groups. But even within the framework existing over the past twenty years it was possible for the government to increase revenue substantially, although, as the evidence suggests, income tax is still being widely evaded. In this connection, the crucial factor appears to be the extent to which improvements can be effected in the machinery for assessment and collection of income tax from own-account workers.

VII

PUBLIC EXPENDITURE AND THE
DEVELOPMENT PROCESS

1. *The Growth of Public Expenditure*

The evolution of economic thinking in Guyana has been accompanied by the government's acceptance of increased responsibility for the promotion of economic development. One result of this has been a sizeable growth in the level of government expenditure. In the previous chapter we indicated the extent of the growth of government revenue from taxation and other sources so as to meet its greatly increased commitments. In this chapter, we analyse the pattern of government expenditure to assess its role in the development process. We shall also carry a stage further the discussion of public undertakings begun in the previous chapter. It may be recalled that the big losses incurred by these undertakings added to the government subsidies, virtually negates the contribution that the growth of public overhead investment can make to the development process.

Table I presents data on the growth of public expenditure between 1952 and 1964, and shows that total expenditure more than doubled between these years. In the former year it represented 20·8 per cent of Gross Domestic Product, and for most of the period it grew at approximately the same rate as domestic product until by 1964 it has risen to 25 per cent. It should be noticed that the development component of total expenditure more than doubled between 1954 and 1955, mainly as a result of the development programme which was launched in the former year. It is evident that the tremendous growth in total public expenditure over these years was accompanied by similar changes in both the recurrent and development components of expenditure, with the latter showing significant increase between 1954 and 1961.

In 1954 recurrent expenditure accounted for 17·4 per cent of

TABLE I

GROWTH OF PUBLIC EXPENDITURE 1952–64

(CURRENT PRICES)

(*Million Guyana dollars: 1952 = 100*)

Year	Recurrent expenditure	Index	Development expenditure	Index	Total expenditure	Index
1952	28·5	100	4·6	100	33·1	100
1953	31·4	110	5·3	117	36·7	111
1954	34·6	121	8·6	189	43·2	131
1955	40·0	141	17·5	385	57·5	174
1956	40·2	142	20·6	452	60·8	184
1957	43·1	151	18·3	402	61·4	186
1958	46·5	163	19·9	437	66·4	201
1959	45·5	160	19·0	418	64·5	195
1960	50·7	178	15·8	347	66·5	201
1961	57·0	201	21·7	476	78·7	239
1962	62·4	219	19·4	426	81·8	248
1963	61·5	216	12·0	236	73·5	223
1964	70·0	245	9·6	213	79·6	236

Source: Estimates, Current and Capital.

Gross Domestic Product, and by 1964 it was absorbing over 21 per cent. The average for the period 1954–64 was just over 19 per cent. In the previous chapter we argued that the capacity to service the national debt measured in terms of the growth of domestic product did not show any significant changes over the period under review. In 1954 only 0·89 per cent of the Gross Domestic Product was absorbed as interest on the public debt, and by 1964 this figure had increased to 3·3 per cent. However, some concern was expressed over the potential increase in the burden of the debt, and this is brought out by the increasing proportion of recurrent expenditure that has to be used for debt charges. This component stood at $1·8 million in 1952, or just over 5 per cent of total recurrent expenditure, but by 1964 it had recorded a fivefold increase and stood at over $10 million, or 15 per cent of recurrent expenditure.

Expenditure on general administrative services doubled between 1952 and 1964 from $7·8 million to $15·8 million. But it declined as a proportion of total recurrent expenditure from

27·4 per cent in 1952 to 23·2 per cent in 1964. However, the general picture presented is a relative constancy in the behaviour of this aggregate. Over the period under review, it absorbed an average of 23·6 per cent of total recurrent expenditure. The high level of expenditure in this section is a reflection of the rising costs of public activity, and is accounted for partly by increases in the salaries of civil servants and other administrative expenses. The growth in the size of administration was contingent upon the increased responsibilities of the government for the promotion of social and economic development, and the need to expand judicial and police services in line with increases in population as well as in the scale of economic activity. It also has a historical connotation, reflecting the increasing emphasis placed on the need to develop an efficient administrative system, a direct legacy of British Colonial rule.

The decision on how much to spend on public service is more acute in relation to social services (especially education, health, housing, and welfare) than it is in regard to the administrative, judicial, or economic services. Countries do not differ widely in the proportions of national income that they spend on general and economic administration. Taking central and local authorities together it is unusual for recurrent expenditure on these items to be less than 5 or more than 7 per cent of national income.[1] In most cases the proportion spent by the less developed tends, if they are ambitious, to exceed the proportion spent by the more developed countries. The latter have claims to better administrative services, and relatively more people engaged in the public service. But in the less developed economies, because of the shortage of educated personnel, the ratio of the salary of a civil servant to *per capita* national income is higher than in the more developed. As countries grow richer, they employ relatively more civil servants, but the percentage of national income that a civil servant receives diminishes, so that the proportion of national income spent on general and economic administration stays within a narrow range. The social services are more flexible. The degree of development of

<hr />

[1] See W. A. Lewis and A. Martin, 'Pattern of Public Revenue and Expenditure', *Manchester School of Economic and Social Studies* (Sept. 1956).

these varies so widely that the percentage of national income spent on them also varies widely.

Expenditure on social services in Guyana increased both absolutely and relative to other budgetary payments. Much of this increased expenditure was made in order to bring the country's social services into line with those considered normal for any civilized country. Expenditure on such services increased from $7·7 million in 1952 to nearly $21 million in 1964. Over the same period it absorbed an average of 30 per cent of total recurrent expenditure, rising from 27 per cent of the total in 1952 to 30·5 per cent in 1964. Between 1954 and 1964 it accounted for an average of over 6 per cent of Gross Domestic Product, rising from 5·14 per cent in 1954 to 6·66 per cent in 1964.[1] Thus while the index for the growth of expenditure on social services stood at 270·2 in 1964 (1952 = 100), that for the growth of total recurrent expenditure stood at 239·1, and that for general administration at 202·2. Thus expenditure on social services has grown much faster than total recurrent expenditure or any of its components, excepting debt charges.

While discussion is usually confined to the allocation of investment within the productive sectors of the economy, it has to be recognized that there are certain social pre-conditions for rapid economic growth. In the allocation of resources, due consideration needs to be given to the basic relationship between economic and social development. There are many activities included under social services that are in fact directly related to economic aims; important among these are vocational and technical education, the spread of elementary and secondary education, scientific research, the development of health services, town and country planning, and the housing of industrial workers. Experience indicates that while, in the early stages, certain productive activities have to be given special emphasis, the stage is soon reached when economic progress slows down or cannot be adequately sustained because of weaknesses concerning the human and social factors of development.

Determination of the proportion of resources that should be allocated to the expansion of social services is a matter of broad

[1] Estimates, Current and Capital.

political and social judgement. However, such decisions need to be preceded by attempts to identify and assess the additional benefits likely to ensue from increased expenditure on social services; the yield on social benefits should at least appear not unreasonable in the light of the general scarcity of resources. The benefits derived from increased expenditure on social services have to be assessed from two points of view. On the one hand social services themselves contribute directly to improvements in the quality of life; better health and educational facilities, for instance, are essential ingredients in the improvement of standard of living. On the other hand, social services help to raise the productivity of the working population and thereby contribute indirectly to the expansion of total output. Virtually all expenditure on social services is likely to make some positive contribution to the improvement of living standards.[1] However, if balanced social and economic development is to be maintained the expansion of social services has to be maintained in some reasonable relationship to the growth in output of commodities and other services; efforts to improve the health of the population, for example, require among other things, that the nutritional standards be improved through the expansion and diversification of agricultural output.

The human need for the expansion of social services in developing countries is clearly great. There are large sections of the communities in low-income groups whose contribution to economic growth is dependent on the development of health, education, and other social services. It is recognized, however, that, on account of the over-all limitation of resources, it may not always be possible to allocate sufficient funds for social services and it may be necessary frequently to adopt a selective

---

[1] The general attitude to social services used to be that they form part of consumption, and are not therefore as important as investment in physical resources. Alternatively, they were held to be not as important as other services that facilitate production, such as transport services or the creation of financial institutions; or as the production of goods that can be exported and earn foreign exchange. But in Guyana it has been recognized that it is as important to expand social services as it is to produce more commodities. Such expenditure can to some extent be justified on the ground that they increase productivity, but even in so far as they are to be justified only as consumption, they rank equally with other kinds of consumption. For an amplification of this argument, see W. A. Lewis, 'Social Services in Development Planning' in *Planning for Economic Development in the Caribbean* (Caribbean Organization, Puerto Rico, 1963), pp. 156–69.

approach in this field. This is only to stress the need for relating educational, health, and other social programmes as clearly as possible to over-all plans for development.

Expenditure in the field of education received the lion's share of funds allocated to social services. In 1952 this amounted to just over $3 million, or 11·08 per cent of total recurrent expenditure, but increased by nearly three and a half times over the years, standing at $10·8 million in 1964, or 15·85 per cent of total recurrent expenditure. The growth in educational expenditure was much faster than that of any other category of social services, and all other items in the recurrent budget except debt charges. It also showed a more rapid rate of increase than recurrent expenditure as a whole. A more detailed treatment of public expenditure in the field of education is given later in this chapter.

Next to education comes expenditure on health which has absorbed an average of 10 per cent of recurrent expenditure over the period. Expenditure on these services doubled from $3 million in 1952 to $6 million in 1964. Like most tropical countries Guyana has had an unsatisfactory health reputation. But with recent improvements in sanitation, water supply, and the elimination of insect-borne diseases, this is no longer the case. We saw in Chapter II that both infant mortality and general death-rates have shown a general decline over the past thirty to forty years. We recall that this was associated with the anti-malarial campaign initiated largely by the sugar companies, and was bound up with the necessity for conserving the labour supply for the sugar industry. Thus the provision of medical attention for the coastal population has always been regarded as a reasonable and economic form of expenditure. No doubt, humanitarian reasons have also been instrumental, but it is a sound enough viewpoint to regard a healthy population as a good economic resource.

The development of the health services has not been given high priority so far and the view has gained ground that, comparatively speaking, the people of Guyana are well served. For example, the World Bank Mission stated flatly, '. . . the medical and health services are faced with no urgent immediate needs for additional facilities'.[1] Although recurrent expenditure has

[1] I.B.R.D., *The Economic Development of British Guiana*, p. 77.

increased considerably and has produced results, it should not be assumed that there is no cause for disquiet. The position of the hospitals, especially the Georgetown Public Hospital, is known to be disturbing in many ways.[1] It is understaffed, poorly equipped, and the turnover of the specialists and medical officers is unfortunately very rapid. Twenty-one rural health centres and a few health outposts which have been provided have extended medical facilities and are a commendable development. But remote parts of the country are badly served, and even on the coastline, there are areas where qualified medical assistance is simply not available.[2]

Malaria has been largely eradicated, and the death-rate and infant mortality rate have fallen very considerably with the extension of medical services. The decline in the mortality rate is a world-wide phenomenon that has had a sharp impact on population figures. Increased population requires fast economic development if there is not to be wide-scale deterioration of the health of the people. The most effective health measure is freedom from want, but that does not mean that the development of health services is a matter of secondary importance and does not need earnest consideration. A health survey of the country should be launched to assess the incidence of disease, general and particular, and to locate the pockets in which this incidence is highest. For the moment however, the fact remains that by the standards of the more advanced countries Guyana's medical services are inadequate; but the increased expenditure has meant that they have become a good deal better than those in many countries at comparable levels of economic development.

Public Works and transport facilities have also absorbed a

[1] The government operates three general hospitals, three specialist (Mental, Tuberculosis, and Leprosarium), and eight small cottage hospitals in rural or remote areas. At the end of 1963 these government hospitals were providing a total of 2,700 beds, and another 300 beds were available in private hospitals and nursing homes as well as 200 beds in sugar estate hospitals which will eventually be taken over by the government. This meant that, in all, around 3,200 beds were available, or 6 beds per 1,000 of the population. *Annual Report of the Director of Medical Services*, 1963.

[2] As far back as 1954, it was recommended that not only should free medical attention be extended to a larger number of people but also that additional facilities such as health centres, cottage hospitals, and increased medical staff would be necessary. See J. H. Richardson, *Report on Social Security in British Guiana* (Georgetown, 1954).

significant proportion of recurrent expenditure. This is to be expected in a country like Guyana where the physical features and the area of physical settlement throw up a very large number of engineering and related problems. Public works absorbed just over $3 million or 11·2 per cent of the recurrent allocation in 1952. By 1964 this expenditure had doubled to $7·3 million, but this represented a slightly reduced percentage (10·8) in relation to the expenditure of 1952. A smaller amount was spent on the provision of transport and harbour facilities. In this case expenditure rose from $1·4 million or 5·8 per cent of total recurrent expenditure to $3·3 million or 4·78 per cent of the total over the same period. The main factors militating against the satisfactory growth of this sector are discussed in a later section of this chapter.

The high proportion of public funds devoted to general administrative services, social services, and the maintenance of infrastructural works have meant that only very small sums could be spent on economic development. This item absorbed an average of 1·8 per cent of Gross Domestic Product between 1954 and 1964. While in general recurrent expenditure includes transactions that occur year by year and the provision for the maintenance of building and equipment, expenditure on 'economic development' includes additions to, or replacement of, the existing capital stock and other outlays, which though not usually regarded as capital formation, are expected to contribute indirectly to an increase in productive capacity.

A characteristic feature of the post-war economic development of Guyana has been the increasing attention given to economic planning. In the next chapter we explore this aspect, in this section, we indicate on a more general level the various directions in which development expenditure was channelled. In this way we hope to throw light on the significance of development expenditure in relation to the allocation of funds from the recurrent budget. The allocation of development expenditure between the two main development periods 1954–9 and 1960–4 is set out in Table 2. During the former period, total expenditure amounted to $105·8 million. A slightly larger amount of $110·7 million was allocated for the 1960–4 period, but the actual expenditure was considerably reduced to $78·5 million. We recall that this reduction had to be effected because of the authorities' failure to raise the requisite proportion of foreign funds for financing their development plan.[1]

The most significant feature of the data is the high proportion of funds allocated to agriculture over these years. This sector

TABLE 2

ALLOCATION OF DEVELOPMENT EXPENDITURE

(Million Guyana dollars)

	1954–9		1960–4		1960–4[a]	
	Expenditure	%	Allocated	%	Expenditure	%
Agriculture						
Drainage and Irrigation	25·6	24·2	28·4	25·7	23·6	30·
Land Development	2·8	2·6	4·3	3·9	1·9	2·
Sea Defences	4·6	4·3	7·4	6·7	7·6	9·
Other	4·6	4·3	4·9	4·4	3·5	4·
Total	37·6	35·4	45·0	40·7	36·6	46·
Forests, Lands, and Mines	3·2	3·0	3·9	3·5	1·5	1·
Transport and Communications	18·6	17·6	12·5	11·3	8·1	10·
Roads	5·8	5·5	14·5	13·1	8·8	11·
Public Buildings	0·6	0·6	2·8	2·5	1·5	1·
Miscellaneous Public Works	1·8	1·7	0·6	0·5	0·7	0·
Education	1·8	1·7	4·1	3·7	3·3	4·
Health	0·8	0·8	1·9	1·7	1·8	2·
Housing[b]	17·6	16·6	5·5	5·0	2·8	3·
Other Social Services	0·8	0·8	2·2	2·0	1·5	1·
Power	2·4	2·3	2·6	2·4	2·7	3·
Water	1·7	1·6	2·9	2·6	1·9	2·
Credits (Industry, Agriculture, and Housing)	10·0	9·5	11·5	10·4	5·3	6·
Miscellaneous	3·1	2·9	0·7	0·6	2·0	2·
	105·8	100·0	110·7	100·0	78·5	100

Source: 1964 Development Estimates. Estimates, Current and Capital, 1965.
[a] 1964 Revised Estimates.   [b] Including Public Officer Housing.

absorbed 35·4 per cent of these funds in the 1954–9 period, and by 1960–4 this had risen to 46·7 per cent. In monetary terms, a total of $37·6 million was spent in this sector over the former period, but in the latter, although $45 million was allocated, only $36·6 million was actually spent.

[1] See Chapter VI, pp. 279–82 above.

Although large amounts were spent on the development of sea defences and land settlement schemes, the drainage and irrigation sector has consistently received the highest proportion of development funds. In 1954–9 it absorbed $25·6 million or 24·2 per cent of development budgets; in 1960–4, this amount was slightly reduced to $23·6 million, but this represented an increased 30·1 per cent of the total. The provision of drainage and irrigation facilities has always presented one of the most intractable problems to the government. The emphasis given to drainage and irrigation has arisen because the coastal area is below sea level, and the provision against flooding has to be given the highest priority. In addition, over the years priority was given to the reclamation of agricultural lands and to the improvement of water control. This need for improved drainage and irrigation was also based on the argument that there was insufficient land under cultivation, and as the rate of growth of population was increasing, this deficiency was expected to become serious; that the employment of the rural population was as urgent as the increase in agricultural production. It was also recognized that more of the new land for cultivation had to be found on the coast despite its special drainage and irrigation problems, and especially since the agricultural prospects of the interior lands were as yet virtually unknown.

In this context the need for a cash crop with a ready market and proper market facilities, and for a crop that can be grown by the peasant farmers with very little initial capital outlay, determined the main trend in cultivation, which was concentrated on the growing of rice. Thus a large part of the available capital was used for strengthening the mono-product economy of the peasant sector, even though rice provided an extremely low return for capital outlay when viewed from an economic standpoint. The expenditure on drainage and irrigation schemes for the expansion of peasant cultivation did not therefore have a very high income-creating potential, and social and political rather than economic factors determined the emphasis on expanding rice lands for the unemployed and underemployed labour. It is likely that as economic development proceeds, and as more and more emphasis is placed on developing the interior areas of the country, with concomitant shifts inwards of the coastal population, the drainage and irrigation problem will be ameliorated. This might possibly lead to a relative reduction of development expenditure in this field. But so long as development is concentrated on the coastal plain, the physical and topographical features of the area will continue to necessitate that huge amounts of capital formation take place in the agricultural sector in the form of better and improved drainage and irrigation to ensure that productivity in agriculture increases.

We noticed earlier that over the years a very high proportion of funds from the recurrent budget has been devoted to the maintenance of transport and communications. This is also the case in the field of development. Over the development period 1954–9 more than $26 million, or 24·8 per cent of total development funds, was allocated to transport and communications, roads, and other public works. During the 1960–4 period this was reduced to an average of $17 million or 22 per cent of the total amount spent. However, it must be remembered that over $27 million was allocated to this sector, and this constituted an average of 26 per cent of the total allocation. It is evident that these are very high figures for a country of Guyana's economic size, but the nature of this expenditure has been warranted by the country's geographical size, and the extremely poor state of its communications. It must however be admitted that this increase has not as yet made any significant inroads on the problems in this sphere.

Social services have also received contributions from the development budgets. The greater part of the expenditure in this category was directed towards capital formation in the form of buildings. The large amount received by the housing sector is noteworthy. During the 1954–9 development period this amounted to $17·6 million, or 16·6 per cent of actual expenditure for the period. This has helped to improve to a considerable degree the poor housing standards; but the present position of housing is still unsatisfactory. With the growing pressure of population the position worsens. All over the world the task of providing satisfactory housing conditions has proved difficult. It involves heavy investment generally varying from 20 to 40 per cent of total capital formation, efficient town and country planning, the relaying of old residential and other areas, the

development of new villages and towns according to the projections of needs, and the application of well-thought-out principles of community development in relation to the requirements of the society, and the choice of building techniques and
a standard of social aesthetics. Housing is a manifestation of the
state of society, its social stratification, disparities of income,
cultural differences, and inherent social stresses. Plans for
housing development have to take all this into account.

Housing development not only involves the application of
large resources, a high standard of engineering skill and performance, and a well-articulated system of communications and
social services, but social engineering of a very high order.
Thinking along these lines is yet to evolve in Guyana, and the
large amounts spent on housing between 1954 and 1959 had
political rather than economic or social implications. It might
be claimed that when an economy is attempting to develop
rapidly, investment in housing receives low priority so that
scarce resources can be diverted to the building up of the productive base. However, in the context of Guyana where
population is rising fast, and where investment programmes in
the future will result in a geographical extension of the economy,
a sizeable programme for housing must be provided. House
building could provide demand for local timber, other local
building materials, and local labour. The furnishing of homes
would also provide incentives to the development of certain
light industries, especially the furniture industry. Moreover,
since development programmes in the future would involve a
certain tightening of import controls in order to reduce the
importation of consumer durables and to release foreign exchange for capital goods, housing may have to become the main
compensation to the population for development effort. Further,
the prospect of house ownership is one of the main incentives to
the kind of routine savings that is required if a greater share of
national investment requirements is to be met by national
savings.

Over the 1954–9 period Industry and Credit received $10
million or 9·5 per cent of development funds. Of the allocation
of $11·5 million in the 1960–4 period, only $5·3 million was
actually spent. These funds were channelled into the Guyana
Credit Corporation, which was expected to allocate them in

accordance with the agricultural and industrial development needs of the country. However, dissatisfaction has been expressed at this institution's failure to help industrial promotion in the country, the greater part of its loans being channelled into the building of houses for the upper and middle income groups, and the criteria used for the allocation of its funds being more or less arbitrary. Although to some extent it was able to meet the pressing demand for agricultural credits and loans in the private sector for houses, it interpreted its enabling statute very conservatively, and thus was unable to supplement the funds received from the central government by drawing on other sources.[1]

An interesting feature of the data presented in Table 2 is the relatively small amount of development funds that have gone into the development of the power and water resources of the country. The electricity consumption in Guyana is extremely low. Compared with the averages in the world or even Latin America, the mere 15,000 kW. installed in public service, with a generation of 50 million kWh. in 1960, corresponding to a consumption of barely 80 kWh. *per capita* per year, is an extremely low figure.[2] The implication here is that in order to achieve vigorous economic development, Guyana will first need forceful development of its electricity capacity. There is no doubt that in order to make a proper appraisement of the present and prospective situations in the field of electric power development, as well as of electricity enterprises, in the most efficient manner, urgent action will have to be taken. An important aspect of this problem is the move to ascertain definitely the existence of hydro-electric sites which could be developed economically for large-scale industrial and general urban purposes, and to discover what conditions must be fulfilled to make such hydro-electric developments possible.

In addition to the material and economic feasibility of the

---

[1] Cf. Thomas, *Monetary and Financial Arrangements*, pp. 156–64.

[2] See Adolfo Dorfman, *Report on the Preliminary Investigations of Problems of Power and Water Resource Development in British Guiana* (Santiago, Chile, 1961). On the other hand electric capacity installed in the mining, industrial, and agricultural enterprises is perhaps three times that figure. This gives a clear idea to what degree the development is uneven, if we compare the main economic activities which are the backbone of Guyana's production on the one hand and general facilities available to urban dwellers on the other.

hydro-electric site itself, the main consideration is, of course, the amount of power the market will be able to absorb. In this connection two different approaches are open; one with a view to supplying hydro-electricity only to Georgetown and perhaps the coastal areas, and a second one where the bulk of the supply would be bought for heavy electro-metallurgical production and a relatively insignificant part transmitted to the coast for general urban, industrial, and agricultural development. The sites suitable for meeting the requirements of the former alternative are not the same as for the latter, and a basic economic policy decision will have to be taken by the government in that respect.[1]

Another problem which has to be given careful study is the supply of electricity to rural areas, which are at present deprived of it. The solution may be envisaged in two different ways: firstly, by supplying the coastal area from Georgetown by means of transmission and distribution lines, or secondly, by creating, as a first step, small generating and distributing centres which would, in due course, merge into a single grid. The answer depends partly on the source of power. If it is to be bulk hydro-electricity, it would possibly be cheaper to build the rural transmission system right away. However, if the supply is thermo-electric the order ought to be reversed. In this context considerable economy will result if the supply of power is looked at in each area or project from the integration point of view combining the industrial, agricultural, pumping, domestic, and other loads to the maximum feasible degree.

Thus as the economic development of the country pressed ahead it was necessary to have expenditure moving in different avenues to provide the institutional and other framework necessary for economic growth. But the impact of the heavy government capital on income has not been very pronounced. It is also possible that government development expenditure has been overstated owing to a loose definition of capital outlays. However, it is obvious that there still exist some significant

[1] The large amounts of funds required in this context means that the government cannot meet its needs entirely from its development budget. Large loans will have to be raised from international bodies, individual donor countries, or consortia of such countries. For an interesting recent discussion of aid-giving by consortia see I. M. D. Little and J. M. Clifford, *International Aid* (Allen and Unwin, 1965).

lacunae in the government's development efforts. These gaps will have to be closed in the future. We may now show the impact of government capital and other expenditures on some areas of the economy that we regard as vital for economic development. We concentrate particularly on education and transport and communications.

2. *Education*

An important aspect of the problem of employment and the generation of income in developing countries which is not generally recognized is that the use of labour ought to be made more profitable and attractive to the economy as a whole through the measures that would improve the performance of the local work force, especially through education and special training programmes. Many studies of economic growth in the advanced countries confirm the importance of non-material investment.[1] These investigations indicate that output has increased at a higher rate than can be explained by an increase in only the inputs of labour and physical capital. The residual difference between the rate of increase in output and the rate of increase in physical capital and labour encompasses many 'unidentified factors', but a prominent element is the improvement in the quality of inputs.[2] The failure to treat human re-

[1] For a compendium of pro-educational arguments see T. W. Schultz, *The Economic Value of Education* (Columbia University Press, New York, 1963).

[2] However, there is a danger of transposing arguments showing the high productivity of education from the advanced countries to the different setting of an underdeveloped economy, notwithstanding the limitations in the pro-education arguments themselves. The danger arises mainly because of certain 'rigidities' and 'resistances' to social transformation and economic development. Cf. H. Myint, 'Education and Economic Development', Special Number of Select Papers on Education presented to the VIIth Latin American Congress of Sociology 1964, *Social and Economic Studies*, Vol. 14, No. 1 (March 1965), pp. 8–20. But the author does recognize that the low quality of the labour force manifests 'economic backwardness'. The lack of emphasis on the investment in human capital explains why some economists have failed to recognize that the problems of 'building the runway', i.e. investment in social infrastructure, education, research, technical skill, health, etc., are rather distinct from the problems of the 'take-off', a problem which falls within the no-man's-land which needs to be jointly explored by economists and other social scientists.

See H. Myint, 'An Interpretation of Economic Backwardness', *Oxford Economic Papers* (June 1954), pp. 132–63, and 'Social Flexibility, Social Discipline, and Economic Growth', *International Social Science Journal*, Vol. XVI, No. 2 (1964), pp. 252–60.

sources as a product of investment has fostered the retention of the classical notion of labour as a capacity to perform manual work requiring little knowledge and skill—a capacity with which, according to this view, labourers are endowed about equally. This notion of labour was wrong then, and is patently wrong now with the growth of more modern techniques of production and economic organization.[1]

We saw earlier that over the period under review the volume of total educational expenditure on both recurrent and capital accounts at current prices more than doubled. Even allowing for price increases this represented a faster rate of increase than was the case for total budgetary expenditure of the country. Leaving aside general price changes, there seems to have been three main reasons for this change: the emergence of strong local opinion, the emergence of world opinion, and population growth. In Chapter II we analysed the demographic influence of such changes. There we saw that the rising birth-rates and decline in infant mortality raised the number of dependants in the population by significant proportions, with a consequential increase in the number of children at school both at the primary and secondary levels.

There is a tendency for government control of education to become more and more comprehensive in response to social demands and thus to restrict the scope for private contributions, which in the course of economic development and rising *per capita* income have often proved to be more elastic than public funds. The financial value of such contributions is usually underestimated. In Guyana, education is financed out of three main sources: the current national budget, the development budget, and various forms of private funds. Local authorities and communities in their capacity as public authorities do not share in the control and finance of education. It is very difficult to get an over-all picture of the proportions spent from different funds, partly because the responsibility on the public side is not fully concentralized, and partly because the private sector cannot be properly assessed in all its different kinds of contribution for lack of statistical information.

[1] H. G. Johnson, 'The Political Economy of Opulence', in his *Money, Trade and Economic Growth* (Allen and Unwin, London, 1962), Ch. 8.

However, in 1960 the government's contribution to education amounted to roughly 67 per cent of recurrent and 38 per cent of non-recurrent expenditure.[1] There were, however, differences in the degree of participation in and towards the several fields. Over the last thirteen years there has been a comparatively fixed structure of government expenditure. This highlights the limited possibilities for one sector to expand at the expense of others, and explains why the rise in the proportion of educational expenditure over this period has been relatively small. However, this rise involves no remarkable achievement in view of the steep increase in debt charges because of big loans on development projects, obligations which should not be neglected even for other urgent requirements. The structure of government revenue underlines the relative rigidity in the allocation of funds. We saw in the previous chapter that more

TABLE 3(a)

NATIONAL INCOME AND EXPENDITURE ON EDUCATION PER CAPITA OF POPULATION AND EXPENDITURE ON PRIMARY SCHOOLS PER CAPITA OF PUPILS ENROLLED, 1952–63

(*At current prices*)

Year	Population	National income per capita	Expenditure on education per capita	Pupils in primary schools	Expenditure on primary schools	
	('000)	($)	($)	('000)	($'000)	($ per pupil)
1952	446·2	326	7·07	78·7	2,557	32·49
1953	459·0	349	7·63	84·1	2,466	29·33
1954	472·2	363	8·91	89·0	2,978	33·46
1955	486·0	361	10·73	94·5	3,622	38·31
1956	500·0	380	12·45	102·1	4,632	45·37
1957	515·1	386	11·99	105·9	4,502	42·51
1958	531·9	360	12·31	111·7	4,743	42·44
1959	549·9	356	12·27	118·4	5,105	43·13
1960	567·0	377	13·32	125·3	5,411	43·17
1961	582·2	390	13·90	130·2	5,669	43·54
1962	598·4	351	14·88	135·3	6,312	46·64
1963	616·4	383	16·49	139·4	7,353	52·75

Source: Germanacos Report.

[1] Report of UNESCO *Educational Survey Mission to Guyana* (*Germanacos Report*) (Georgetown, 1965).

than 80 per cent of the revenue is derived from taxation, mainly from customs and excise, reflecting a high degree of dependency in spending capacity on external developments.

Despite these difficulties, the government of Guyana has accepted in principle that education plays a significant role in the economic and social development of its citizens,[1] and this is reflected in the increasing absolute volume of expenditure on

TABLE 3(b)

(INDICES OF GROWTH)

NATIONAL INCOME AND EXPENDITURE ON EDUCATION PER CAPITA OF POPULATION AND EXPENDITURE ON PRIMARY SCHOOLS PER CAPITA OF PUPILS ENROLLED, 1952–63 (1952 = 100)

(*At current prices*)

Year	National income *per capita* of population	Education expenditure *per capita* of population	Expenditure on primary schools *per capita* of	
			Population	Pupils enrolled
1952	100·0	100·0	100·0	100·0
1953	107·1	107·9	93·7	90·3
1954	114·4	126·0	110·1	103·0
1955	110·7	151·8	130·0	117·9
1956	116·6	176·1	161·6	139·6
1957	118·4	169·6	152·5	130·8
1958	110·4	174·1	155·7	130·6
1959	109·2	173·6	162·0	132·7
1960	115·6	188·4	166·5	132·9
1961	119·6	196·6	170·0	134·0
1962	107·7	210·5	184·1	143·6
1963	117·5	233·2	208·2	162·4

education over the years. This can be seen from Table 3 which shows national income and expenditure on education *per capita* of population and expenditure on primary schools *per capita* of pupils enrolled for the years 1952–63. The data reveal that expenditure on education *per capita* more than doubled between these years. This was also the case for expenditure on primary schools *per capita* of the population, although the growth in the

[1] Cf. *White Paper on Educational Policy*, Ministry of Education and Social Development (Georgetown, 1962).

TABLE 4

EXPENDITURE ON EDUCATION 1952–63

(Thousand Guyana dollars—at current prices)

	1952	1953	1954	1955	1956	1957	1958	1959	1960	1961	1962	1963
Primary Schools[a]	2,633	2,643	3,273	2,953	4,917	4,876	5,081	5,437	5,858	6,430	7,923	7,675
General Budget	2,557	2,489	3,013	3,665	4,671	4,562	4,813	5,179	5,502	5,751	6,407	7,475
Development Budget	76	154	260	288	246	305	268	258	356	679	1,516	200
Government Training College	34	33	55	63	115	99	97	116	146	153	154	143
General Budget	34	33	55	63	115	99	97	116	146	153	154	143
Secondary Schools[b]	193	233	298	367	398	437	621	751	747	787	819	917
General Budget	193	233	298	367	398	437	581	661	705	754	802	917
Development Budget	—	—	—	—	—	—	40	90	42	33	17	—
Vocational Schools[c]	148	161	207	229	242	255	257	258	253	273	323	351
General Budget	148	144	181	222	242	255	234	247	253	273	323	351
Development Budget	—	17	26	7	—	—	23	11	—	—	—	—
Special and Reformatory	76	78	89	95	103	107	106	107	104	109	124	138
General Budget (Education)	76	78	89	95	103	107	106	107	104	109	124	138
Higher Education[d]	183	362	300	393	401	456	523	180	689	836	871	1,060
General Budget	183	362	300	393	401	405	522	180	689	836	871	1,060
Development Budget	—	—	—	—	—	51	1	—	—	—	—	—

Miscellaneous Expenditure												
Ministry of Education[e]	137	129	141	185	199	245	261	244	280	377	366	1,096
General Budget	137	129	141	185	199	227	261	244	280	366	366	410
Development Budget	—	—	—	—	—	18	—	—	—	11	—	686
Other Ministries[f]	289	309	448	717	735	905	1,038	997	1,124	1,111	1,149	1,461
General Budget	289	309	441	687	680	869	1,006	951	1,060	1,031	1,084	1,255
Development Budget	—	—	7	30	55	37	32	46	64	80	65	206

Sources: Annual Reports of the Accountant General, 1952–1964. Estimates Current and Capital. Development Estimates. Annual Reports of the Director of Education.

[a] Including practical instruction courses.
[b] Including government payment to grant aided schools.
[c] Government Technical Institute and Carnegie School of Home Economics.
[d] Contribution to the University of the West Indies, Subsidies for Students' Welfare abroad, Students' Loans and Contributions to various international education agencies.
[e] Including administration, i.e. Department of Education.
[f] Includes school medical and dental services, teachers' pensions and gratuities, maintenance of government schools, broadcasts to schools, Amerindian education, etc.

latter was much less spectacular. Expenditure on primary schools *per capita* of pupils enrolled increased by 62 per cent over these years.

Table 4 presents data on the functional division of expenditure on education between 1952 and 1963. Over the period 1952 to 1963 total expenditure on primary education accounted for an average of 70 per cent of the total education budget, rising from $2·7 million in 1952 to $7·7 million in 1963. An average of 90 per cent of this amount was allocated to recurrent expenditure, e.g. the salaries of teachers, while the remaining one-tenth catered for capital expenditure including the building programme. It should also be noticed that the pace of capital formation was increasing absolutely faster over the period 1961–2 compared with the situation for recurrent expenditure.

Taking 1954 as the base year, the relative increase in the total primary education bill ranged from around 20 per cent over 1955, to over 100 per cent from 1961 onwards. Generally, the trend has been a fairly rapidly rising one. While the trend in recurrent expenditure—the more dominant element—conformed very closely to the general one in so far as the behaviour of the annual rate of increase was concerned, the trend of capital expenditure was also a rising one. The intensification of the school building programme and teacher training activities is reflected in the relatively high figures for 1961 and 1962.

Although expenditure on primary education has been steadily rising the country's background still remains confused, and this is strongly reflected in the poor quality of the labour force. Compulsory primary education has a long history, almost as long as in the United Kingdom.[1] This extensive system of primary education produces a reasonably well-educated school-leaver with general certificates of education, but the system, which is primarily based on the English tradition, is not geared to the problems of development. The educational system produces good civil servants, lawyers, doctors, and teachers but few skilled or semi-skilled artisans such as plumbers,

[1] Since 1876 primary education has been legally compulsory, but this imitation of the British Education Act of 1870 was not rigorously applied, particularly to the East Indian population living on the sugar plantations. Today primary education is compulsory from the age of 6 to 14 years where accommodation is available. For an indication of the growth of primary education between 1876 and 1962 see *Germanacos Report*, appendix.

builders, mechanics, and technicians. At the secondary level, the increase in the demand for this type of educational service represented one of the most interesting educational developments over the period. The increase in the population was again an instrumental variable in this regard. It has been estimated that the population in secondary schools comes to about 15,500 out of an estimated total pupil population in primary and secondary schools of approximately 156,000, i.e. 10 per cent of the children in schools are in secondary schools; of the children of the age-range 12–18, 18 per cent are catered for. Government secondary schools contain less than 10 per cent of the children in secondary schools, the grant-aided schools over 55 per cent. The large number in the uncontrolled private schools is especially significant as the education provided in the majority of these is of the poorest quality; the government's efforts to provide alternative facilities is more than warranted.

Total expenditure on government secondary and aided schools totalled over $6 million between 1952 and 1963. This was just under one-tenth of the expenditure on primary education. Of this proportion, the lion's share went towards subsidizing the salaries of teachers, with capital expenditure representing less than one-sixth of the total. Consequently, it would appear that this source of expenditure has been marginal in its influence. But it must be remembered that the majority of the buildings used by the secondary schools are not owned by the government, and teacher training as such has not been its direct responsibility. It could therefore be appreciated what the financial implications would be for the future when the provision for secondary education becomes a free public service.

On the other hand, it could be argued that the government has been working through the private sector in order to maintain an indirect influence on the pattern. The income elasticity of demand for education may have been an important factor in this connection. We saw that a large proportion of development funds has been channelled into the agricultural sector, and principally into the rice industry. With favourable prices and relatively satisfactory harvests, farmers' incomes were rising, and in most cases the impact was reflected in changes in the consumption pattern of households, including the purchase of more educational services. At the same time employment opportunities created in other sectors of the economy had a similar kind of impact. Colonial Development and Welfare Grants enabled the initiation and completion of various projects in the public sector. All in all the impact was to reinforce the government's indirect influence on the demand for secondary education.

The question remains as to the appropriate relationship between the number of pupils at different levels of the educational pyramid. A recent UNESCO report suggests that in the underdeveloped countries the relationship should be of the order of 100:26:2.[1] In other words, for every 100 pupils attending primary schools, there should be 26 attending secondary schools and two attending institutions of higher learning. Guyana falls terribly short of such standards. In 1963, the secondary school enrolment amounted to 11 per cent of the number enrolled in primary schools.

There is even further cause for disquiet if we consider the geographical distribution of secondary schools in Guyana. The interior of the country is not served at all; this is hardly surprising when one considers the vast area and its thinly scattered population. Greater Georgetown with more than one-fourth of the population has two-thirds of the total pupil population. The densely populated area of the east and Corentyne coast is the only rural area that has attracted the attention of voluntary organizations to build secondary schools. The government's efforts, which had been confined to Georgetown, have now been directed to Essequibo where a third school is building up year by year. When we consider the total pupil population in Georgetown and the Greater Georgetown all-age schools in relation to the secondary-school population—a ratio of 2·7:1— and compare this with the similar figure for the rest of the country, a ratio of 27:1, we see the distinct advantage the Georgetown children have in comparison.[2]

The need for secondary-school graduates will become even

---

[1] UNESCO, E.D. 192. *Report of Conference at Karachi and Tokyo*, 1963.
[2] In fact quite a sizeable proportion of the children in the secondary schools at Georgetown travel by train, by road, by ferry, or on foot from the environs and outlying districts. The fact that rural Guyana is badly served causes concentration in and upon Georgetown at great expense to parents and fatigue to the children. It also helps to explain the sudden and recent blossoming of private secondary schools in the rural areas.

more acute in the future. The required number must necessarily depend on the pace at which economic development
proceeds. The annual output of the secondary schools in
Guyana is still unable to fill all the positions for which this type
of training is usually regarded as desirable, and the government
is planning to increase the present enrolment over the next few
years.[1]

For technical education, the pattern was similar to the case
just considered. Expenditure on education at this level was just
around half of what it was for secondary education. The main
source of technical training in Guyana is the Government
Technical Institute, established in 1950, and currently serving
approximately 900 students. Apart from this institution, the
only substantial contributions to technical training occur at the
trade schools of Bookers Sugar Estates and the Demerara
Bauxite Company. The number of skilled personnel turned out
by these institutions is too small to meet the required needs.

The success of the investment and development effort is dependent on the availability of sufficient skilled and professional
manpower. The basic dilemma confronting the economic effort
in Guyana is that there exists large-scale unemployment, while
at the same time many jobs remain vacant, owing to the unavailability of trained personnel.[2] This unavailability often
prevents both private enterprise and government from em-
barking upon projects which could contribute to the over-all
employment situation and raise the standard of living. It is
obvious what a heavy price the country's economy is paying for
its past neglect of technical and professional training, and
strenuous efforts must be made to ensure that the economy is
not similarly handicapped in the future.[3]

---

[1] Under the 1966–72 Development Programme the present government has
allocated over $6 million for the provision of another 17,000 secondary school
places, *Development Plan, 1966–72*, Ch. 10.

[2] In the public service alone over 450 professional and technical positions were
vacant as of March 1965 owing to the lack of suitably qualified applicants. There
were also almost 200 vacancies for professional workers and 400 vacancies for
craftsmen, technical workers, and other non-professional workers with specialized
training, counting the vacancies only in firms employing 5 or more people and in
government. It was also revealed that the work of over 160 craftsmen was reported
as unsatisfactory, counting only firms employing over 5 people and excluding
government. *Manpower Survey*, 1965, Ch. 4.

[3] Over the 1966–72 Development period it is envisaged that over $6 million

At the University level, there has been a steady absolute increase in public funds (except in 1959) for the training of officers in both the professional and technical fields of the public service. Around $8 million including grants from the United States Information Service were spent in this way, and a little under 75 per cent of this amount was financed by loans and revenue. This amount excludes students going abroad on their own financial resources. Primary education aside, training at this level appears to have been better treated than technical training and all other aspects of education. Compared with technical education, the amount expended on higher education is absolutely bigger, and represents around 20 per cent of total expenditure on primary education. One of the main reasons for this emphasis is the immediate needs of the economy for all kinds of specialists.

The other items on which public funds were expended fall into a heterogeneous group, including Adult Education, Amerindian Development, the Department of Education, Reformatory Schools, pensions and gratuities for teachers, dental school service and schools broadcasts, and education expenditure by other ministries. This group absorbed around $10 million of public funds, and as a group they outrank the position held by higher education. But from the point of view of investment the reverse is the case, for less than $3 million of this sum represented capital investment compared with over $7 million in the case of University training. It is a point of significance that almost all this investment has been taking place in the training of agricultural personnel, in the research and survey projects of other ministries, and the trend of expenditure shows that for every year after 1954, the increases both absolute and relative have been considerable.

3. *Transport and Communications*

The relatively heavy investment by the government in transportation reflects the importance of this sector in the Guyanese

would be spent on the improvement of facilities for technical education. The government intends to increase the facilities now offered by its Technical Institute, and School of Home Economics, as well as the building of three new technical colleges. Cf. *Development Programme 1966–72*, Ch. 9.

context. The demand for transport and communications, like the demand for power, is a derived demand. This demand depends upon the volume and dispersal of economic activity, that is, the need to shift men and goods from one place to another. There may of course be need for provision for transport and communications for non-economic reasons such as can be justified on grounds of national security. But the greater part of transport and communications facilities are subservient to the needs of production and distribution of goods and services within the geographical areas of the country and across them to the markets with which the economy is linked.

(a) *Roads.* Guyana has in all some 531 miles of public roads. About 354 miles of these are in the coastal and riverain areas; the remainder are in the interior. There are approximately 0·008 miles of motor roads for every square mile of territory. This ratio compares very unfavourably with the prevailing situation in most underdeveloped countries.[1] But the provision of an adequate road network is marred by the fact that between 85 and 90 per cent of the country's population is settled on the coastal and riverain areas, and these two areas are served by roughly 274 miles of roads, or just over a half of the total road mileage in the country. This coastal concentration of population has also meant that the greater part of industrial and economic activity has been concentrated in this area.

In Guyana all the forms of inland transport are a financial burden on the government and thereby on the taxpayer. An attempt is therefore made in this section to assess in outline the cost to the country of the roads. Table 5 presents data on the actual recurrent expenditure for the year 1964. The principal spending department is the Roads Division in the Ministry of Works and Hydraulics. The annual allocation of funds is not sufficient for full maintenance of the existing conditions of the entire road system. Appreciable improvements are shown in a number of short sections, but this is at the cost of the deterioration of the network as a whole, slowly but steadily worsening

---

[1] For example Barbados has 705 miles of road and in Jamaica there are approximately 1·1 miles of road for every square mile of territory. In East, West, and Central Africa, the ratio tends to be of the order 0·10 miles of road per square mile of land area. See E. K. Hawkins, *Roads and Road Transport in an Underdeveloped Country—A case Study of Uganda.* Colonial Research Study No. 32 (H.M.S.O. 1962), p. 23.

under the growing weight of traffic. The maintenance of the roads in the towns of Georgetown and New Amsterdam just keeps in step with increasing traffic. The townships benefit from government grants towards the costs. The contribution made by other departments is insignificant.

The following factors help to explain the existence of a backlog of road improvements and maintenance: the unusually soft clay soil for road foundations and difficult drainage conditions; inadequacy of road maintenance and improvement funds; the inadequate number of trained road engineering personnel and of supporting staff; inadequacy of equipment. Alluvial clay is the basic foundation of the coastal roads, and the parallel

TABLE 5

ANNUAL RECURRENT EXPENDITURE ON ROADS

(*Million Guyana dollars*)

Ministry of Works and Hydraulics, Roads Division	
Establishment, administration	0·35
Road maintenance	1·8
Arrear in maintenance	0·3
Ministry of Home Affairs	
Road costs	0·37
Contribution to Georgetown and New Amsterdam	0·13
Georgetown	
Road maintenance	0·2
New Amsterdam	
Road maintenance	0·04
Rural Districts	
Road Maintenance	0·05
Traffic Police	0·1
Licensing vehicles	0·1
Hospital emergencies, accidents	0·4
Ministry of Agriculture, Forests and Lands	
Roads in development schemes	0·1
Ministry of Communication	
Road signs, education, grants	0·04
Ferries, attributable to road vehicles	0·16
Lighting of roads	0·1
Town and Country Planning	0·1
Total expenditure	4·3

Source: Estimates, Current and Capital, 1964.

proximity of drainage trenches encourages erosion and inundation of this foundation. In addition many of the roads are surfaced with earth, sand, sand-clay or burnt-earth. Given the volume of traffic they bear and the seasonal occurrence of heavy rainfall this type of road can last only for a short period of time. Consequently, maintenance activity has to be a regular and costly exercise, if tolerable standards are to be maintained. There is also an imbalance between maintenance by hand and mechanized work, and between the labour force and mechanical plant available. Labour, in so far as the roads are concerned, is underemployed and a large number of the workers every year is temporarily transferred to other forms of employment such as sea defences.

Over the 1960–4 period the Roads Division of the Ministry of Works and Hydraulics spent around $8·5 million on road maintenance. Given a total expenditure on maintenance, road development, and surveys, of just over $17 million over the

TABLE 6

EXPENDITURE ON ROAD MAINTENANCE, CONSTRUCTION, AND SURVEYS

(*Million Guyana dollars*)

Projects	1960	1961	1962	1963	1964
Maintenance	1·54	1·74	1·70	1·65	1·88
Development					
Parika-Bartica Road	0·66	1·03	2·75	0·06	—
Bartica-Potaro Road	0·48	0·51	0·15	—	—
East Bank Demerara Road	0·54	0·60	0·40	0·12	0·20
East Coast Road (Abary Bridge)	0·01	0·55	0·03	—	—
Lethem–Wichibai–Dadanawa Road	—	0·02	0·01	—	—
Surveys					
Potaro–Lethem Road	0·16	0·13	0·01	—	—
East and West Coast Road	—	0·40	0·01	—	—
Atkinson Field–Mackenzie	—	—	0·05	0·20	0·04
West Coast Demerara Road	—	—	—	—	0·05
Total	2·79	4·98	5·11	2·03	2·17

Source: Accounts, Roads Division, Ministry of Works and Hydraulics. *Development Estimates, 1964–65.*

23—E.D.G.

same period, the contribution to road maintenance was approximately 50 per cent of the total allocation. The position is set out in Table 6 above. The average expenditure over the five-year period 1960–4 was $3·414 million, of which approximately $2·388 million and $1·028 million represented the amount of work carried out annually by government forces and by contractors respectively. In 1960 maintenance expenditure was approximately $1·54 million and for every succeeding year expenditure kept above this level. However, this rising trend of maintenance expenditure was still inadequate to cope with the pace at which the public roads had been deteriorating. The rising expenditure on maintenance also has the implication that smaller sums are available for development of new roads systems.

There can be no doubt that the priorities in any road programme must be the initiation of greater monetary control, financial balance, and the maintenance of every existing mile of road at least in the condition it is now. In the past it has not been possible to organize maintenance so as to keep in step with the normal increase of traffic demands. Within the available resources it was impossible to strike a proper balance between maintenance of the entire road system and improvement demands in dispersed sections. A comparison of funds expended on the annual upkeep of roads and the growth of vehicle traffic between 1959 and 1964 is shown in Table 7. The rise in the cost

TABLE 7

EXPENDITURE ON ROAD UPKEEP AND GROWTH
OF VEHICLE TRAFFIC

Year	Cost of road upkeep ($'000)	Up by (%)	Number of vehicles registered					
			Cars	Up by (%)	Lorries, buses	Up by (%)	All vehicles	Up by (%)
1959	1,242	—	7,365	—	2,594	—	18,627	—
1960	1,544	24	8,503	15	2,757	6	21,924	17
1961	1,738	13	9,504	12	2,990	8	24,846	13
1962	1,744	2	10,177	7	3,079	3	26,612	7
1963	1,700	0	8,077	—	2,015	—	28,403	7
1964	2,000	13	11,000	9	3,714	20	30,000	5

Source: Reports, Roads Division, Ministry of Works and Hydraulics.

figures includes a certain amount caused by decline in the value of money. If we accept 1963 as an exceptional year of prolonged work stoppages, the table shows that the increase in traffic has not been of a size to make it entirely responsible for the worsening of road conditions, although this may have been influenced to some extent by speed and weight increases. The cause may be attributed to either lack of efficiency in maintenance, workmanship, materials, equipment, or lack of sufficient funds. However, the work actually accomplished cannot be found inefficient. On the contrary it shows ample proof of commendable achievement with limited resources. The conclusion must therefore be that deficient funds with unavoidable repercussions on materials and plant has been until now the main cause of deterioration.

In planning the creation of a worthy road system and its future expansion, it is essential for the government to analyse both the costs of providing the roads and maintaining them to proper standards as well as the financial resources to be made available to meet the costs. This must be an integral part of a wider analysis to determine the total 'cost to the country' of the inland transport system and to examine the possibility of balancing this over-all cost between the different forms of transport at the lowest attainable level.[1]

(b) *Railways.* The railway system of Guyana embraces about 130 route miles. The East Coast Railway which runs from Georgetown to Rosignol is $60\frac{1}{4}$ miles long. The West Coast Railway running from Vreed-en-Hoop on the West Bank of the Demerara River estuary to Parika on the East Bank of the Essequibo River estuary is $18\frac{1}{2}$ miles long. The remaining 51 miles consist of private lines owned by the Demerara Bauxite Company at Mackenzie.

The services of the East Coast Railway earned $621,188 as total revenue in 1955. By 1964 revenue increased by 38 per cent to $715,844. Total expenditure was $1,218,263 in 1955. By 1964 it had increased by 32 per cent to $1,609,301. Thus while the deficit in 1955 was $597,075, by 1964 it had grown by

---

[1] Such an analysis of roads and road transport has not yet been made for the simple reason that so many different authorities, departments, and operators are involved, unlike the other parts of inland transport where financial results are easily assessed, recorded, and published.

almost 50 per cent to $893,457. On the West Coast Railway the deficit grew from $93,746 in 1955 to $272,783 in 1964, an increase of 190 per cent. The general picture is one of annual deficits for both railways, and since 1957 the government's financial subsidy to the railways kept to well over $700,000 every year. By 1964 it had risen to well over $1 million, an increase of almost 70 per cent since 1955.[1]

The passenger services comprise the largest revenue earners on both railways. In 1956, from the combined total revenue of $1,021,381, passenger traffic accounted for $670,054 or 65·6 per cent. This proportion was almost 70 per cent in 1962, and was maintained in 1964.[2] Putting aside the fact that fares are subsidized for certain categories of workers, since 1952 there has been no increase in rail fares, though since May 1964 first and second-class fares were abolished leaving just third-class fares. This resulted in a loss of revenue of over $200,000 by the end of the year. Passenger traffic grew over the period 1956 to 1962, and remained constant between 1962 and 1964. But when we take into account what was happening to railway fares over the same period, a growth of passenger traffic between 1956 and 1964 is indicated.[3] The other main revenue earners are goods traffic, parcels, and mails. Table 8 shows the main revenue items of the East Coast Railway for the period 1956–62.

TABLE 8
REVENUE ITEMS—EAST COAST RAILWAY
(Guyana dollars)

	1956	1958	1960	1962
Passengers	411,271	454,771	527,642	629,187
Parcels	105,051	105,401	114,388	110,829
Special services	16,003	16,982	13,137	16,607
Mails	3,950	3,950	3,950	3,950
Goods	121,562	147,844	155,405	166,983
Miscellaneous receipts	25,568	28,106	30,733	37,357
Deficit on working year	548,667	655,678	612,711	628,048
Total	1,232,072	1,413,732	1,457,966	1,592,961

[1] Transport and Harbours Department, *Annual Reports*.
[2] Ibid.
[3] Ibid.

The revenue-earning capacity of this line has been greatly hampered by road competition. This competition mainly from hire car services, and buses, and in terms of fares and convenience, is keenest in the areas between Georgetown and Mahaica. The area possesses one of the best stretches of coastal roads. This facilitates easy movement of motor vehicular traffic along the public road and in the villages. The region also has one of the heaviest concentrations of the coastal population. The close proximity of the road to most of the villages and settlements affords convenient door-step transport. In addition, where the railway fare appears to be about the same or a bit lower than that of the taxi or bus, convenience of carriage gives the advantage to the road. Table 9 below gives a general comparison of single fares charged by buses, taxis, and the railways.

TABLE 9

COMPARATIVE STATEMENT OF SINGLE JOURNEY FARES BY RAIL AND ROAD SERVICES ON THE EAST COAST

Stations from Georgetown to	3rd class single ($)	Railway		Taxi Single ($)	Bus Single ($)
		7-day return ($)	4-day return ($)		
Plaisance	0·24	0·16	—	0·25	0·20
Beterverwagting	0·33	0·22	—	0·36	0·30
Buxton	0·44	0·30	—	0·50	0·30
Enmore	0·56	0·38	—	0·50	0·36
Golden Grove	0·60	0·40	—	0·50	0·36
Belfield	0·64	0·43	—	0·50	0·40
Clonbrook	0·68	0·51	—	0·75	0·48
Mahaica	0·68	0·59	0·44	0·75	0·52
Mahaicony	1·21	0·81	0·61	0·80	0·80
Burma	1·33	0·89	0·67	—	0·80
Belladrum	1·45	0·97	0·73	—	1·00
Lichfield	1·57	1·05	0·79	—	1·00
Fort Wellington	1·75	1·17	0·88	—	1·00
Rosignol	2·05	1·37	1·02	2·00	1·00

Source: Transport and Harbours Department, Georgetown, Guyana.

The picture is even more complicated than Table 9 indicates. Certain categories of users of this service purchase season tickets which are valid for periods of 4 days, 4 and under 7 days, 1 month, 3 months, and 6 months. These season tickets are subsidized by the government in order to maintain and expand the volume of passenger traffic using the service. The rates of season tickets are as follows:

	Month (per mile)	3 Months (per mile)	6 Months (per mile)
	¢	$	$
For the first 11 miles (adults)	65	1·67	3·13
For the first 11 miles (children)	38	0·97	1·82
For the next 11 miles (adults)	63	1·61	3·03
For the next 11 miles (children)	37	0·96	1·80
Over 22 miles (adults)	52	1·33	2·50
Over 22 miles (children)	37	0·80	1·50

From these rates, an adult would pay $14·08 for a month's season ticket between Georgetown and Mahaica (22 miles) travelling twice daily. This means that an adult could make 60 journeys at a fare a little below 25 cents for each journey. For the same distance, the single fare by rail costs 88 cents, by taxi 75 cents, and by bus 52 cents. In short, the average contractual fare between Georgetown and Mahaica is about 25 per cent of the single fare by rail, 30 per cent of the fare by taxi, and 44 per cent of the fare charged by the buses. Thus there is some question as to whether these contractual fares serve the purpose of attracting to the railway a sufficient volume of passenger traffic to justify the system on economic grounds.

TABLE 10

REVENUE ITEMS—WEST COAST RAILWAYS

(*Guyana Dollars*)

	1956	1958	1960	1962
Passengers	258,783	280,456	348,532	371,119
Parcels	10,603	12,824	20,714	37,760
Special services	2,633	2,966	2,529	2,072
Mails	1,650	1,650	1,650	1,650
Goods	60,924	57,512	69,892	59,771
Miscellaneous receipts	3,383	2,432	3,423	2,047
Deficit on working year	103,100	188,335	145,615	175,274
Total	441,076	546,175	592,355	649,693

Source: Transport and Harbours Department, *Annual Reports.*

The table below shows the revenue position for the West Coast Railway. Here again contractual fares are subsidized by the government to an average of 20 per cent of the single rail journey and 40 per cent of the fare for taxi or bus.

Table 11 presents data on the commodity traffic flows on the East and West Coast Railways in 1964. From this it can be seen that goods traffic on the East Coast Railway consists very largely of bulk cargoes of molasses and rice coming 'inwards', the proportion of 'outward' traffic being very small. On the West Coast Railway the traffic is more evenly distributed in that substantial tonnages of goods for shops and building materials are carried on 'outward' journeys to balance the shipment of molasses and rice on the 'inward' journeys.

But the commodity cargo traffic moved by the railways is better understood in relation to the total commodity cargo

TABLE 11

COMMODITY TRAFFIC FLOWS ON EAST AND WEST
COAST RAILWAY IN 1964

	East Coast				West Coast			
	'Out' traffic		'In' traffic		'Out' traffic		'In' traffic	
	(tons)	(cwt.)	(tons)	(cwt.)	(tons)	(cwt.)	(tons)	(cwt.)
Shop goods	197	7	277	12	4,740	3	60	14
Lumber and building materials	809	12	—	—	1,504	5	7	18
Molasses	582	14	19,545	9	1	10	6,278	2
Rum	21	17	877	0	23	17	—	1
Coal	2	8	—	—	2	15	—	—
Wood	5	5	—	—	2	17	3	16
Lime and manure	380	11	—	—	—	—	—	—
Oils	153	18	1	17	107	8	2	9
Machinery	288	2	5	18	24	9	1	13
Rice	—	—	11,883	9	—	9	3,878	9
Paddy	4	5	50	18	70	5	64	5
Coconut and copra	3	9	—	4	—	11	17	4
Other agricultural produce	57	6	10	2	5	13	341	0
Bran	—	—	596	1	—	—	—	—
Perishables	—	—	—	—	4	3	26	19
Matchwood	—	—	—	—	—	—	1,403	3
Non-paying cargo	63	0	—	15	96	9	27	8
Sundries	410	10	48	2	776	13	278	19
Total	2,980	4	33,297	7	7,378	7	12,392	0

Source: Transport and Harbours Department, *Annual Reports. Direct Requests.*

traffic moved along the entire coastal area. The statistical data limits the exercise to a comparison with government ferries, coastal and river shipping services; the relevant data for the period 1960–4 are given in Table 12. The most interesting point that emerges is that the combined railways moved just under two-fifths of the commodity cargo traffic carried by the government transport services on the coastal and riverain areas over the period 1961–4. Within the general pattern, however, there

TABLE 12

COMMODITY TONNAGE CARRIED BY GOVERNMENT
RAIL, FERRY, AND COASTAL AND RIVER SHIPPING
SERVICES 1960–4

Railway Services	1961	1962	1963	1964
East Coast	52,591	54,958	34,569	36,214
West Coast	22,529	21,823	17,568	16,033
Total	75,120	76,781	52,137	52,247
Coastal and River Services				
Demerara Ferry	21,171	22,741	14,553	16,216
Berbice Ferry	2,273	2,166	2,044	2,993
Georgetown/Bartica	9,871	10,107	6,312	8,428
Georgetown/Adventure	30,874	27,122	19,170	26,225
Georgetown/North West	3,934	4,609	3,728	5,038
Essequibo Islands Adventure Passenger Service	460	546	518	819
New Amsterdam/B'ce River Steamer	3,290	2,601	1,635	2,462
New Amsterdam/B'ce River Launch	216	220	118	139
New Amsterdam/Canje Launch	302	415	285	354
Georgetown/New Amsterdam Cargo	43,578	37,607	27,550	41,022
Georgetown/Springlands Cargo	—	—	—	3,477
Total	115,969	108,314	75,913	107,173
Grand Total	191,089	184,915	128,050	159,420

Source: Transport and Harbours Department, *Annual Reports. Direct Requests.*

has been a noticeable decline in the proportion carried by the railway compared with that of the coastal and river services.

We may now take a brief look at the expenditure accounts of the railways as shown in Tables 13 and 14. We saw earlier that the deficits incurred by these undertakings have been increasing from year to year and that there have been no significant changes on revenue account to compensate for this. Unfortunately, the expenditure side of the account is not altogether

TABLE 13

EXPENDITURE ITEMS—EAST COAST RAILWAY

Items	1956 ($)	1958 ($)	1960 ($)	1962 ($)	% of total expenditure 1960
Maintenance and repair of ways and works	261,096	280,042	305,114	350,256	20·9
Maintenance and repair of rolling stock	107,667	135,350	184,321	219,963	12·7
Locomotive running expenses	201,030	266,766	276,796	283,868	19·6
Traffic expenses	454,841	464,745	399,312	405,057	27·4
General charges	200,509	247,621	239,095	302,350	16·4
Compensation (accidents and losses)	6,929	451	423	94	—
Workmen's compensation	—	1,467	2,283	9,649	0·2
Mechanical equipment	—	14,938	20,026	21,224	1·4
Other items: Workmen's fac. ord.	—	—	9,706	—	—
Back pay factories ord. Back pay F.U.G.E.	—	2,352	20,890	—	1·4
Total	1,232,072	1,413,732	1,457,966	1,592,961	100·0

Source: Transport and Harbours Department, Annual Reports.

satisfactory. Maintenance and repair expenses of ways and works for both railways amounted to $348,711 in 1956, but by 1962 it had increased by 34 per cent to $466,535. Expenditure within this field was rising every year.

There exists a basic difficulty in this field. It was estimated that at 1962 prices about $355,000 per annum is required to keep the East Coast Railway track and structures in good

TABLE 14

EXPENDITURE ITEMS—WEST COAST RAILWAY

Items	1956 ($)	1958 ($)	1960 ($)	1962 ($)	% of total expenditure 1960
Maintenance and renewal of ways and works	87,615	95,304	100,485	115,779	17·0
Maintenance and renewal of rolling stock	39,449	66,615	81,657	88,591	13·8
Locomotive running expenses	78,065	101,212	106,149	123,644	17·9
Traffic expenses	176,732	215,222	230,731	236,363	38·9
General charges	52,766	65,163	62,920	79,566	10·6
Compensation: (accidents and losses)	6,449	578	298	2	0·1
Workmen's compensation	—	85	671	816	0·1
Mechanical equipment	—	987	1,383	4,733	0·2
Back pay factories ord.	—	1,009	2,394	199	0·4
Back pay F.U.G.E.	—	—	5,667	—	1·0
Total	441,076	546,175	592,355	649,693	100·0

Source: Transport and Harbours Department, Annual Reports.

condition.[1] In all the years since 1956, this level of expenditure was never realized. The inadequacy of recurrent funds meant inadequate maintenance. On account of this rail fractures are of frequent occurrence, embankments need reinforcing, extra ballast is required, and urgent works need to be carried out at bridges and culverts. Another aspect of the problem is that this section of the railway is very labour intensive. It could be claimed that it was a tacit part of the government's policy to keep as many people from the coastal areas employed on the railways in amelioration of the crucial employment situation in certain areas such as West Berbice.

Maintenance and renewal expenses in the case of rolling stock more than doubled between 1956 and 1962 ($147,116 in 1956 to $308,554 in 1962). The expenses here show a rising trend because of old coaching stock and locomotives which rapidly deteriorate because of old wooden underframes and buffers. The situation is further aggravated because this stock

[1] B. J. Smodlaka, Report on Transport and Communications Problems in British Guiana (United Nations Bureau of Technical Assistance Operations, Feb., 1962), p. 20.

of equipment is inadequate in terms of increasing passenger traffic and, to maintain normal services, the ageing equipment has to be kept working.

Although there may be an explanation for the high proportion of expenditure that goes towards maintenance, repair, and renewal of ways and works and rolling stock, scepticism may be raised about the large amounts spent on 'traffic expenses'. For both railways this formed the largest single item between 1956 and 1962.[1] To a large extent this item comprises mainly the salaries of railway employees who are not employed on maintenance. The labour-intensive nature of the enterprise is again underlined. It also seems that the 'traffic expenses' and 'general charges' contain very many unidentified and miscellaneous items in the railway budget, which in fact may be a gloss for inefficiency and waste in several of the operations of these undertakings. Furthermore, expenditure on maintenance works and ways, rolling stock, locomotives, and other operating expenses including traffic and general charges is compulsory from year to year in order that the service may be maintained. The consequence of this is that sizeable deficits show up in the transport budgets. As a first step towards the reorganization of railway finance, a detailed investigation of the above items of expenditure ought to be carried out so as to ascertain in what directions waste and inefficiency arise, and to delineate the avenues into which these funds are channelled.

It would seem that there is little prospect of significantly improving the financial position of the railways in the near future. We have seen that in the case of the East Coast Railway, especially between Georgetown and Mahaica, there is tremendous competition from buses, taxis, and other road vehicles. The villages and settlements beyond Mahaica are very sparsely populated and somewhat nearer to the road than the railway, so this section of the line is not frequently used. There is little income from goods traffic and the long-run case for closing down this railway is manifest. There can be no substitutes for good coast roads. However, it has been recommended that the West Coast Railway service should not be withdrawn, but should be maintained in service for passenger

[1] Except for 1956 in the case of the East Coast Railway.

and goods traffic. It has been further suggested that steps should be taken to operate it on the basis of a tramway system with additional halts and crossing facilities.[1]

4. *Conclusion*

The process of drawing up an expenditure programme is an exercise in the allocation of scarce economic resources, i.e. it is concerned with a series of marginal choices between different uses or combinations of land, labour, and capital. The analysis of the behaviour of the revenue and expenditure accounts of road and rail transport serve to highlight the fact not so much of a misallocation of public funds, but the failure of these investments to fructify because of administrative and other reasons. If any misallocation occurred, it was in maintaining an inefficient transport network on the coastal area when more effort should have been directed in extending the transport system inwards.

The increase in income that will accompany structural changes in the economy will mean an increase in the production for the domestic market on a much larger scale than at present and a much more diversified volume of goods for export. By 1980, at least, a series of light engineering and other manufacturing industries will be established. The rationalization of the rice and sugar industries, and the adoption of mixed and diversified farming will lead not only to a larger volume of agricultural products but to a fuller utilization of the coastal belt, the intermediate zone, and the riverain areas. In support of these developments, the traffic originating from the coastal belt and elsewhere would have increased very significantly.

In keeping with the concept of economic planning that has been adopted in Guyana, the government's avowed aim has been to channel public expenditure into uses that supplement the activities of the private sector by providing those services deemed essential for economic development but which would not normally be provided by private investors. This involves a deliberate choice of priorities by the authorities. There is always a limit on the amount of funds that can be borrowed, taxed, or

[1] *Smodlaka Report*, pp. 17, 18.

created, and that can be spared from financing the current operations of the government. The availability of resources sets limits to the extent to which expenditure can be raised in one direction without lowering it in another.

In strict economic terms, a rational allocation of government capital expenditure would involve investments in projects for which the present discounted values of future benefit streams bear the most favourable relationship to the present value of the total cost stream over the period. Only by discounting to the present can allowance be made for the fact that benefits that will be enjoyed some time ahead are not so attractive as those that can be quickly enjoyed, while costs that will not have to be incurred for some years will be easier to bear than those that have to be shouldered right away, more especially as there should be larger supplies of all kinds which can be drawn upon.

A crucial decision concerns the rate of discount or the social time preference which is to be used for this exercise. The higher the rate chosen the more quick-maturing investments will appear attractive in relation to the long gestation projects and vice-versa. Hence the rate to be chosen depends on when it is desired that the benefits should accrue. In a development country where supplies of all sorts of equipment are meagre and the expectation of life is still short, it would be natural to suppose that a high social time preference rate of discount would be appropriate.

In Guyana, the government is constantly under pressure to channel scarce investment funds into projects that would not receive priority in a rational scheme of resource allocation. Furthermore the available statistical information has not yet reached the level of refinement to enable public investments to be made in accordance with the criterion referred to above. But even in the absence of such refined computations, it would appear that some important areas of the economy, considered vital for economic development, have been neglected or given insufficient attention. These areas include electric and hydro-electric power, harbours and ports, and perhaps technical education. These must be given high priority in any future development schemes.

VIII

ECONOMIC PLANNING—RETROSPECT
AND PROSPECT

1. *Introduction*

After the end of hostilities in Europe in 1945, a large measure of responsibility for internal affairs was conceded to the elected representatives of the people of Guyana. With the formation of political parties came a new seriousness in economic planning. It had become obvious that complete reliance on market forces would not lead to economic development and the government would have to play a more positive role.

To some, this meant that the government should first decide its goals and then, by various fiscal incentives, encourage private investors to pursue these goals. In this view the true goals of the government should be the provision of education and health services, the extension of services to agriculture and other such basic social investments.[1]

But to others, the concept of 'planning' is much more comprehensive. They would prefer to see the economy fashioned on the model used in the Communist States where the principal means of production are owned and managed either by the State or by co-operatives.

The individual enterprises are not guided by reference to market forces, but are instead directed to conform with the national plan. Plans have therefore a different function in these

---

[1] Recent French four-year plans are perhaps the most comprehensive type of planning yet attempted in a mixed economy. This sort of planning embraces the whole economy, but so far as production in the private sector is concerned it operates by persuasion, not compulsion. Control of consumption in the private sector has been exercised almost wholly through the fiscal system (tax on value added) with a small amount of support from credit control. For an interesting account of French planning see J. Hackett and A. M. Hackett, *Economic Planning in France* (Allen and Unwin, 1963), and Pierre Bauchet, *Economic Planning, The French Experience* (Heineman, London, 1964).

countries from that in market economies and the State can channel resources into any sector of the economy depending on the scale of priorities [1] of the planners and the availability of productive inputs. Some economists are of the opinion that this method approximates most closely to the type of planning needed by economically backward countries that want to develop quickly. For example, Professor Myrdal asserts: 'the plan must determine this overall amount [2] and must in addition determine the proportion of capital to be allocated in different directions'.[3] It is evident that only a government that actually controlled the resources could ensure that such a programme is carried out.

The path the government of Guyana has chosen can be described as a *quasi-inducement approach,* somewhere between the two extremes outlined above. It has not only enunciated certain policy goals, and attempted to provide incentives, but has also been tried to influence the over-all allocation of resources. This approach did not meet with much success in that private investors were not willing, or able, to co-operate. Government participation in the economic life of the country is small; publicly owned enterprises are few and, broadly speaking, Guyana is a country where private enterprise dominates the economic scene.

One factor that seems to have influenced the government against too much regulation and control of the economy appears to have been the desire to attract capital from foreign sources in large enough quantities to supplement the inadequate local supply. But a factor that must have had extraordinary importance was the uncertain political climate. Foreign investors are reluctant to invest in a country in which uncertainty is increased by what they regard as excessive bureaucratic controls. But the same can be said for domestic capitalists, many of whom have exported their capital because local conditions were unfavourable to enterprise. The evidence presented in a previous chapter suggests that a substantial amount of capital was

---

[1] For a recent and interesting discussion of this and related concepts used in Soviet-type economies, see A. Nove, 'Planners' Preferences, Priorities, and Reforms', *The Economic Journal,* Vol. LXXVI, No. 302 (June 1966), pp. 267–77.

[2] That is, investment.

[3] Myrdal, *Economic Theory and the Underdeveloped Regions,* pp. 80–1.

exported through the commercial banks. Capital exports can be regulated by statute. But such regulations are exceedingly difficult to enforce in practice. To this extent it is no more easy to direct investments by domestic capitalists than those of foreign capitalists. The government was hampered in carrying out even the modest tasks it had set itself by the absence of certain vital institutions. We saw that a Central Bank was not established until late in 1965, so that during the period reviewed in this study, the government had to operate without the tools of monetary policy.

2. *Economic Planning 1945–64*

The evolution of economic planning in Guyana has been mainly a post-war phenomenon. It can be traced to 1945 when an allocation of $12 million was received under the Colonial Development Welfare Act of 1945. But the first rudimentary attempt at planning was made in 1947 when a Ten-Year Development Plan 1947–56 was drawn up. Expenditure in this plan was broadly allocated under the following main heads: $6·5 million on three major drainage and irrigation projects, $11·2 million on social welfare, justice, and public buildings, and $10·3 million mainly on economic services including agriculture, forestry, transport, surveys, and research. It was proposed to spend about $20 million in the first five years and another $6 million later. During the period 1947–50 only $2 million was spent. There were, however, a number of new schemes advanced for consideration after the plan was launched and in 1950 a revision was necessary so that some of these schemes might be included in the plan. The two important schemes included in the revised programme were a telecommunications system and the rehabilitation of transport and harbours.[1]

In 1953 after the first five years of the ten-year plan, a general economic survey mission organized by the International Bank for Reconstruction and Development visited the country at the request of the government of Guyana and submitted a report on economic development, in which a Five-Year

[1] Papers relating to Development Planning, Legislative Council Paper No. 6/1960.

Development Programme 1954-8 was recommended.[1] The investment programme recommended for 1954-8 aimed at increasing national income by 20 per cent and income per head by 6 per cent in five years. In order to achieve these objectives, four principal aims were outlined:[2] (1) to strengthen as rapidly as the technical resources of the country permit, those sectors that appear most urgently in need of improvement, in order to provide better balance in the economy; (2) to provide for continued progress in those sectors where the economy is already strong; (3) to provide a programme of technical research and experimentation in agriculture and related fields as well as soil, geologic, hydrographic, topographic, and other surveys, as a prerequisite for the development of the colony's resources, both during the next five years and thereafter; (4) to stimulate local savings and investment, both public and private, in order to reduce the dependence of the economy on external capital inflows and external grants.

The Mission estimated that gross investment in the years prior to 1954 had been running at the rate of over 20 per cent of national income, and for the five-year programme they assumed a rate of 24 per cent, the extra amount to be supplied mainly by the government, while private investment would be maintained at the existing level.

The salient features of the recommended programme have been summarized in Table 1. To some extent the pattern of recommendation set out by the Bank followed the pattern in Guyana started under the previous Development and Welfare Schemes. Two major drainage and irrigation schemes had already been started, and the need for better communications was already considered a priority item. In this respect the report served mainly to justify and consolidate the type of development expenditure to which the country was already committed. In particular it emphasized the prevailing tendency to concentrate development on the improvement and expansion of coastal lands. The immediate objectives as regards the interior were seen to be in the form of more surveys of agricultural and mineral possibilities rather than actual investment. One of the weaknesses of the Bank's report and of subsequent expenditure

[1] I.B.R.D., *The Economic Development of British Guiana.*   [2] Ibid., p. 23.
24—E.D.G.

TABLE I

FIVE-YEAR GOVERNMENT DEVELOPMENT PROGRAMME 1954–8 AS RECOMMENDED BY I.B.R.D. MISSION

(Thousand dollars)

Sources of funds		Investment programme	
1. Government funds and revenues	41,800	1. Agriculture	24,487
a. Funds from annual revenue	23,000	a. Drainage and irrigation projects	10,780
b. Additional funds from annual revenues		b. Land settlement	1,150
(1) From savings on State subsidies	4,000	c. Rice Development Corporation	5,000
(2) From savings on operating loss of State enterprises	3,500	d. Other agricultural projects	1,106
		e. Research and surveys	2,251
c. Loan funds not disbursed, end of 1953	5,300	f. Agricultural credits	4,200
d. Estimated surpluses, end of 1953	3,000	2. Transport and communications	22,304
e. Repayment of Agricultural Bank and other State loans	1,000	3. Forestry	2,280
f. Other credits repayable during the period	2,000	4. Social Welfare	7,450
2. Colonial Development and Welfare Grants	11,100	5. Public Works (including sea defences)	5,450
		6. Industrial credits	1,500
a. Allocated for 1954–6	6,600	7. Hydro-electric power (Tumatumari project)	1,440
b. Estimated possible, 1957–8	4,500	8. Surveys (geologic, etc.)	400
3. New Loans	13,100	9. Credit Corporation	600
Total	66,000	Total	65,911

Source: I.B.R.D., *The Economic Development of British Guiana*, pp. 30–6; 43.

has been a tendency to draw sharp lines of distinction between the 'interior' and the 'coast'. More attention might, for instance, have been given to planning the development of access communications, such as the gradual construction of roads as ancillary communications to rivers, and thus benefiting the riverain lands which were already receiving attention from private investment.

It might, however, be argued that the detailed programme of the Mission was oriented towards projects that promised the highest returns in the light of the financial resources available, the technical staff and manpower, and the time needed for engineering planning. It can be seen from Table 1 that stress was laid on public investments in the field of agriculture, excluding sugar and mining. It could have been claimed that at that time sugar and mining were relatively quite advanced and therefore needed no government projects. It was also assumed that private industry was fully capable of making the necessary investments. But although it was realized that the need for the diversification of agriculture was of paramount importance in the interest of further growth and progress of the economy, most of the schemes were for expanding the rice industry. Social reasons apart, this enormous bias given to rice was misguided in that the meagre returns to investment in land settlement, land reclamation, and drainage and irrigation did not justify it. The transport programme was closely tied to agricultural development, aiming to reduce costs of transport of agricultural products and to open new areas for agricultural development.

The government considered that a larger programme than the one recommended by the Mission was required for the country, and an initial programme for 1954-5 was drawn up to be absorbed subsequently in a long-term development programme. A total of $44 million was allocated in this regard, $33 million for economic development, and the remainder for social services.[1] In accordance with the original intention that the

[1] From the outset it was realized that expenditure of this magnitude which would be more than treble that of the average of the preceding three years was unlikely to be achieved in the opening period of the long-term programme. In fact the programme was not achieved until March 1954 and financial sanction of the Legislative Council was not obtained until the end of May. New Departments of Housing,

initial programme for the years 1954–5 should be later absorbed into a long-term plan, the government prepared a Five-Year Development Programme for the period 1956–60 framed on the recommendations of the International Bank with the addition of a number of new projects.[1]

No firm assessment of this plan is available, but a comparison of gross domestic product over the years 1956–9 may provide a useful measure of its effectiveness. Gross Domestic Product at factor cost stood at $207 million in 1956, and by 1959 had risen to $239·4 million. This is not a spectacular change, but the un-impressive behaviour of this aggregate over these years must be considered against the background of considerable setbacks in the production of sugar, timber, and bauxite during the years 1958 and 1959, and rice during 1958. These were years of re-cession which must have had adverse effects on the income-creating potential of the government programmes.

We may, however, gain a more realistic picture of the per-formance of the economy during these years if the expenditure programme is viewed in its proper perspective. These expendi-tures were merely a continuation of those that were initiated in 1947 under the Colonial Development and Welfare Schemes.

Land Settlement, and Drainage and Irrigation, and the organization of the Credit Corporation had to be established and staff recruited and trained. Time had to be spent in carrying out preliminary investigations, preparing plans, and securing machinery and equipment. Despite these difficulties and the loss of the early months of the year, 60 out of 79 schemes in the programme were in progress at the end of 1954. The year 1954, however, was one of preparation and it was not until 1955 that the programme began to gain momentum. Certain initial diffi-culties unfortunately continued and the lack of qualified and experienced tech-nicians in certain fields hampered progress. Nevertheless, expenditure on development schemes in 1955 amounted to over $17 million—a total of $26 million for the two-year period; and it was evident that the foundations were laid for the stimulation of economic activity throughout the country. Sessional Paper, No. 5/1959, p. 7.

[1] Unexpended balances from the 1954–5 programme were incorporated into this plan. The programme envisaged expenditure over the 5-year period of $61 million for the economic development, and $30 million for social development—a total of $91 million. Emphasis was placed on drainage and irrigation schemes, roads and transport services, a new telephone system, a programme for research for natural resources, construction of public buildings, hospitals, schools, and land settlement. Sessional Paper, No. 5/1959, op. cit.

Towards the end of 1958 it was decided to shorten the programme by one year, i.e. to the end of 1959. Thereafter development was intended to continue under a new 5-year programme, 1960–4, which was expected to provide for the continua-tion of projects not completed at the end of 1959.

Thus if we discount the years 1958 and 1959, a good idea of the impact of these expenditures can be gained by an examination of the behaviour of the main aggregates between 1948 and 1957. The net national income of Guyana, the mid-year population, and the national income per head of population from 1948 to 1957, together with their percentage increases are given below.

TABLE 2

NET NATIONAL INCOME

Year	Net national income at factor cost ($ Mn.)	Mid-year population ($'000)	National income *per capita* ($)
1948	100·4	397	253
1949	108·0	408	265
1950	120·6	420	287
1951	135·9	431	315
1952	144·2	445	324
1953	159·1	459	347
1954	175·0	472	371
1955	174·4	486	359
1956	188·6	500	377
1957	199·2	516	386
% increase 1948–57	98·4%	32%	52·5%

Source: Sessional Paper No. 5/1959.

The figures disclose that between 1948 and 1957, the national income rose by 99 per cent, but as population also rose—by 32 per cent—the increase in national income per head of population was only 52·5 per cent. If account is taken of the rise over the same period in the level of prices, the increase in the real national income was around 11 per cent. This increase is the true measure of the economic progress of the country over the period. It may be said therefore that public expenditures may have had some effect in raising incomes, but its effectiveness was probably somewhat reduced by the high rate of growth of population; for only if the income of the community increases faster than the rate of increases in population and in prices together can it be said that the standard of living of the people is improving.

In 1959 a new programme was considered necessary and one was drawn up on the recommendations of Mr. Kenneth Berrill.[1] The main assumption of the Berrill Report and the Programme of which it formed the basis was that the rate of growth of national product was high. 'The decade 1948–57 saw national product increase by over a half in real terms' (5 per cent per annum), while 'between 1952–7 the growth of output averaged 6 per cent'. This apparently provided justification for assuming that 'over the next five years, 1960–64, the economy will continue the fast rate of growth of the pre-1957 period'.[2] In other words, it was assumed that the rate of economic growth would be 6 per cent per annum in real terms as compared with 5 per cent in the decade 1948–57. It was decided that the government could help this expansion most in the field of non-plantation agriculture, particularly in rice, since diversification of agriculture would take much longer to yield a return than rice.

The programme aimed at both the economic and social development of the country, but greater emphasis was placed on projects that were expected to increase productivity and strengthen the economic sector. It was argued that, 'only by doing this will it be possible to raise permanently the general standard of living of the people and improve the lot of those who are at present living at the bare subsistence level. Not till the national income is substantially raised can there be a good acceleration in the production of social services, which is the ultimate aim of development'.[3]

Table 3 presents data on the main resources and expenditures of the programme. A close look at the projects shows that the main objective of the programme was the expansion of primary production. Special emphasis was placed on increasing the area

---

[1] At the end of the Financial Talks in the United Kingdom in August 1959 on the outline of a Development Programme for the country over the five-year period beginning 1 January 1960, there was general agreement between Her Majesty's government and the government of British Guiana that a continuing programme of development on large scale was needed, not only in the immediate future, but also in 1965–9, if land and other assets were to be available for the ever-growing labour force. It was under these circumstances that Mr. Berrill carried out an investigation and submitted a Report in June 1959, details of which were laid before the Legislative Councillate in 1959.

[2] *Berrill Report*, pp. 7–8.

[3] Sessional Paper No. 5/1959, p. 6.

TABLE 3

DEVELOPMENT PROGRAMME 1960-4

(Thousand Guyana dollars)

Sources of fund		Allocation of expenditure	
1. Government funds and revenues	15,000	Economic Sector	92,407
a. Budget surplus	15,000	1. Agriculture (incl. sea defences, drainage and irrigation and land development)	49,040
2. Colonial Development and Welfare Grants	23,200	2. Transport and Communications	25,457
		3. Forestry	550
a. Unspent, end of 1959	3,000	4. Surveys (geological, etc.)	4,700
b. New	19,200	5. Public Buildings	1,300
c. Further expected	1,000	6. Credits, agricultural and industrial	11,000
3. Loans	71,800	Social Sector	
		1. Education	4,140
		2. Health	893
a. Exchequer loan 1960-2	19,200	3. Housing	6,000
b. Exchequer loan 1962-4	19,200	4. Rural Water supply	2,882
c. Local borrowing	10,000	5. Social Welfare	750
d. Expected from I.B.R.D., C.D.C., U.N. Special Fund and U.S. Govt. Development Loan Fund	23,400	6. Credit, housing	2,000
		7. Miscellaneous (Local Government reorganization and rural self-help)	1,568
Total	110,000	Total	110,280

Source: Development Programme 1960–64, Sessional Paper No. 5/1959.

of cultivable land by 200,000 acres by the end of 1964, and on exploring the possibility of expanding the production of livestock and of a variety of crops such as coconuts, cocoa, cotton, peanuts, pulses, and vegetables. Considerable expenditure was made on drainage and irrigation, land development, and sea defences. Geological surveys to assess the mineral potentialities and improvement of timber manufacturing for exports were also stressed. Finally grants and credit were to be made for agricultural and industrial purposes to develop the private sector, especially for the benefit of small producers.

The 1960–4 Development Programme attracted much criticism and discussion owing mainly to its premise that agricultural expansion is the major answer to the economic problems of Guyana.[1] Newman severely criticized the programme and put forward arguments for heavy industry in Guyana based on bauxite, manganese, and timber as a basis for long-run economic growth. The transitional problems of income and employment would, however, need help from agriculture through mixed farming, rice, and light industry. Thus, according to Newman, in the future planning for heavy industry stress should have been given to hydro-electricity and the exploration of oil and mineral resources.

The comments of Thorne, Cumper, and Boulding were generally in favour of Newman as regards the principles of planning and the long-run economic future of Guyana. However, Berrill defended his Report, saying that since the potentialities of heavy industry were not known and since past trends did not show the Guyana government could obtain more funds, the 1960–4 programme was the most that could be achieved with limited resources. In this respect, and as the events after 1961 have shown, Berrill and the government of Guyana were on the right lines. It must also be remembered that this develop-

[1] See P. Newman, 'The Economic Future of British Guiana', *Social and Economic Studies*, Vol IX, No. 3 (September 1960), pp. 263–96. K. E. Berrill, 'Comments on the "Economic Future of British Guiana" by Peter Newman', ibid., Vol. X, No. 1 (March 1961), pp. 1–5. A. P. Thorne, 'British Guiana's Development Programme', ibid., Vol. X, No. 1 (March 1961), pp. 6–17. G. E. Cumper, 'Investment Criteria; A Comment', ibid., Vol. X, No. 1 (March 1961), pp. 18–24. K. E. Boulding, 'Social Dynamics in West Indian Society', ibid., Vol. X, No. 1 (March 1961), pp. 25–34. P. Newman, 'Epilogue on British Guiana', ibid., Vol. X, No. 1 (March 1961), pp. 35–41.

ment programme was not drawn up for the whole economy, but was mainly an expenditure programme of the government.

But the defects of the 1960–4 Development Programme must be examined within the context of the entire planning effort between 1954 and 1964. In this respect a comparison between development expenditure realized during the period of the 1954–9 plan and that of the 1960–4 period may not be out of place. In the previous chapter we saw that actual expenditure over the 1954–9 plan amounted to $105·8 million, and although the planned expenditure for the 1960–4 plan was slightly higher ($110·7 million), actual expenditure amounted to $78·5 million, or just over 70 per cent of the expenditure realized for the former plan period. We recall from Chapter VI that this failure to reach the planned target was mainly a result of the shortfall in government revenue and the inability of the government in power to raise foreign loans and grants in large enough quantities.

However, certain unifying features of both plans stand out. In 1954–9 the highest priority was shared by housing and drainage and irrigation. In 1960–4 drainage was pre-eminent. Both plans neglected roads, basic surveys, agricultural extension, and education. Drainage is a good priority, especially if coupled with roads. But we have emphasized that the drainage expenditures of the last decade have not paid off. In the first place, too much was spent in each area; the same money spent less intensively on more schemes would have opened up more land to cultivation and added more to output.[1] Secondly, when lands have been prepared so expensively, good husbandry must be a condition of occupancy, and farmers who fail to use the land effectively must give way to others. The drainage and irrigation expenditures of the last decade violated both these principles.

Thus the period 1945–64 was one of 'piece-meal' rather than *national* planning. Although it is evident that the government was in many instances thinking in national terms, the 'plans' were simply statements of how the government proposed to spend its financial resources, and lacked any conscious efforts at co-ordinated economic development. Many viable projects

[1] Alternatively, a large proportion of these funds could have been diverted to the development of new agricultural areas away from the overcrowded coastlands.

were begun and finished in the years prior to 1964, but an integrated approach to economic planning has yet to become a reality. The post-war approach to economic planning in Guyana raises problems which were either glossed over in these earlier attempts, or, for reasons of expediency, were never solved. In the remaining section of this chapter, therefore, we discuss the main variables that ought to predominate in future economic policy. This telescoping is based on our earlier findings on the structural weaknesses characterizing the Guyanese economy, and the lacunae in earlier economic planning.

3. *Future Horizons*

The fundamental problem for Guyana is how to increase the national product whilst absorbing the increasing labour force in gainful employment, so that the *per capita* income rises steadily. It is a problem of both *income* and *employment*. The solution must include not only a statement of the desired rate of economic growth in the context of the general objectives of the society, but also a consideration of the appropriate investment strategy required to make this a reality.

The problem of development is technical, social and economic. A purely technical problem involves the choice of the right means from a multiplicity of adequate means to achieve a single given end. An economic problem considers a system (multiplicity) of adequate means in relation to a system (multiplicity) of possible ends. Where there is a multiplicity of ends, some may be in partial conflict with others. To achieve more of one end may be possible only at the expense of achieving less of another end. Moral and political considerations give different values to the various ends. In the event, the national community will determine explicitly or implicitly a hierarchy of ends. By comparing and contrasting the various permutations possible in the system of means, in relation to its own system (hierarchy) of ends, the society expresses its choice of economic and social policy. In this choice it is guided by its knowledge of its own human and natural resources and the power of its technology.

Guyana is a young nation and its goals have not yet crystal-lized. But we may suppose that the country seeks an accelerated rise in national income and in the living standards of its people; it seeks a real equality of opportunity, and eradication of the inequalities of income, wealth, and economic power; in general, it seeks the attainment of greater economic independence. The attempt to realize these goals through a series of development plans requires their consistent formulation and a clear statement of the means of achieving them.[1] It also requires a conscious acceptance of priorities and of certain assumptions that must underlie any concrete programme of action. At any given time there are definite factors that exercise constraints on the pace at which the standard of living of the people can be improved. It is the task of policy to remove these constraints progressively since they cannot be eliminated all at once.

The apparently simple objective of improving the living standards of the people poses a choice between the present and the future and a whole range of related choices between alternative patterns of investment and production. Whatever the actual choice, it has wide implications.[2] Thus a chosen rate of savings or pattern of investment in the current period influences the rate and pattern of development not only in the present but in subsequent years as well. It is to be realized that in a higher standard of living is the end product of development. A higher standard of living can be afforded on a solid basis only after economic growth has advanced sufficiently to be able to proceed on its own steam. At the same time there must be a perceptible change in the standard of living of the people and their welfare if they are to work energetically for economic progress. But any decision to increase consumption in the present is in fact a restriction on the possibility to increase it later. Thus while the case for sacrifice in the present can be responded

---

[1] Although the prevailing political and social circumstances, as well as the level of development, not only determine the general aims and purposes of planning, but also delineate the boundaries within which choices between policy instruments can be made, the aims of plans and the means selected for their implementation, however, are not choices that can be made independently of one another. If the methods of implementation have to be appropriate to the objectives, it is also true that the objectives have to be realistically chosen in the light of the measures for implementation available to the government.

[2] For a concise discussion of these issues, see S. Chakravarty and R. S. Eckaus, 'Choice Elements in Intertemporal Planning', in P. N. Rosenstein-Rodan (ed.), *Capital Formation and Economic Development*, Studies in the Economic Development of India, No. 2 (Allen and Unwin Ltd., 1964), pp. 68–82.

to only if the promises of higher standards of living look redeemable in the not-too-distant future, the case for improvement in the future must be supported at the same time by some current improvement. The problem of choice connected with intertemporal planning cannot be easily solved, and all that can be attempted in this study is an indication of the nature of the problem.

There is also a certain vagueness connected with the second objective—social justice. This becomes evident whenever a deliberate attempt is made to define its scope if its implications are to be incorporated into development plans. Whether we define the concept of social justice to include the provision of a basic minimum of education and other amenities to all citizens irrespective of their means, or whether we extend the scope of social justice to include objectives such as a reduction of inequalities of incomes, wealth, and economic power, or an extension of public ownership of the means of production, it is clear that it becomes extremely difficult to incorporate these ingredients into development plans without having to face the problem of priorities and without some narrowing of the area of conflict among different objectives by suitable instruments of policy.

The attempt at greater economic independence, that is, the attempt to make the economy less vulnerable to unsettling influences emanating from abroad and therefore more controllable by domestic policy, raises several problems of choice. The replacement of imports by domestic production has to be consistent with the *economic* use of domestic resources. The promotion of exports or the stabilization of external markets might entail forging closer economic relations with neighbouring countries and new trading partners. The implication is that the objective of economic independence ought not to be interpreted in contradistinction to the maintenance of a certain degree of interdependence in relation to other countries, and the constant search for trade channels where this is feasible. The conclusion emerges that it is extremely difficult to arrive at a neat reconciliation of all the objectives that a development plan tries to achieve simultaneously and a reconciliation that will be in harmony with all points of view. A certain amount of arbitrary goal adjustment is inevitable.

Underlying the final choice of strategy and the pattern of investment to be made in Guyana is the major necessity of widening and diversifying the narrow productive base of the economy. The aim must be to make the economy less vulnerable to unfavourable changes in world market conditions and more capable of sustaining continuous economic growth on the basis of its own resources. There is also the need to create sufficient employment opportunities to match the increase in the labour force which is the result of rapid expansion in the population during the past fifteen years or so and which promises to continue unabated for some time to come. The fulfilment of these aims will involve a major effort in terms of an investment programme much larger than has ever been initiated. Part of this effort must be devoted to the fuller realization of the potential of the currently dominant sectors of sugar, rice, and bauxite, and to an improvement of their competitive position in world markets. But the real thrust towards future economic development must be in new fields of economic activity and largely in new areas inland.

The main instrument for the realization of this strategy consists in an appropriate pattern of investment. The working out of this investment pattern requires close consideration of the following inter-related choices in respect of:

(1) the distribution of investment funds between social and economic sectors;

(2) the size of the investment in the infrastructure or economic overheads as against investment in what are called directly productive sectors;

(3) the balance between investment in 'industry' as against investment in 'agriculture';

(4) the allocation of investment for industry between heavy industry on the one hand and light industry on the other;

(5) the geographical regions in which investment should be concentrated, i.e. on the Coastlands, the Intermediate White Sand Belt or the Interior;

(6) the allocation of investment between different projects and areas within regions.[1]

---

[1] One of the drawbacks of the *Berrill Report* was that its treatment of the problem of efficient allocation of investment funds was very elementary. The allocations were evolved, 'after a brief visit to the Colony', and although 'local expert know-

We suggested earlier that any choice between economic and social sectors must of necessity be arbitrary, for it is difficult to assign relative quantitative weights to these factors. The difficulty is further compounded by the fact that in the longer run all the sectors of the economy may be considered 'economic' although the contribution to productivity of the more 'social' investments may be more indirect in nature.[1] But where a choice between the two becomes necessary, resources can be allocated to the social sector only if the remaining allocation to the economic sector could yield the requisite amount of income and employment. But without a fairly precise measure of the income and employment generating potential of possible projects, it is impossible to say what resources can be released for investments in the social sectors. But the indications given from our examination of the performance of the economy between 1953 and 1964 suggest that past investments in the economic sector have not led to any significant rise in income and employment. This points to the stepping up of investments in the economic sector.

As a corollary of the above argument, the acceptance of targets of growth of income in the future may require a change in the composition of investment in the social sector rather than a fall in the share of the latter in social investment. For example, it may be necessary to redirect the resources that might on earlier patterns have gone to health or social welfare services towards housing if the number and types of houses designed can provide opportunities for generating income and employment in the construction sector and in industries supplying building materials. Similarly it may be necessary to switch resources away from traditional types of education towards technical

ledge and experience deserve to be given full weight when any final programme is drawn up, the final programme is in fact identical with that advocated by the Report'. The heavy emphasis placed on agriculture was because 'it has been said many times that for the next fifteen years at least agriculture must supply most of the expansion in British Guiana', so that 'there seems to be no alternative to very heavy expenditure on water control measures'. Manufacture received very little emphasis because 'the home market is tiny and there has been little tariff protection even for that. The possibilities for export are generally poor, for Guyana has no cheap power and raw materials' (*Berrill Report*, pp. 30, 32, 12, 11, respectively). The rationale for the concentration on rice was given in the statement, 'British Guiana farmers know how to grow rice' (ibid., p. 11).

[1] This problem has been discussed more fully in Chapter VII, Section 1.

education if such a switch could create cadres needed to realize the opportunities for directly productive investment in the economic sector. But it must be emphasized that much of social investment, and therefore part of the problem of assigning value to the one or the other, is really a problem of choosing social investments of a type that would boost productive activity in the short run either by helping to break supply bottlenecks, like that found in technical education, or by providing effective demand, e.g. a large-scale programme of timber and clay-brick houses, for idle domestic resources.

With regard to the choice between investment in infrastructure and in directly productive activities, the evidence suggests that the low real return on investment in both the public and private sectors is closely connected with the unfamiliarity of the population at large with the techniques of promoting and running efficient enterprises. For historical reasons, unlike many other developing countries, and also owing to the concentration of almost the whole of the population on the coastal strip, true cottage or household industry carried out by family labour has had little or no impact on the economy. The majority of the rural population have until recently been working as landless labourers on the sugar estates and have not acquired much experience of methodical farming as independent farmers. They are not familiar with proper techniques of land preparation and water control nor are they used to mixed farming.

These conditions show up in the apparent lack of enterprise and a preference for wage labour. In the few instances where enterprise and initiative are exercised they show up in preference for activities that utilize existing skills and opportunities and conform best with prevailing attitudes. If diversification and expansion of the narrow productive base and the fulfilment of output potential in sectors other than sugar, bauxite, and rice are accepted as major objectives underlying income and employment targets, then the investment programme must provide for a programme of reform of basic institutional conditions. In terms of investment allocation this would mean primarily investment in education and training particularly in an effective agricultural extension service. This would tend to increase the share of infrastructural investment in total investment.

Since the strategy envisaged will attempt to develop the economy along fresh lines by way of extensive diversification and geographical expansion of the productive base, the need for infrastructural investment would become more demanding. We have seen that the system of transport and communications, drainage and irrigation works, and the development of public utilities in general have all in the past been largely determined by the requirements of economic activity on the coastal belt, mainly on sugar and rice. The attempts to relieve the dependence of the rural economy on this mono-culture will require a fresh network of roads, an extension and rationalization of water control works and an increased demand for public utilities. It is therefore to be expected that the share of infrastructure investment to the total would be relatively large if the economy is to expand physically into completely new geographical regions.

The question of the geographical allocation of investment is intimately connected with the investment strategy to be pursued in agriculture, industry, and infrastructure, and a fuller account will be given later. Thus the balance between infrastructure investment and investment in directly productive activities cannot be settled in isolation from the question as to whether new geographical areas are to be opened up. This question, is itself related to the further question whether heavy industry is to be developed or whether attention in the short run should be concentrated on light manufacturing industry. For if heavy industry is to be established it would have to be in the up-country districts where the mineral and water resources are located; if light industry is to be emphasized then these are likely to be concentrated around the towns, with easy access to domestic markets and ports. We may therefore now turn to consider the possibilities and prospects in the fields of heavy and light industry.

It has been suggested that the key to the long-run future of Guyana lies with the exploitation of mineral and water resources as a basis for establishing heavy industry.[1] This argument may have some validity, but this must remain a very long-run prospect since the *known* mineral resources are limited. The basic geological exploration for minerals other than

---

[1] Newman, *The Economic Future of British Guiana.*

bauxite and the technological research into the possibilities of exploiting minerals known to exist in small quantities or complex combinations are only now under way. It is true that Guyana has large reserves of mixed aluminous nnd ferruginous material in the form of laterites but the combinations in which they occur render them refractory to normal iron-smelting processes. The future of these deposits lies in the development of a process for separating iron and alumina. Research along these lines has already started but until a breakthrough is achieved and exploitable mineral resources other than bauxite and manganese are located, heavy industry investment will have to be confined to bauxite and manganese and to research.

The issues involved in the development of light industry are quite clear. The need to provide employment for a growing number in both urban and rural areas, the need to provide outlets for the potential supplies of raw materials and other produce of the primary sectors, and the real demand for manufactured and processed commodities now supplied by imports make it necessary to establish light industries. It has been estimated that some $30 million, or some 20 per cent of all imports, are potentially substitutable for domestic produce.[1] This total is almost entirely comprised of foodstuffs, household furnishings, and panelling and construction materials. Thus, on the surface, opportunities for the expansion of the agricultural, stock-raising, and forestry sectors, and therefore related manufacturing and processing activities, do exist. A report submitted in 1960 on the industrial possibilities of Guyana concluded that the country has most of the pre-requisites for rapid industrial development, but that it lacks some better co-ordination of its existing private initiative and some better foreign assistance, particularly in planning and evaluating new industrial opportunities. Consequently, it may be possible to make rapid progress in the development of industry with available private resources.[2]

A host of industrial activities, including electric power, grid and local distribution systems, wood fuel production, wood

[1] W. L. David, *The approach to import substitution in Guyana* (Development Secretariat, Georgetown, 1967).

[2] E. A. Tenenbaum, et al., 'Industry for British Guiana', Sessional Paper No. 3/1960, Legislative Council British Guiana, 1960.

distillation for chemicals and charcoal, cement, prefabricated concrete products, pre-finished wood floorings, glass, pottery, paper, cannery, bicycle manufacturing and tyres, storage batteries, textiles, tanning, and related projects were briefly examined. It was suggested that efforts should be directed towards the initiation or substantial expansion of most of the industries during the next year or so depending on the results of a more careful study. A detailed analysis of the industries recommended was taken up later. But from 1957, the government has been investigating the possibility of a number of minor industries including coir products, cane furniture and straw articles, and pottery. Recently investigations have been started for large-scale manufacture of glassware, cement, paints, alcohol from broken rice, canning, paper, and light building materials.[1] As each project is studied and declared feasible, the Guyana Development Corporation is expected to make efforts to attract private investors.

The prospects for the development of heavy industry in the near future are slight, and although the light manufacturing industries by themselves promise fruitful investment opportunities in terms of income generated per unit of investment they do not by themselves provide an effective answer to raising income and employment of the scale needed in the country. An effective answer has to be sought in the development of agriculture, horticulture, stockraising, and the industries connected with them. It is in these fields that a breakthrough will have to be attempted. This leads back to a consideration of the focal points towards which the development efforts will have to be directed, and therefore to an examination of the comparative potentialities of the Coastlands, the Interior, and the Intermediate White Sand Belt.

Hitherto agricultural development has been concentrated only on a small proportion of the total land surface of the

[1] Limits to these industrial possibilities are set by the fact that much of the unemployed labour in the towns and elsewhere is inadequately trained for industrial work, that supplies from the primary sectors are not yet flowing as smoothly and in such large quantities as are necessary for the running of efficient processing or manufacturing plants. Moreover, the total domestic demand for many of these products is small in relation to the capacity of the technical units of production of even the minimum size. For a fuller list of industrial investment opportunities and statement of the country's industrial development policy, see *Guyana Development Programme 1966–72*.

country and mainly on the relatively fertile clayey soils of the coastal strip and the banks of the major rivers. The need for expensive sea defences and water control systems in these areas militated against the diversification and expansion of agricul- tural output. The expansion and diversification of agriculture are closely related. The cost of expansion being high, only an industry like sugar, which can afford expensive capital works and which possesses the technical resources to make the best of investment, could expand. But we have shown that even this industry would not be able to exist without subsidized prices. The other major use to which the coastal and riverain areas have been put is rice farming, probably because paddy cultiva- tion does yield some return even if the type of farming practised is not very scientific. Thus the average efficiency of investment on the coastlands has not been very high and is likely to remain unchanged unless scientific techniques of farming and intensive cultivation are adopted, and high-value crops are introduced so as to offset the effect of high land development and maintenance costs. The developed parts of the coastlands and riverain areas because of their high fertility must be recognized as one of the scarcest factors in the economy and every effort ought to be made to maximize the output from these scarce factors.

Parts of the coastal region are at an advantage. Being the areas where the vast majority of the population is concentrated, they have the bulk of the domestic market on location and port facilities for shipping domestic produce and receiving import supplies. Social overheads in the form of schools and hospitals are already installed and important overhead investments rep- resented by sea defences, drainage and irrigation works, and roads are already there. There is thus a prima facie case for concluding that the efficiency of the investment in the already developed and settled areas of the coast is likely to be high. This is reinforced by further evidence that with the existing tech- niques the investment in recent years in the coastal areas is not fully utilized. But it is certainly necessary to guard against an exaggeration of the importance of the social and economic overhead investments that already exist on the coast, since there is an acute shortage of power, while a network of roads compatible with development does not really exist. Moreover, other facilities demanded by the population are unavailable.

On close examination, the sea defences and drainage and irrigation channels are the only real facilities that exist. Even the villages would have to be re-designed and many of the houses rebuilt if morale on the coast is to be maintained at a high enough level to support a modern and scientific agrarian economy. Moreover, the size of the domestic market available is in any event so small that the advantages of having it close at hand may not be so great. In view of the above considerations, investment on the coast should emphasize the need to pick up all the slack that exists there, but investment in new areas on the coast, where there are no new sea defences or drainage and irrigation facilities, should be postponed as it may prove easier to start afresh in the Intermediate Zone.

It would, however, in any event have been a natural course in considering the long-term development possibilities for agriculture to consider the possibility of exploiting land resources in all parts of the country. In the light of the difficulties to be faced in increasing output on the coast, there is all the more reason why a close examination of the possibilities of development of other areas will have to be undertaken. The problem here is to find areas where the long-run average efficiency of investment is higher than that of the coast. Both the White Sand Zone and the Interior appear to offer sizeable advantages as large areas, the development of which would not demand extensive and high-cost drainage costs or any sea defences, though the problem of drainage will remain in nearly all areas.

The Interior comprises two separate regions, the Rupununi savannahs, and a region of igneous rocks overlaid by sands and laterite clays, which is for the most part under forest cover. In both areas the soils are reputed to be almost everywhere of low fertility and any attempts to use these soils for agricultural purposes would require large amounts of fertilizer like nitrogen and lime. It would clearly be unprofitable to use fertilizer on such a large scale in these areas unless the cost of marketing it and of moving the resulting produce to markets is fairly low in proportion to the value of the product. Thus the problem of transport and communications looms large in these areas. In addition, there may also be need for the provision of drainage facilities. In view of all this the Interior has to be regarded as providing the lowest investment priority as far as agriculture is concerned. However, on grounds other than economic, such as the need to integrate isolated Amerindian communities more fully into Guyanese society, some investment in the Interior, e.g. in the Rupununi, may become necessary. Naturally, if there are substantial mineral finds which lead to the establishment of communities in that region and which require the building of roads, it may also be wise to establish some agricultural settlements nearby. But with regard to the large-scale land development for agricultural purposes, this must remain a task for the longer run.

In view of the difficulties of opening up the interior and of developing new lands in the coastal region, any further extension of the physical base of the economy has to be in the Intermediate Zone. This zone has as its southern boundary a line passing through the mouth of the Pomeroon River, Bartica, Mackenzie, and Orealla, and constitutes a land mass of about 7,000 square miles. It includes both savannah country and large tracts of bush and forest-covered expanses. The soils are of white sand formation interspersed with outcrops of brown sand, but the medium has only a little humic material in the upper few feet and, like the soils of the Interior, would require extensive fertilization if they are to be profitably exploited for agriculture. Thus it may appear that this region has problems similar to those of the Interior, and that the only difference lies in the fact that the cost of bringing supplies out will be much lower for this region.

But the region has several advantages over the Interior and the Coast. This is particularly true of the brown sand belts of the region. These brown sand areas covering roughly 3,000 square miles are located on either side of the Berbice River, around Ebini. This location gives the brown sand belt a special advantage because of its proximity to the river. Moreover, part of the area is open savannah country which would not need clearing and can serve as the focal point for the opening up of the region.[1] Furthermore these brown sand soils easily lend themselves to mechanization both because of their physical structure and their occurrences in wide expanses. Thus mecha-

[1] See W. L. David 'Planning for Economic Development in Guyana' (Mimeo, University of Guyana, 1967).

nization can be introduced without running the risk of under-utilizing machinery. We noted earlier that the tractorization of rice farming on the coastland does not lead to the optimum utilization of available resources, and the suggestion was made that from a purely economic point of view the situation warrants that preference be given to labour-intensive techniques. We also argued that it is possible to establish large-sized farms in the Intermediate Zone, which might not only provide work for the currently under-utilized farm machinery on the coast, but also make the more capital-intensive technology economically justifiable.

Since the need for sea defences and drainage of the sandy soils would not exist, the need for extensive drainage schemes would be avoided, with a consequent reduction in the cost of land development. Furthermore, being virgin area with no vested interests it would be possible to introduce new crops and products. This possibility is technically feasible because the soils have a good physical structure for most types of agriculture and horticulture, though chemical fertilizers or plant nutrient would have to be added before the promise of success is realized. Given the fertilizer and requisite irrigation, there is a wide range of possibilities such as (a) pasture for grazing. This will involve the introduction of special grasses such as 'pangola'. Since introduction and cultivation of such grasses are very costly, the pastures would have to be used for raising high-class beef and dairy cattle; (b) tobacco and cotton which can serve as industrial raw materials); (c) tree crops such as citrus, avocado, breadfruit, and other tropical fruit; (d) rootcrops such as onions, peanuts, ginger, tumeric; (e) sorghum, millet, peas, tomatoes, pineapples, and a range of other fruits and vegetables. It is evident that many of these crops are high-value ones. This is particularly true of food-grains, vegetables, industrial raw materials, fruits, and above all, meat and dairy products. Besides, markets for most of these products are available domestically as well as in the West Indian region.

In addition, most of the produce could be processed in the area by the establishment of canning, processing, and fabricating plants. Processing plants for condensed, sterilized or powdered milk, plants for the production of cheese, butter, and corned beef, and canning plants for fruits, juices, vegetables,

and tanneries for processing hides and skins will all become
necessary complements to the successful development of agriculture. The Intermediate Zone therefore has the possibilities
of developing *agro-industrial* centres, balanced technical-econo-
mic combinations, the intermingling of different ethnic groups,
and in course of time will provide the nuclei for further growth
by virtue of having become points of large-scale settlement.
Since complementary investments in industrial plants are vital
to the success of agriculture, it is necessary to programme their
location in such a manner that the flow of raw materials to the
processing and other plants is maintained at a high level of
efficiency. The Zone has the advantage of making this smooth
flow possible because it is unencumbered, and also because it is
possible to set up a network of roads. Road-building in this area
is immeasurably easier than on the coast because of the nature
of the terrain and the greater availability of road-building
materials.

  If all the advantages mentioned above are to be realized the
material and institutional requisites of success will have to be
provided. The most important material requisites are power and
fertilizer. Given the high cost of imported fertilizer and the
absence of power in the Intermediate Zone, the success of the
scheme depends upon whether an effective solution of these two
problems can be found. Recently, a very attractive solution in
the form of the 'biogas process' has been put forward. This
process converts organic waste (which in this region could be
forest waste) into high quality organic fertilizer which can be
directly applied to the soil; at the same time the process produces significant quantities of gas of a high calorific value which
can be readily converted into electric energy. If this process
proves technically feasible in the context of this region the twin
problem of fertilizer and power will be solved. But the success
of this strategy is not necessarily bound up with the 'technical
possibilities' of the 'biogas process', though a viable solution in
the latter respect would be very beneficial.

  It is encouraging that several hydro-electric sites are available
for development within close reach of the region. Of these sites,
the most exhaustive survey of the technical and economic
aspects has been made at Tiboku, on the Mazaruni River. A
one-hundred foot development having a total installed capacity

of 306 MW has been recommended at an estimated cost of US\$114 million (including transmission, sub-stations and access roads). It is envisaged that the bulk of the power generated will be utilized for aluminium smelting by the Demerara Bauxite Company, but the scale of operations contemplates the release of considerable excess power capacity which could be used in agro-industrial development of the Intermediate Zone and other suitable areas.

If the power problem is solved by way of hydro-electricity rather than by the 'biogas process', this will mean the importation of fertilizer. But most of importation could be considerably reduced by bulk buying and domestic mixing and the extensive use of bauxite ships. Nevertheless, it will remain a high-cost input and it follows that the development of this region must emphasize high-valued products and scientific farming. The development of this area will also necessitate complementary investment in infrastructural works in the form of farm schools for research and training, and most fundamentally, the establishment of an efficient system of transport and communications.

We have been arguing that the main thrust forward in the next 15 to 20 years is to be up the Berbice River into the brown sands of the Intermediate Zone. This means that the area around Ebini must become a crucial inland nodal point, with a road system radiating from there. One of these two road systems will link up the Ebini-Ituni area with Mackenzie. Two others could cut through the brown sands on the two sides of the Berbice River. Another would provide a link with Crabwood Creek and Orealla on the Courentyne. Finally, a road along the river bank to the coast will complete the circuit. In the road system envisaged, the road from Georgetown to Atkinson Field will be extended to Mackenzie. This road will permit access to the Intermediate Zone by way of the Demerara Valley. Since we envisage very little development on the Essequibo side of the country in the scheme outlined in this chapter, the Atkinson-Field-Mackenzie road link would give farmers on the Essequibo access to the Intermediate Zone. In addition to the road linking Atkinson with Mackenzie, it may also be necessary to build a road linking Bartica with the Intermediate Zone at Atkinson. This road system will facilitate the transportation of fertilizers inwards, and the exportation of meat, dairy products, and other agricultural produce to the Caribbean and other markets. The road system can be supplemented by an adequate system of canals and similar means of transport.

We may conclude that, in the light of the evidence made available, the future of the economy will be closely bound up with the development in the agricultural while manufacturing industries will depend in turn on this sector for their main sources of raw materials. Despite the channelling of a relatively high proportion of government developmental expenditure into this sector its rate of growth has been well below that of gross domestic product, and food production for the domestic market has not kept pace with the needs of the economy as dictated by the growth of population and *per capita* income.

Consequently increasing quantities of scarce foreign exchange had to be utilized for importing food supplies—the greater proportion of which could be produced locally, on idle lands, without restricting the production of crops intended primarily for export. The relative stagnation of the agricultural sector has set limits to the extent to which secondary industry could expand. Thus in planning for future growth priority will have to be given to measures designed to bring under cultivation all the cultivable lands as well as on the renewed assault on the problem of farming methods. In the latter connection, experience over the post-war era seems to suggest that success will turn not so much upon the amount of financial resources invested as upon the working out, through experimentation, of forms of organization that will enable the farmers to maximize their income.

IX

CONCLUSION

WHERE an economy is open and decision-making is decentralized, all the problems connected with the discovery of techniques to make income targets compatible with employment targets, to bring supply and demand and the balance of payments into equilibrium, to match planned savings and investment, and so on, have to be consciously tackled. In Guyana where the economy is very open in the sense that external considerations exercise a great influence on the behaviour of the domestic economy, and highly decentralized in the sense that direct public sector action has exercised only a minimal impact on behaviour, the task of planning is difficult in spite of the simplicity of the economy.

Any scientific attempt at recommending the future paths for the desired increases in income and employment must be preceded by an indication of how the economy functions. Thus in this study of the Guyanese economy at the crossroads we have attempted to show how income and employment and increases in them are currently generated, and how the open and decentralized nature of the economy affects the behaviour of the main aggregates, i.e. income, employment, consumption, investment, and their components. This picture has revealed the major issues of policy in respect of the necessity for direct action by the public sector in order to promote the desired behaviour of income and employment; for indirect action by the public sector (monetary, fiscal, industrial, commercial, etc.) within the existing institutional framework; and for institutional reforms in order to enhance the effectiveness of direct and indirect action and to ensure fulfilment of the chosen targets and objectives.

During the period surveyed in this study, there was a very high rate of investment, the ratio of investment to Gross Domestic Product averaging 24 per cent between 1954 and 1964. Government development expenditure has also been at a high level, amounting to about one-third of gross investment and nearing two-fifths of all public sector expenditure in most years. But the impact of high investment and heavy government capital expenditure on incomes has not been very pronounced. This means that the heavy investment in Guyana has not proved to be a sufficient condition for, or a decisive determinant of, rapid growth in income and employment. We estimated the incremental capital output ratio at 5:1 in a period when the terms of trade effect on income was particularly favourable. This leads us to infer that the operative constraints on development from the viewpoint of future economic planning are to be found in the basic structural and institutional weaknesses of the economy.

During the twelve-year period reviewed, income per head remained almost static during the first ten years, and then showed a tendency to decline in an atmosphere of political and social stress. Increases in output were eaten up by the rapid growth of population which was faster than the capacity of the economy to absorb the increasing number of persons into gainful employment. The level of unemployment increased from 18 per cent of the labour force in 1956 to 20·9 per cent in 1965. Besides the rising population an important causative factor has been excessive mechanization. As wages have risen, employers have substituted machinery for labour especially in bauxite, sugar, rice, and construction. Thirdly, there was the lack of access to cultivable land, due to insufficiency of roads and drainage. Finally, there have not been enough expanding industries.

With sugar contracting in its employment, the only sectors that could expand their labour force significantly were bauxite, rice, and government service, but the employment generated in these activities was not sufficient to absorb the rising labour force. The government's aim at encouraging the development of labour-intensive industries is still at its seminal stage, and no attempt has yet been made to reduce ultra-mechanization in the rice sector. There is evidence that agriculture could be made much more labour intensive, thus opening up many desirable employment opportunities. Furthermore, in areas of the export sector, such as sugar, where the government has resisted the mechanization of certain operations, the indications are that such a policy cannot be sustained for much longer without deleterious effects on the growth of the economy.

In the absence of any outlets for emigration, the increasing unemployment suggests a need for a sensible population policy aimed at reducing the fertility rate of those sections of the population whose rate of increase has been most prolific.[1] Such policies are not costless, but they will contribute towards the solution of the country's income and employment problems in the short run. But on the more positive side, the real solution must encompass the expansion of the narrow productive base of the economy, with a concomitant inward shift of the coastal population, and the promise of a greater number of employment opportunities.

The governing dynamic of the economy was the foreign-owned export sector comprised of sugar and bauxite. But although this sector contributes the lion's share of domestic product, it is related to the national economy in a very restricted way, contributing to national income mainly through payments to households in the form of wages and to the government in the form of taxes. But a large proportion of both household and government leaks abroad immediately through purchases of imports. The government has to buy imported materials for public investment projects. In this case, the leakage is direct and complete, subject to distributive margins. Alternatively, it pays wages to households for administrative services or work on investment projects. Here the size of the leakage depends on the size of the average and marginal propensities to import; both are expected to be very high.[2] In so far as margins are taken by distributors, brokers, bankers, transporters, etc., incomes are created in the services sector in the process of the leakage. What does not leak out immediately is either spent on domestic services, commodities produced in one of the four dependent productive sectors, or saved in liquid or near liquid

[1] That is, the rural East Indian and Negro elements. However, recommendations for family planning and similar measures for fertility reduction have to be handled very cautiously and delicately since they may be politically and socially explosive in a country where voting has been mainly along racial lines, where the survival of governments may depend on this factor, and where the fear by one race of domination by another is real.

[2] In so far as the government accumulates foreign balances there is also a leakage (capital inflow), but this has been insignificant.

form,[1] thus offering an indirect inducement to activity in agriculture and domestic manufacturing, and sometimes, as in the case of rice, via public sector investment.

In the case of sugar, it is unlikely that the long-run demand will grow much faster than 2 per cent per annum, assuming that the relatively favourable market structure of the present remains unaltered and provided there are no abnormal shifts in quota allocations under the Commonwealth Sugar Agreement or in the United States market. Thus if sugar is to maintain a long-run rate of growth of income equal to population growth, the full burden will rest on upward movements in prices. Meanwhile, employment, under the pressure of mechanization, shows a tendency to decline at a rate above the rate of increase of the labour force, and the increase in wage costs has led to a reduction in the industry's competitive position.

The prospects for the bauxite-based industries are more favourable. In this case income generated is likely to rise steadily, although the very capital-intensive nature of the industry will always prevent it from making a very significant contribution in the field of employment. Demand has been expanding at the rate of 9 per cent per annum between 1952 and 1962, and it is forecast by the industry that growth will continue at a high rate well into the future owing to the widening of uses for the metal in developed countries and to sizeable increases in consumption as the industrialization of the developing countries proceeds. But part of the country's problem lies in reaching new terms of collaboration with the industry so as to increase the share of the increment in product accruing to national income. Another part of the problem arises from uncertainty as to whether the expansion of international demand for bauxite products would lead to an increase in productive capacity, and to the erection of smelting facilities. In this connection the contribution of the bauxite-based industries towards accelerating the rate of growth and transformation of the structure of the economy will depend very largely on the

---

[1] This is where monetary policy should come into play to ensure that real resources represented by monetary or quasi-monetary assets are utilized to the full for domestic growth. But as we have shown, money and credit are unmanaged, and the intermediaries tend to act in ways incompatible with domestic growth.

country's ability to find willing partners with capital, the requisite skills, and acceptable terms of collaboration.

A conclusion that has emerged from this study is the relative stagnation of the manufacturing sector especially in the light industrial field. A constraint in this case has been the unavailability of domestic savings to finance investment.[1] As household incomes increased, both potential demand for manufactured commodities and the potential supply of domestic savings also increased, but to the extent that the one grew, the other was restricted. But in so far as there was a big backlog of demand for manufactured goods met by importation, there is prima facie warrant for concluding that one of the main restraints on the contribution this sector may have made to national income was the tendency for household income to be directed to the purchases of foreign rather than domestically produced commodities.

The shortage of household savings, or the failure to channel potential household saving into the manufacturing sector, is another part of the problem. So is also the fact that the available techniques of producing manufactured commodities both require quantities of capital which are more than can be supplied from domestic sources and at the same time also promise to establish minimum productive capacity much greater than total domestic demand. However, to the extent that there do exist technical possibilities of establishing industries for which there is adequate demand, it is clear that the 'shortage' of household savings has been a restrictive factor on the growth of income and employment. A contributing factor restricting income generation in the manufacturing sector has been the smallness and narrowness of the domestic agricultural sector. The absence of supplies of agricultural raw materials as inputs into processing and manufacturing industry has been a partial deterrent to investment there.

The relative stagnation of the dependent agricultural sector which contains an average of 40 per cent of the total labour force sets limits to the extent to which secondary industry can expand in the absence of access to large export markets. The

---

[1] An important aspect of this problem has been the lack of indigenous entrepreneurship and the failure of previous governments to provide the necessary assistance and encouragement to local efforts.

development of the manufacturing sector during the period reviewed was largely based on industries processing primary products. While there is still some scope for this process to continue, it appears that any further expansion of the manufacturing sector will hinge not only on the degree of success achieved in the raising of the incomes of the rural population and the extension of the processing of new agricultural products; but hopes for the growth of the manufacturing sector will hinge very much on competitive costs of production. But even if this obstacle could be overcome, the country would still have to contend with adverse commercial policies in the countries most capable of importing the sort of manufactured goods which Guyana may be able to produce.[1]

Thus the future of the economy will be closely bound up both directly and indirectly with developments in the agricultural sector. Despite the channelling of a relatively high proportion of government expenditure into this sector, its rate of growth has been well below that of domestic product, and food production for the domestic market has not kept pace with the needs of the economy as dictated by the growth of population and household net incomes. Consequently, increasing quantities of scarce foreign exchange have to be utilized for importing food supplies—a large proportion of which could be produced locally, without restricting the production of crops intended primarily for export. Agricultural development has so far been confined to the narrow coastal strip along the coast and major rivers. The expensive infrastructural investment necessary for utilizing such lands has hindered major agricultural development. Any long-term development plan must therefore investigate the possibility of utilizing other lands, particularly the White Sand Region immediately behind the coast.[2]

But success in exploiting the Intermediate Zone as a major growth point will depend principally on whether a farming

[1] However, the potential domestic demand that is expected to be captured consequent upon a policy of effective import substitution is likely to be significant.

[2] But as we have argued, this emphasis on the Intermediate Zone ought not to lead to the total neglect of valuable lands on the coast and elsewhere. In particular new emphasis is being given to the north west district of the Essequibo which promises many possibilities especially in the mineral field. New finds of minerals other than bauxite in this area may give the country's economy just the fillip it needs.

class, skilled in scientific mixed farming can be created. Up to the present, the emergence of such a class has been inhibited by the functioning of the plantation system on the coastlands, and the very elementary techniques used in rice cultivation. Attitudes to agriculture and husbandry and the composition of skills have been largely governed by the dependence of the rural work force on wagework on sugar estates. And where they do farm their own lands, as in the case of rice farmers, they tend to concentrate on one cash crop, ignoring the possibilities of using by-products and neglecting to investigate improved methods of culture and husbandry. Thus heavy expenditure will be required in the training of cadres of all kinds and in the establishment of infrastructure, especially communications. This means that the public sector must play a greater and more responsible part in the future guidance of economic activity.

SELECT BIBLIOGRAPHY

(1) RECURRENT REPORTS OF THE FOLLOWING GOVERN-
MENT DEPARTMENTS, STATUTORY AND INSTITUTIONAL
BODIES:

Accountant General
Agriculture, Department of
Agriculture, Ministry of, *Agricultural Statistics*
Budget Speeches, Legislative Council
Census Reports
Central Statistical Bureau, *Analysis of Domestic Product* (first compiled
in 1965 in an attempt to provide a comprehensive set of statistics
for use in the preparation of the 1966–72 Development Plan);
Digests of Statistics; *Quarterly Review of Financial Statistics*
Credit Corporation
Development Estimates as passed by the Legislative Council
Drainage and Irrigation, Department of
Education, Department of
Estimates Current and Capital, Legislative Assembly
External Trade, Annual Accounts relating to, Department of
Customs and Excise
Forest Department
Income Tax, Department of
Labour, Department of
Lands and Mines, Department of
Land Settlement Department
Post Office Savings Bank
Public Works, Department of
Registrar General
Rice Marketing Board
Rice Producers' Association
Special Funds
Sugar Producers' Association, Annual and Special Reports
Transport and Harbours, Department of
Treasurer, Department of

(2) REPORTS, SURVEYS, ETC., PERTAINING TO THE GUYANA
ECONOMY

BEN-ARI, A., *Report on Land Settlement in British Guiana*, Ministry of
Foreign Affairs, Israel, 1962.

26—E.D.G.

BERRILL, K., *Report on the British Guiana Development Programme, 1960–64*, Sessional Paper No. 2/1960, Legislative Council, British Guiana, 1959.

BISHOPP, D. W., *The Bauxite Resources of British Guiana and their Development*, Georgetown, 1955.

British Guiana: *Draft Development Plan, 1966–72*, Government Printery, Georgetown, 1965.

CAMACHO, R. F., *General Review of Drainage and Irrigation on the Coastal Plain and Reports for the Years 1957, 1958, 1959*, Ministry of Natural Resources, Georgetown, 1960.

Caribbean Commission, Committee on Agriculture and Forestry of the Caribbean Research Council, *The Sugar Industry in the Caribbean*, Washington, D.C., 1947.

Colonial Office: *Colonial Development and Welfare in the West Indies: Agriculture in the West Indies*, Col. No. 182, H.M.S.O., 1942.

—, *Industrial Development in Jamaica, Trinidad, Barbados, and British Guiana*, Report of Mission of United Kingdom Industrialists, Col. No. 294, H.M.S.O., London, 1953.

—, *Report of a Commission of Inquiry into the Sugar Industry of British Guiana*, Col. No. 249, H.M.S.O., 1949.

—, *Report of a Commission of Inquiry into Disturbances in British Guiana in February, 1962*. Col. No. 354, H.M.S.O., London, 1962.

—, Colonial Annual Reports on British Guiana.

D'ANDRADE, W. P., and PERCIVAL, D. A., *The National Economic Accounts of British Guiana*, Daily Chronicle, Ltd., Georgetown, 1958.

DUMONT, Rene, *Report to the Government of British Guiana on Planning Agricultural Development*, F.A.O., Rome, June 1963.

FLEMMICH, C. O., *Report to the Government of British Guiana on the Marketing of Wood and Wood Products with special reference to the Export of Timber*, Report No. 1737, F.A.O., Rome, 1963.

Files, Departmental
Central Planning Unit
Central Statistical Office
Department of Agriculture
Industrial Development Corporation
Ministry of Finance
Ministry of Economic Affairs
Ministry of Trade and Industry.

GERMANACOS, G. L., et al., *Report of the UNESCO Educational Survey Mission to British Guiana*, Ministry of Education, Georgetown, 1965.

GYANCHAND, M., *Report on the Three Year Plan, 1964–65–66 for British Guiana*, Central Planning Unit, Georgetown, 1963.

International Labour Office, *Report to the Government of British Guiana on a Survey of Family Expenditures, 1956*, I.L.O., Geneva, 1957.

—, *Report to the Government of British Guiana on Employment, Unemployment and Underemployment in the Colony in 1956*, Geneva, 1957.

JACOBS, K. C., *British Guiana: Report on the Financial Position*, Col. No. 358, H.M.S.O., 1964.

KALDOR, N., *Proposals for a Reform of Taxation of British Guiana*, Ministry of Finance, Georgetown, 1962.

MARSHALL, A. H., *Report on Local Government in British Guiana*, Georgetown, 1962.

ORESCANIN, D., STANKOVIC, S., JELOVAC, V., and HAMBERGER, E., *Draft Report to the Government of British Guiana on Forest Inventory Development*, Ministry of Economic Affairs, Georgetown, 1965.

PARTIN, W., *A Report on Vocational Education in British Guiana*, Ministry of Education, Georgetown, May 1965.

REES, T. I., *Forest Inventory Report to the Government of British Guiana*, Report No. 1762, F.A.O., Rome, 1962.

Report of the Royal West India Commission, 1897, Col. 8655.

Report of the Royal West India Commission, 1945, Cmnd. 6607.

Report of the British Guiana Constitutional Commission, 1954.

Robertson Report, Cmnd. 9274.

Report on the Bauxite-Aluminium Industry of British Guiana, United Nations Technical Assistance Operations, March 1964.

SMODLAKA, B. J., *Report on the Transport and Communications in British Guiana*, United Nations Technical Assistance Operations Bureau, 1962.

Survey of Manpower Requirements and the Labour Force, British Guiana 1965: Preliminary Report, Ministry of Labour and Social Security, Georgetown, British Guiana, 1965.

SPENCER, A. O., *Memorandum on the Financial Position in British Guiana, 1920–46*, Government House, Georgetown, 1946.

THOMAS, C. Y., *Monetary and Financial Arrangements in a Dependent Monetary Economy: A study of British Guiana, 1945–62*. Institute of Social and Economic Research, University of the West Indies, 1965.

(3) OTHER PUBLICATIONS CONSULTED ON THE GUYANESE ECONOMY

ABBOTT, G. C., 'The West Indian Sugar Industry with some Long Term Projections of Supply', *Social and Economic Studies*, Vol. 13, No. 1, March 1964, pp. 1–37.

BERRILL, K., 'Comments on "Economic Future of British Guiana" by Peter Newman', *Social and Economic Studies*, Vol. 10, No. 1, March 1961, pp. 1–5.

BOULDING, K. E., 'Social Dynamics in West Indian Society', *Social and Economic Studies*, Vol. 10, No. 1, March 1961, pp. 25–34.

BREWSTER, H., and THOMAS, C. Y., *The Dynamics of West Indian Economic Integration*, Studies in Regional Integration, Vol. 1, University of the West Indies, 1967.

Caribbean Organisation, *Planning for Economic Development in the Caribbean*, Puerto Rico, 1963.

CLEMENTI, Sir Cecil, *A Constitutional History of British Guiana*, Macmillan, London, 1937.

CUMPER, G. E., 'Investment Criteria: A Comment', *Social and Economic Studies*, Vol. 10, No. 1, pp. 18–24.

—, 'West Indian Household Budgets', *Social and Economic Studies*, Vol. 9, No. 3, September 1960, pp. 355–65.

— (ed.), *The Economy of the West Indies*, University of the West Indies, 1960.

FARLEY, R., 'The Rise of the Peasantry in British Guiana', *Social and Economic Studies*, Vol. 2, No. 4, 1954.

—, 'Kaldor's Budget in Retrospect: Reason and Unreason in a Developing Area: Reflections on the 1962 Budget in British Guiana', *Inter-American Economic Affairs*, Vol. XVI, No. 2, Winter 1962, pp. 25–63.

GIRVAN, N., *The Caribbean Bauxite Industry*, Studies in Regional Integration, Vol. 2, No. 4, University of the West Indies, 1967.

Kundu, A., 'The Economy of British Guiana, 1960–75', *Social and Economic Studies*, Vol. 12, No. 3, September 1963, pp. 307–80.

—, 'Rice in the British Caribbean Islands and British Guiana, 1950–75', *Social and Economic Studies*, Vol. 13, No. 2, June 1964, pp. 243–81.

LEWIS, W. A., 'The Industrialisation of the West Indies', *Caribbean Economic Review*, Vol. 12, No. 1, May 1950, pp. 1–61.

McINTYRE, A., *Aspects of Development and Trade in the Commonwealth Caribbean*, Economic Commission for Latin America, May 1965.

NATH, Dwarka, *A History of Indians in British Guiana*, Nelson, London, 1950.

NEWMAN, P., 'The Economic Future of British Guiana', *Social and Economic Studies*, Vol. 9, No. 3, September 1960, pp. 263–96.

—, 'Epilogue on British Guiana', *Social and Economic Studies*, Vol. 10, No. 1, March 1961, pp. 35–41.

—, *British Guiana: Problems of Cohesion in an Immigrant Society*, Oxford University Press, 1964.

O'LOUGHLIN, C., 'The Economy of British Guiana 1952–56: A national Accounts Study', *Social and Economic Studies*, Vol. 8, No. 1, 1959, pp. 1–104.

—, 'The Rice Sector in the Economy of British Guiana', *Social and Economic Studies*, Vol. 7, No. 2, 1958.

REUBENS, E. P., and REUBENS, B. G., *Labour Displacement in a Labour-surplus Economy: The Sugar Industry of British Guiana*, Institute of Social and Economic Research, University of the West Indies, 1962.

ROBERTS, G. W., 'Prospect for Population Growth in the West Indies, *Social and Economic Studies*, Vol. 2, No. 4, December 1962, pp. 333–50.

—, 'Note on Population Growth', *Social and Economic Studies*, Vol. 7, No. 3, 1958.

RODWAY, J., *History of British Guiana* (3 vols.), Georgetown, 1891–4.

SMITH, Raymond T., 'Land Tenure in Three Negro Villages in British Guiana', *Social and Economic Studies*, Vol. 4, No. 1, 1955, pp. 70–8.

—, 'Economic Aspects of Rice Production in an East Indian Community in British Guiana', *Social and Economic Studies*, Vol. 6, No. 4, 1957, pp. 502–22.

SMITH, Raymond T., *Ethnic Difference and Peasant Economy in British Guiana*, in (eds.) Firth, R., and Yamey, B. S., *Capital, Saving and Credit in Peasant Societies*, George Allen and Unwin, Ltd., London, 1964, pp. 305–29.

—, *British Guiana*, Oxford University Press, 1962.

THORNE, A. P., 'British Guiana's Development Programme', *Social and Economic Studies*, Vol. 10, No. 1, March 1961, pp. 6–17.

—, 'Reflections on British Guiana', *Social and Economic Studies*, Vol. 12, No. 2, June 1963.

WEBER, A. R. F., *A Centenary History and Handbook of British Guiana*, The Argosy Co., Georgetown, 1931.

YOUNG, Allyn, *The Approaches to Local Self-Government in British Guiana*, Longmans, London, 1958.

(4) BRIEF LIST OF WORKS CONSULTED ON PROBLEMS OF INVESTMENT AND ECONOMIC DEVELOPMENT

BATOR, F. M., 'On Capital Productivity, Input Allocation and Growth', *The Quarterly Journal of Economics*, February 1957, pp. 86–106.

BLOOMFIELD, A. J., 'Monetary Problems in Underdeveloped Countries', *Public Policy*, Vol. 17, Harvard, 1956.

BRUTON, H. J., 'Growth Models and Underdeveloped Countries', *Journal of Political Economy*, August 1955, pp. 322–36.

CHENERY, H. B., 'The Application of Investment Criteria', *The Quarterly Journal of Economics*, Vol. 67, 1953, pp. 76–96.

—, 'Comparative Advantage and Development Policy', in *Surveys of Economic Theory*, Vol. 2: *Growth and Development*, prepared for the American Economic Association and the Royal Economic Society, Macmillan, 1965, pp. 125–55.

COALE, A. J., and HOOVER, E. M., *Population Growth and Economic Development in Low Income Countries*, Oxford University Press, 1959.

DAVIS, Kingsley, 'The Amazing Decline of Mortality in Under-developed Areas', *American Economic Review*, Papers and Proceedings, May 1956, pp. 305–18.

DEANE, Phyllis, *The Measurement of Colonial National Incomes*, Cambridge University Press, 1948.

—, 'Long Term Trends in World Economic Growth', *Malaysian Economic Review*, October 1961, pp. 14–22.

DELL, S., *Trade Blocs and Common Markets*, Constable, London, 1963.

ECKSTEIN, O., 'Investment Criteria for Economic Development and the Theory of Intertemporal Welfare Economics', *The Quarterly Journal of Economics*, February 1957, pp. 56–85.

EDWARDS, D., *An Economic Study of Small Farming in Jamaica*, University of the West Indies, 1961.

EICHER, C., and WITT, L., *Agriculture in Economic Development*, McGraw Hill Book Company, New York, 1964.

ELLIS, H. S., and WALLICH, H. C., *Economic Development for Latin America*, Proceedings of a Conference held by the International Economic Association, Macmillan, 1962.

FLANDERS, M. J., 'Prebisch on Protectionism: An Evaluation', *The Economic Journal*, June 1964, pp. 305–26.

GREAVES, Ida, *Colonial Monetary Conditions*, H.M.S.O., London, 1953.

GALENSON, W., and LEIBENSTEIN, H., 'Investment Criteria, Productivity and Economic Development', *The Quarterly Journal of Economics*, August 1955, pp. 243–310.

HAZLEWOOD, A. D., 'The Economics of Colonial Monetary Arrangements', *Social and Economic Studies*, Vol. 3, 1954, pp. 291–315.

HICKS, U. K., *Budgeting for Development*, Bulletin, Central Bank of Ceylon (Colombo), Nos. 6, 7, 8, June, July, August 1957, pp. 8–14, 10–17, and 14–21.

—, *Development Finance: Planning and Control*, Oxford, 1965.

—, *Development from Below*, Oxford, 1961.

HICKS, U. K., 'The Economics of Educational Expansion in Low-Income Countries', *Three Banks Review*, March 1965, pp. 3–29.

HUGGINS, H. D., *Aluminium in Changing Communities*, Andre Deutsch in Association with the Institute of Social and Economic Research, University of the West Indies, 1965.

JOHNSTON, B. F., and MELLOR, J. W., 'The Role of Agriculture in Economic Development', *American Economic Review*, September 1961, pp. 566–93.

JOHNSON, H. G., *The World Economy at Crossroads*, Clarendon Press, Oxford, 1965.

KAHN, A. E., 'Investment Criteria in Development Programmes', *The Quarterly Journal of Economics*, February 1951, pp. 38–61.

KALDOR, N., *Essays in Economic Policy*, Vols. 1 and 2, Gerald Duckworth and Co. Ltd., London, 1964.

LEWIS, W. A., *The Theory of Economic Growth*, George Allen and Unwin Ltd., London, 1955.

—, 'Education and Economic Development', *Social and Economic Studies*, Vol. 10, 1961, pp. 113–27.

—, 'Employment Policy in an Underdeveloped Area', *Social and Economic Studies*, Vol. 7, No. 3, September 1958.

—, 'Economic Problems of Development', in *Restless Nations*, Council of World Tensions, George Allen and Unwin Ltd., 1962.

—, 'Some Reflections on Economic Development', *Economic Digest, Institute of Development Economics* (Karachi), Vol. 3, No. 3, Winter 1960, pp. 3–5.

—, *Development Planning*, George Allen and Unwin Ltd., 1965.

LITTLE, I. M. D., and CLIFFORD, J. M., *International Aid*, Allen and Unwin Ltd., 1965.

MARTIN, A., and LEWIS, W. A., 'Patterns of Public Revenue and Expenditure', *Manchester School of Economic and Social Studies*, Vol. XXIV, No. 3, September 1956, pp. 203–44.

MAJUMDAR, D., 'Size of Farm and Productivity: A Problem of Indian Peasant Agriculture', *Economica*, Vol. XXXII, May 1965, pp. 161–173.

MEIER, G. M., *Leading Issues in Development Economics*, Oxford University Press, 1964.

MEYER, R. L., *Developmental Planning*, McGraw Hill Book Company, New York, 1965.

MILIKAN, M. F. (ed.), *Investment Criteria and Economic Growth*, Centre for International Studies, Massachusetts Institute of Technology, 1954.

MORGAN, T., 'The Long Run Terms of Trade Between Agriculture and Manufacturing', *Economic Development and Cultural Change*, Vol. 8, 1959, pp. 1–21.

MYINT, H., 'Education and Economic Development', *Social and Economic Studies*, Vol. 14, No. 1, March 1965, pp. 8–20.

—, *The Economics of Developing Countries*, Hutchison, London, 1964.

—, 'The Interpretation of Economic Backwardness', *Oxford Economic Papers*, New Series, Vol. 6 (1954), pp. 132–63.

—, 'Social Flexibility, Social Discipline and Economic Growth', *International Social Science Journal*, Vol. XVI, No. 2, 1964, pp. 252–60.

MYRDAL, G., *Economic Theory and Underdeveloped Regions*, Gerald Duckworth and Co. Ltd., London, 1957.

NEISSER, H., 'Investment Criteria, Productivity and Economic Development', *The Quarterly Journal of Economics*, November 1956, pp. 644–67.

NEVIN, E., *Capital Funds in Underdeveloped Countries*, Macmillan and Co. Ltd., London, 1961.

NEWLYN, W. T., and ROWAN, D. C., *Money and Banking in British Colonial Africa*, Oxford University Press, 1954.

NOVE, A., 'Planners Preferences, Priorities and Reforms', *The Economic Journal*, Vol. LXXXVI, No. 302, June 1966, pp. 267–77.

OSHIMA, H. T., 'The Share of Government in Gross National Product for Various Countries', *American Economic Review*, June 1957, pp. 381–90.

ONITIRI, H. M. A., 'Nigeria's Balance of Payments and Economic Policy, 1946–60', Unpublished Ph.D. Thesis, London, 1963.

ROBINSON, E. A. G. (ed.), *Problems in Economic Development*, Proceedings of a Conference held by the International Economic Association, Macmillan and Co. Ltd., London, 1965.

ROSENSTEIN-RODAN, P. N. (ed.), *Capital Formation and Economic Development*, Studies in the Economic Development of India, No. 2, Allen and Unwin Ltd., London, 1964.

—, *Pricing and Fiscal Policies*, Studies in the Economic Development of India, No. 3, Allen and Unwin Ltd., London, 1964.

SEERS, D., 'The Role of National Income Estimates in the Statistical Policy of an Underdeveloped Area', *Review of Economic Studies*, Vol. XX (1952–3), pp. 159–68.

—, 'Economic Programming in a Country Newly Independent', *Social and Economic Studies*, March 1962, pp. 34–43.

—, 'The Mechanism of an Open Petroleum Economy', *Social and Economic Studies*, Vol. 13, No. 2, June 1964, pp. 233–42.

SEN, A. K., *The Choice of Techniques: An Aspect of the Theory of Planned Economic Development*, Basil Blackwell, Oxford, 1962.

SCHULTZ, T. W., *The Economic Value of Education*, Columbia University Press, New York, 1963.

SCHULTZ, T. W., *Economic Crises in World Agriculture*, The University of Michigan Press, 1965.

—, *Transforming Traditional Agriculture*, Yale University Press, 1964.

THOMAS, C. Y., 'The Balance of Payments and Money Supplies of a Colonial Monetary Economy', *Social and Economic Studies*, Vol. 12, No. 1, March 1963, pp. 27–36.

TUN WAI, U., 'Taxation Problems of Underdeveloped Countries', *International Monetary Fund Staff Papers*, Vol. IX, No. 3, November 1963.

VAKIL, C., and BRAHMANAND, P., *Planning for an Expanding Economy: Accumulation, Employment and Technical Progress*, New York, 1956.

WALINSKY, L. J., *Planning and Execution of Economic Development*, McGraw Hill, New York, 1963.

WOLF, C., and SUFRIN, S., *Capital Formation and Foreign Investment in Underdeveloped Areas*, Syracuse University Press, 1958.

ZIMMERMAN, L. J. (ed.), *Economic Planning*, Mouton, The Hague, 1963.

INDEX

Administrative services, expenditure on, 305–7, 311
Africa, population growth, 45 n. 2; roads, 329 n. 1; sugar, 135 f., 153
Africans, 64; population increase, 51–4, 374 n. 1; free Negro villages, 54 n. 2
Agricultural Census, 94
Agricultural Thrift and Credit Societies, 96
Agriculture, xxii f., 14, 73–5, 77, 80 ff., 84–167, 342, 346–9, 353 f., 364–71, 376–8; exports, 86 and n. 1, 87; investment in, 89; labour force, 87 and n. 3, 88, 90; machinery imported, 271; output, 7, 13–14, 31; processing, 14, 74 f.; *and* economic development, 84
See also Land development; Livestock; Rice; Sugar; *and under* Mechanization
Agriculture, Department of, 165
ALCAN, 195 n. 1, 200, 208, 222
Alumina, 7, 17, 30, 38, 145, 184, 220, 234, 256, 263; capital, 209; exports, 186, 200–4, 226–8, 254; investment, 188 f.; labour force, 188, 190 f.; labour/capital ratio, 190; production, 186, 188, 197 f., 201, 222, 363; wages, 192–3
Aluminium, 199; capital, 209; demand, 193, 200, 220–2; prices, 217, 219 f.; production, 195 n. 1, 198 f.
See also ALCAN
Amerindians, 47, 53, 160, 328, 367
Anna Regina, size of farms at, 98
Annai, cattle, 160
Antigua, sugar, 146
Area of Guyana, xix, 24, 64
See also Regions
Argentina, aluminium, 222
Asia, population growth, 45 n. 2, 122

Atkinson Field, roads, 370
Australia, aluminium, 222; bauxite, 197; chocolate, 165; sugar, 135 f., 146

Balance of payments, 22, 145, 204, 244–52, 254, 263, 372; terminology explained, 244
Banks, 256, 263–4, 271 f., 301 f., 346. Central Bank, 302 and n. 1. 346. International Bank, 280. International Bank for Reconstruction and Development (I.B.R.D.), 346–9
Barbados, area, 64; oil and soap, 164; rice, 112, 114; roads, 329 n. 1; sugar, 139, 146; timber, 178; trade with, 240–3, 252, 257
Bartica, 75, 367, 370; labour force, 78; unemployment, 78
Bauxite, xxii, 7, 9, 17 f., 185, 234–6, 350, 354, 359, 361, 363, 370, 373 ff.; calcined, 197 and n. 2, 199–200, 203, 252; capital, 188 f., 209, capital/labour ratio, 217; exports, 186, 199–204, 218, 226–8; investment, 30 f., 39 f., 188; labour force, 190 f., 217–18; prices, 209–220, 292; processing, 197–8; production, 186, 193–8, 222; quality, 197 and n. 1, 222; statistical data, 187–8; taxation, 218 and n. 1, 219 f., 292; transportation, 205–8; wages, 192–3; world price and production, 193–8, 210–17
See also Demerara Bauxite Company; Mechanization; Surinam
Berbice, labour force, 71 f., 78; population, 44; rice production, 92 ff., 100, 103; tractors, 101; unemployment, 78 f., 340
Berbice River, 161, 166, 205, 208, 367, 370